Disney

Tangled

SHIORI KANAKI

AUG 18

TOKYOPOP®

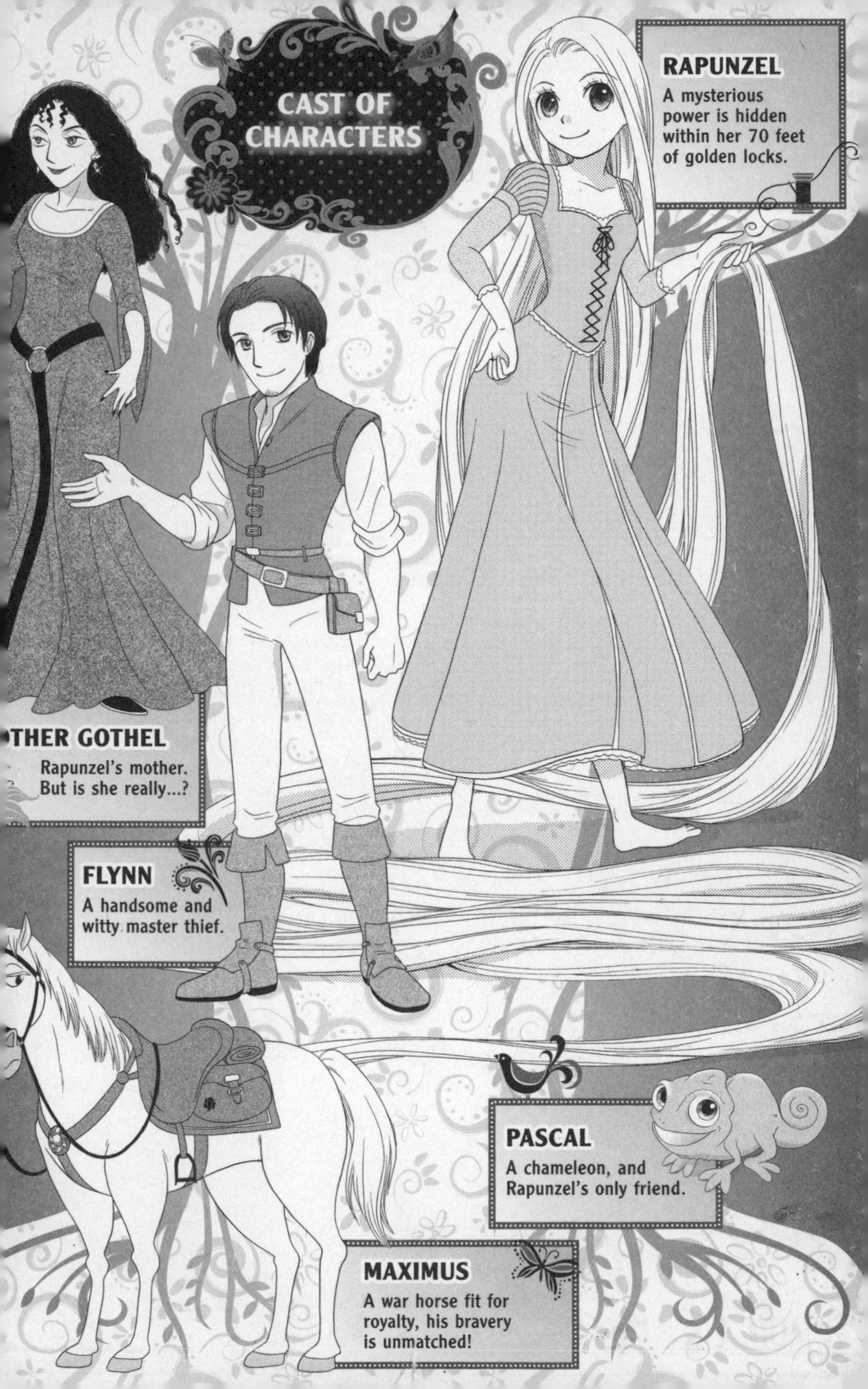
CAST OF CHARACTERS
RAPUNZEL
A mysterious power is hidden within her 70 feet of golden locks.
THER GOTHEL
Rapunzel's mother. But is she really...?
FLYNN
A handsome and witty master thief.
PASCAL
A chameleon, and Rapunzel's only friend.
MAXIMUS
A war horse fit for royalty, his bravery is unmatched!

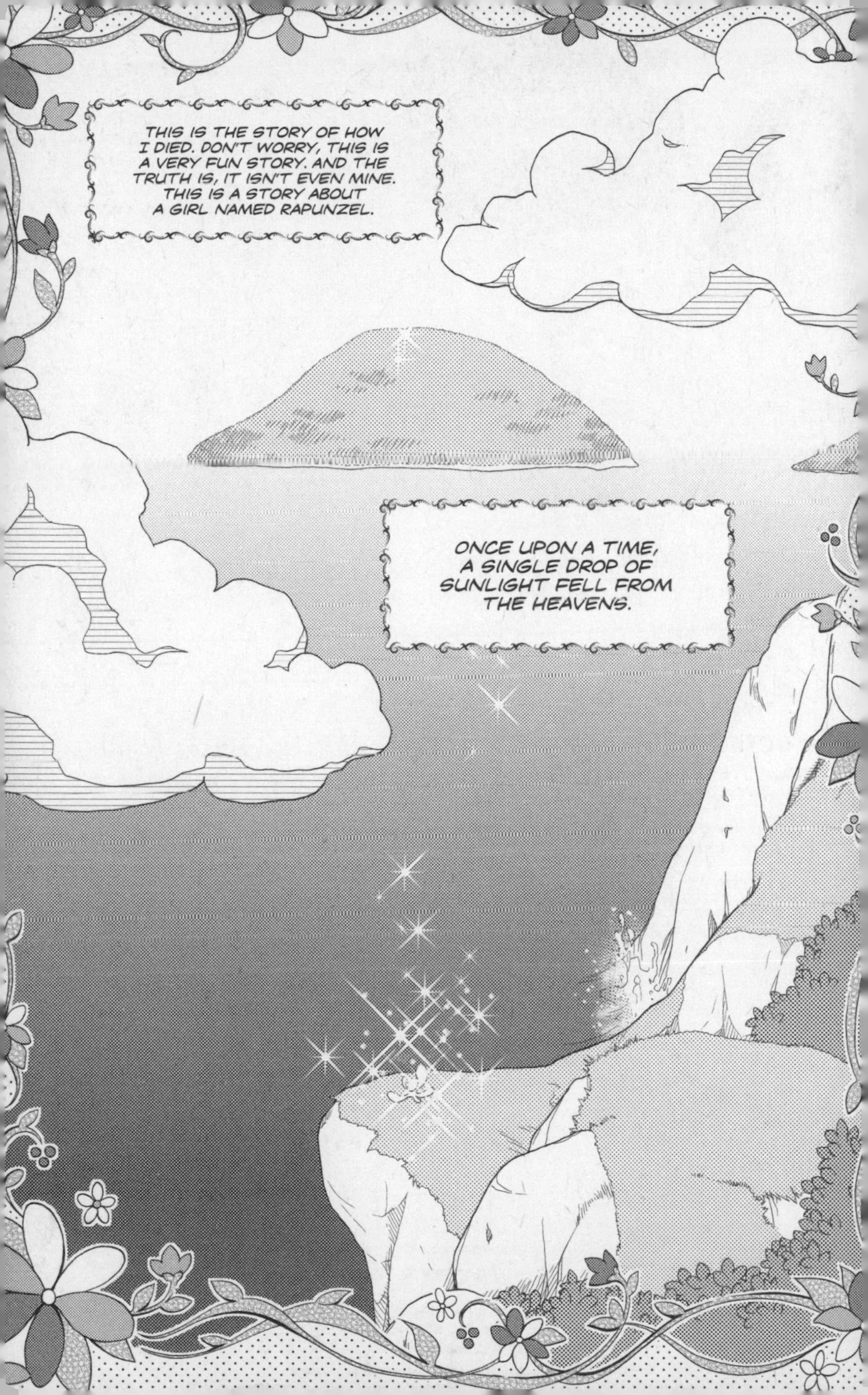
THIS IS THE STORY OF HOW I DIED. DON'T WORRY, THIS IS A VERY FUN STORY. AND THE TRUTH IS, IT ISN'T EVEN MINE. THIS IS A STORY ABOUT A GIRL NAMED RAPUNZEL.
ONCE UPON A TIME, A SINGLE DROP OF SUNLIGHT FELL FROM THE HEAVENS.

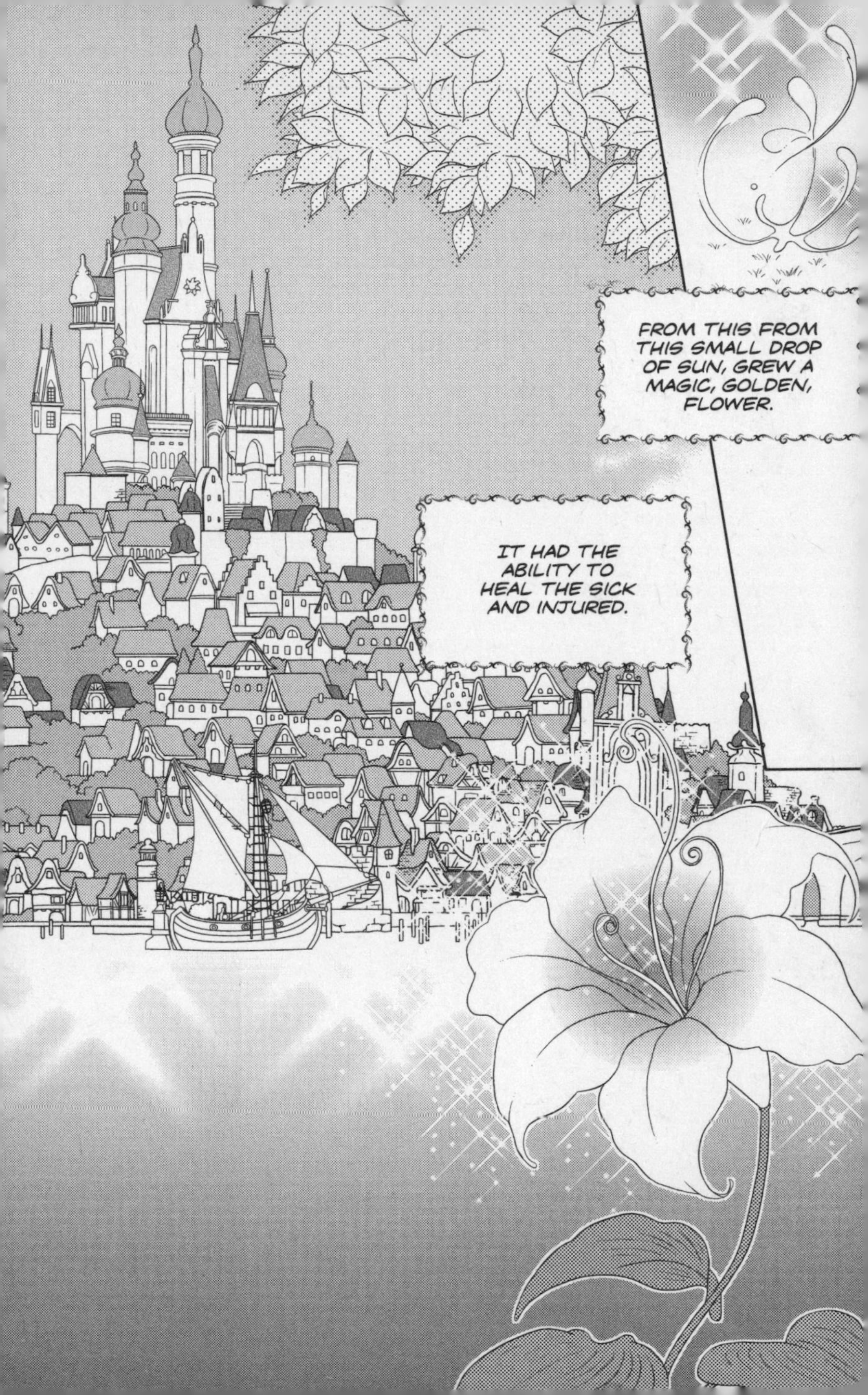
FROM THIS FROM THIS SMALL DROP OF SUN, GREW A MAGIC, GOLDEN, FLOWER.
IT HAD THE ABILITY TO HEAL THE SICK AND INJURED.

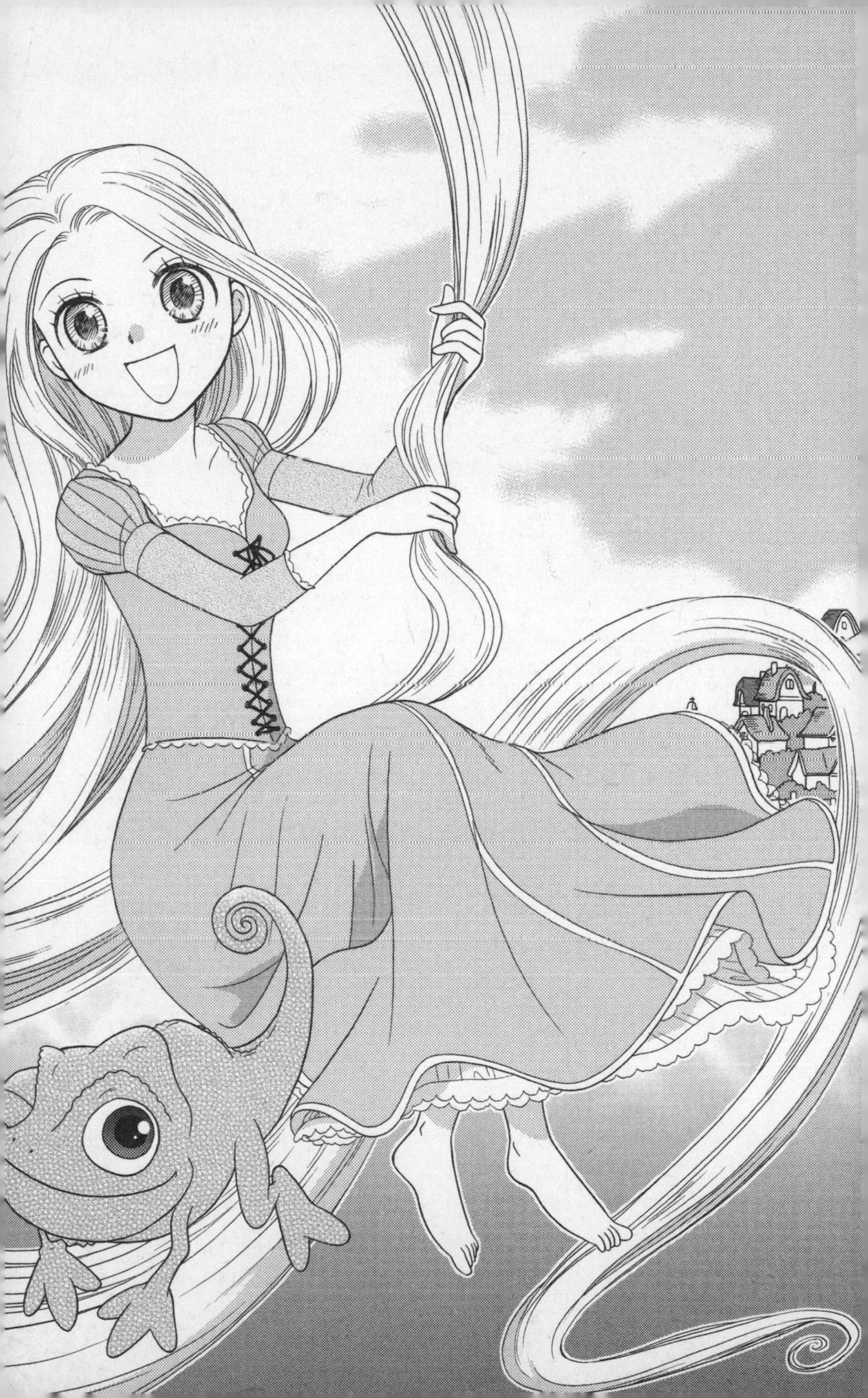

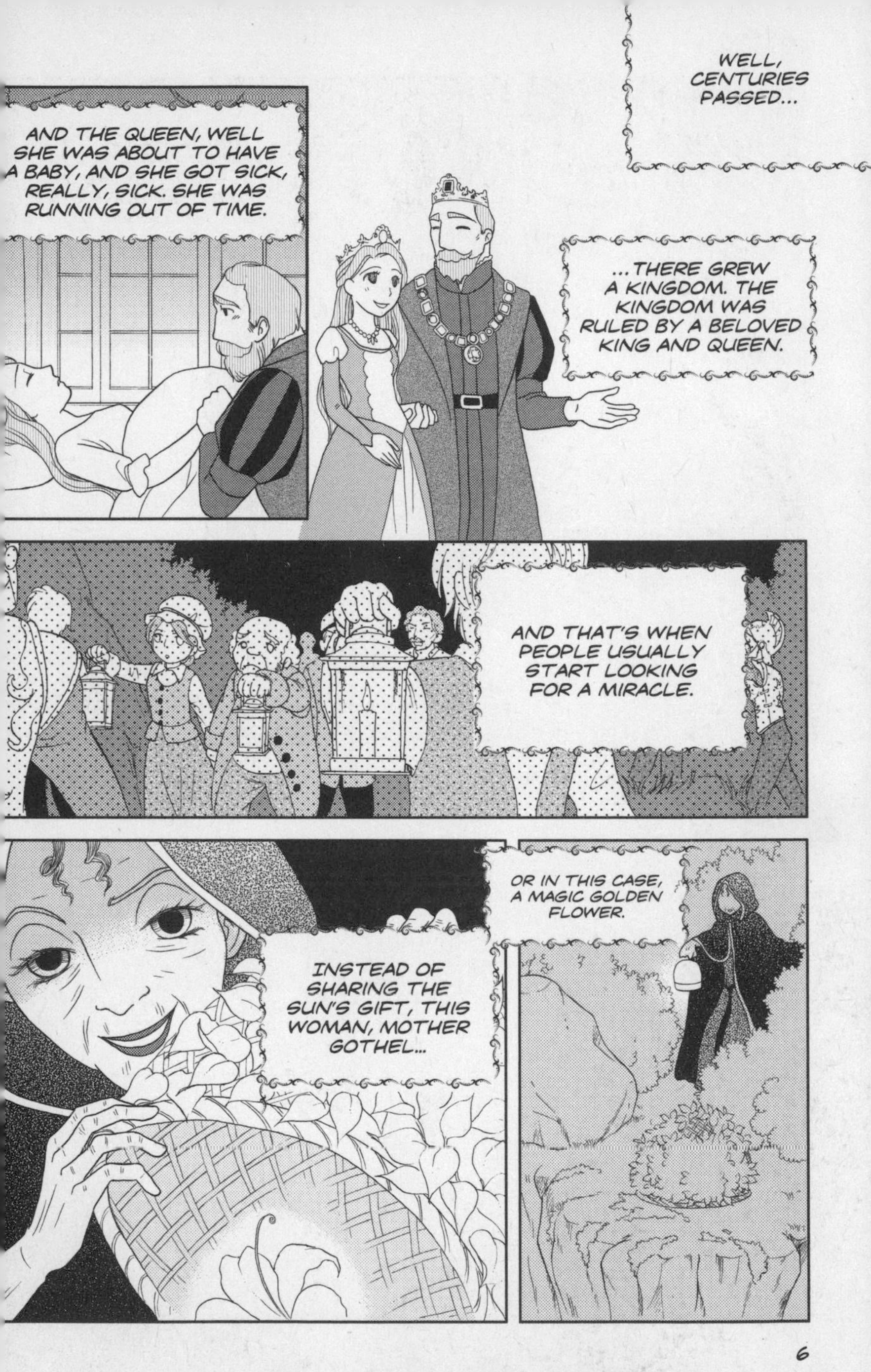
WELL, CENTURIES PASSED...
...THERE GREW A KINGDOM. THE KINGDOM WAS RULED BY A BELOVED KING AND QUEEN.
AND THE QUEEN, WELL SHE WAS ABOUT TO HAVE A BABY, AND SHE GOT SICK, REALLY, SICK. SHE WAS RUNNING OUT OF TIME.
AND THAT'S WHEN PEOPLE USUALLY START LOOKING FOR A MIRACLE.
OR IN THIS CASE, A MAGIC GOLDEN FLOWER.
INSTEAD OF SHARING THE SUN'S GIFT, THIS WOMAN, MOTHER GOTHEL...

READ THIS WAY

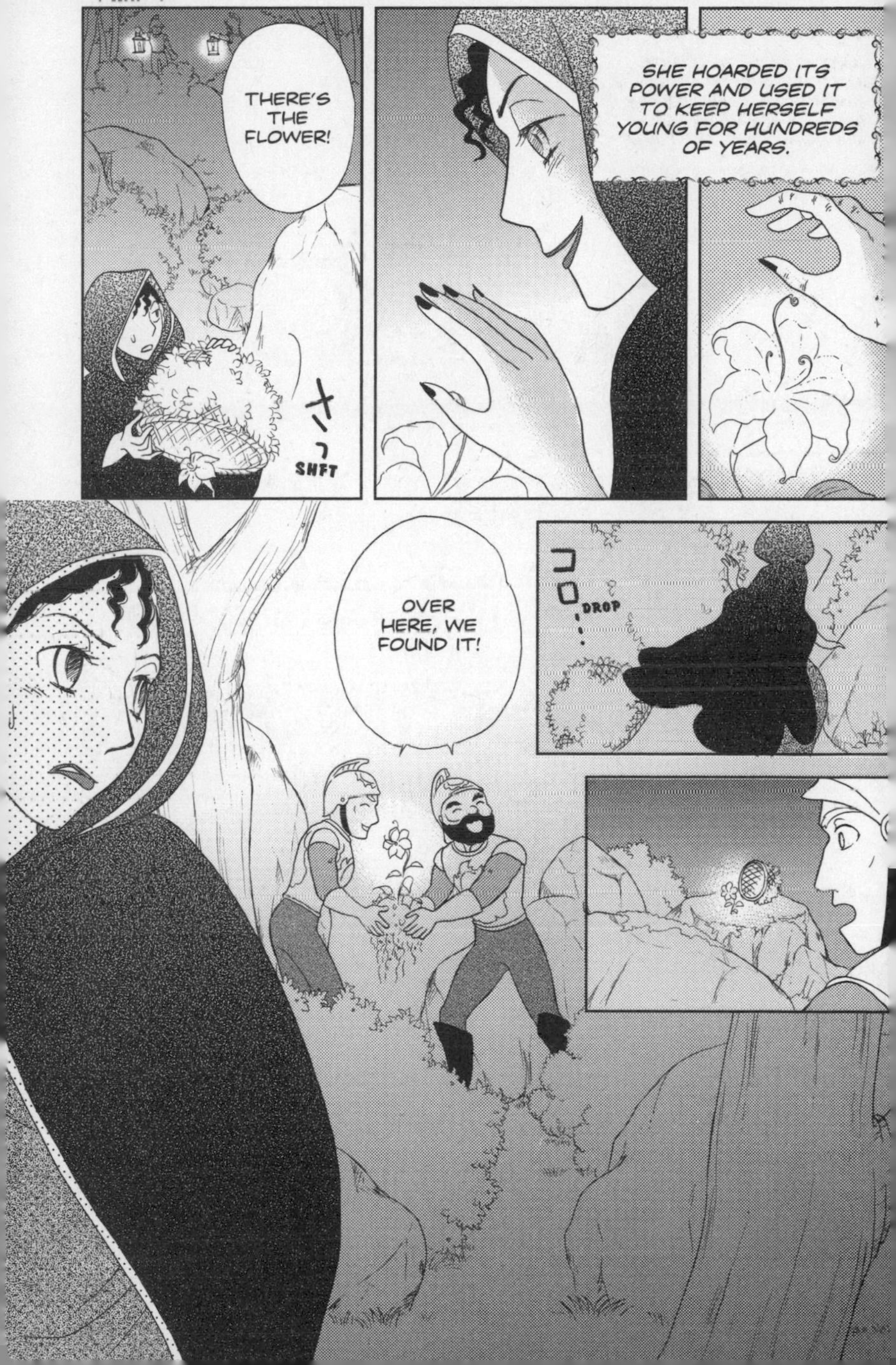
SHE HOARDED ITS POWER AND USED IT TO KEEP HERSELF YOUNG FOR HUNDREDS OF YEARS.
THERE'S THE FLOWER!
さっ
SHFT
コロ...
DROP
OVER HERE, WE FOUND IT!

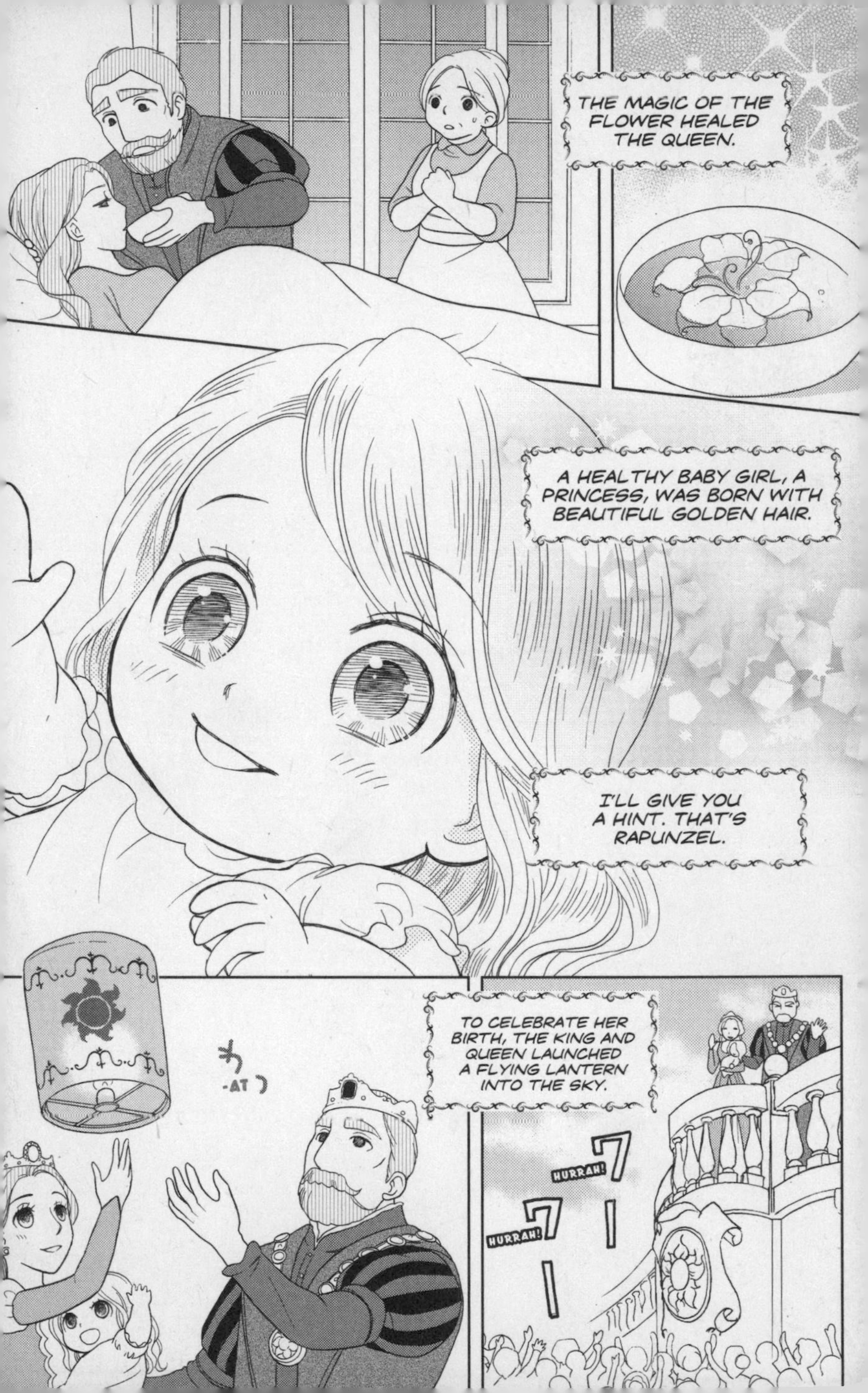
THE MAGIC OF THE FLOWER HEALED THE QUEEN.
A HEALTHY BABY GIRL, A PRINCESS, WAS BORN WITH BEAUTIFUL GOLDEN HAIR.
I'LL GIVE YOU A HINT. THAT'S RAPUNZEL.
TO CELEBRATE HER BIRTH, THE KING AND QUEEN LAUNCHED A FLYING LANTERN INTO THE SKY.
HURRAH!
HURRAH!

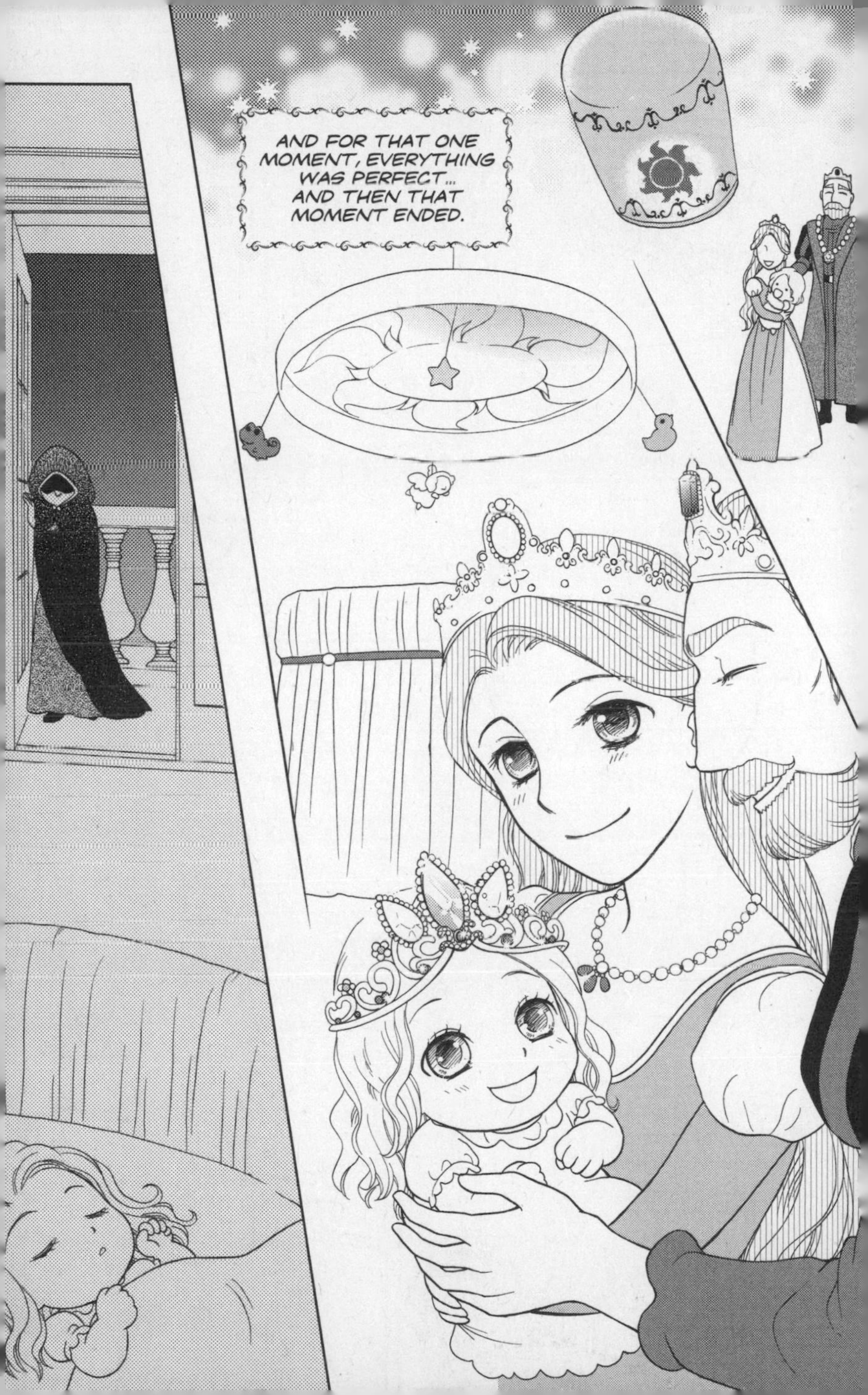
AND FOR THAT ONE MOMENT, EVERYTHING WAS PERFECT... AND THEN THAT MOMENT ENDED.

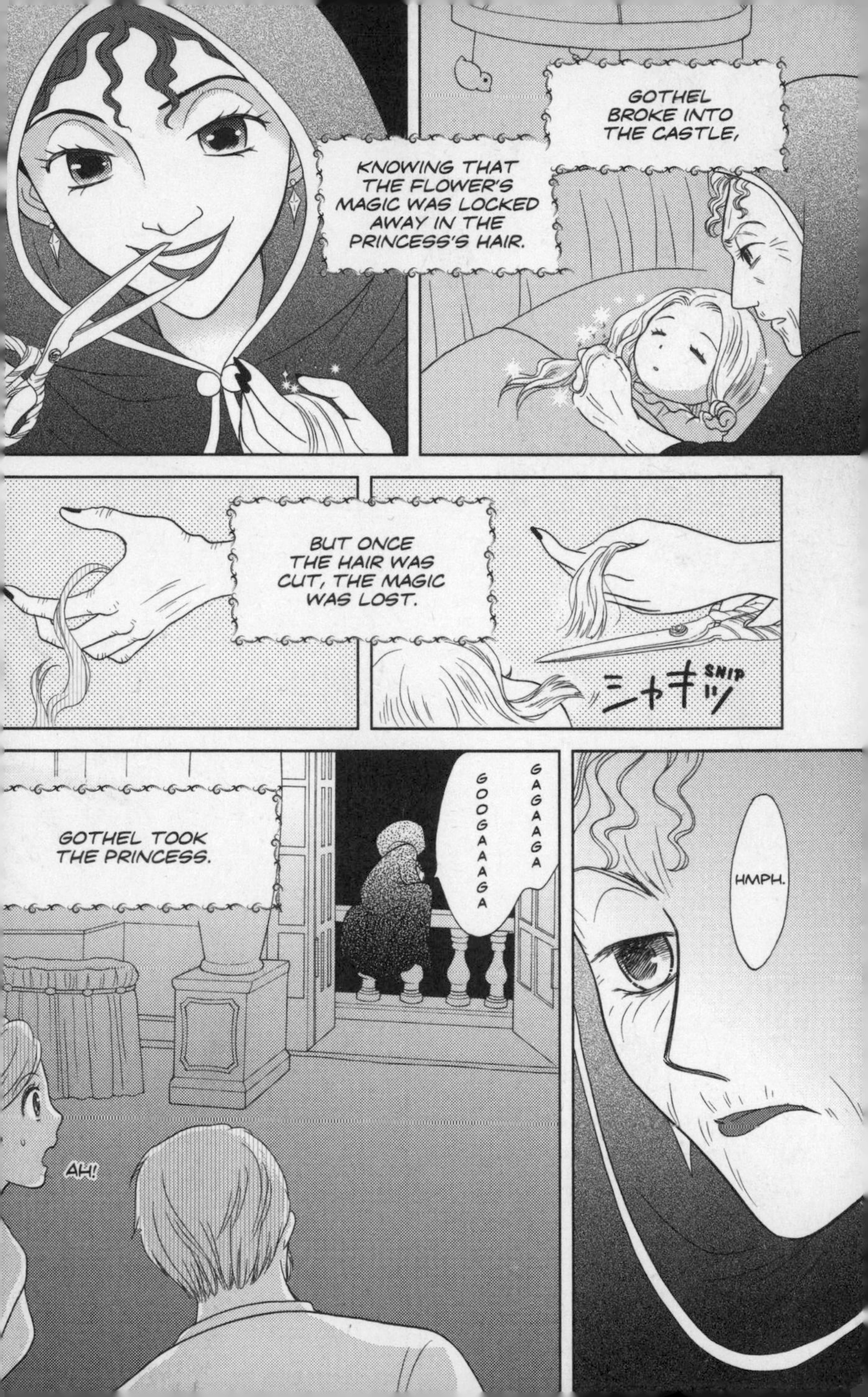
GOTHEL BROKE INTO THE CASTLE,
KNOWING THAT THE FLOWER'S MAGIC WAS LOCKED AWAY IN THE PRINCESS'S HAIR.
BUT ONCE THE HAIR WAS CUT, THE MAGIC WAS LOST.
シャキッ SNIP
HMPH.
GOTHEL TOOK THE PRINCESS.
GAGAAGA GOOGAAAGA
AH!

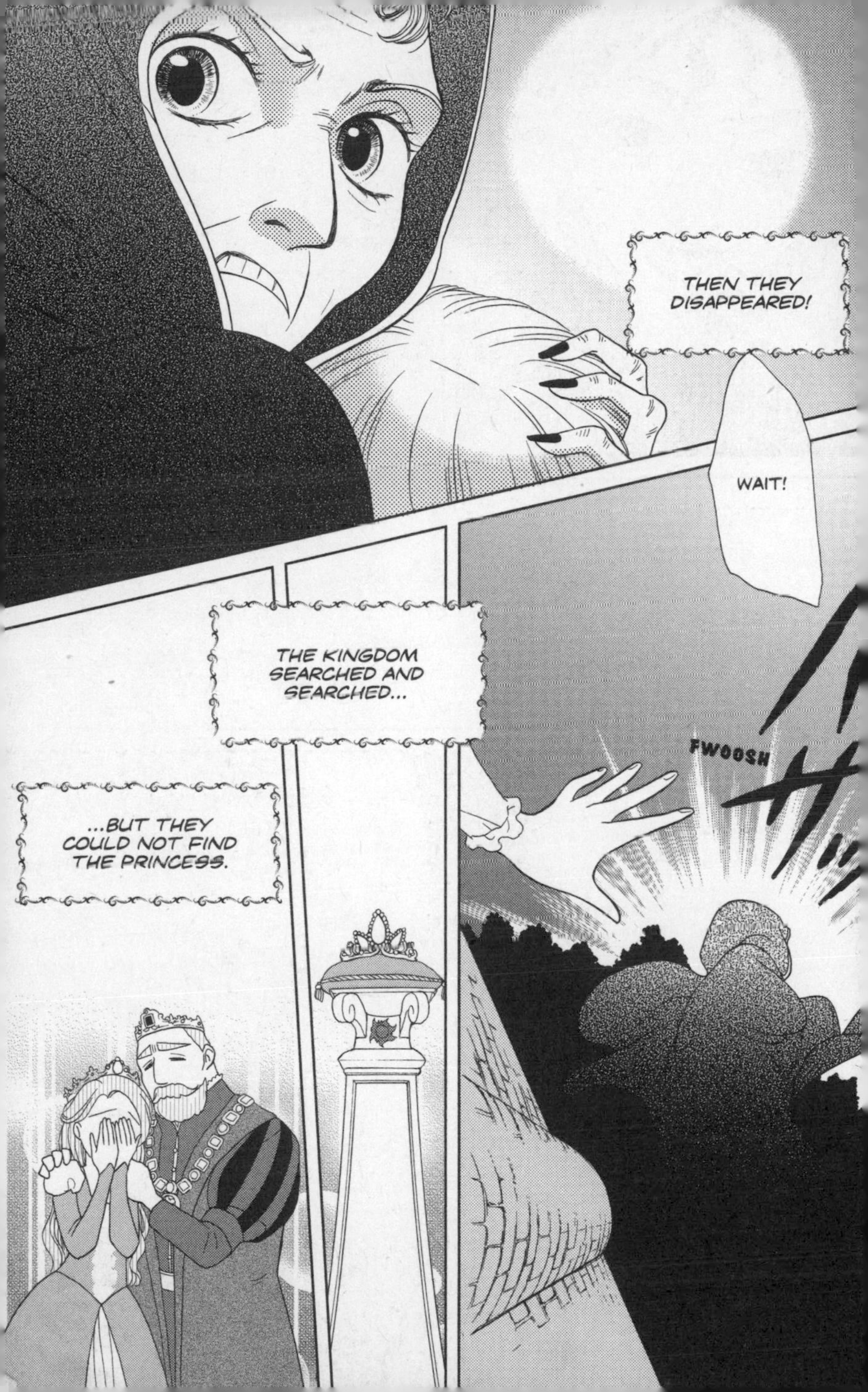
THEN THEY DISAPPEARED!
WAIT!
FWOOSH
THE KINGDOM SEARCHED AND SEARCHED...
...BUT THEY COULD NOT FIND THE PRINCESS.

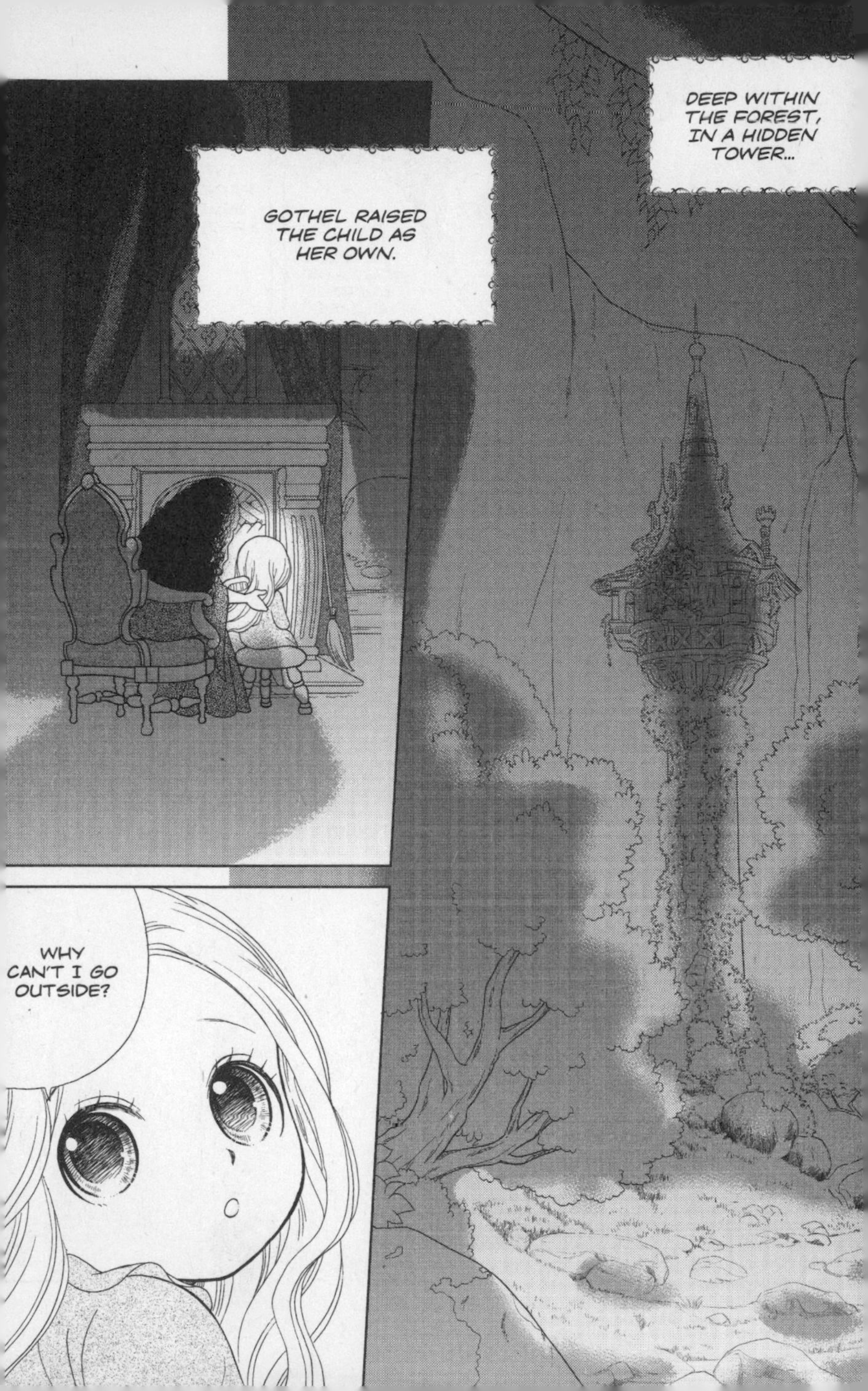
DEEP WITHIN THE FOREST, IN A HIDDEN TOWER...
GOTHEL RAISED THE CHILD AS HER OWN.
WHY CAN'T I GO OUTSIDE?

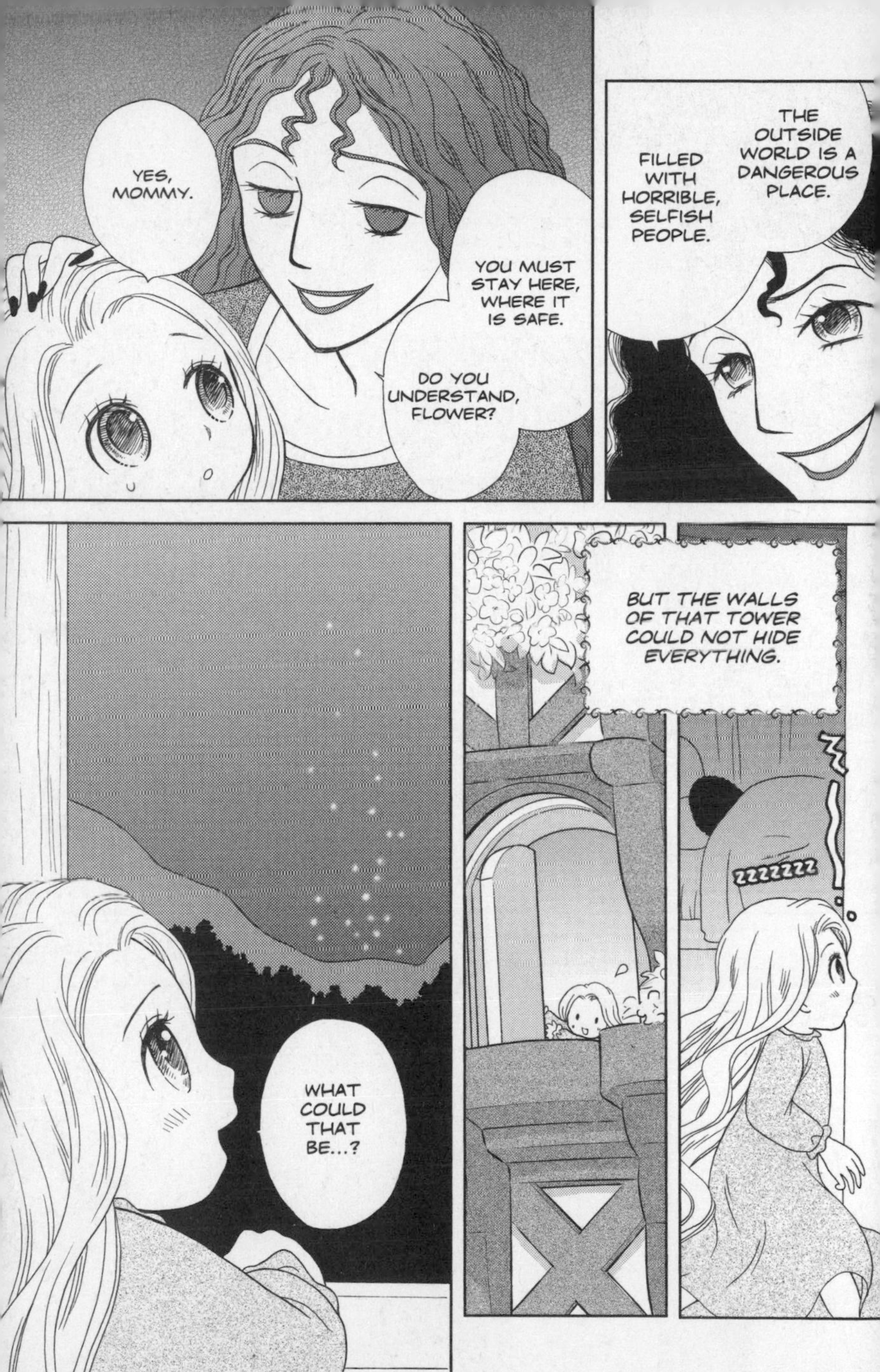
THE OUTSIDE WORLD IS A DANGEROUS PLACE.
FILLED WITH HORRIBLE, SELFISH PEOPLE.
YOU MUST STAY HERE, WHERE IT IS SAFE.
DO YOU UNDERSTAND, FLOWER?
YES, MOMMY.
BUT THE WALLS OF THAT TOWER COULD NOT HIDE EVERYTHING.
ZZZZZZZ
WHAT COULD THAT BE...?

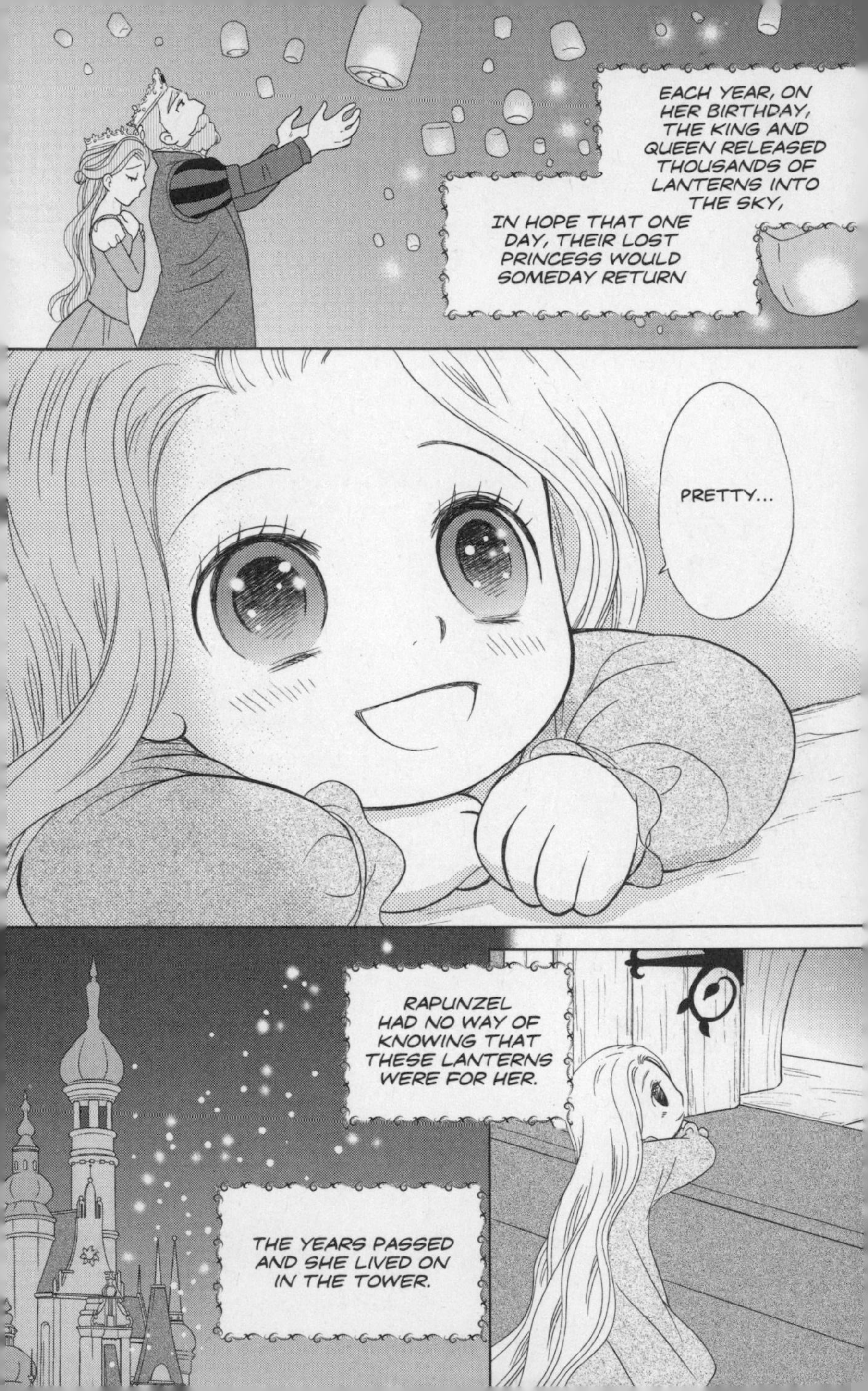
EACH YEAR, ON HER BIRTHDAY, THE KING AND QUEEN RELEASED THOUSANDS OF LANTERNS INTO THE SKY,
IN HOPE THAT ONE DAY, THEIR LOST PRINCESS WOULD SOMEDAY RETURN
PRETTY...
RAPUNZEL HAD NO WAY OF KNOWING THAT THESE LANTERNS WERE FOR HER.
THE YEARS PASSED AND SHE LIVED ON IN THE TOWER.

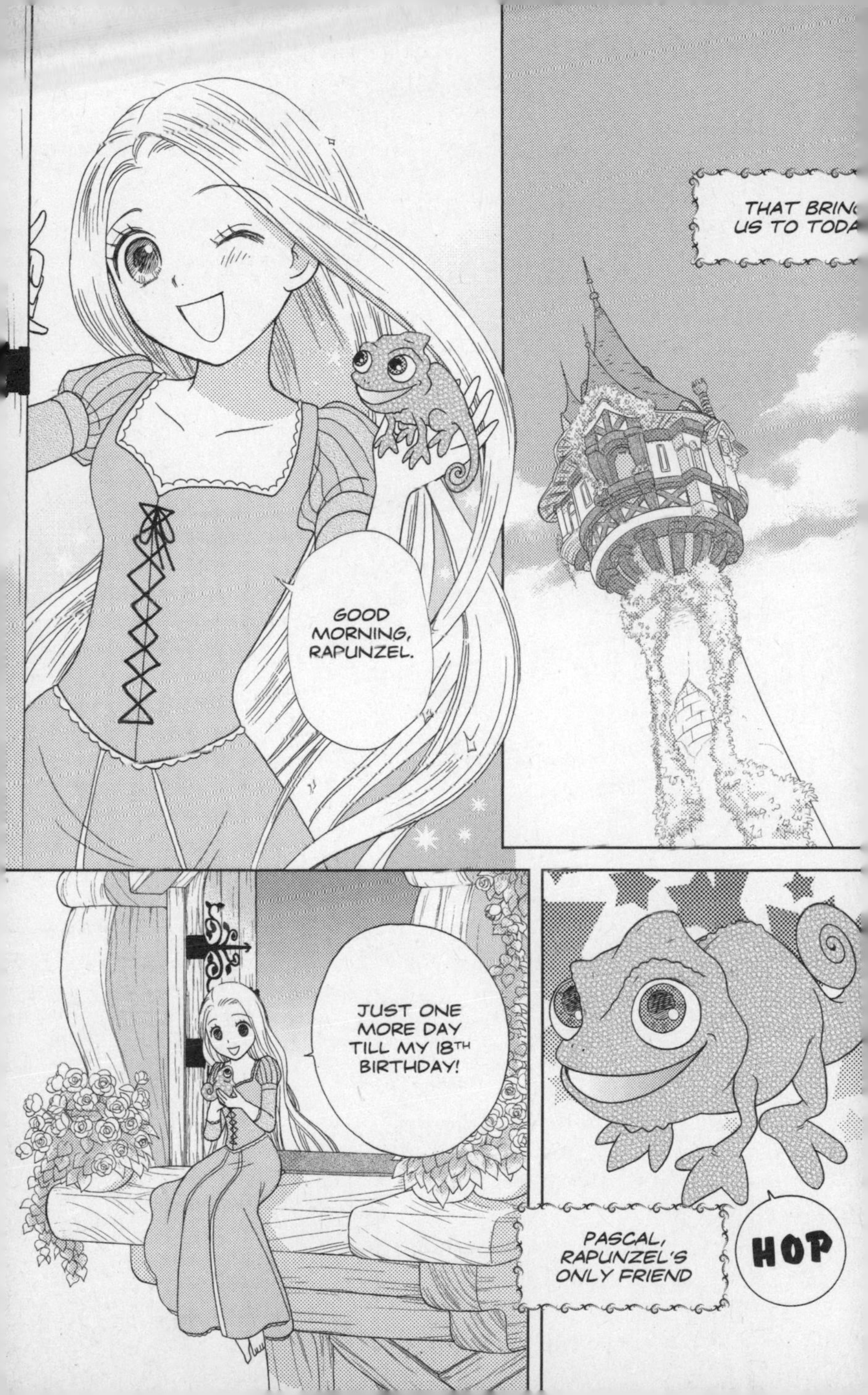
THAT BRING
US TO TODA
GOOD MORNING, RAPUNZEL.
HOP
PASCAL, RAPUNZEL'S ONLY FRIEND
JUST ONE MORE DAY TILL MY 18TH BIRTHDAY!

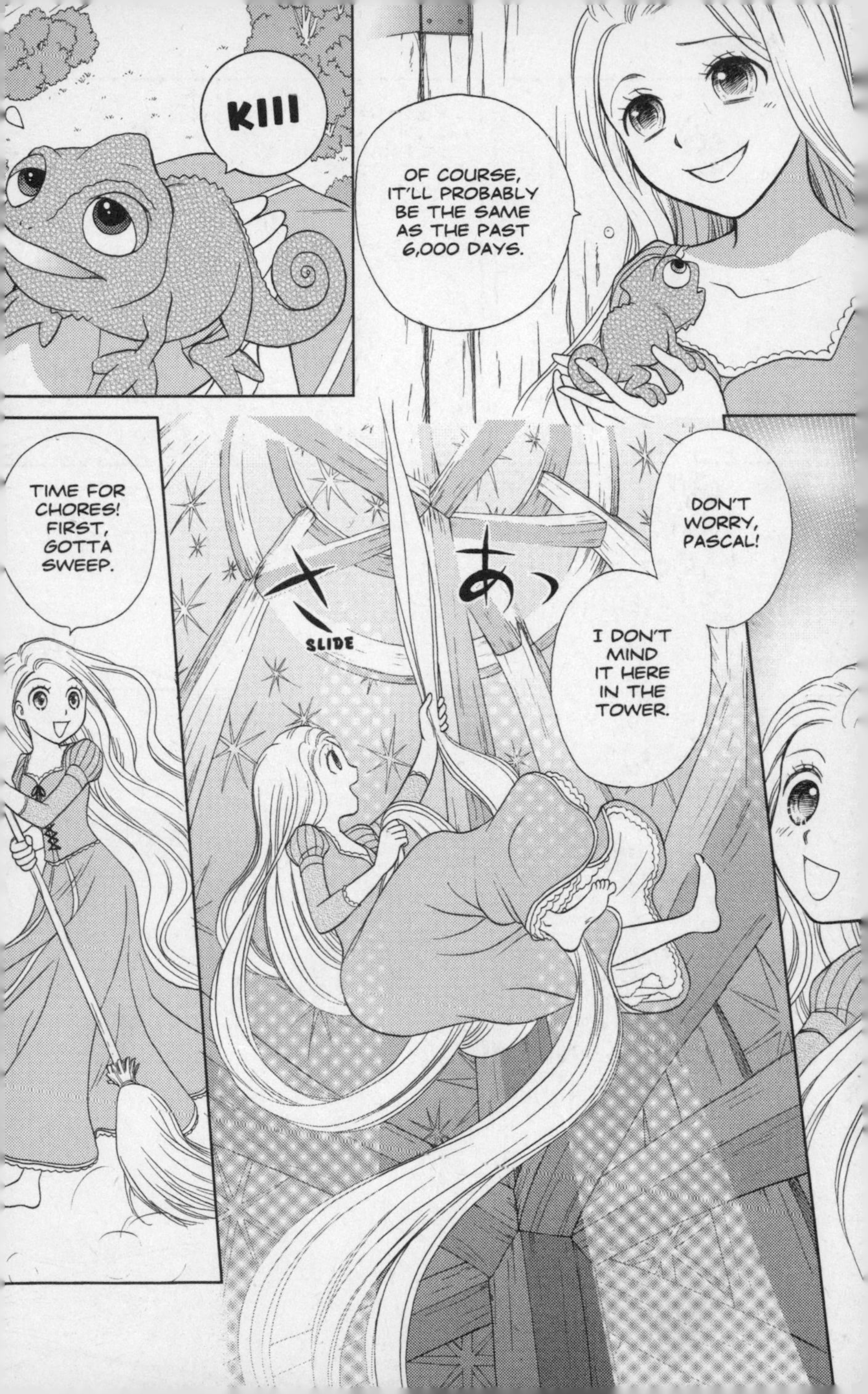

OF COURSE, IT'LL PROBABLY BE THE SAME AS THE PAST 6,000 DAYS.
KIII
DON'T WORRY, PASCAL!
I DON'T MIND IT HERE IN THE TOWER.
あっ
SLIDE
TIME FOR CHORES! FIRST, GOTTA SWEEP.

READ THIS WAY

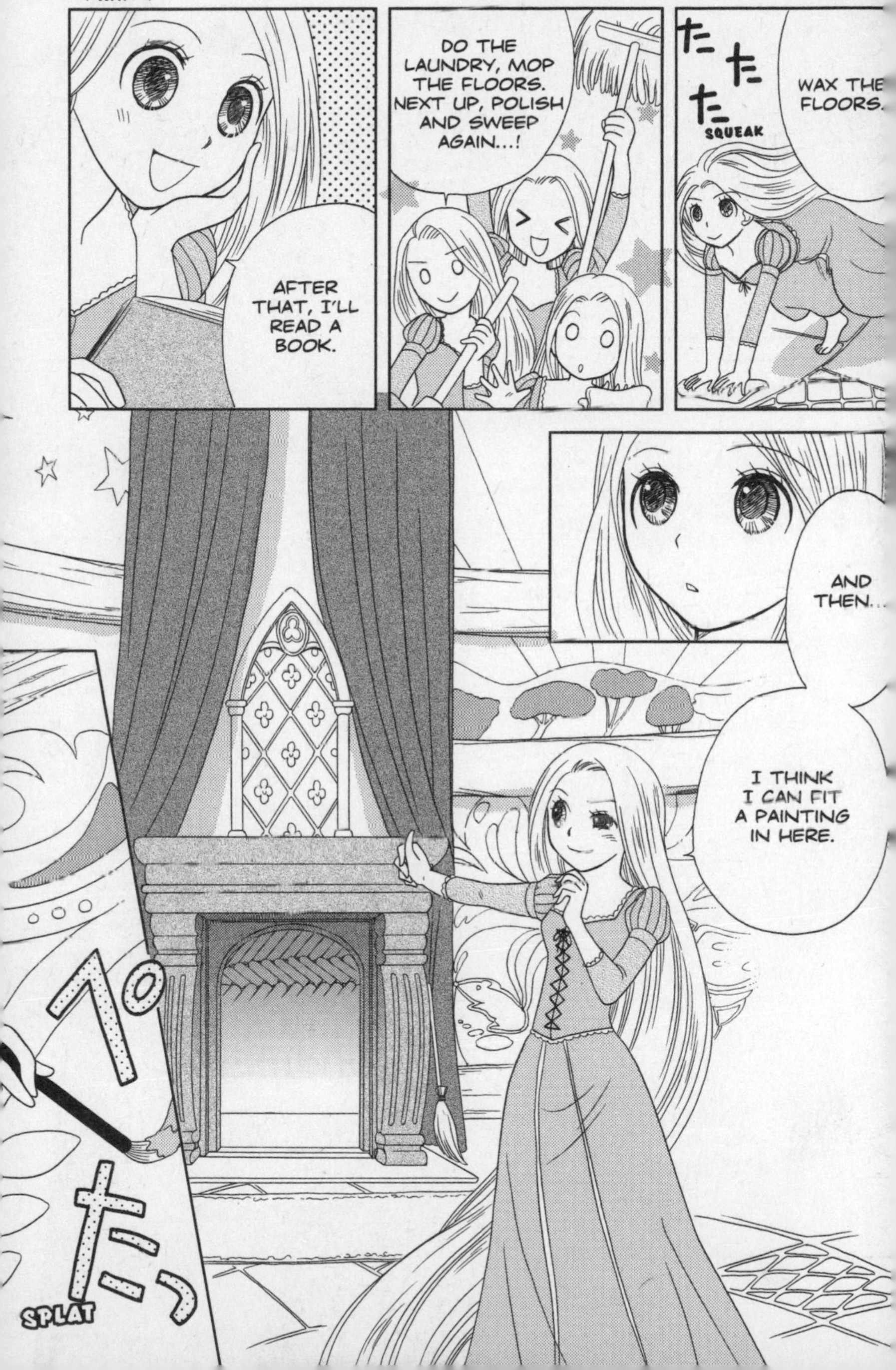

WAX THE FLOORS.
たたた
SQUEAK
DO THE LAUNDRY, MOP THE FLOORS. NEXT UP, POLISH AND SWEEP AGAIN...!
AFTER THAT, I'LL READ A BOOK.
AND THEN...
I THINK I CAN FIT A PAINTING IN HERE.
ぺたっ
SPLAT

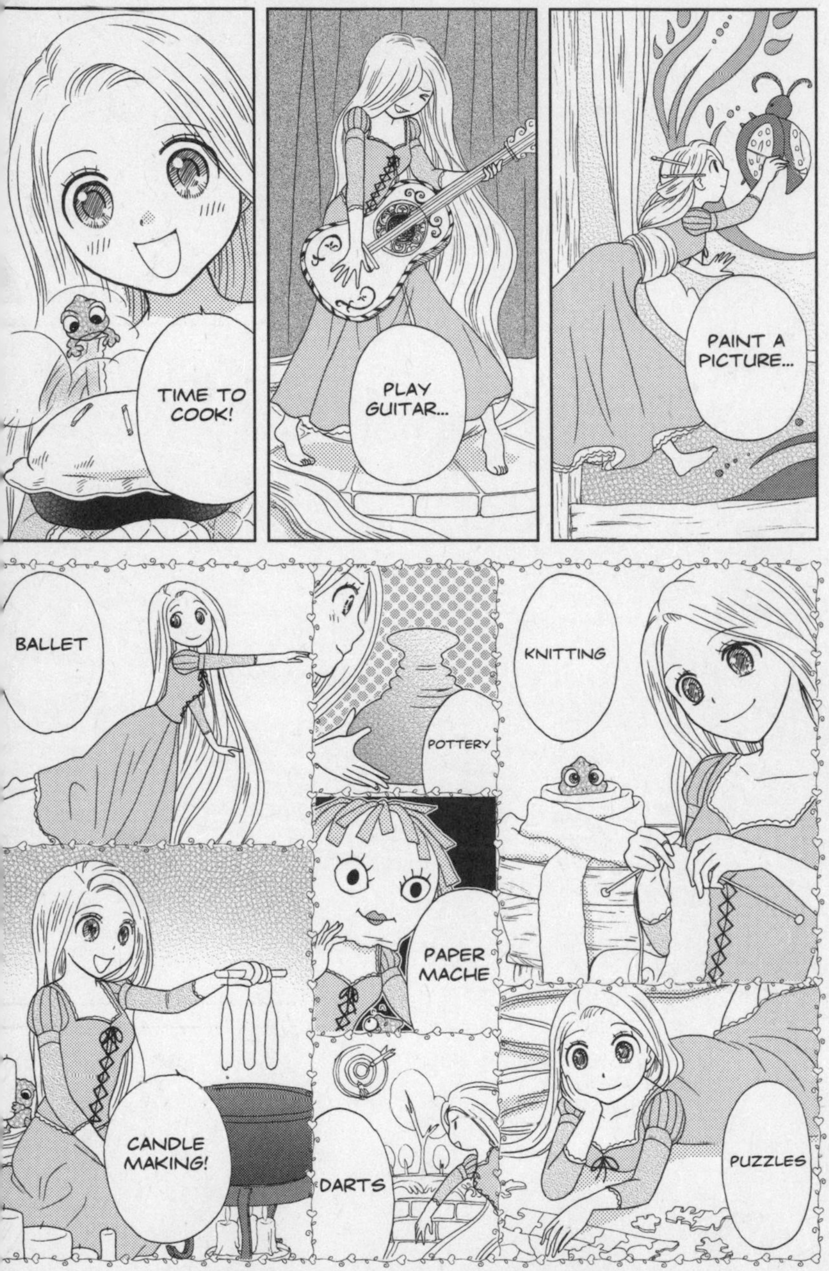
PAINT A PICTURE...
PLAY GUITAR...
TIME TO COOK!
KNITTING
POTTERY
BALLET
PAPER MACHE
PUZZLES
DARTS
CANDLE MAKING!

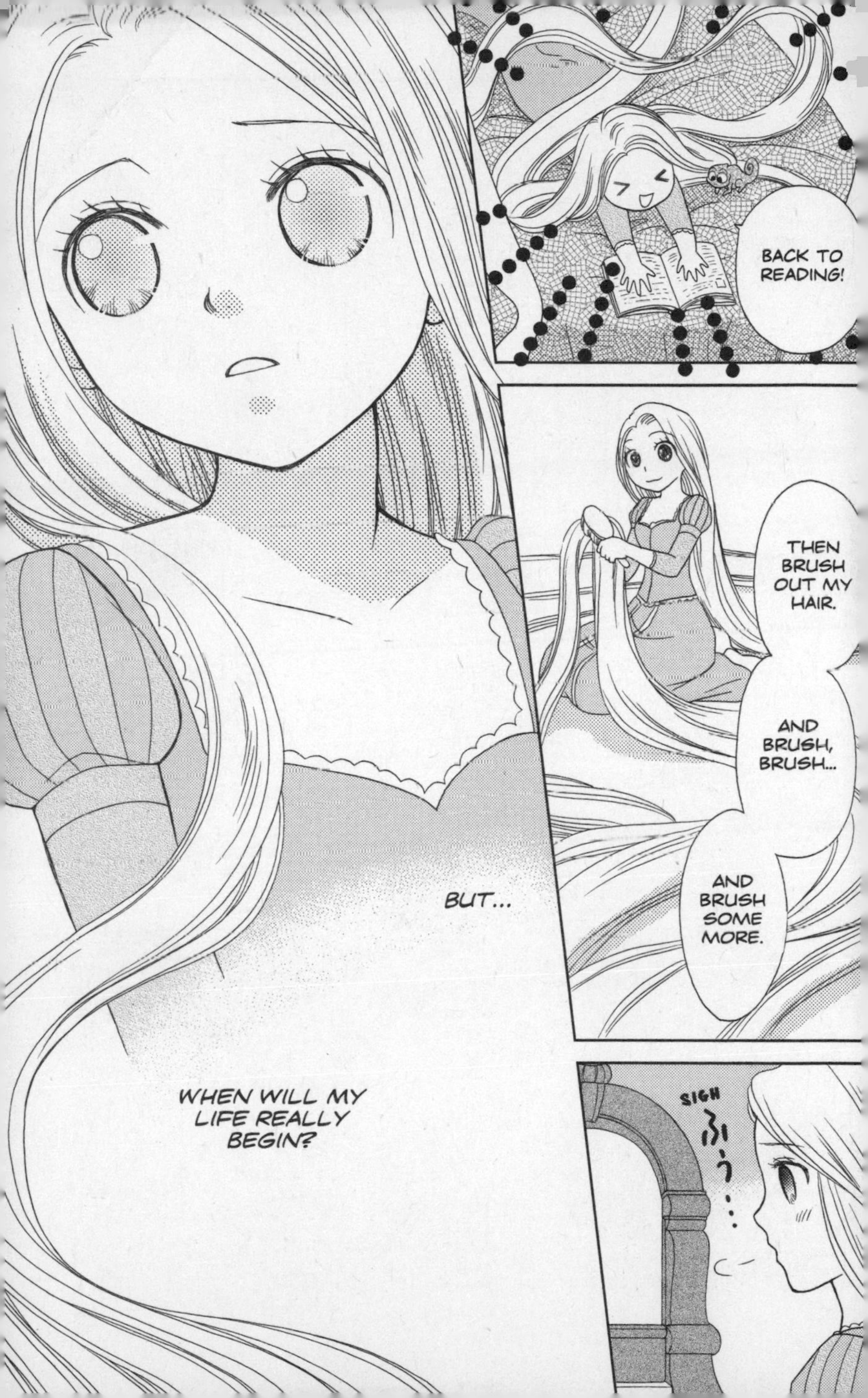
BACK TO READING!
THEN BRUSH OUT MY HAIR.
AND BRUSH, BRUSH...
AND BRUSH SOME MORE.
SIGH
ふぅ…
BUT...
WHEN WILL MY LIFE REALLY BEGIN?

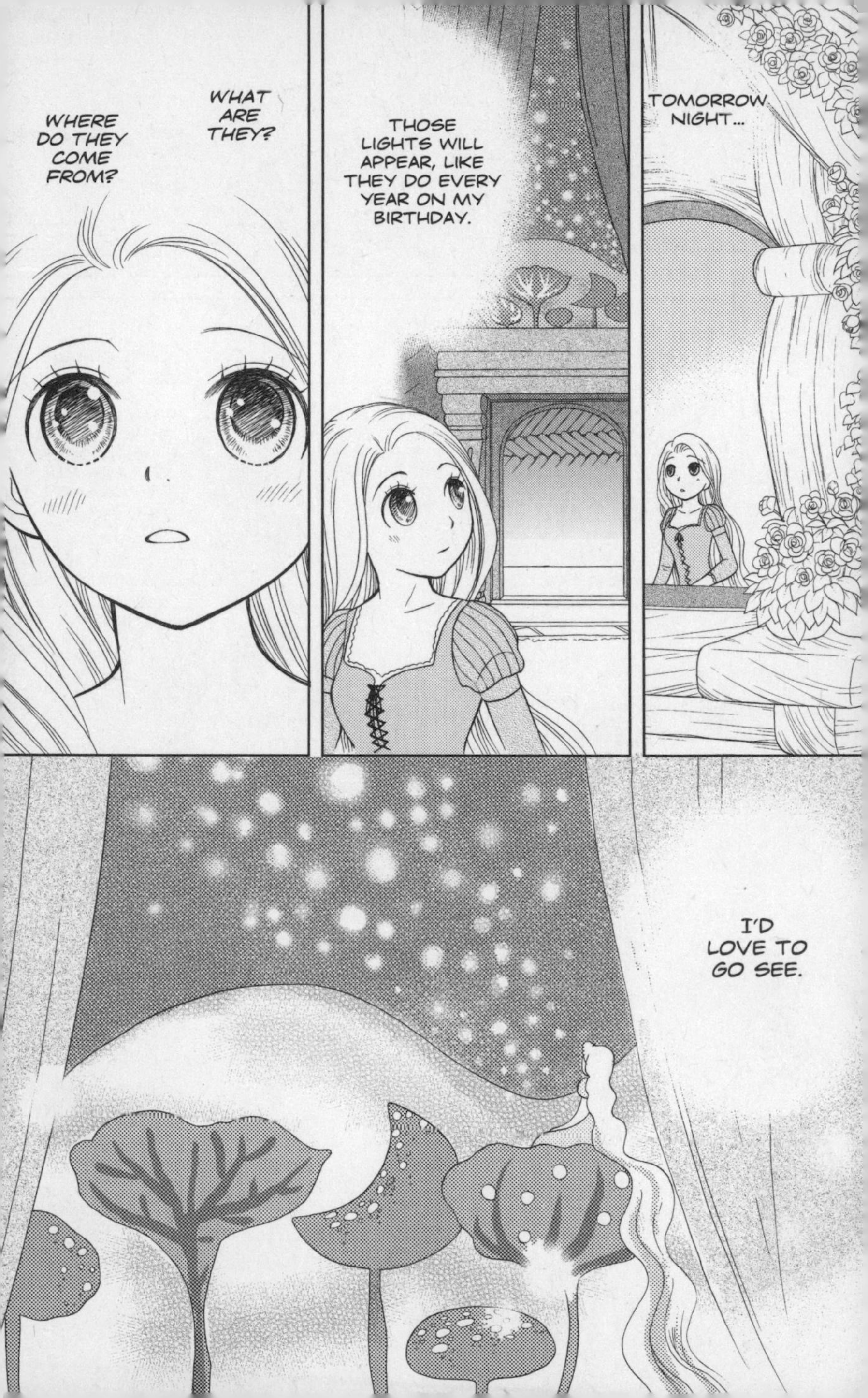
TOMORROW NIGHT...
THOSE LIGHTS WILL APPEAR, LIKE THEY DO EVERY YEAR ON MY BIRTHDAY.
WHAT ARE THEY?
WHERE DO THEY COME FROM?
I'D LOVE TO GO SEE.

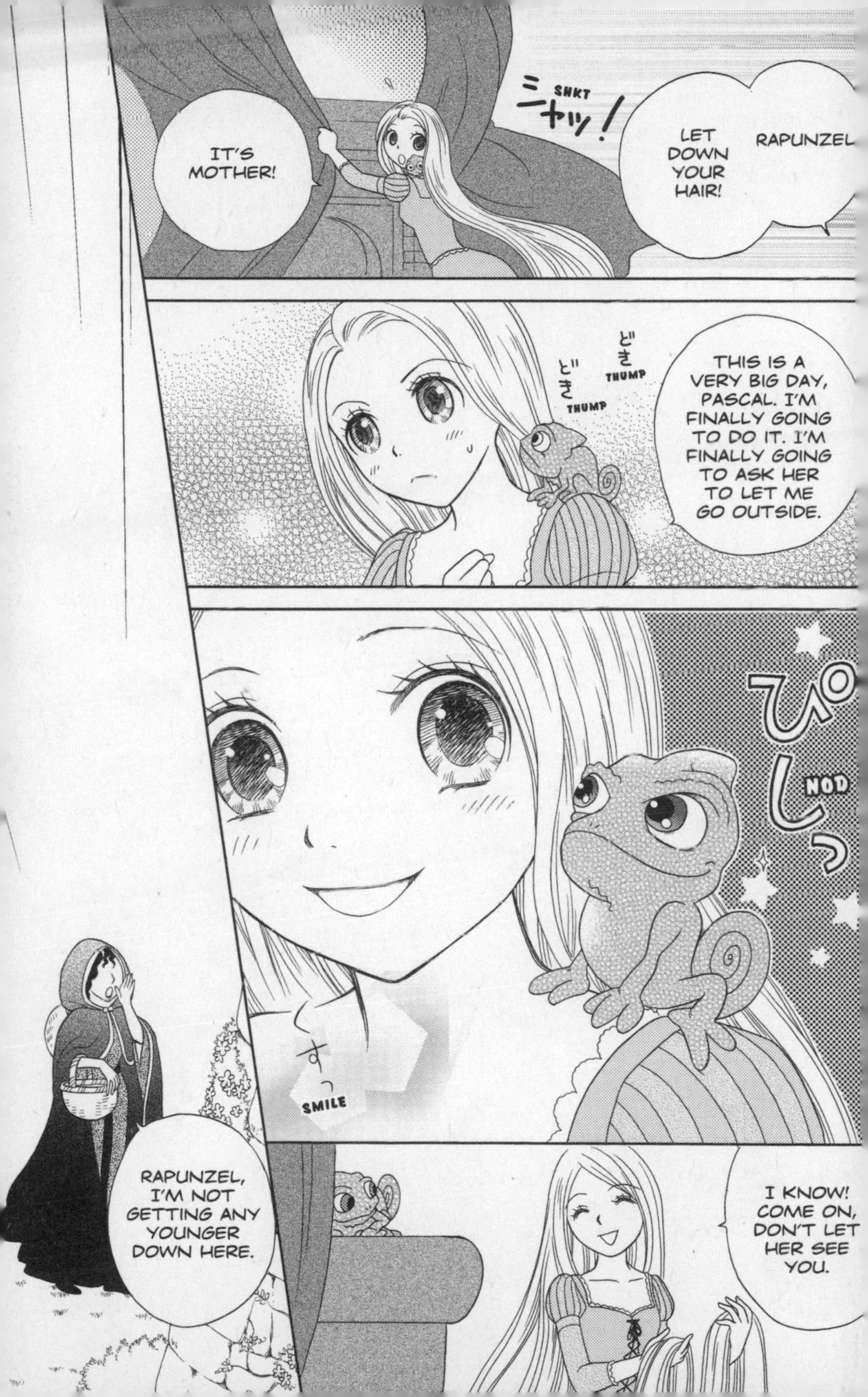
RAPUNZEL
LET DOWN YOUR HAIR!
シャッ! SHKT
IT'S MOTHER!
THIS IS A VERY BIG DAY, PASCAL. I'M FINALLY GOING TO DO IT. I'M FINALLY GOING TO ASK HER TO LET ME GO OUTSIDE.
どき THUMP
どき THUMP
ぴしっ NOD
すっ SMILE
I KNOW! COME ON, DON'T LET HER SEE YOU.
RAPUNZEL, I'M NOT GETTING ANY YOUNGER DOWN HERE.

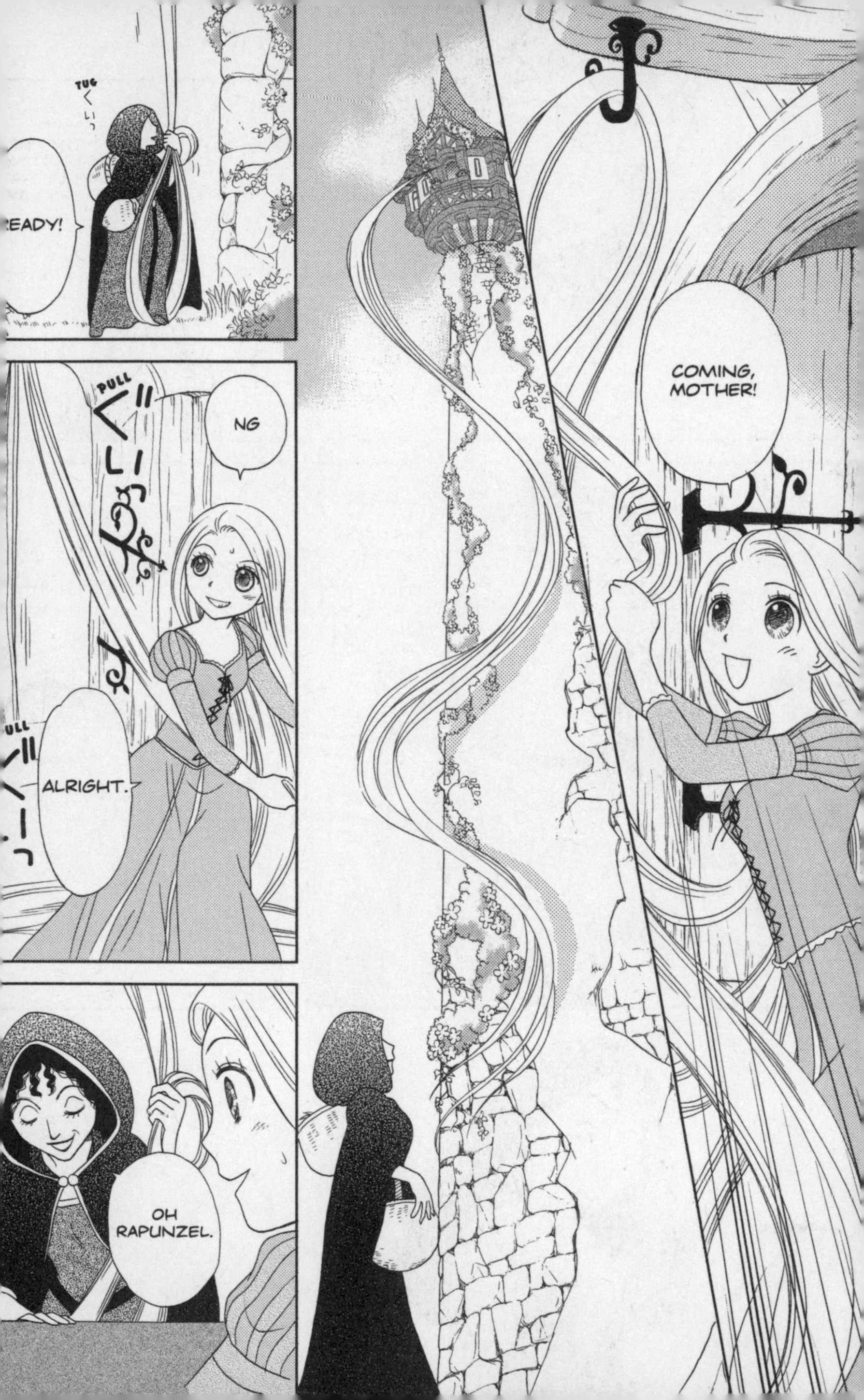
COMING, MOTHER!
TUG
READY!
PULL
NG
PULL
ALRIGHT.
OH RAPUNZEL.

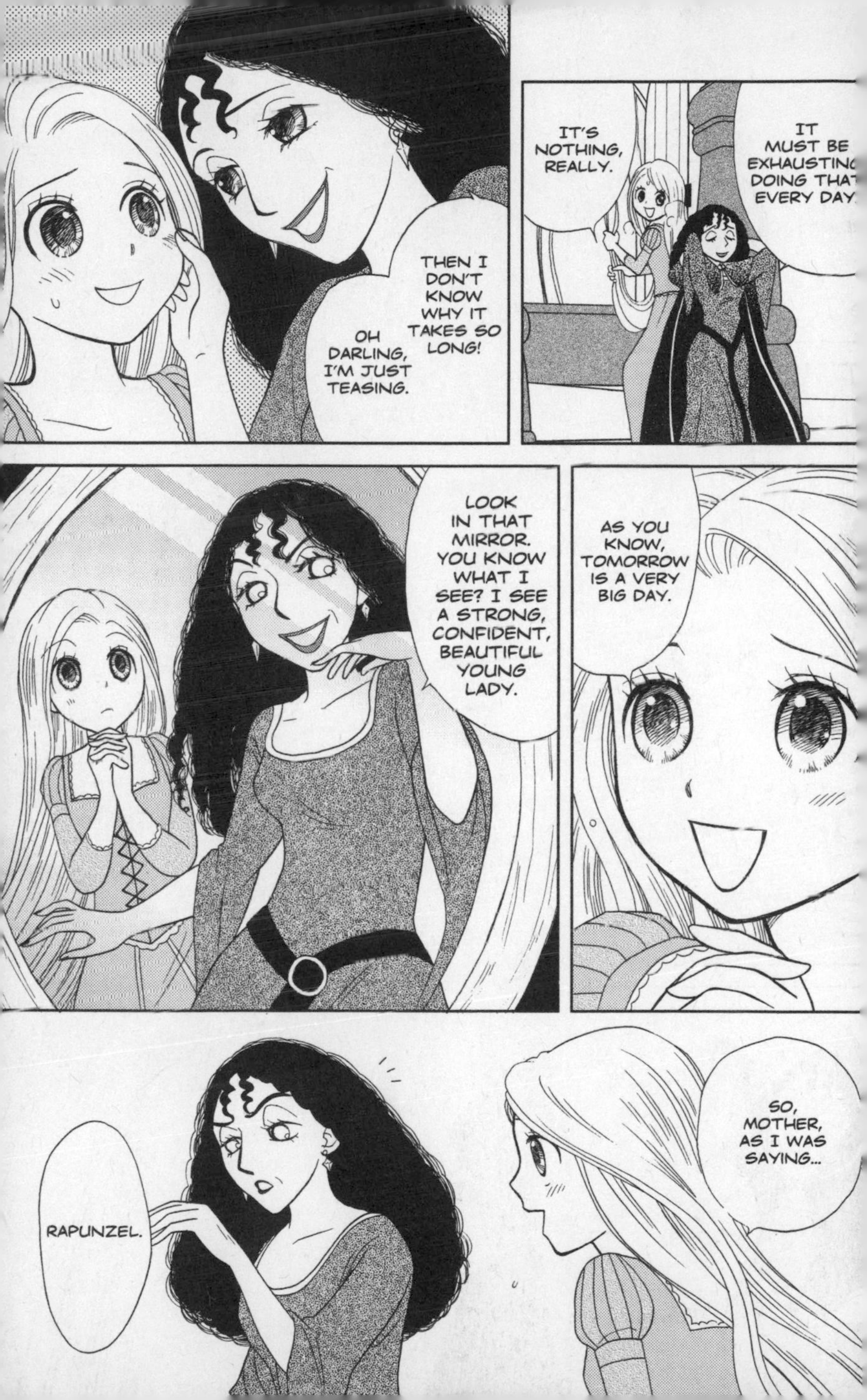
IT MUST BE EXHAUSTING DOING THAT EVERY DAY.
IT'S NOTHING, REALLY.
THEN I DON'T KNOW WHY IT TAKES SO LONG!
OH DARLING, I'M JUST TEASING.
AS YOU KNOW, TOMORROW IS A VERY BIG DAY.
LOOK IN THAT MIRROR. YOU KNOW WHAT I SEE? I SEE A STRONG, CONFIDENT, BEAUTIFUL YOUNG LADY.
SO, MOTHER, AS I WAS SAYING...
RAPUNZEL.

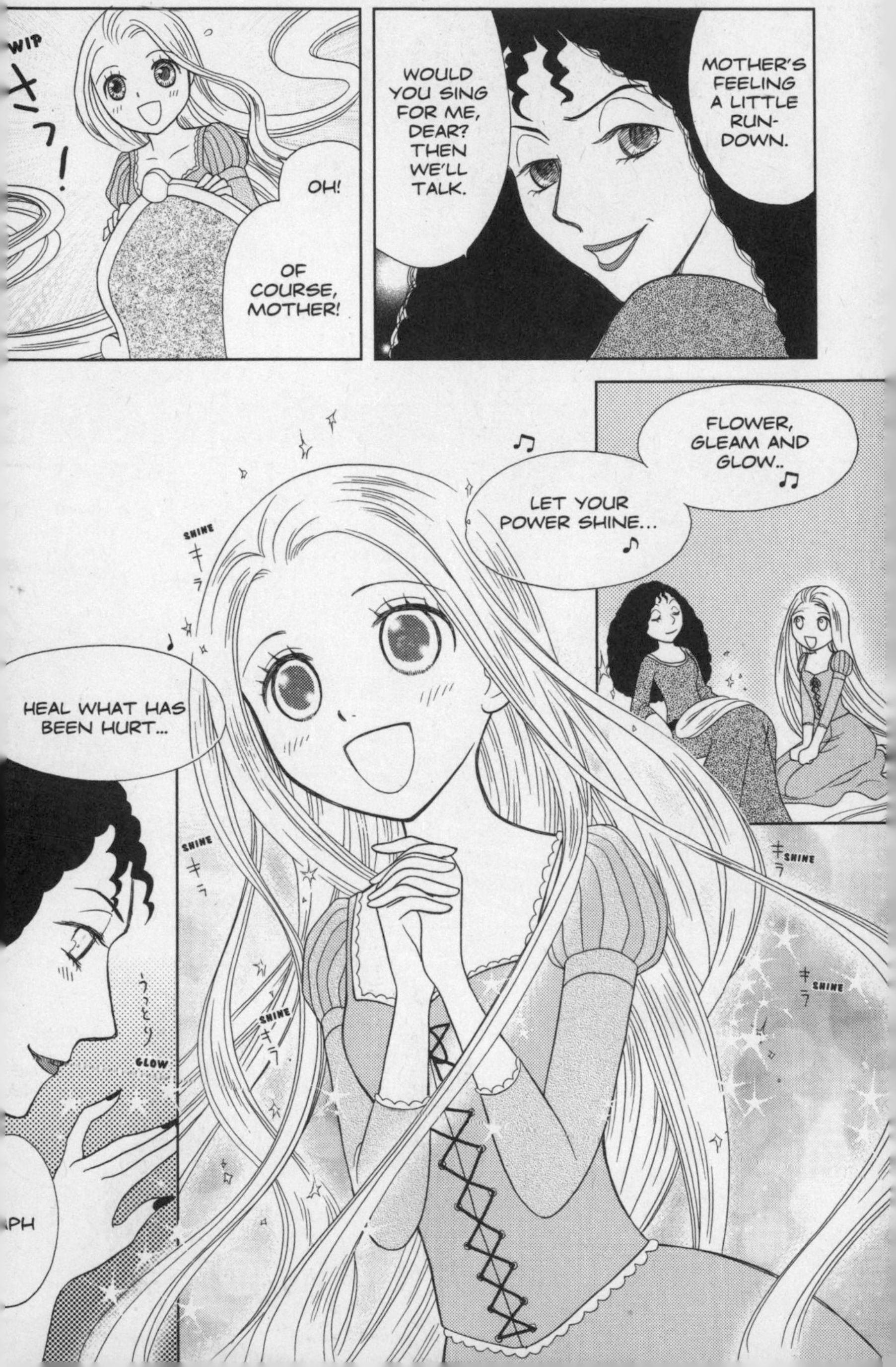
MOTHER'S FEELING A LITTLE RUN-DOWN.
WOULD YOU SING FOR ME, DEAR? THEN WE'LL TALK.
WIP
OH!
OF COURSE, MOTHER!
FLOWER, GLEAM AND GLOW.. ♫
LET YOUR POWER SHINE... ♪
SHINE
SHINE
SHINE
SHINE
SHINE
HEAL WHAT HAS BEEN HURT...
GLOW

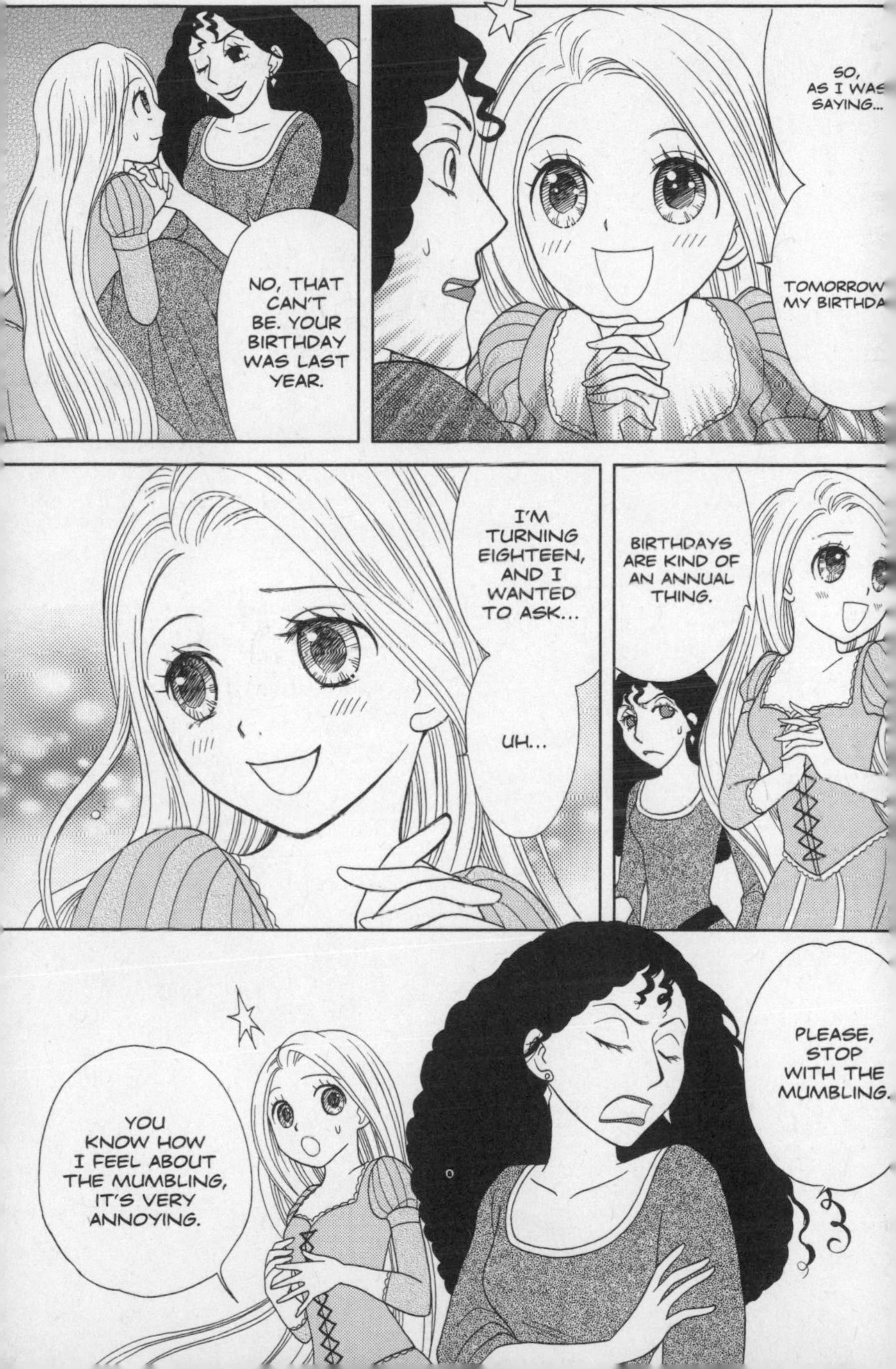
SO, AS I WAS SAYING...
TOMORROW MY BIRTHDA
NO, THAT CAN'T BE. YOUR BIRTHDAY WAS LAST YEAR.
BIRTHDAYS ARE KIND OF AN ANNUAL THING.
I'M TURNING EIGHTEEN, AND I WANTED TO ASK...
UH...
PLEASE, STOP WITH THE MUMBLING.
YOU KNOW HOW I FEEL ABOUT THE MUMBLING, IT'S VERY ANNOYING.

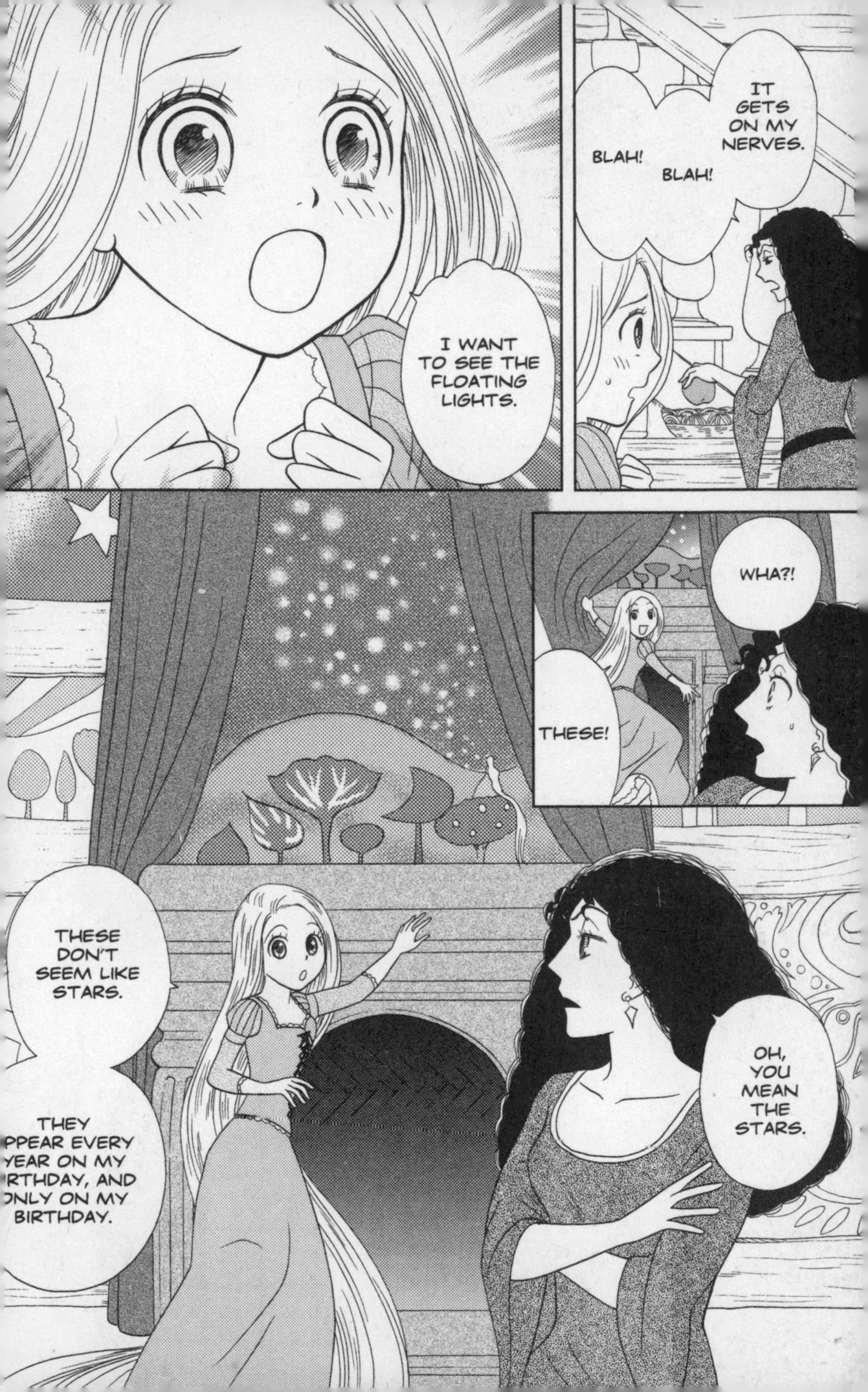
IT GETS ON MY NERVES.
BLAH!
BLAH!
I WANT TO SEE THE FLOATING LIGHTS.
WHA?!
THESE!
OH, YOU MEAN THE STARS.
THESE DON'T SEEM LIKE STARS.
THEY PPEAR EVERY YEAR ON MY RTHDAY, AND NLY ON MY BIRTHDAY.

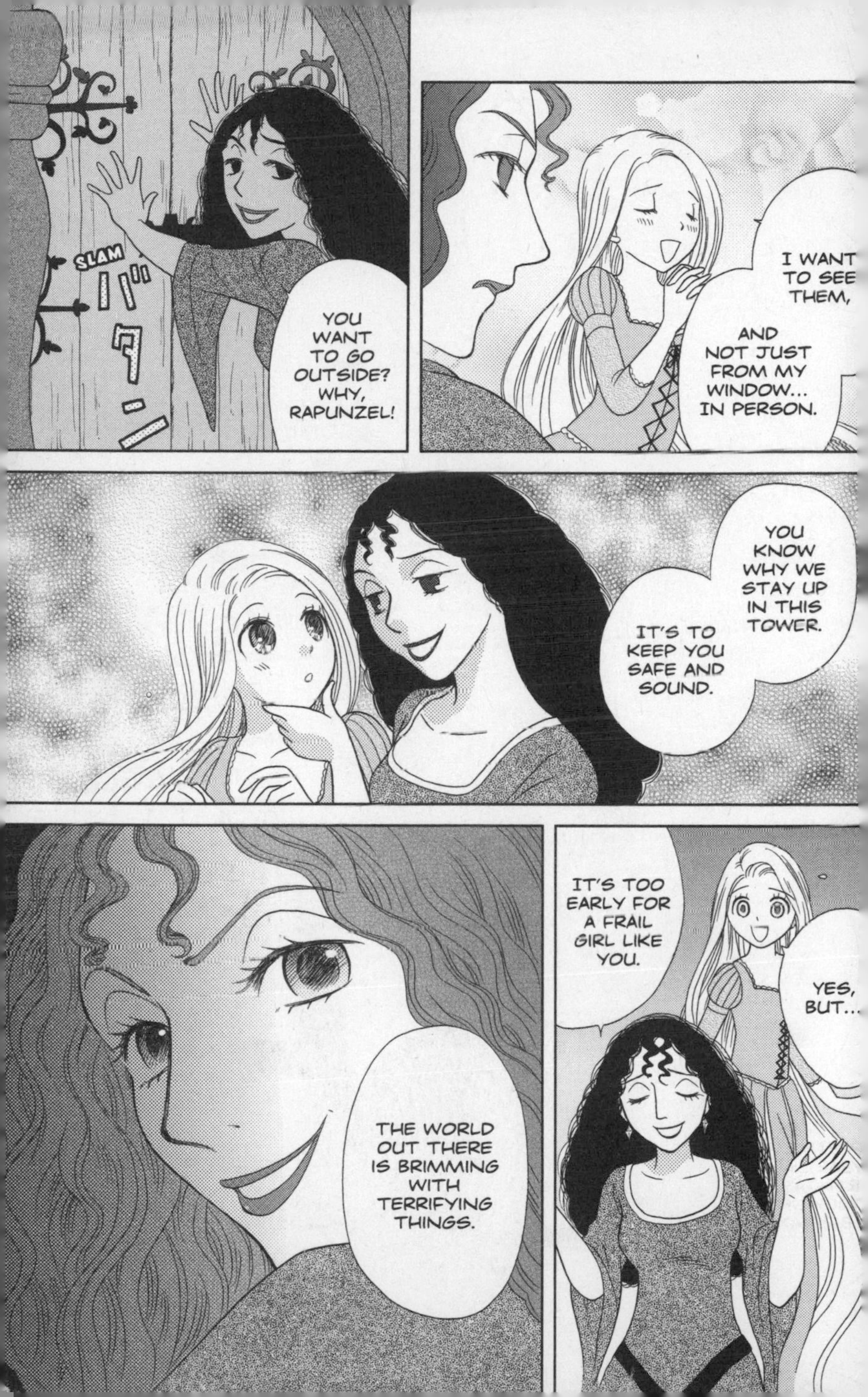
I WANT TO SEE THEM,
AND NOT JUST FROM MY WINDOW... IN PERSON.
SLAM
YOU WANT TO GO OUTSIDE? WHY, RAPUNZEL!
YOU KNOW WHY WE STAY UP IN THIS TOWER.
IT'S TO KEEP YOU SAFE AND SOUND.
YES, BUT...
IT'S TOO EARLY FOR A FRAIL GIRL LIKE YOU.
THE WORLD OUT THERE IS BRIMMING WITH TERRIFYING THINGS.

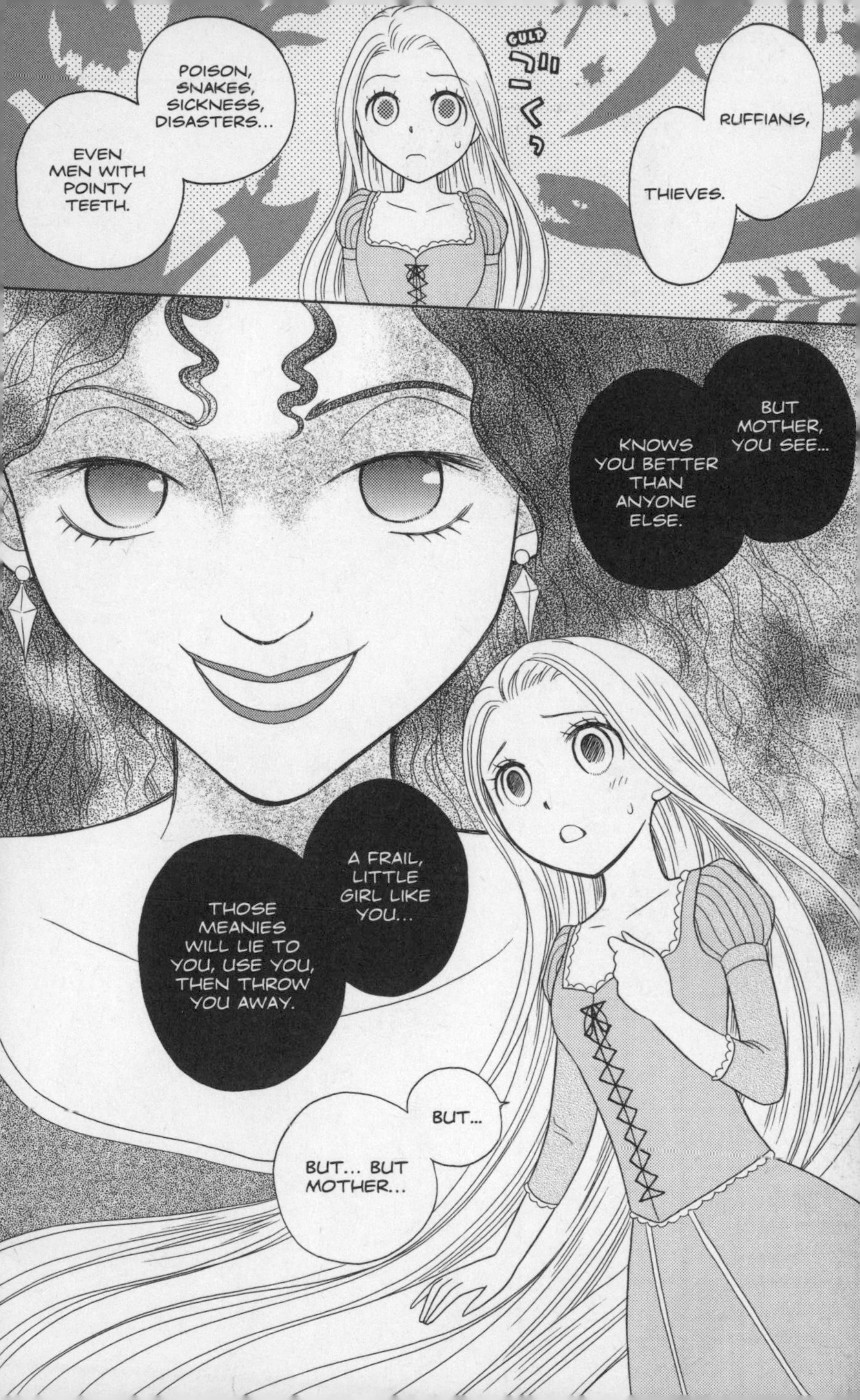
RUFFIANS,
THIEVES.
GULP
POISON, SNAKES, SICKNESS, DISASTERS...
EVEN MEN WITH POINTY TEETH.
BUT MOTHER, YOU SEE...
KNOWS YOU BETTER THAN ANYONE ELSE.
A FRAIL, LITTLE GIRL LIKE YOU...
THOSE MEANIES WILL LIE TO YOU, USE YOU, THEN THROW YOU AWAY.
BUT...
BUT... BUT MOTHER...

READ THIS WAY

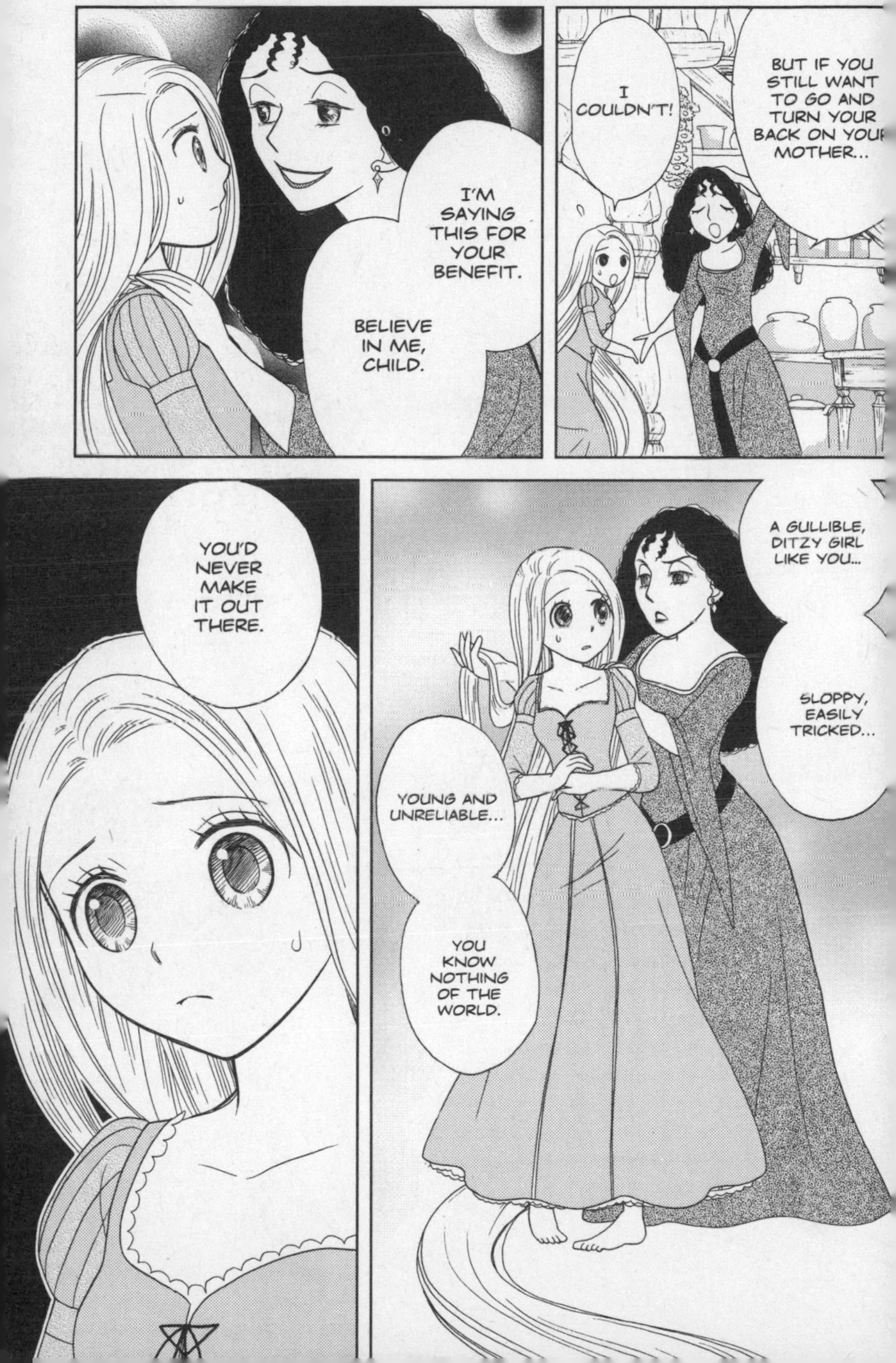

BUT IF YOU STILL WANT TO GO AND TURN YOUR BACK ON YOUR MOTHER...
I COULDN'T!
I'M SAYING THIS FOR YOUR BENEFIT.
BELIEVE IN ME, CHILD.
A GULLIBLE, DITZY GIRL LIKE YOU...
SLOPPY, EASILY TRICKED...
YOUNG AND UNRELIABLE...
YOU KNOW NOTHING OF THE WORLD.
YOU'D NEVER MAKE IT OUT THERE.

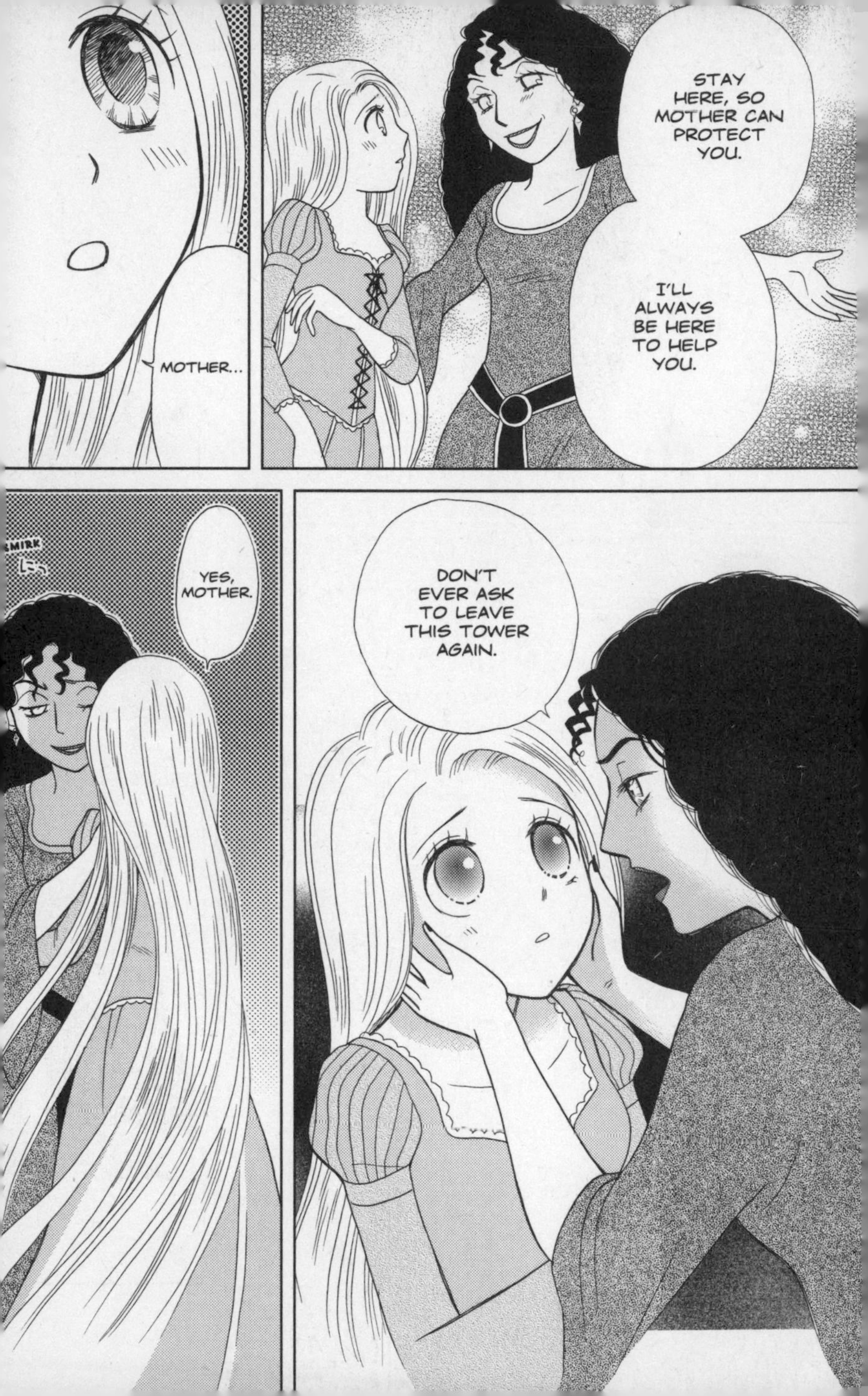
STAY HERE, SO MOTHER CAN PROTECT YOU.
I'LL ALWAYS BE HERE TO HELP YOU.
MOTHER...
DON'T EVER ASK TO LEAVE THIS TOWER AGAIN.
SMIRK
YES, MOTHER.

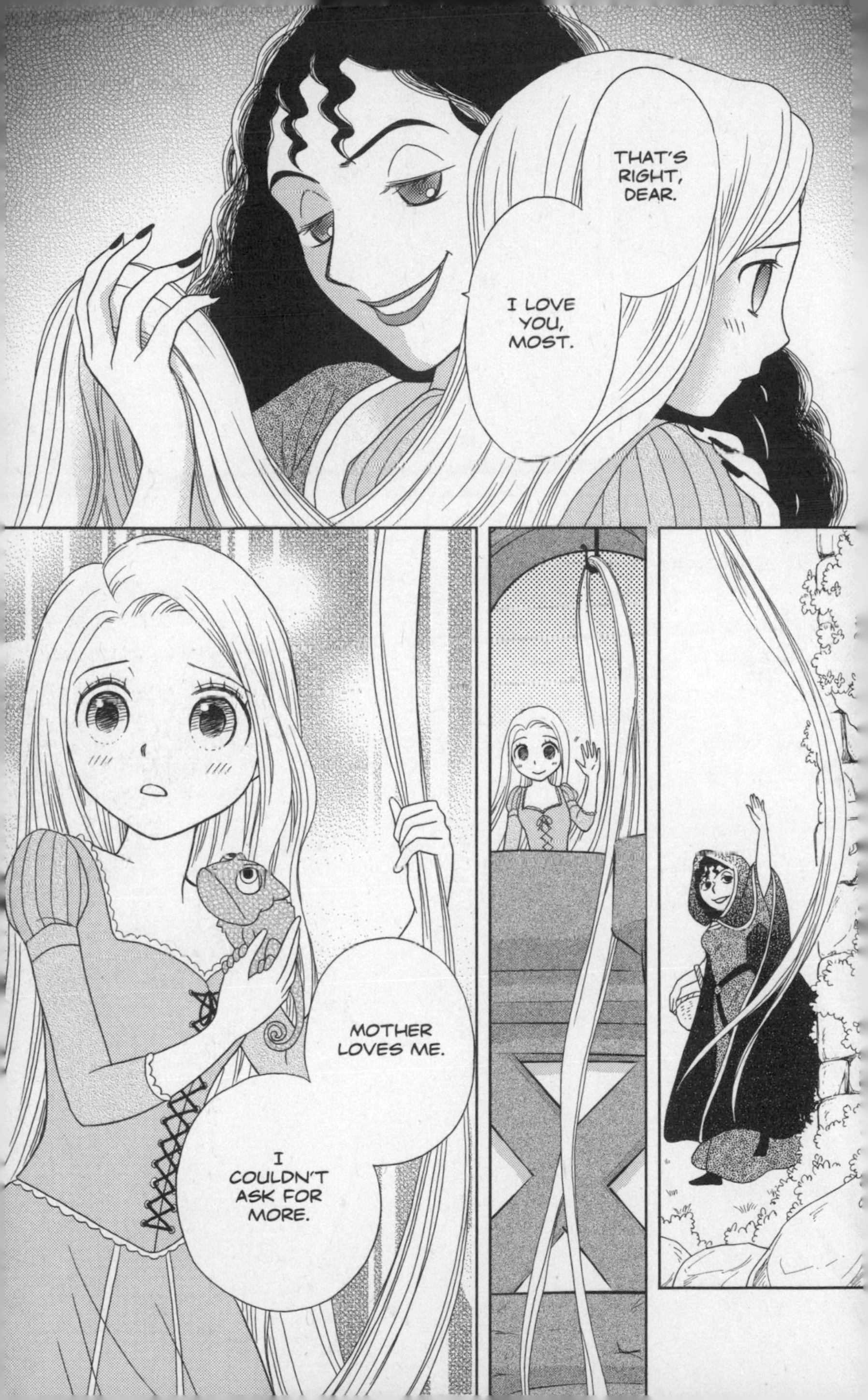
THAT'S RIGHT, DEAR.
I LOVE YOU, MOST.
MOTHER LOVES ME.
I COULDN'T ASK FOR MORE.

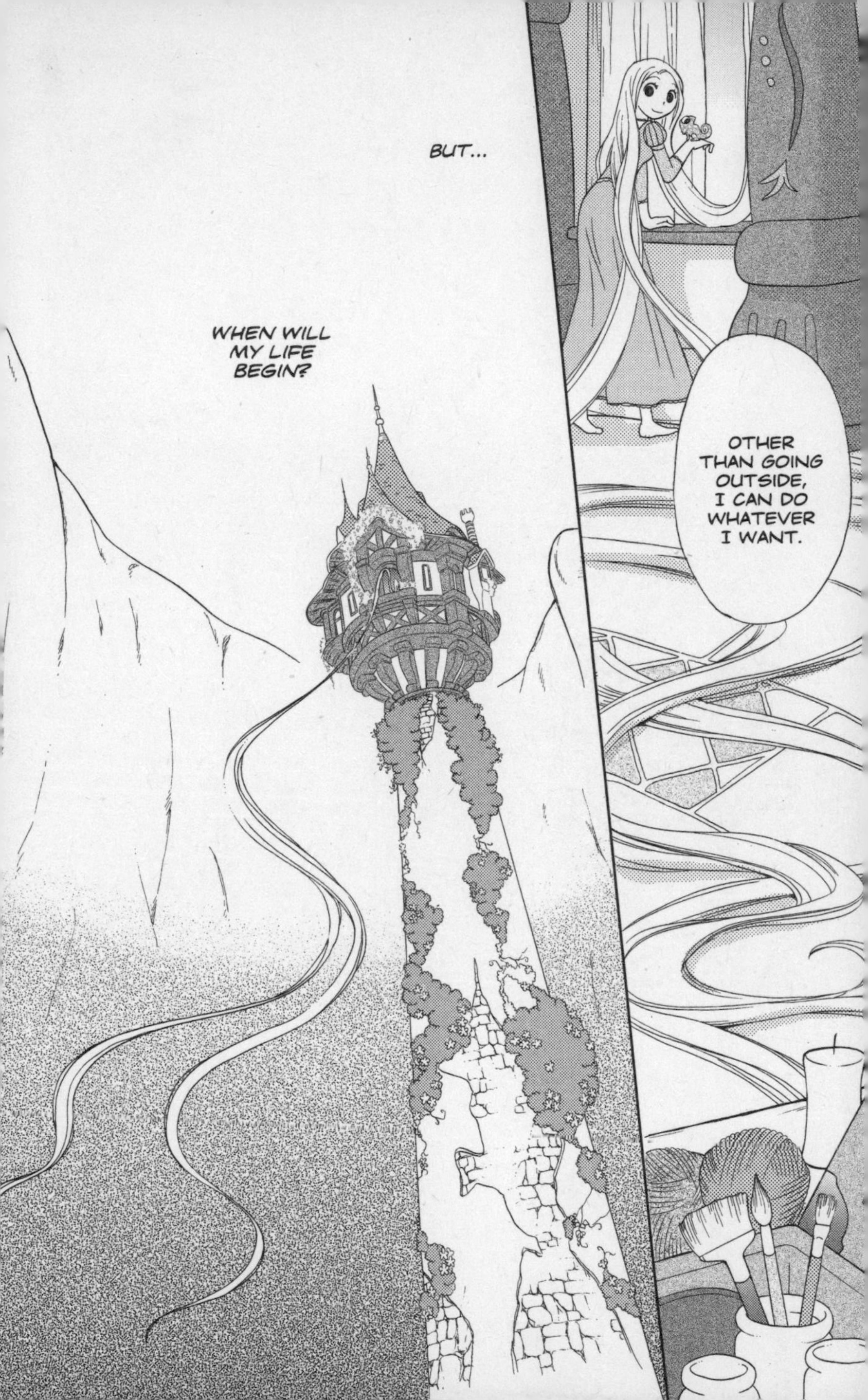
OTHER THAN GOING OUTSIDE, I CAN DO WHATEVER I WANT.
BUT...
WHEN WILL MY LIFE BEGIN?

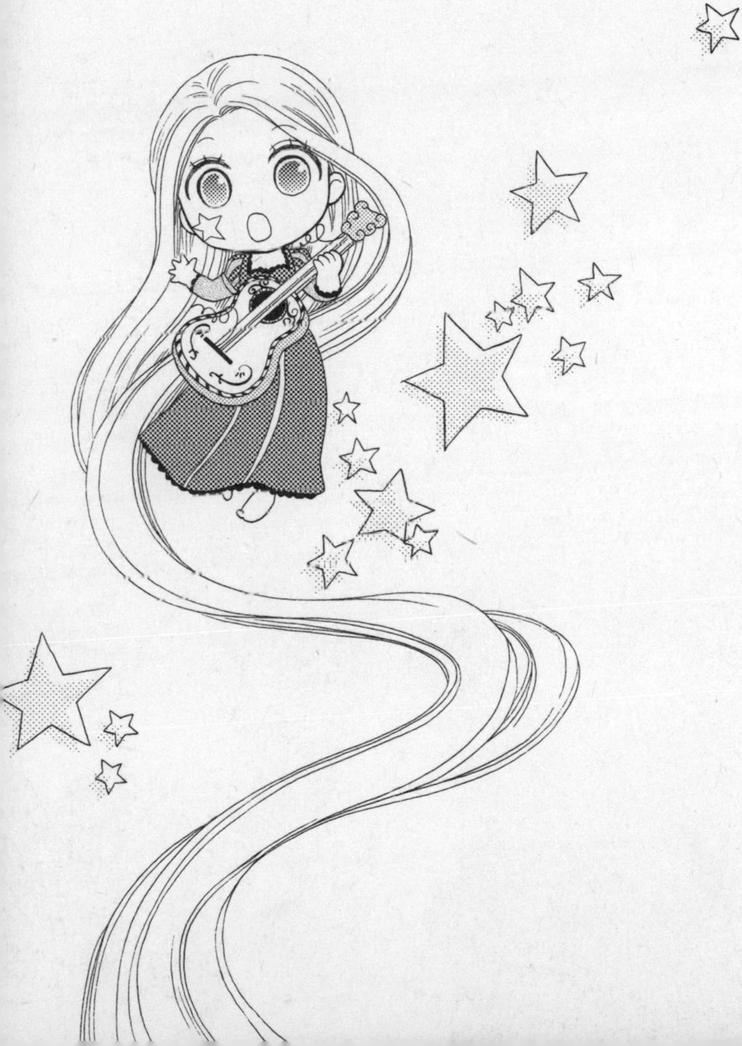

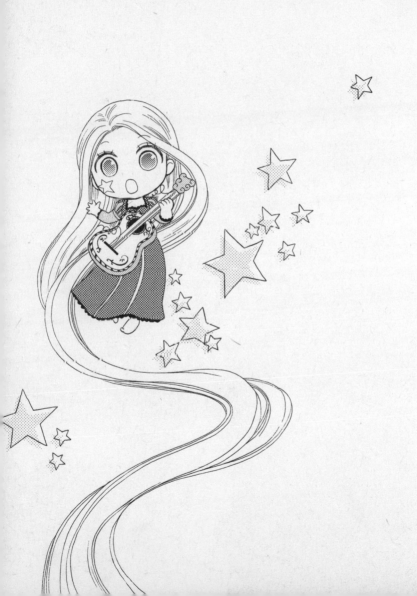

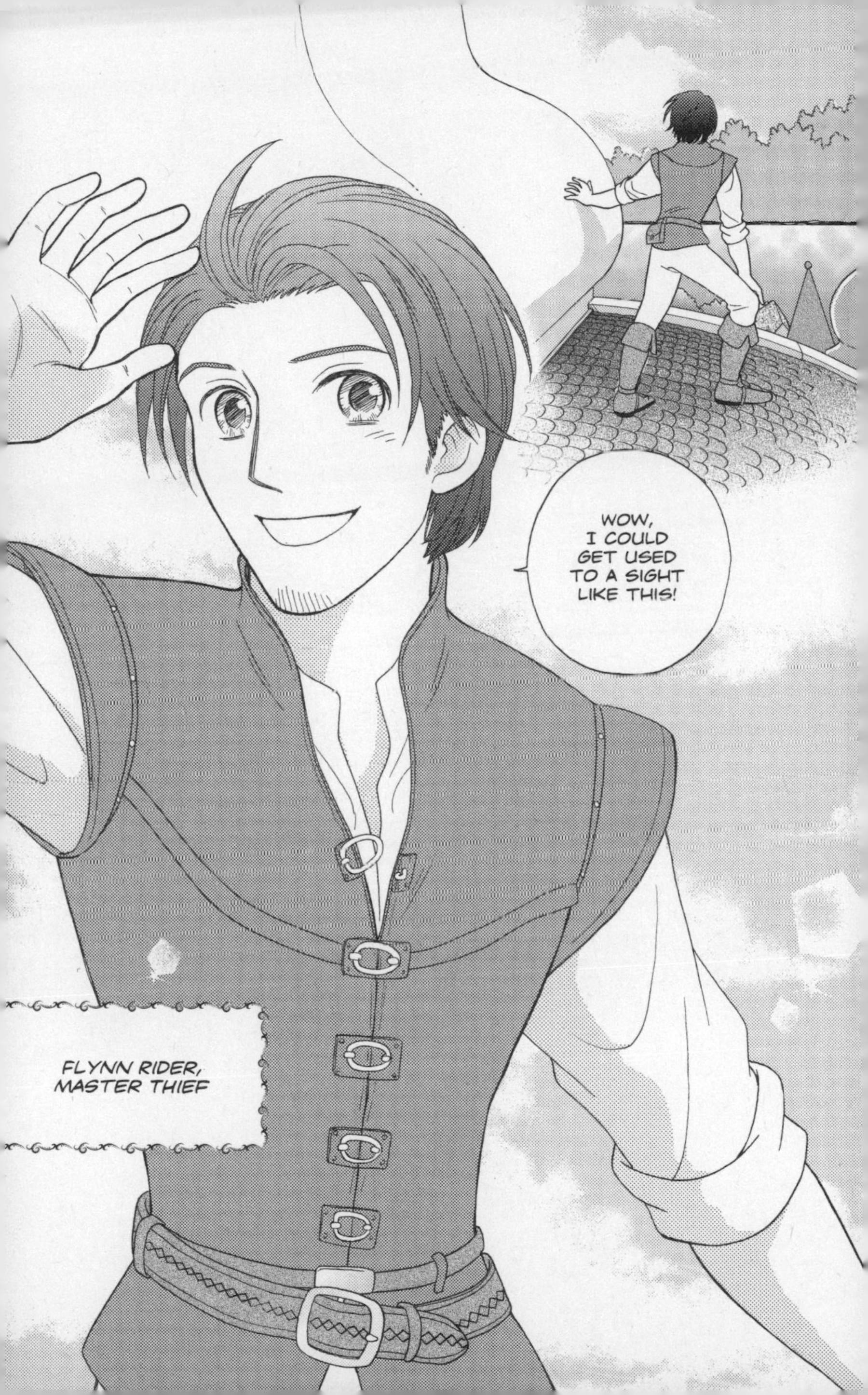
WOW, I COULD GET USED TO A SIGHT LIKE THIS!
FLYNN RIDER, MASTER THIEF

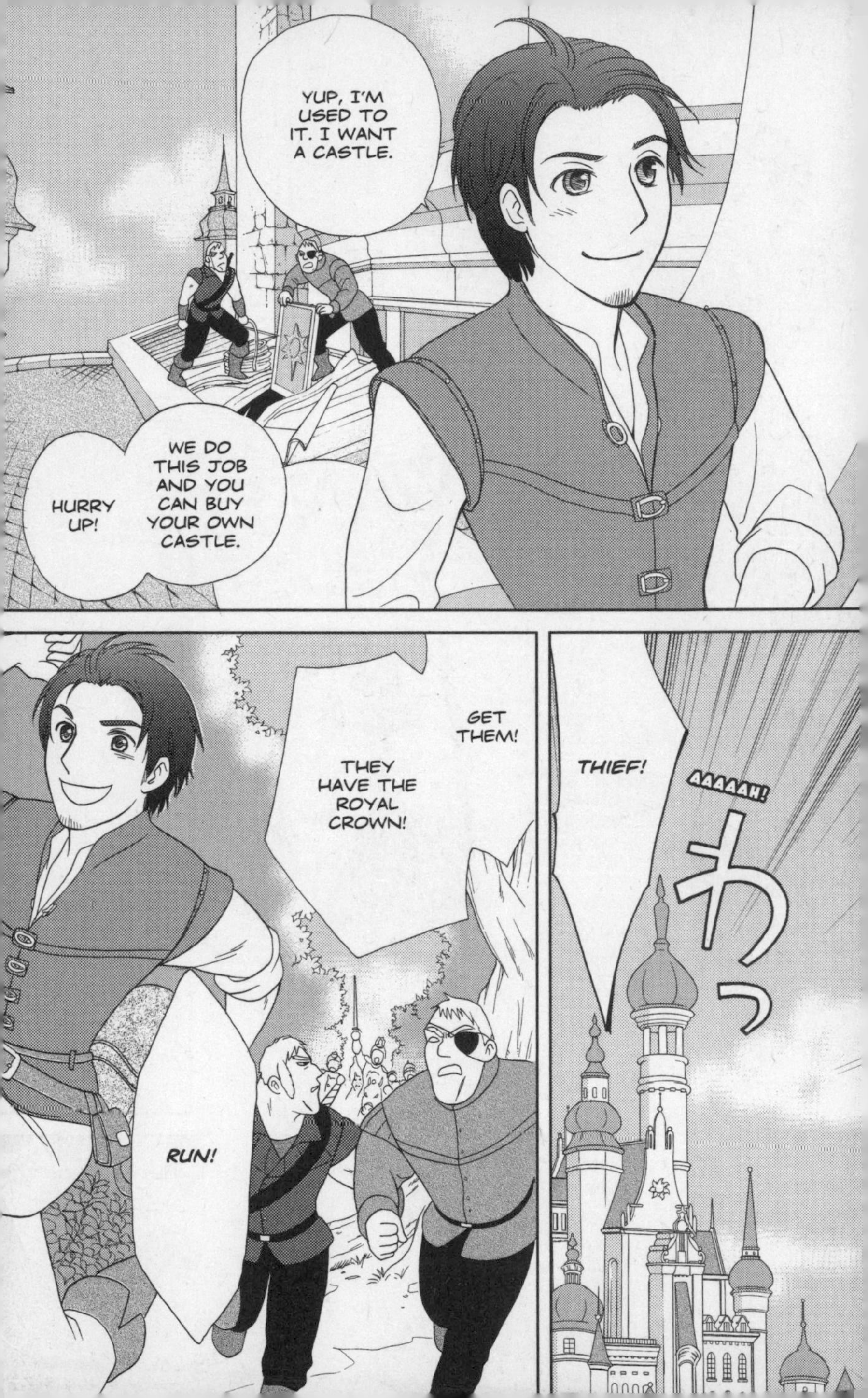
YUP, I'M USED TO IT. I WANT A CASTLE.
WE DO THIS JOB AND YOU CAN BUY YOUR OWN CASTLE.
HURRY UP!
AAAAAH!
わっ
THIEF!
GET THEM!
THEY HAVE THE ROYAL CROWN!
RUN!

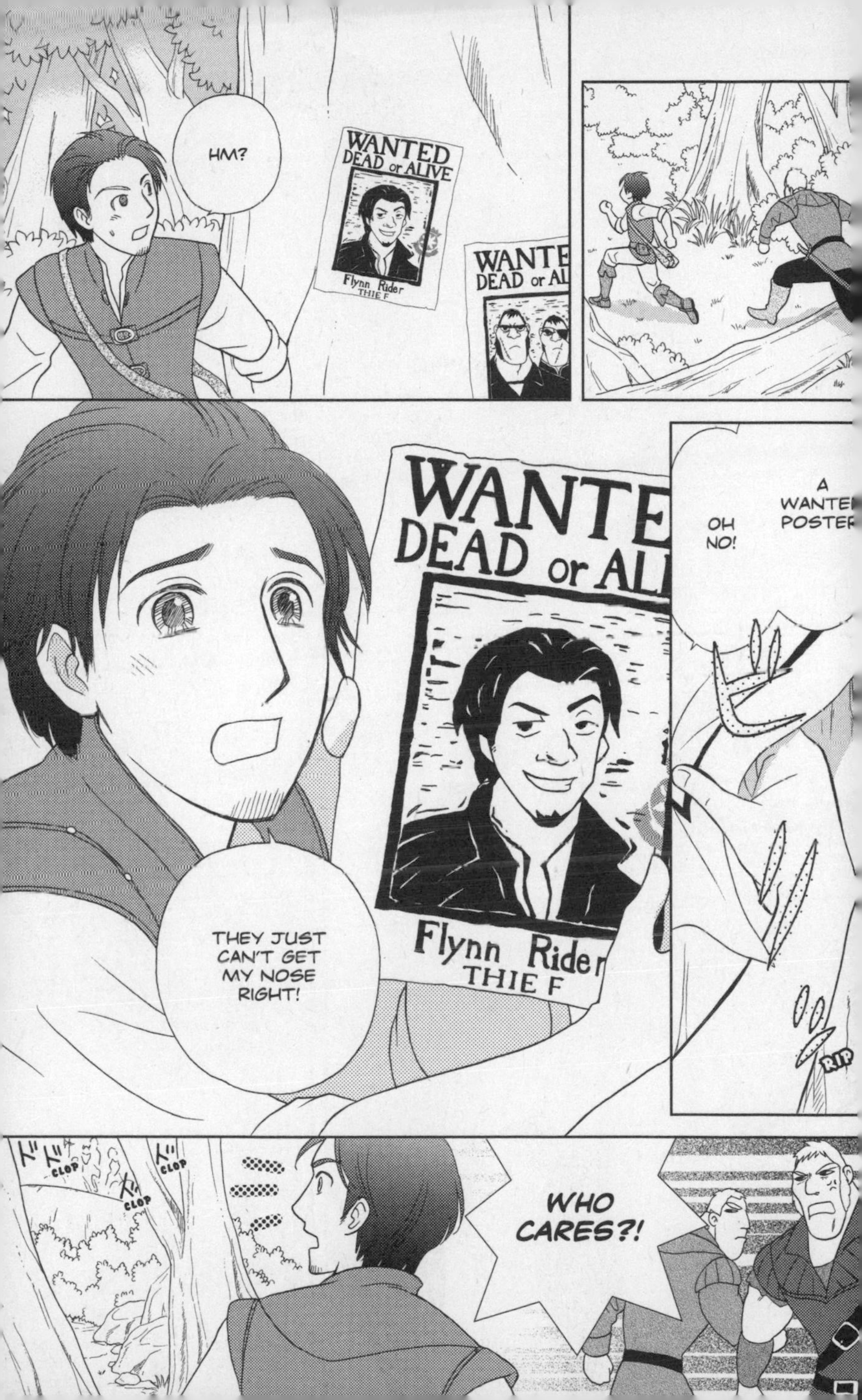
HM?
WANTED DEAD or ALIVE
Flynn Rider THIE F
WANTE DEAD or AL
A WANTE POSTEF
OH NO!
RIP
WANTE DEAD or AL
Flynn Rider
THIE F
THEY JUST CAN'T GET MY NOSE RIGHT!
WHO CARES?!
CLOP
CLOP
CLOP

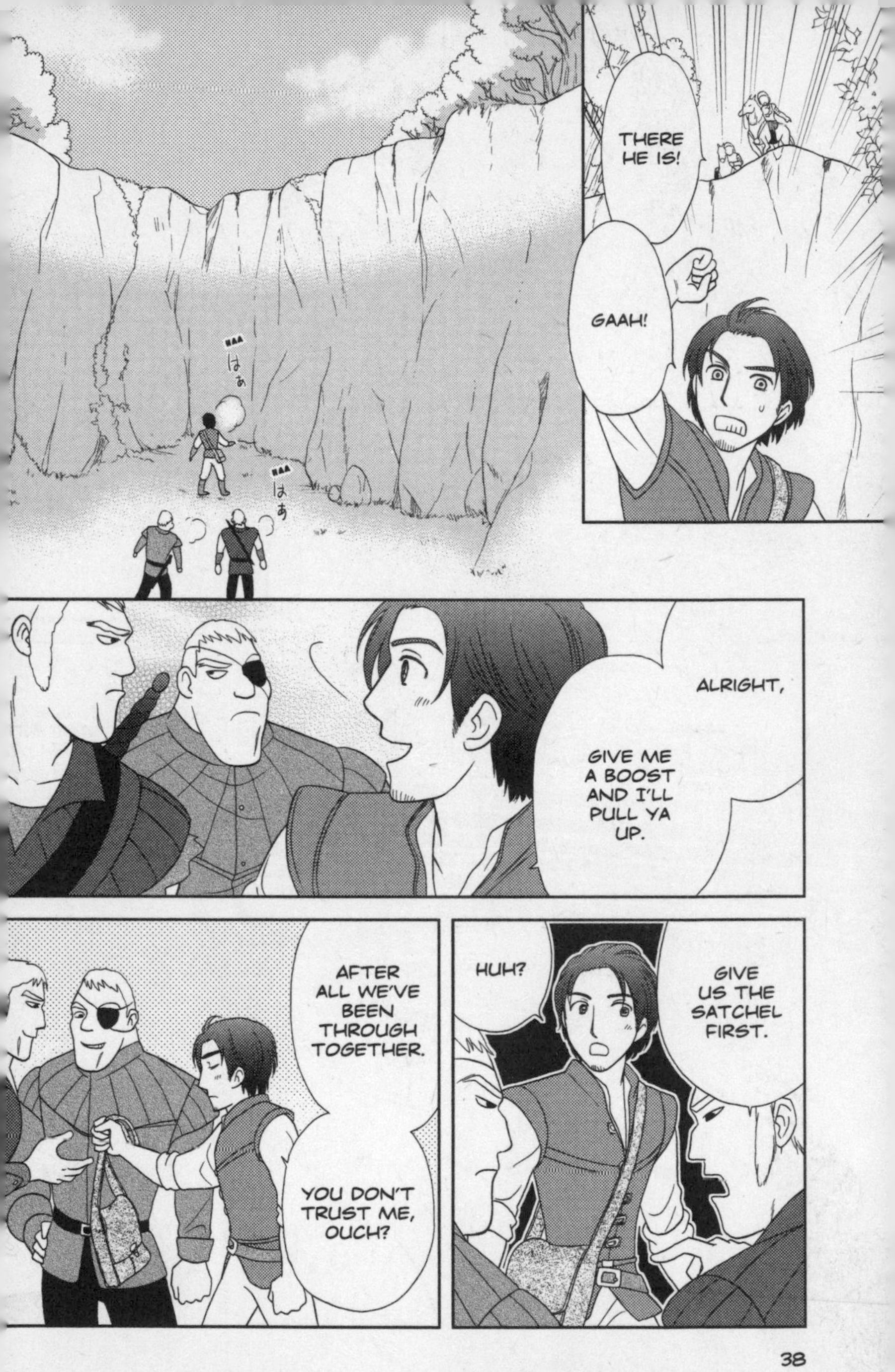
THERE HE IS!
GAAH!
HAA
はぁ
HAA
はぁ
ALRIGHT,
GIVE ME A BOOST AND I'LL PULL YA UP.
GIVE US THE SATCHEL FIRST.
HUH?
AFTER ALL WE'VE BEEN THROUGH TOGETHER.
YOU DON'T TRUST ME, OUCH?

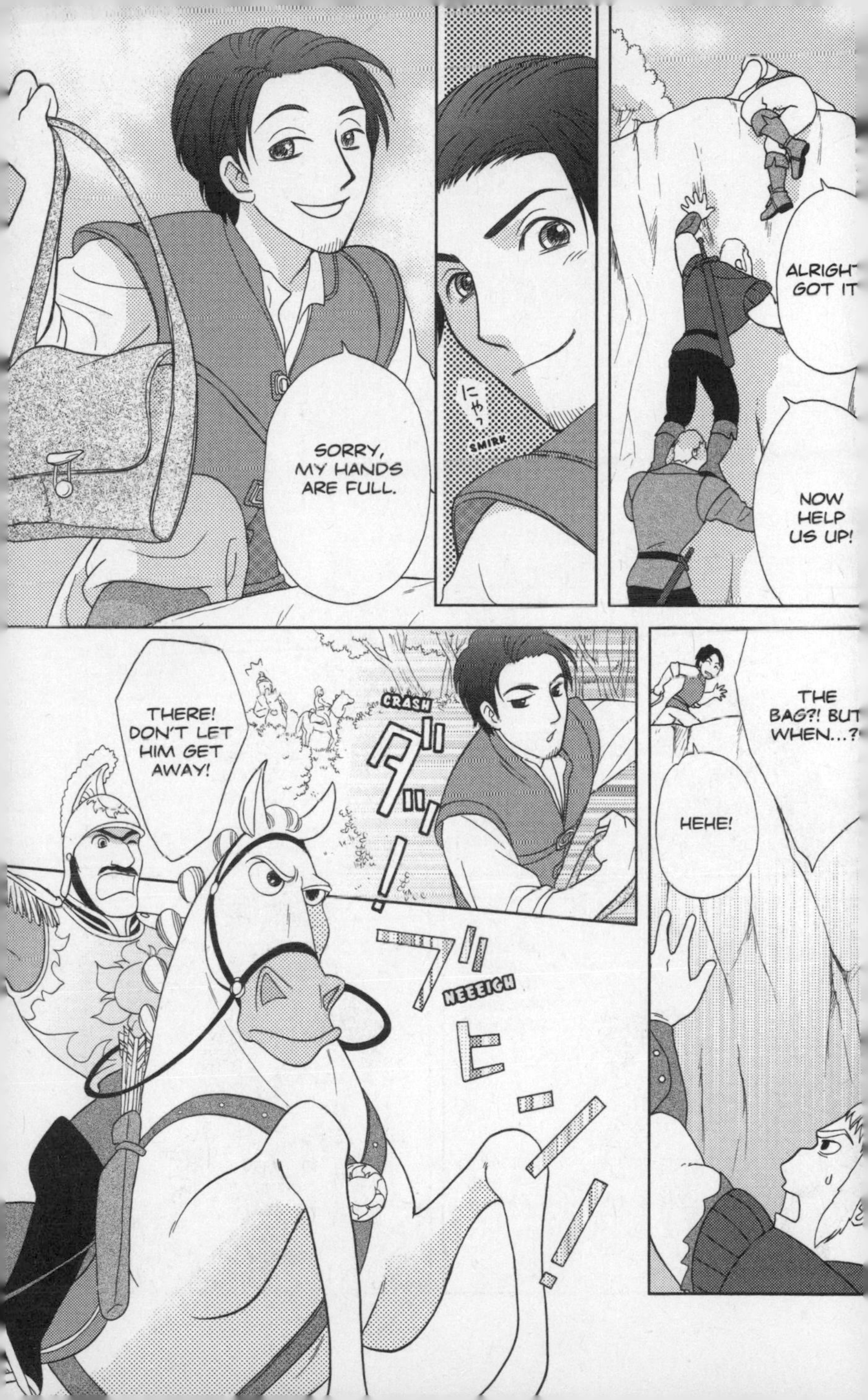
ALRIGHT GOT IT
NOW HELP US UP!
にやっ
SMIRK
SORRY, MY HANDS ARE FULL.
THE BAG?! BUT WHEN...?!
HEHE!
CRASH
ダーッ!
THERE! DON'T LET HIM GET AWAY!
ブヒー!!
NEEEIGH

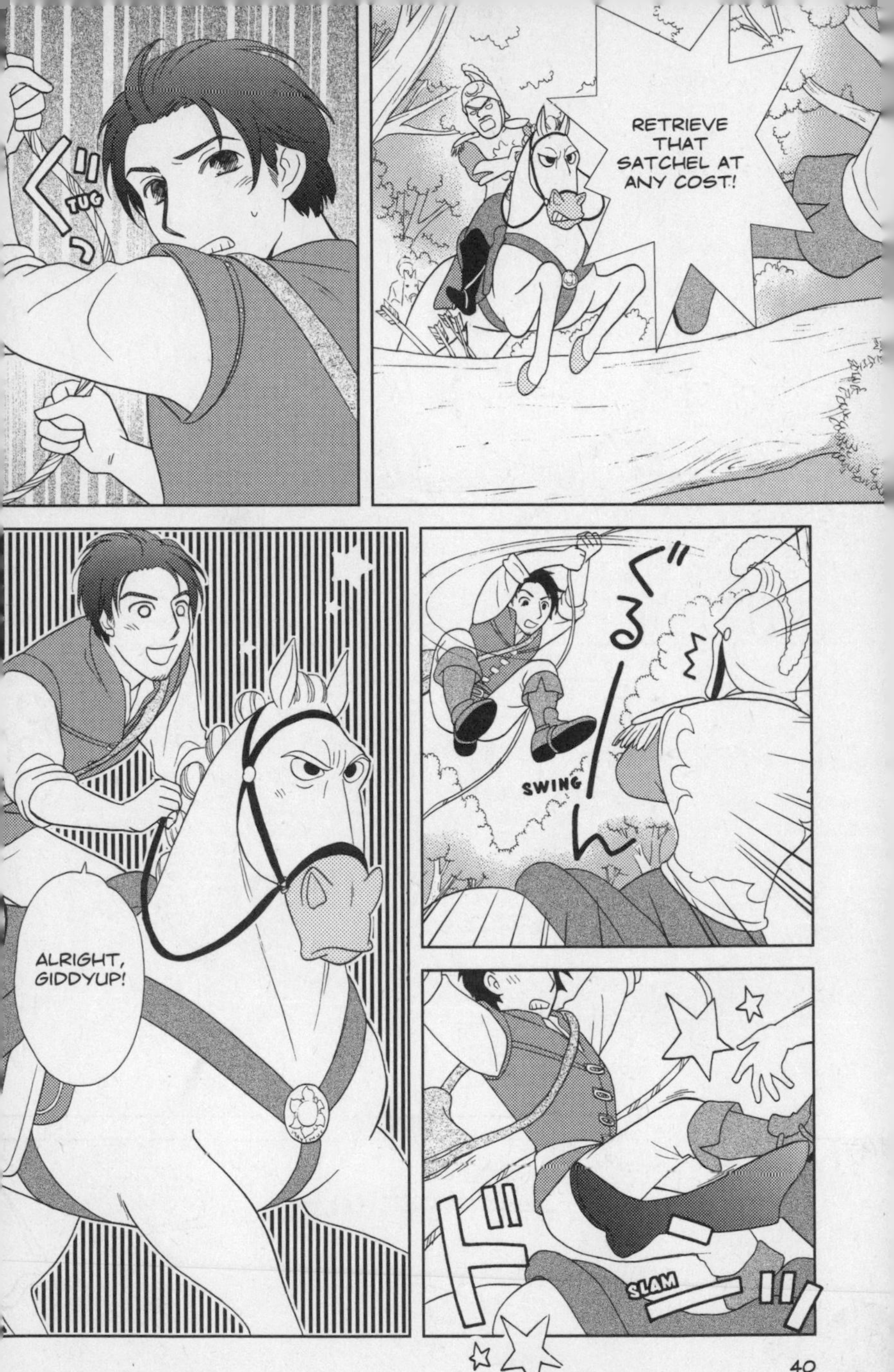
RETRIEVE THAT SATCHEL AT ANY COST!
TUG
SWING
SLAM
ALRIGHT, GIDDYUP!

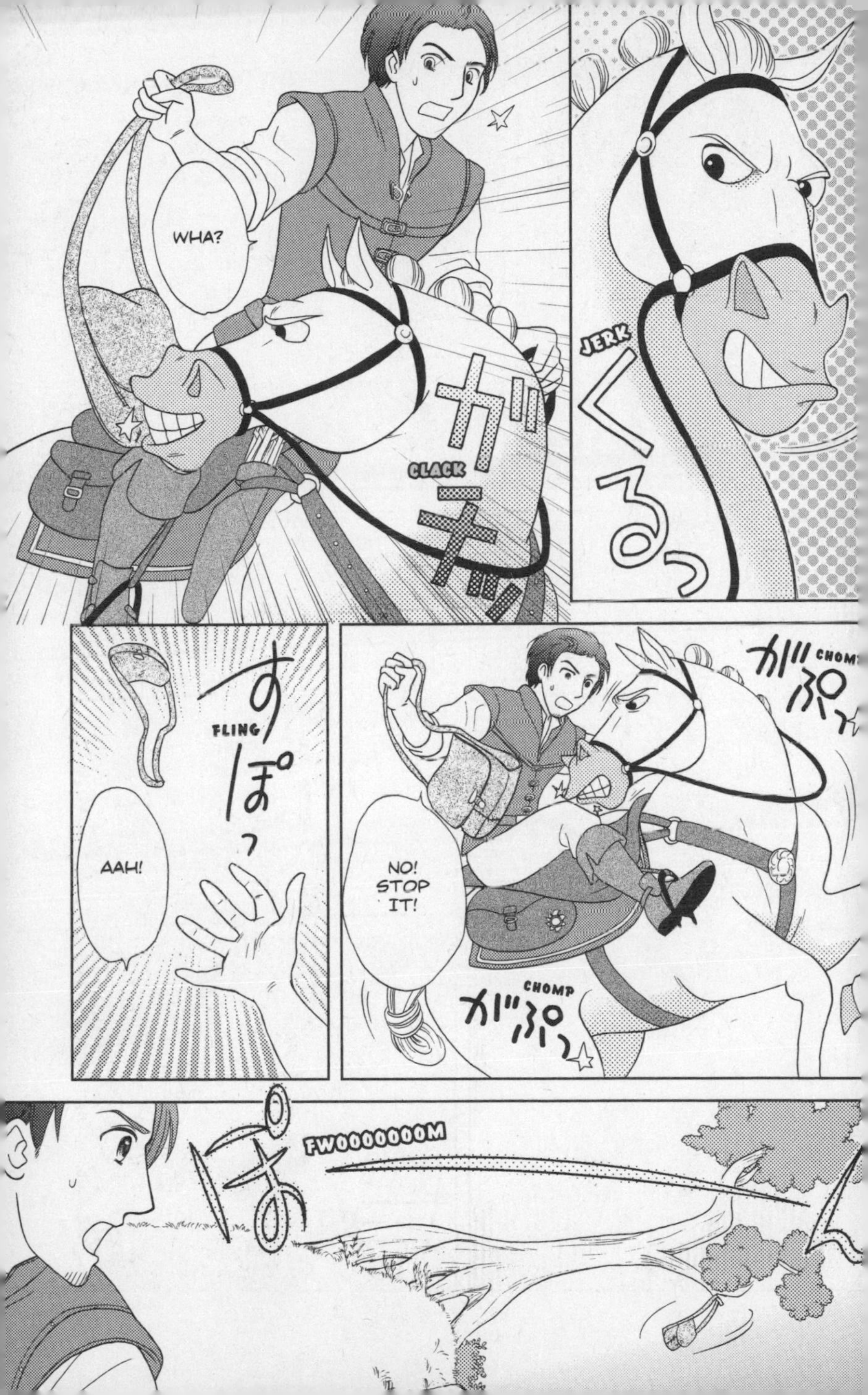

くるっ
JERK
WHA?
ガチッ
CLACK
がぶっ
CHOMP
NO! STOP IT!
がぶっ
CHOMP
すぽっ
FLING
AAH!
ぽ〜ん
FWOOOOOOOM

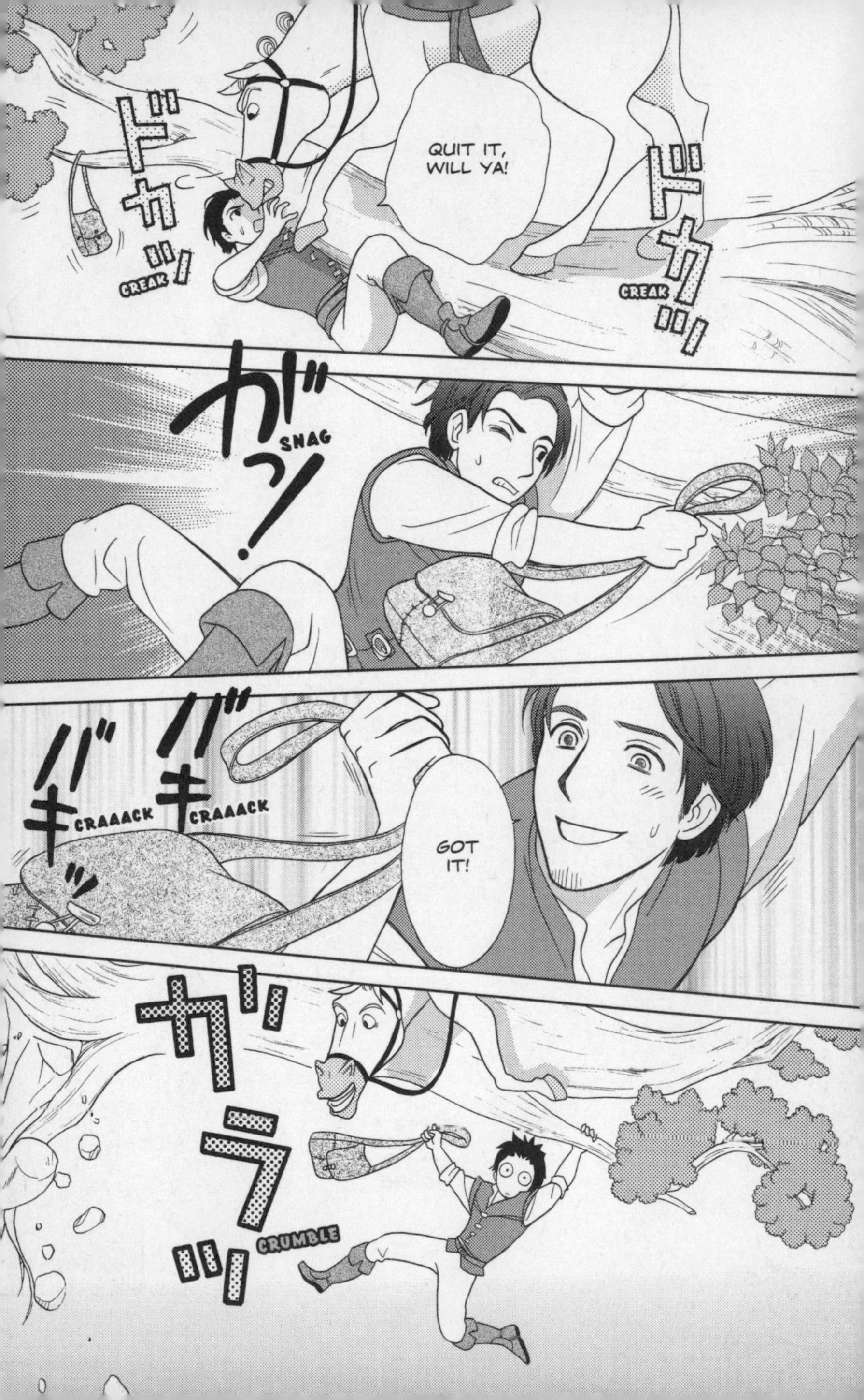
ドカッ
CREAK
QUIT IT, WILL YA!
ドカッ
CREAK
がっ!
SNAG
GOT IT!
バキ
CRAAACK
バキッ
CRAAACK
ガラッ
CRUMBLE

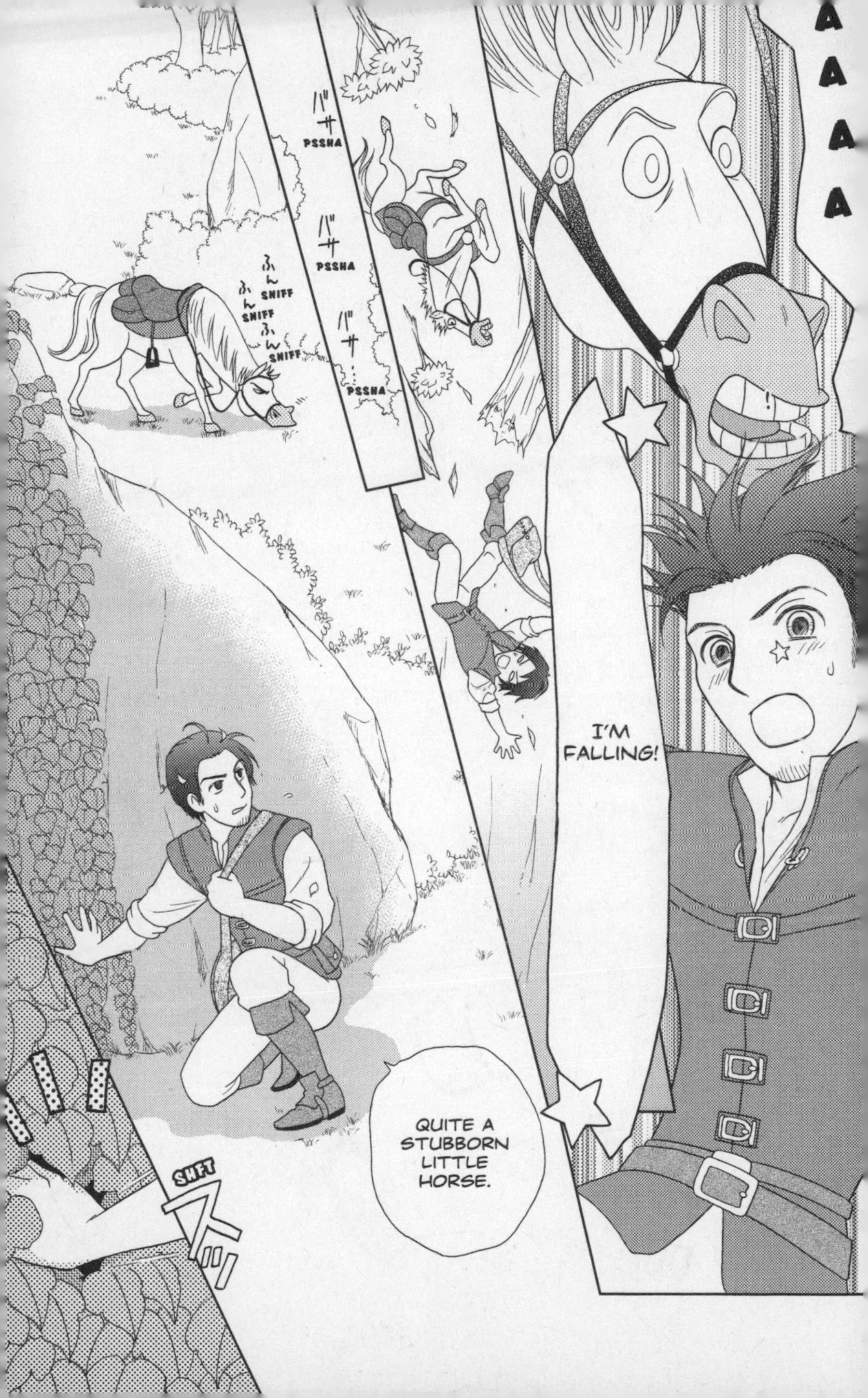
AAAA
I'M FALLING!
バサ PSSHA
バサ PSSHA
バサ… PSSHA
ふん SNIFF
ふん SNIFF
ふん SNIFF
QUITE A STUBBORN LITTLE HORSE.
SHFT

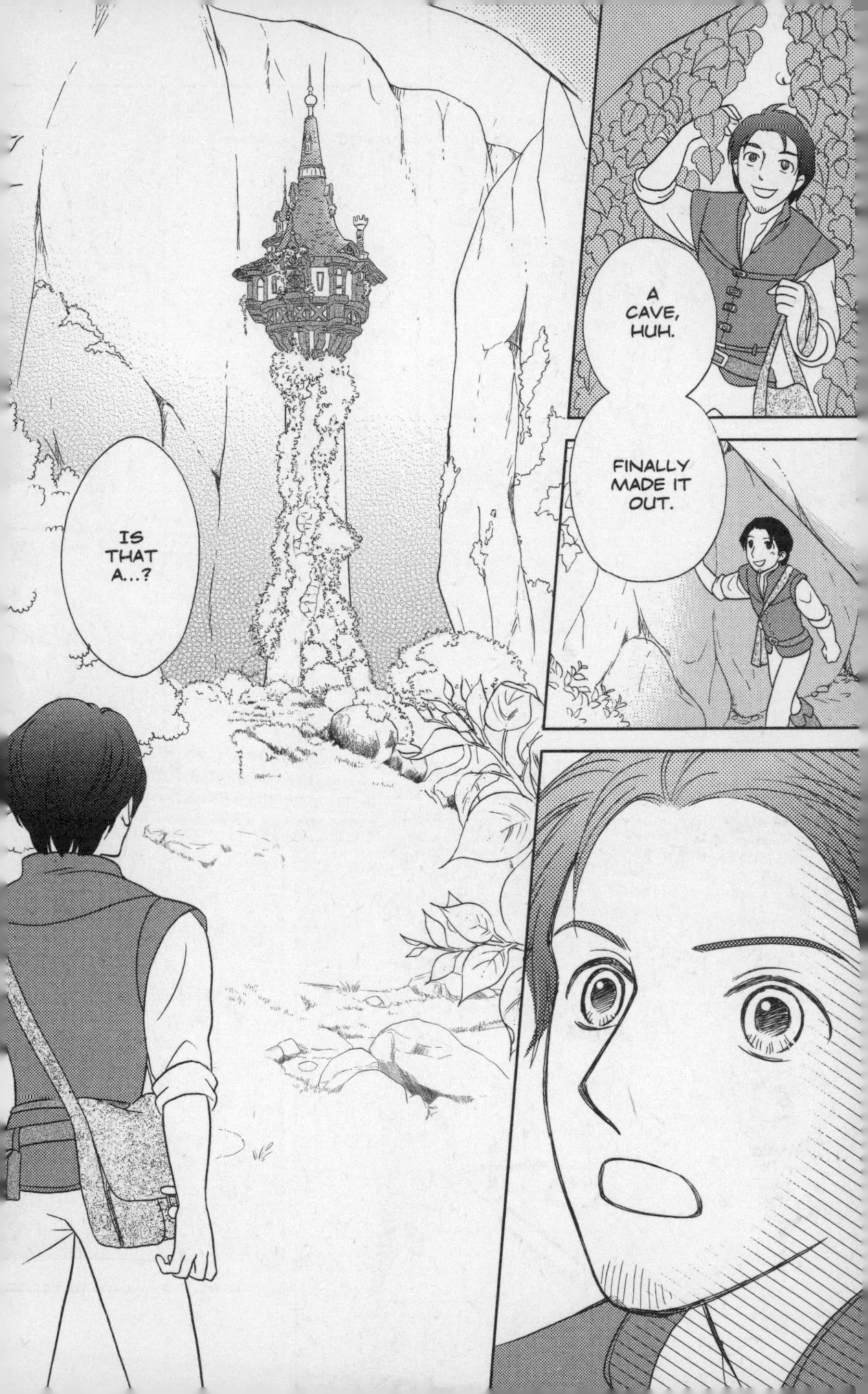
A CAVE, HUH.
FINALLY MADE IT OUT.
IS THAT A...?

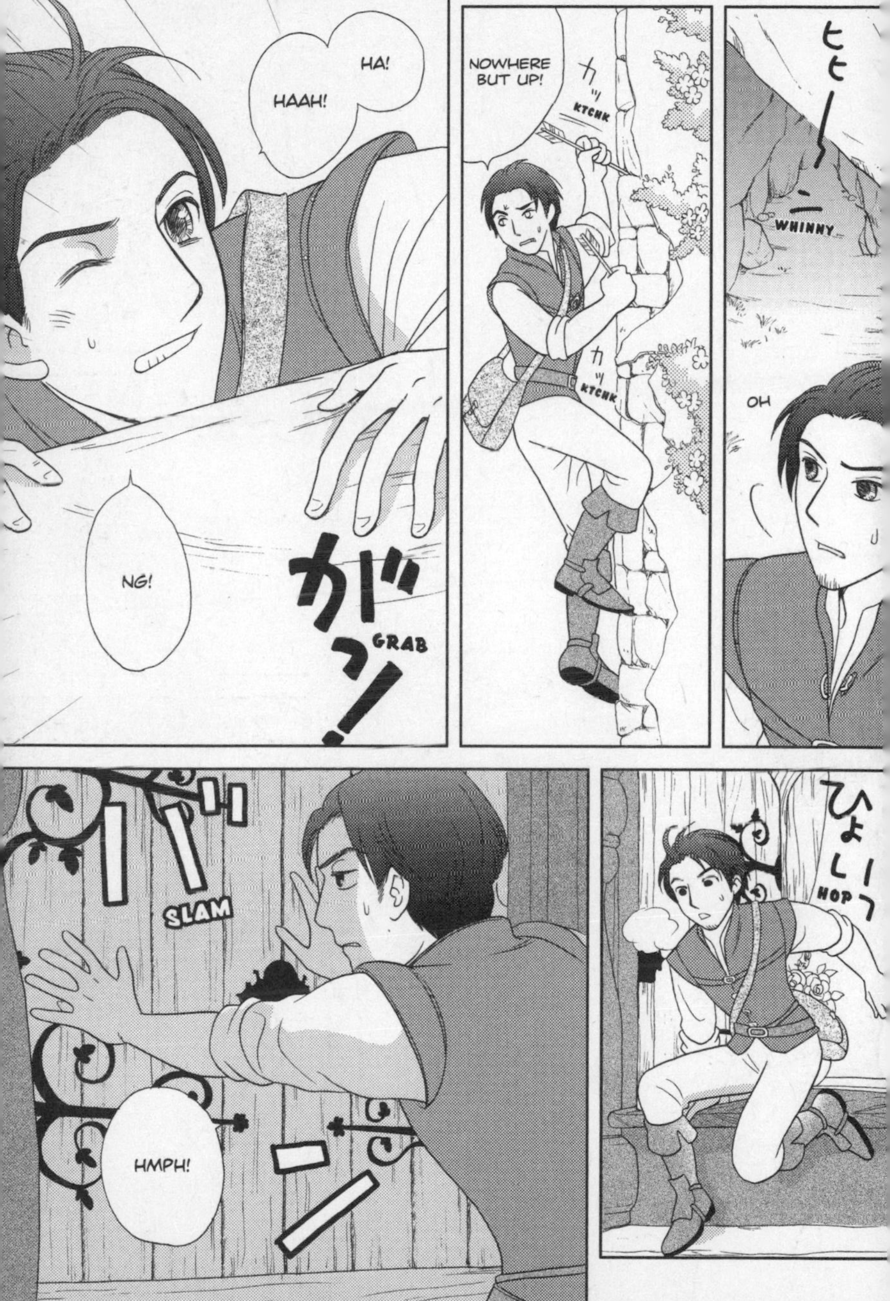
WHINNY
OH
NOWHERE BUT UP!
カッ
KTCHK
カッ
KTCHK
HA!
HAAH!
NG!
がッ!
GRAB
ひょいっ
HOP
SLAM
HMPH!

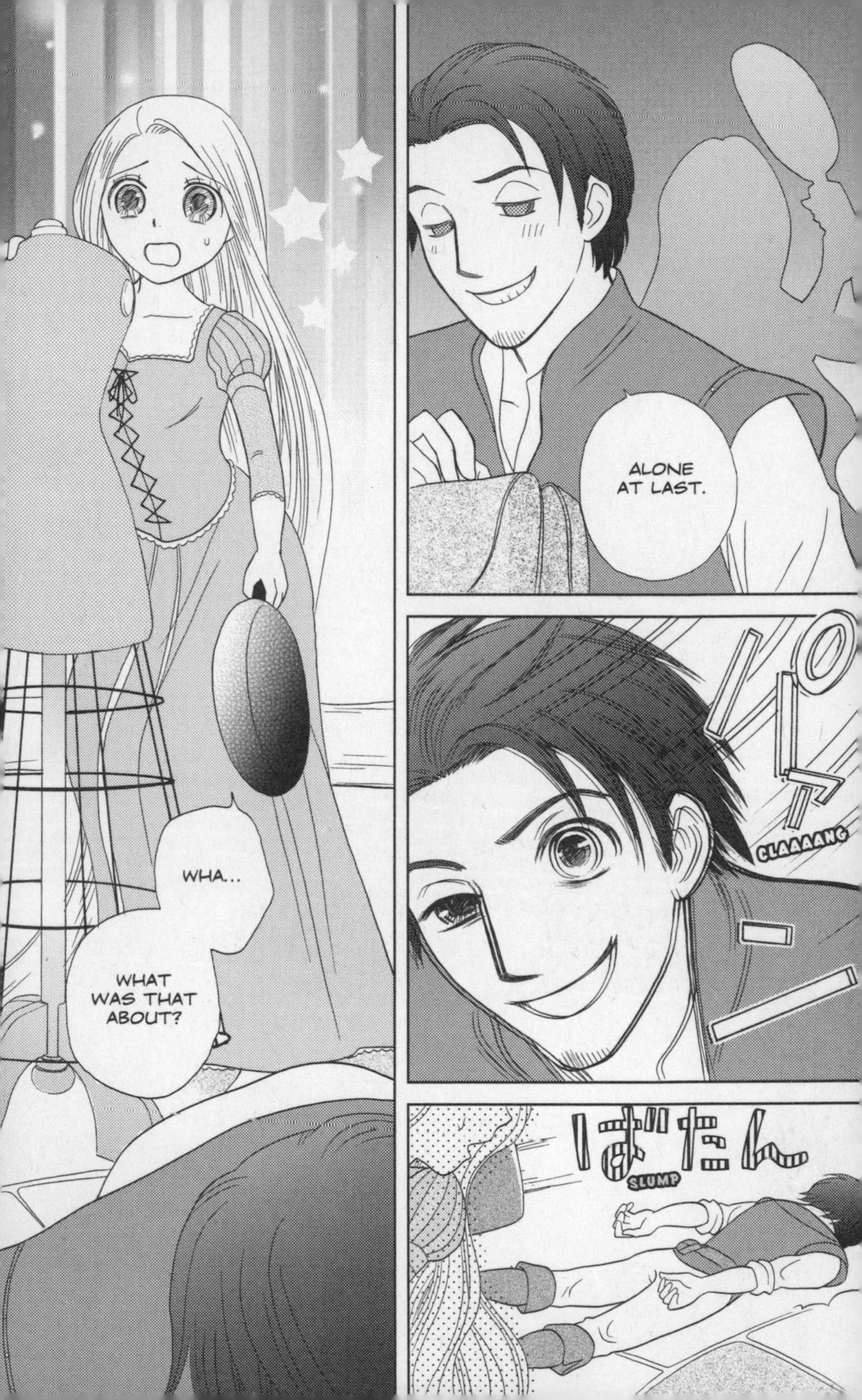
ALONE AT LAST.
CLAAAANG
ばたん
SLUMP
WHA...
WHAT WAS THAT ABOUT?

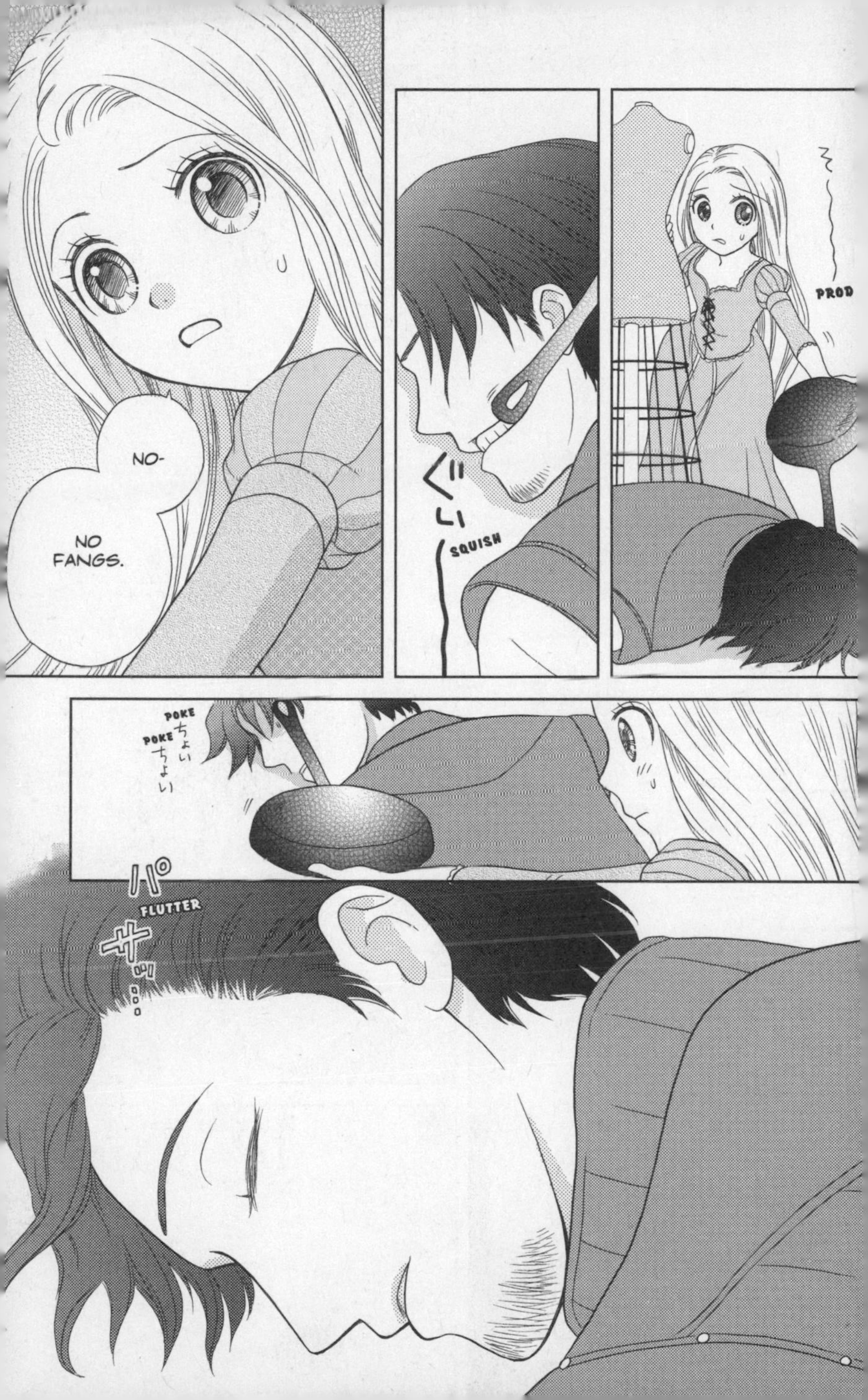
PROD
ぐに
SQUISH
NO-
NO FANGS.
POKE
ちょい
POKE
ちょい
パサッ...
FLUTTER

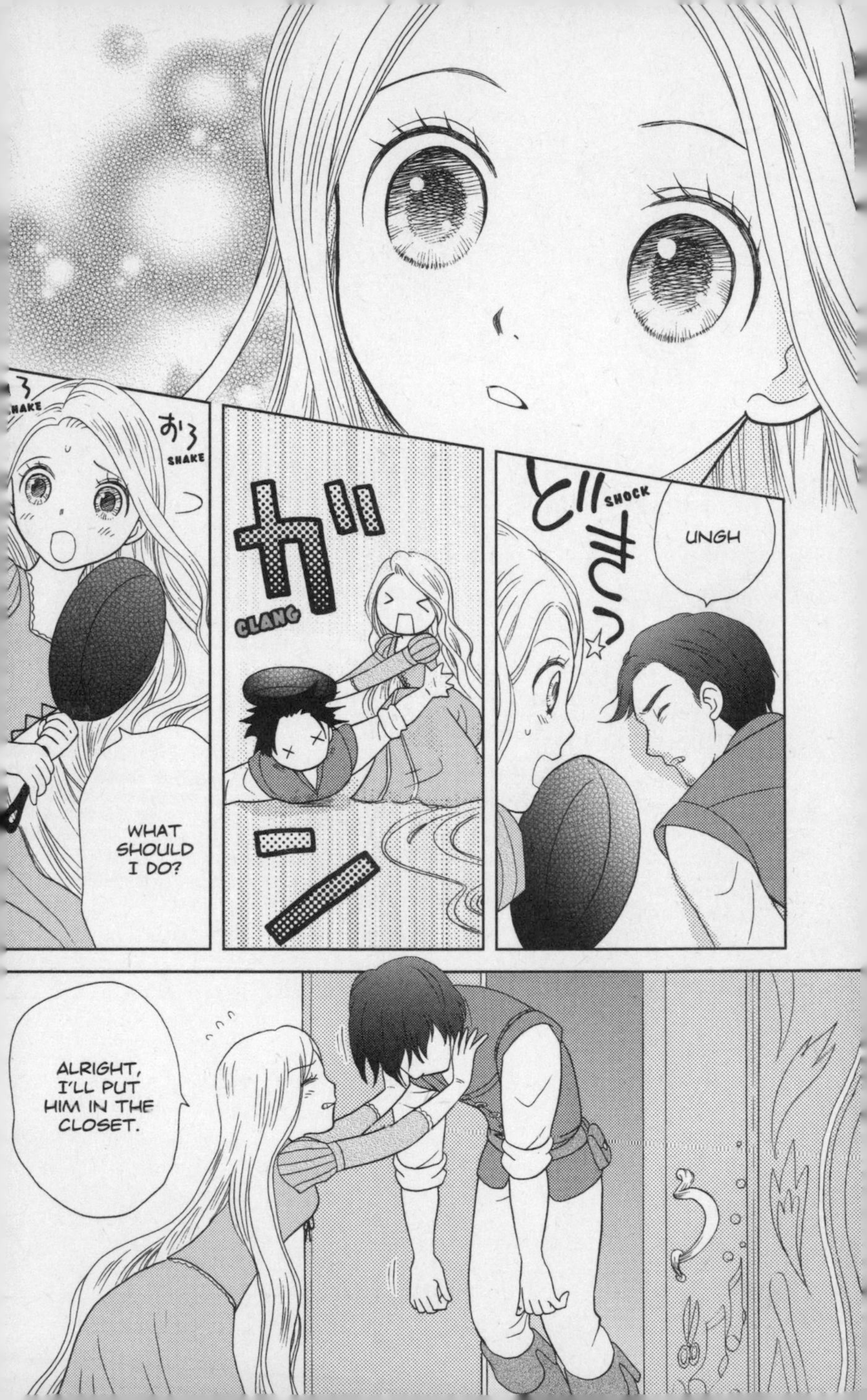
どきっ
SHOCK
UNGH
ガーン
CLANG
おろ
SHAKE
SHAKE
WHAT SHOULD I DO?
ALRIGHT, I'LL PUT HIM IN THE CLOSET.

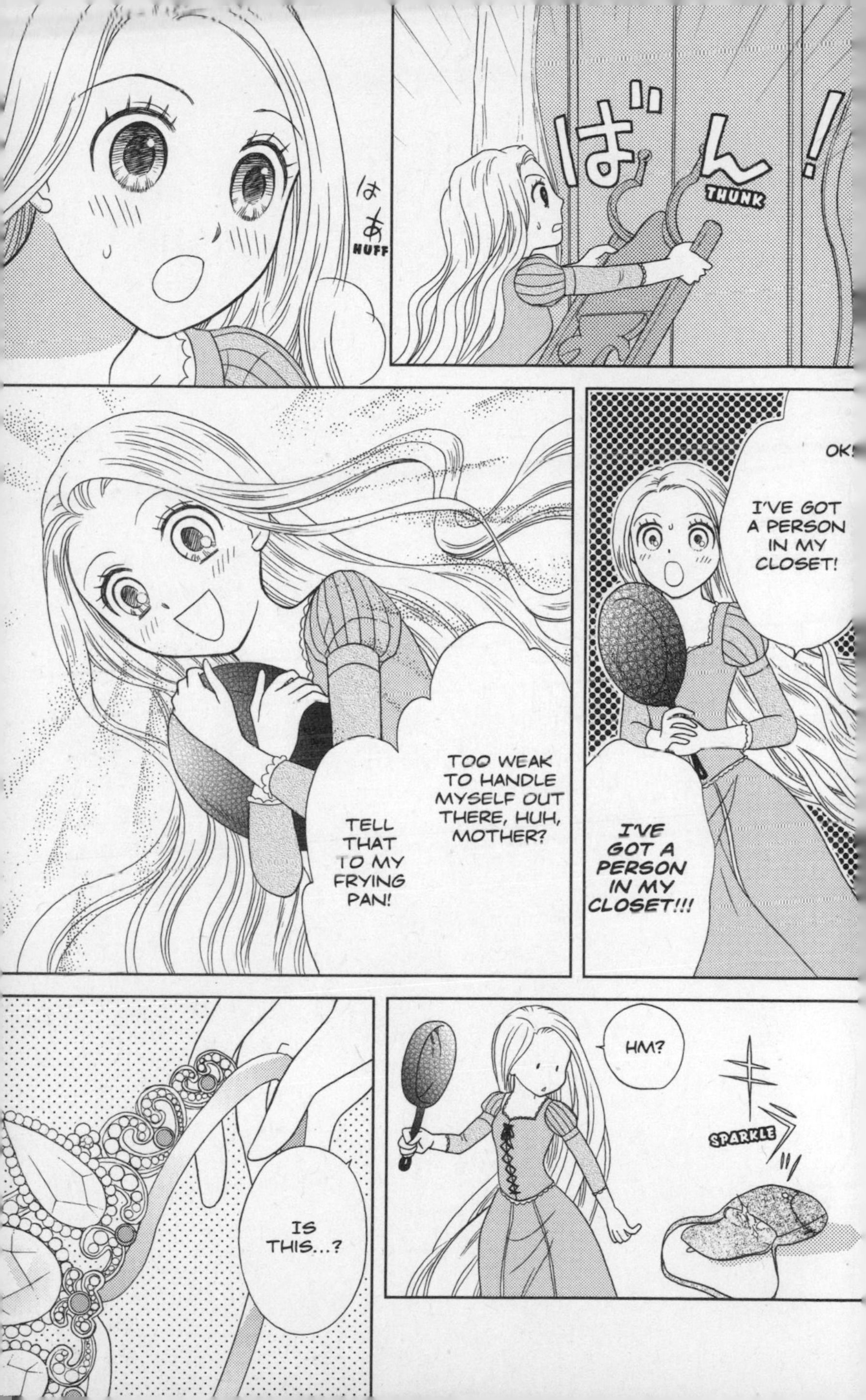
ばん!
THUNK
はあ
HUFF
OK!
I'VE GOT A PERSON IN MY CLOSET!
I'VE GOT A PERSON IN MY CLOSET!!!
TOO WEAK TO HANDLE MYSELF OUT THERE, HUH, MOTHER?
TELL THAT TO MY FRYING PAN!
HM?
SPARKLE
IS THIS...?

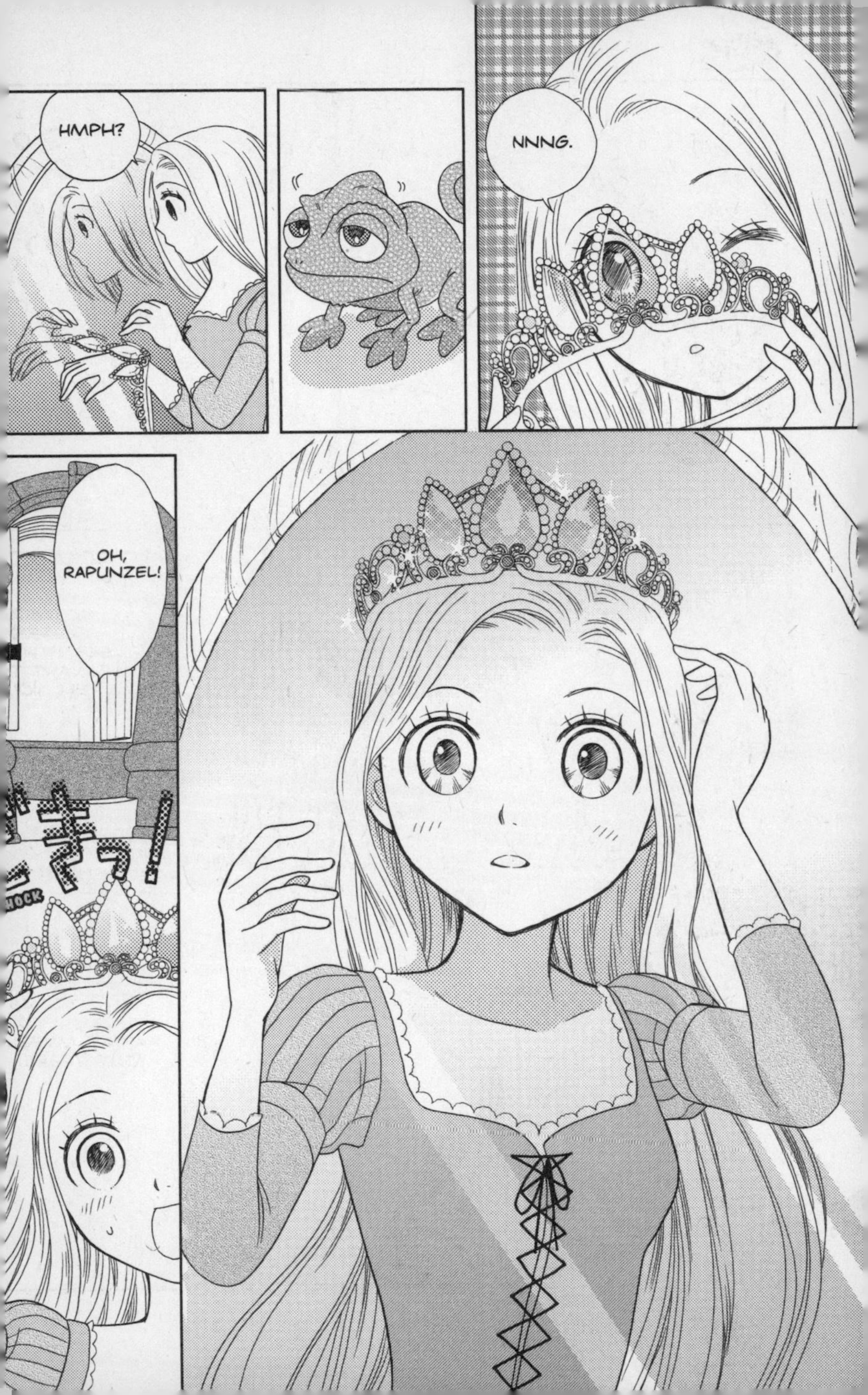
NNNG.
HMPH?
OH, RAPUNZEL!

READ THIS WAY

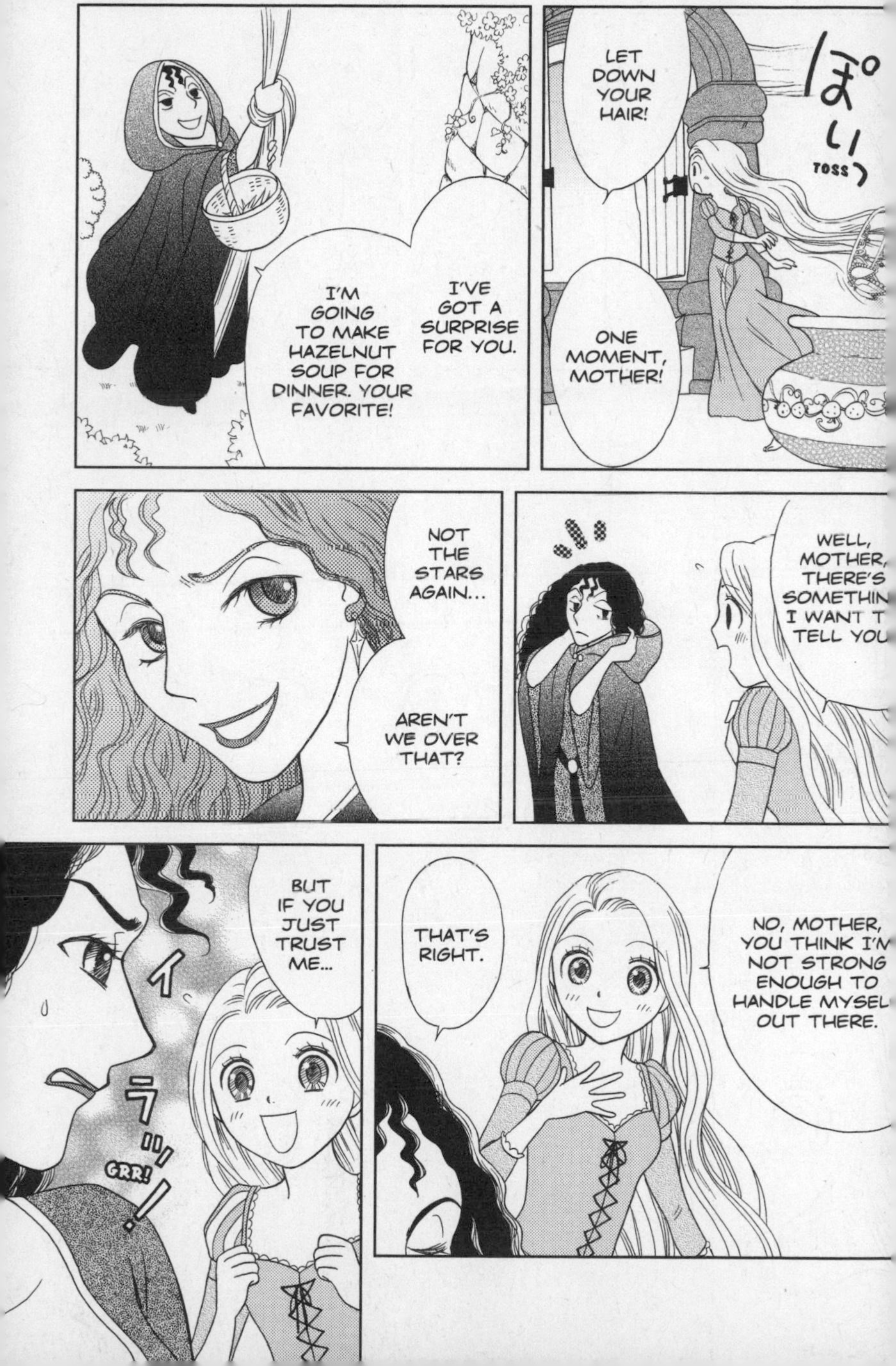
LET DOWN YOUR HAIR!
ぽい
TOSS
ONE MOMENT, MOTHER!
I'VE GOT A SURPRISE FOR YOU.
I'M GOING TO MAKE HAZELNUT SOUP FOR DINNER. YOUR FAVORITE!
WELL, MOTHER, THERE'S SOMETHIN I WANT T TELL YOU
NOT THE STARS AGAIN...
AREN'T WE OVER THAT?
NO, MOTHER, YOU THINK I'M NOT STRONG ENOUGH TO HANDLE MYSEL OUT THERE.
THAT'S RIGHT.
BUT IF YOU JUST TRUST ME...
イラッ
GRR!
!

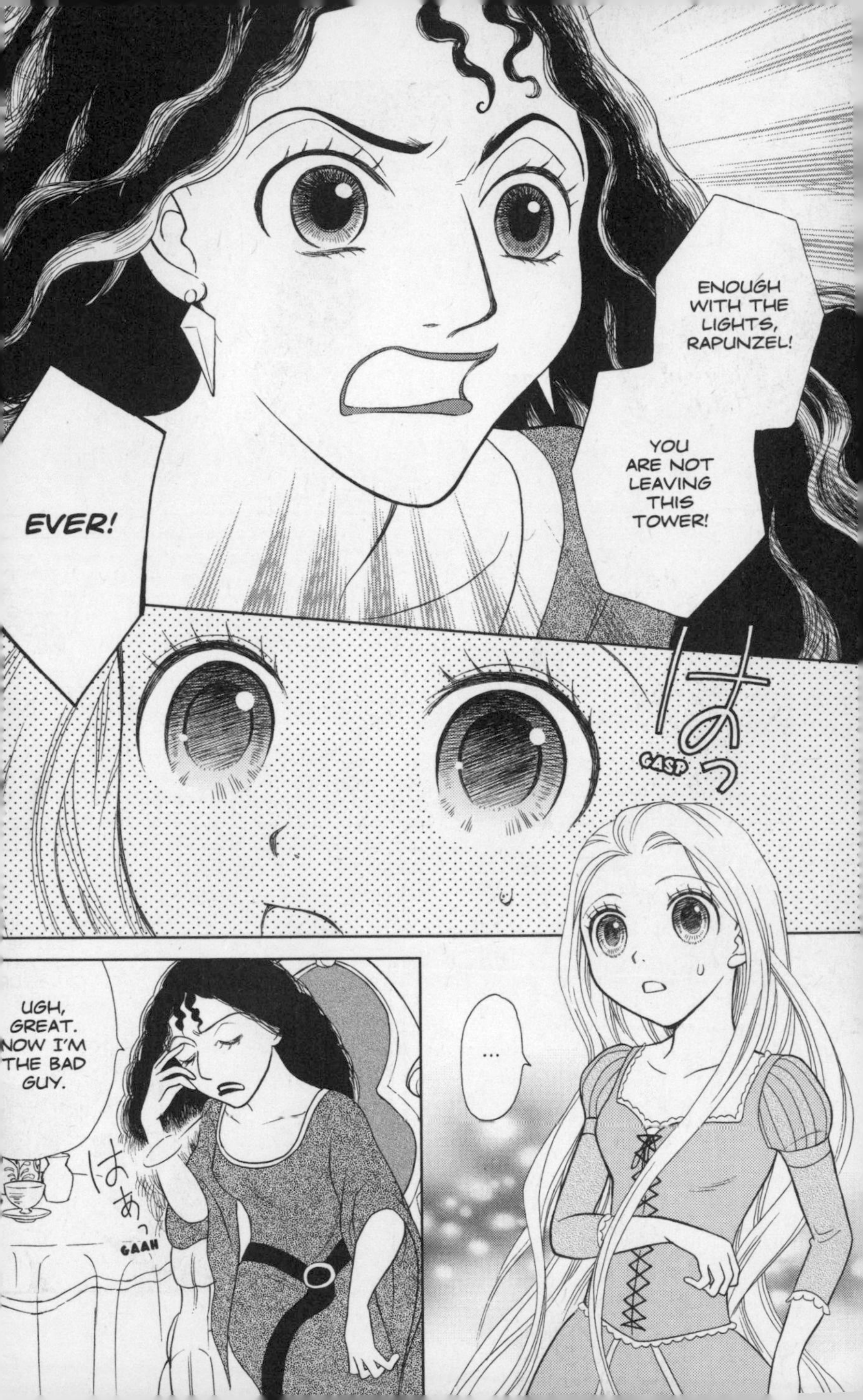
ENOUGH WITH THE LIGHTS, RAPUNZEL!
YOU ARE NOT LEAVING THIS TOWER!
EVER!
はっ
GASP
...
UGH, GREAT. NOW I'M THE BAD GUY.
はあっ
GAAH

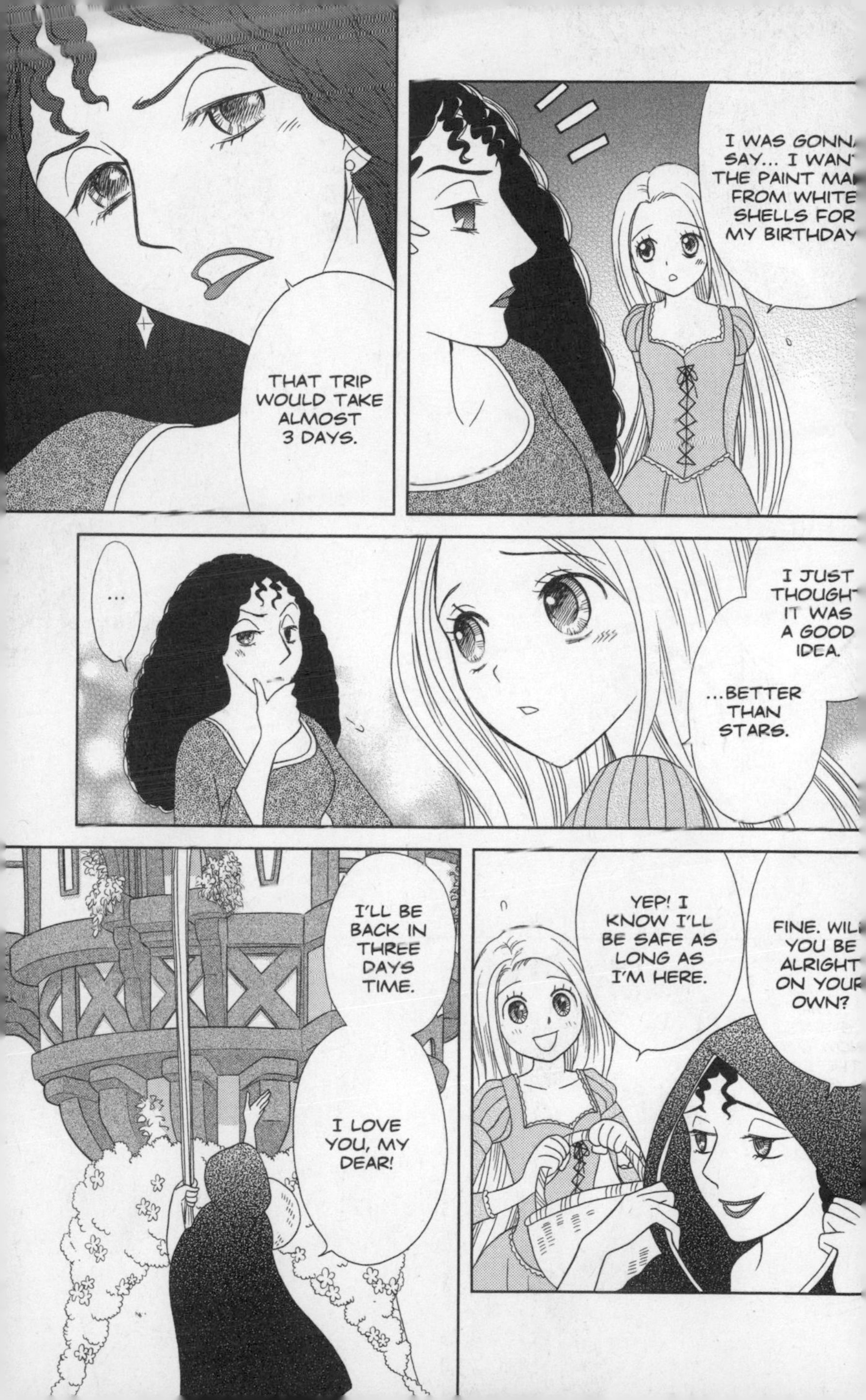
I WAS GONN SAY... I WAN THE PAINT MA FROM WHITE SHELLS FOR MY BIRTHDAY
THAT TRIP WOULD TAKE ALMOST 3 DAYS.
I JUST THOUGH IT WAS A GOOD IDEA.
...BETTER THAN STARS.
...
FINE. WIL YOU BE ALRIGHT ON YOU OWN?
YEP! I KNOW I'LL BE SAFE AS LONG AS I'M HERE.
I'LL BE BACK IN THREE DAYS TIME.
I LOVE YOU, MY DEAR!

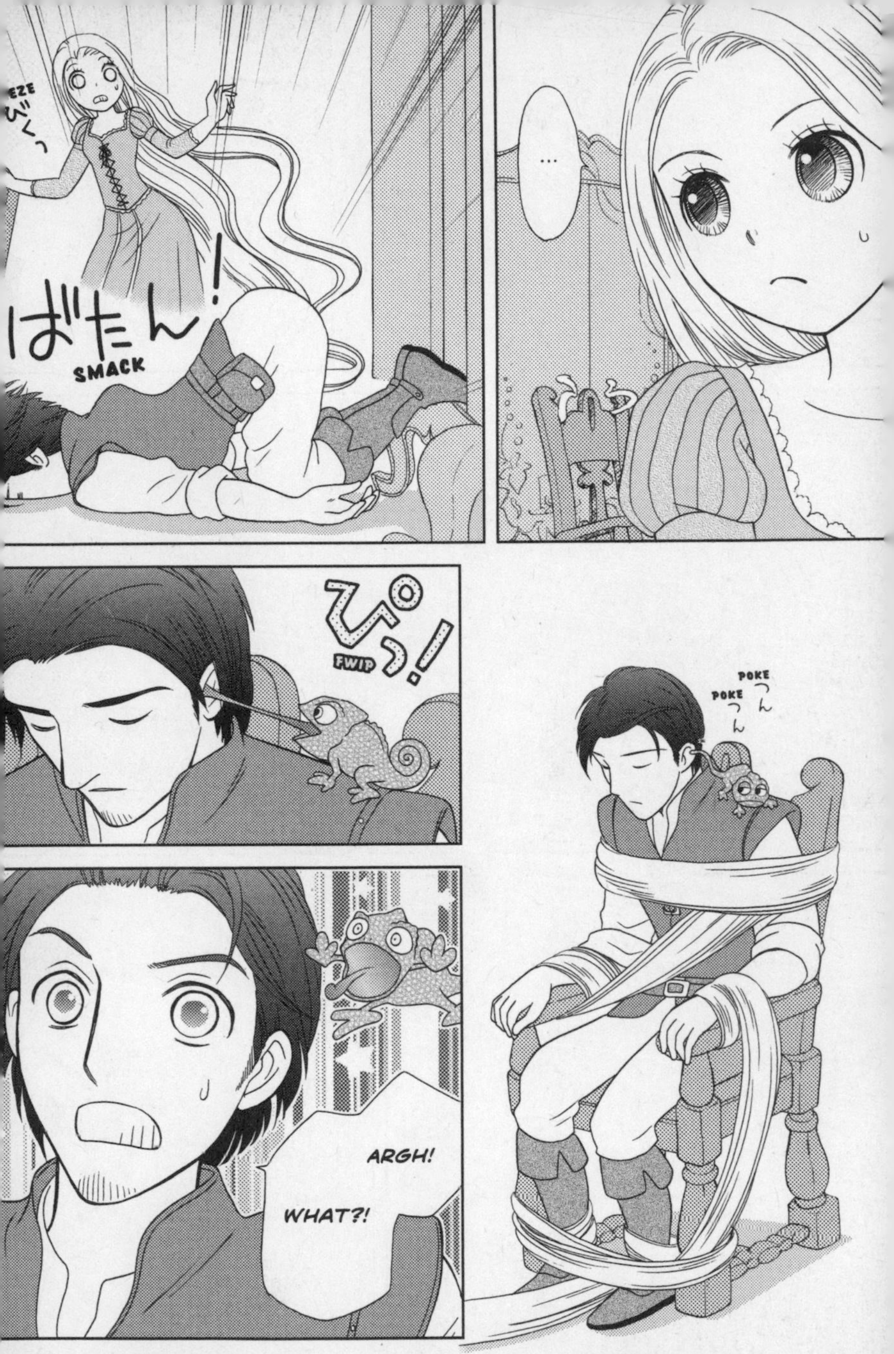
...
EZE
びくっ
ばたん!
SMACK
POKE
つん
POKE
つん
ぴっ!
FWIP
ARGH!
WHAT?!

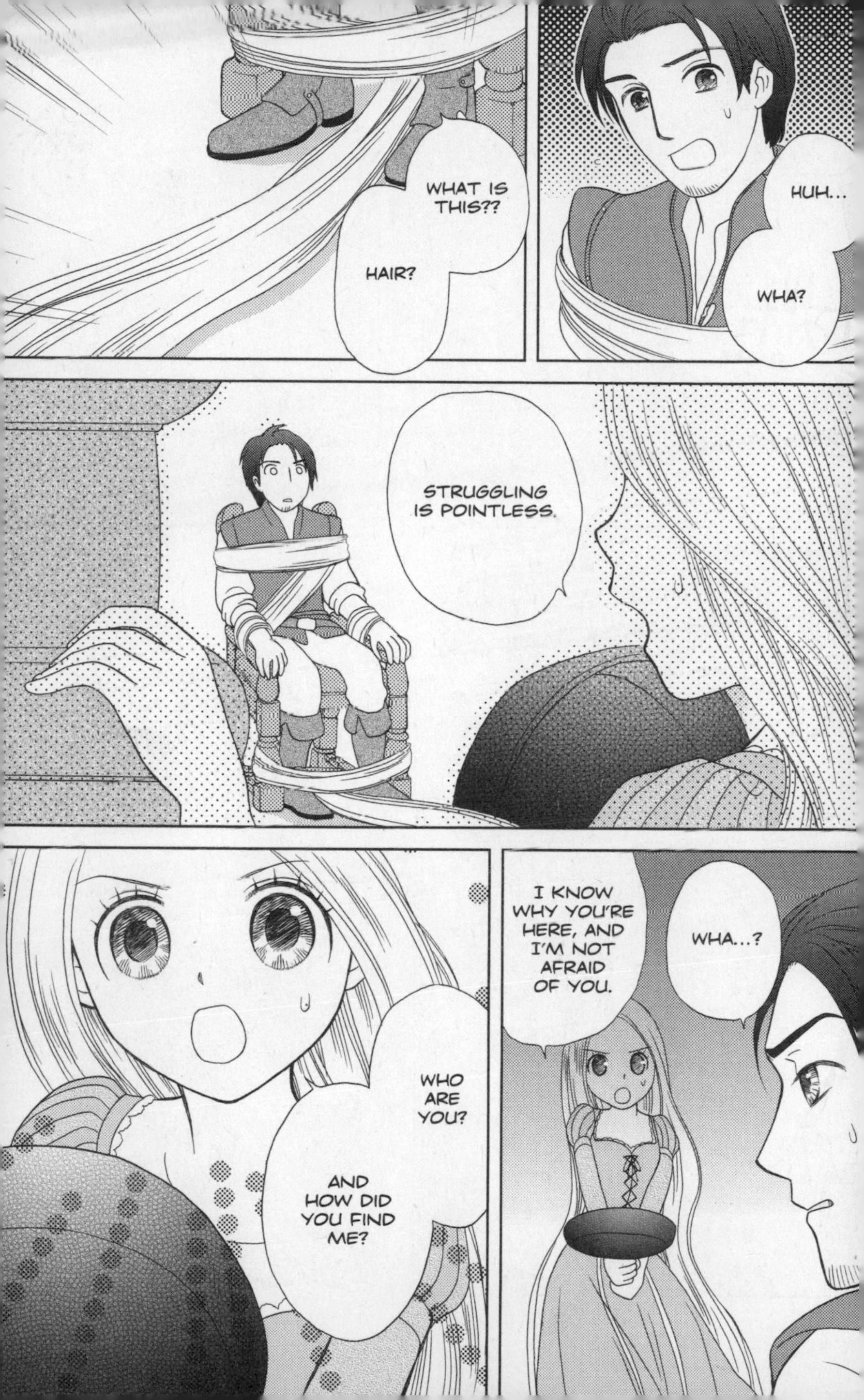
HUH...
WHA?
WHAT IS THIS??
HAIR?
STRUGGLING IS POINTLESS.
WHA...?
I KNOW WHY YOU'RE HERE, AND I'M NOT AFRAID OF YOU.
WHO ARE YOU?
AND HOW DID YOU FIND ME?

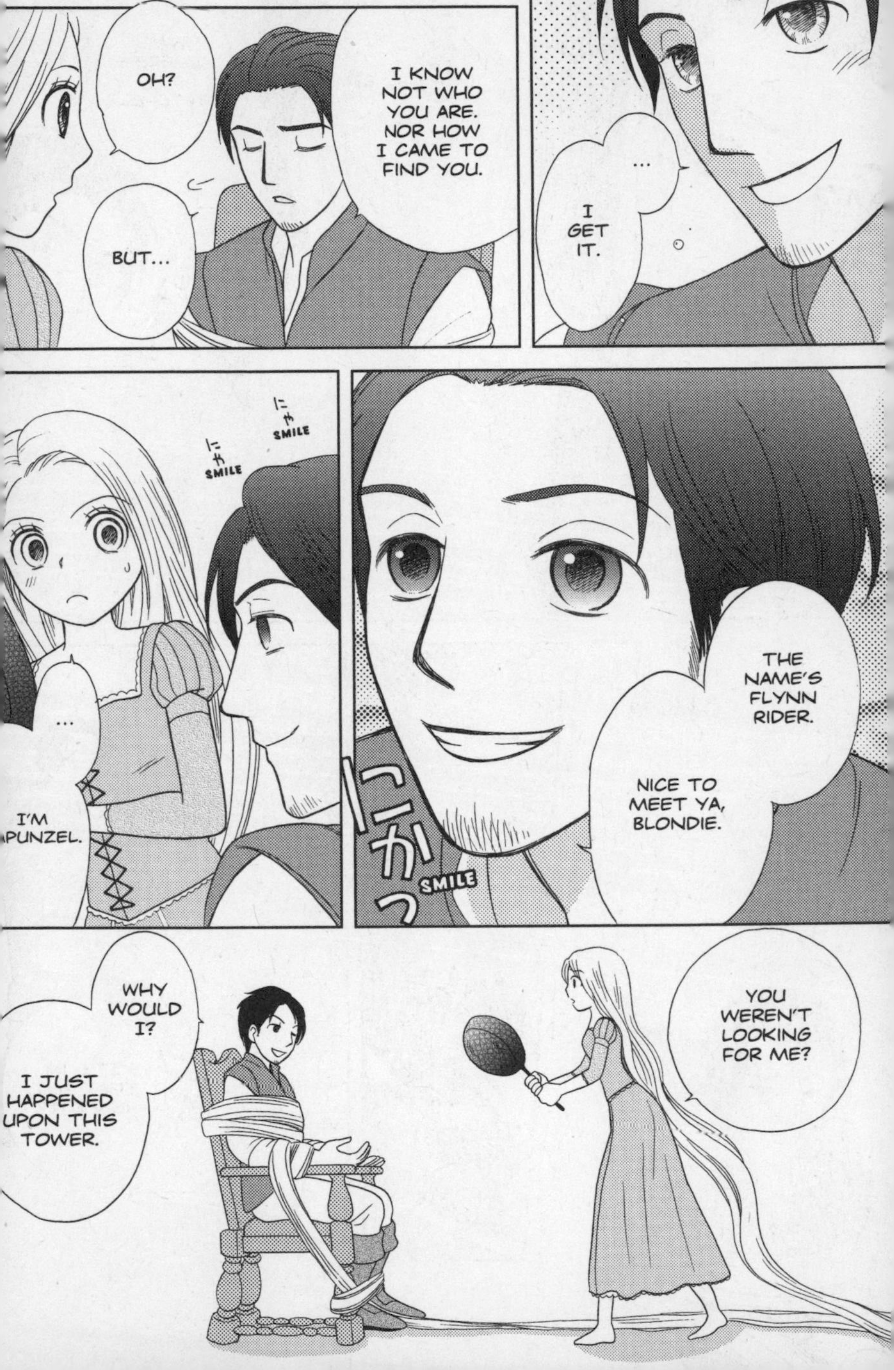
...
I GET IT.
I KNOW NOT WHO YOU ARE. NOR HOW I CAME TO FIND YOU.
OH?
BUT...
THE NAME'S FLYNN RIDER.
NICE TO MEET YA, BLONDIE.
にかっ
SMILE
にゃ
SMILE
にゃ
SMILE
...
I'M APUNZEL.
YOU WEREN'T LOOKING FOR ME?
WHY WOULD I?
I JUST HAPPENED UPON THIS TOWER.

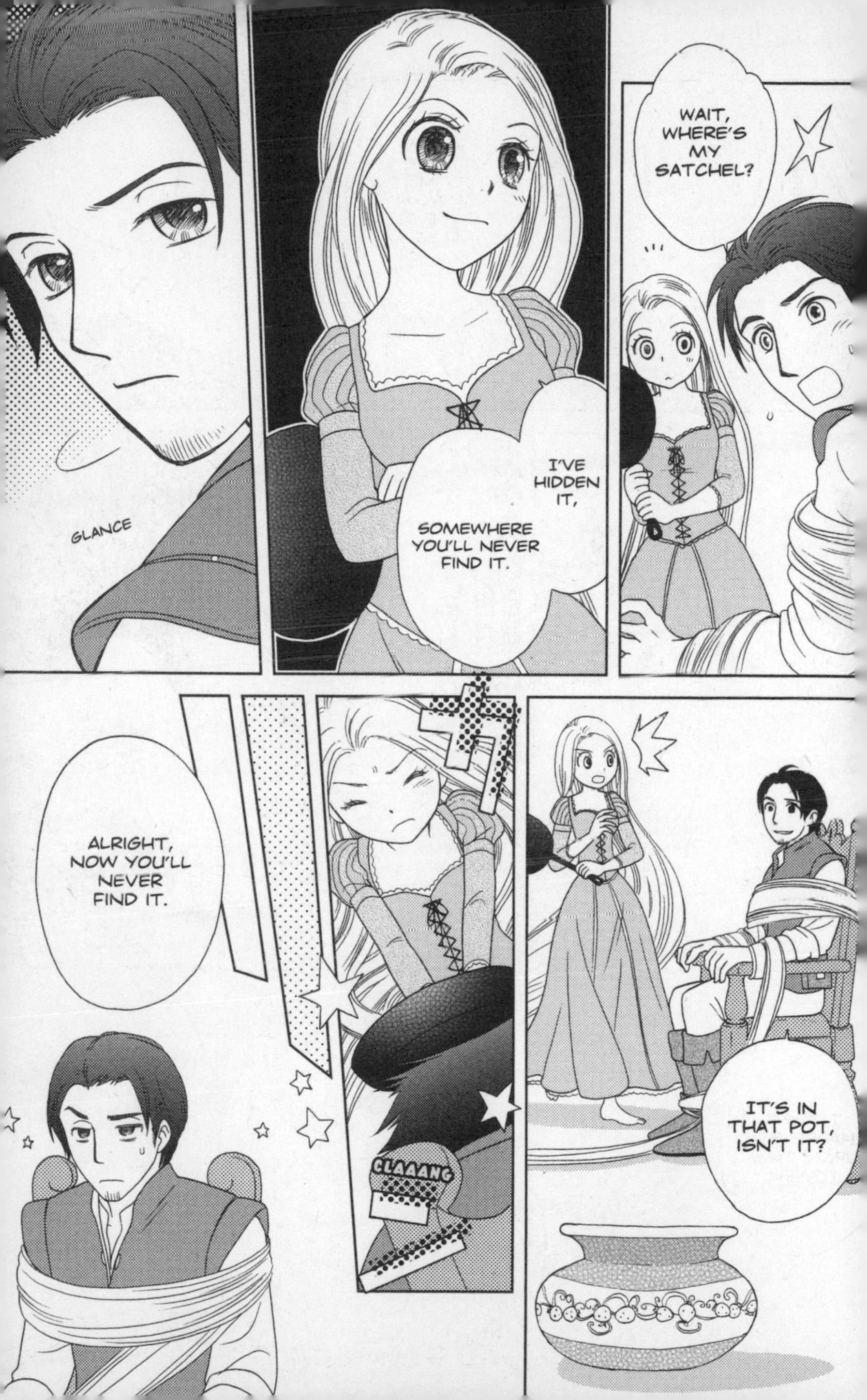
WAIT, WHERE'S MY SATCHEL?
I'VE HIDDEN IT,
SOMEWHERE YOU'LL NEVER FIND IT.
GLANCE
IT'S IN THAT POT, ISN'T IT?
CLAAANG
ALRIGHT, NOW YOU'LL NEVER FIND IT.

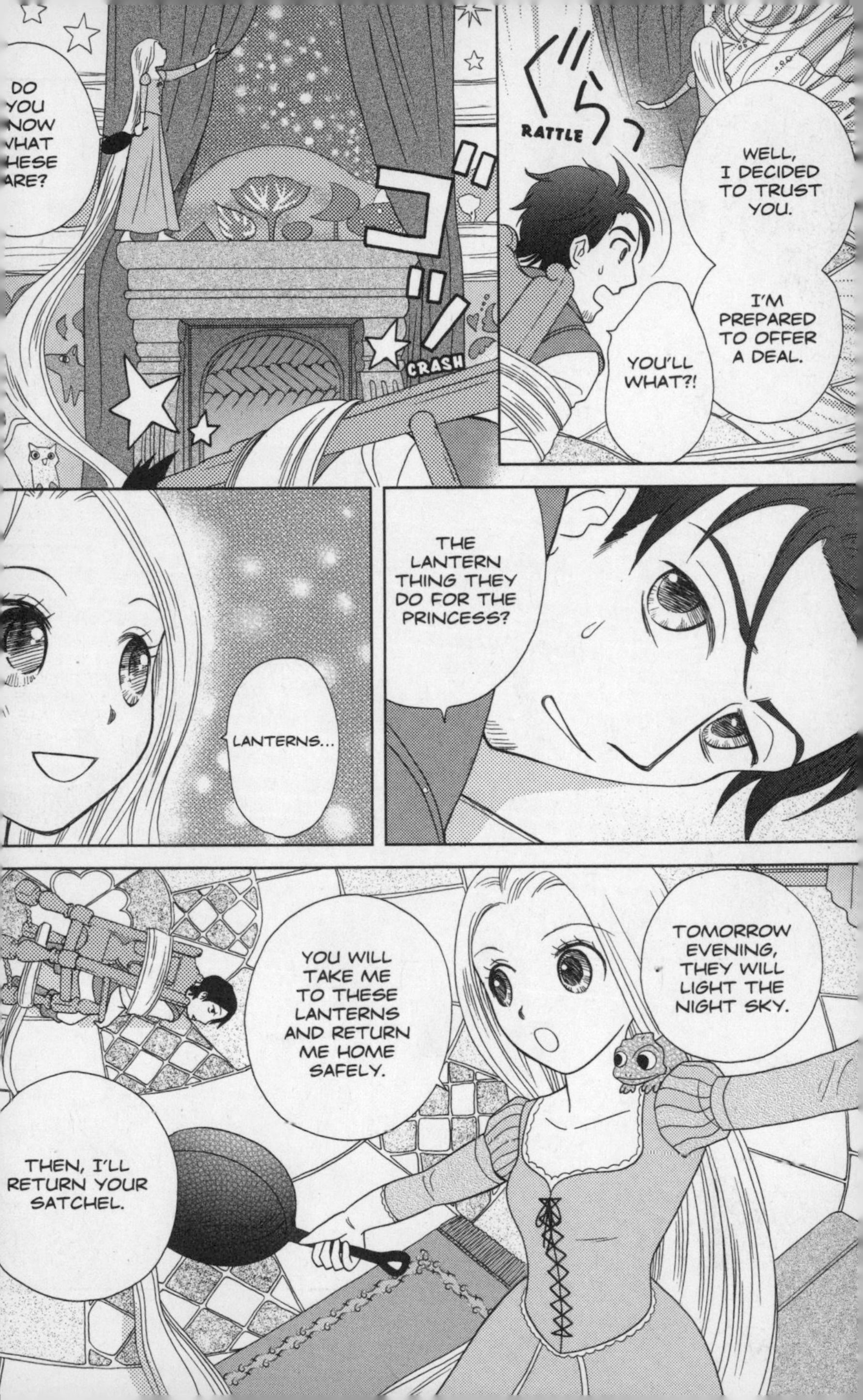
ぐらっ
RATTLE
WELL, I DECIDED TO TRUST YOU.
I'M PREPARED TO OFFER A DEAL.
YOU'LL WHAT?!
DO YOU NOW WHAT HESE ARE?
CRASH
THE LANTERN THING THEY DO FOR THE PRINCESS?
LANTERNS...
TOMORROW EVENING, THEY WILL LIGHT THE NIGHT SKY.
YOU WILL TAKE ME TO THESE LANTERNS AND RETURN ME HOME SAFELY.
THEN, I'LL RETURN YOUR SATCHEL.

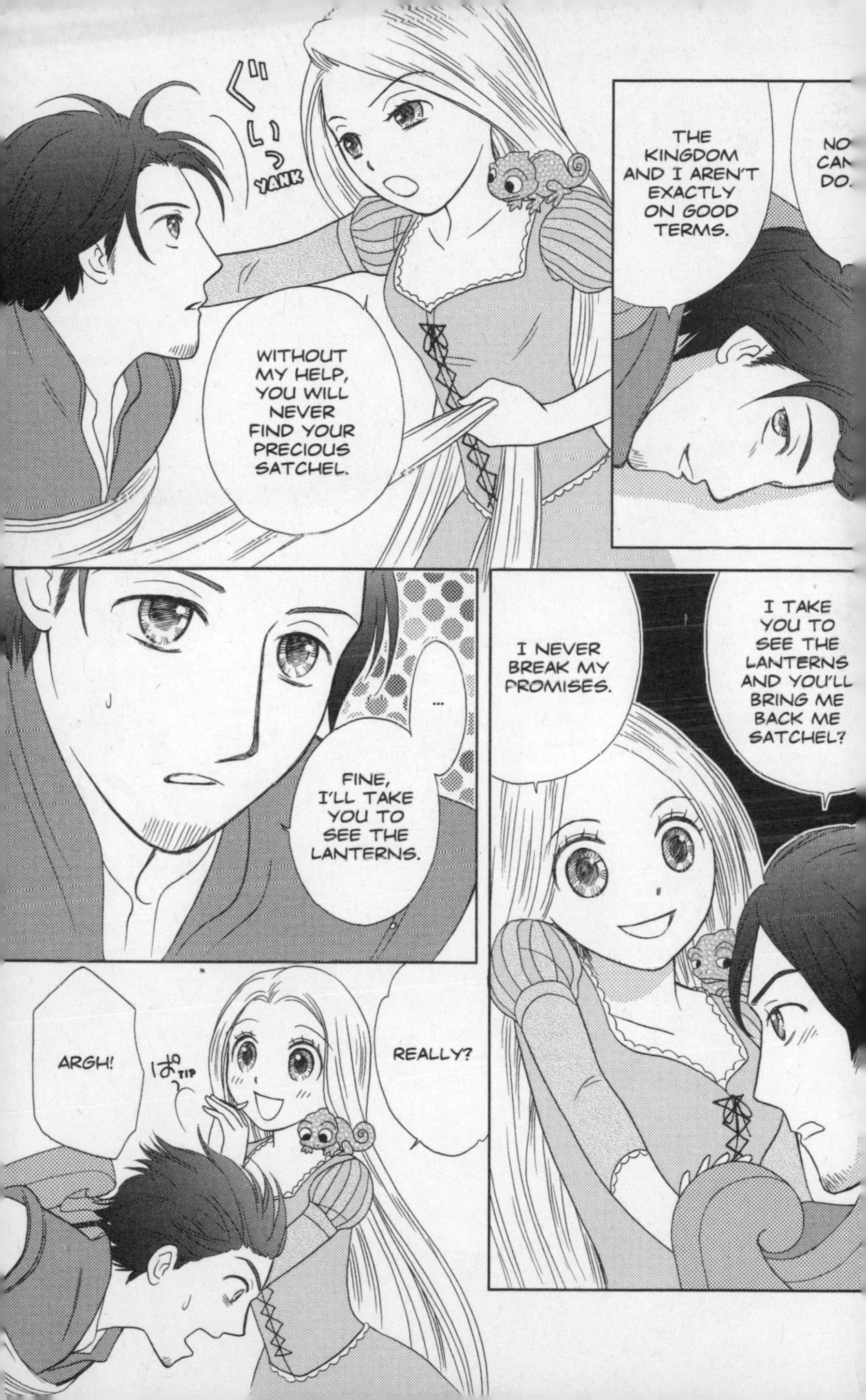
NO
CAN
DO.
THE KINGDOM AND I AREN'T EXACTLY ON GOOD TERMS.
ぐいっ
YANK
WITHOUT MY HELP, YOU WILL NEVER FIND YOUR PRECIOUS SATCHEL.
I TAKE YOU TO SEE THE LANTERNS AND YOU'LL BRING ME BACK ME SATCHEL?
I NEVER BREAK MY PROMISES.
...
FINE, I'LL TAKE YOU TO SEE THE LANTERNS.
REALLY?
ぱ
TIP
ARGH!

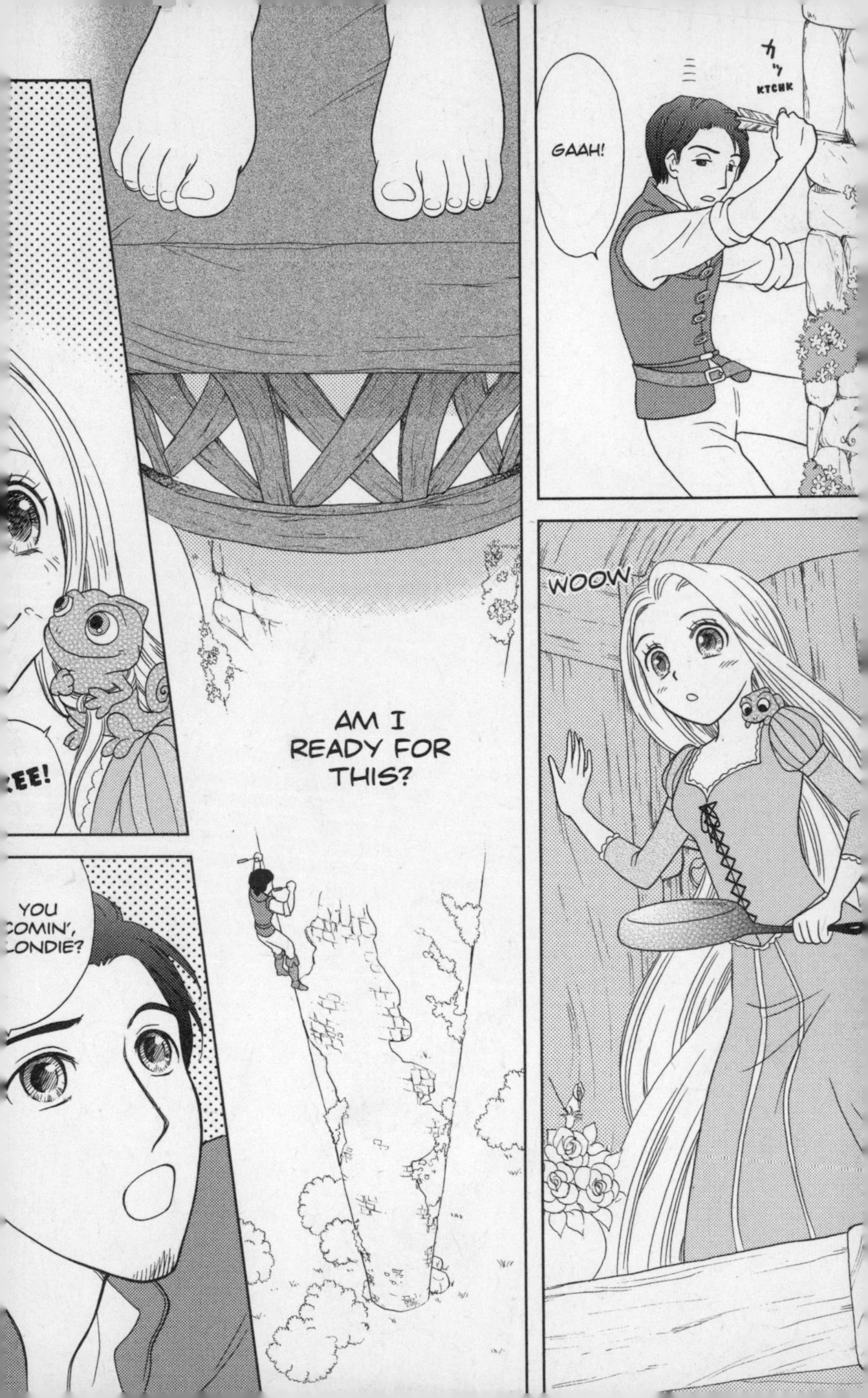
カッ
KTCHK
GAAH!
WOOW
AM I READY FOR THIS?
EE!
YOU COMIN', LONDIE?

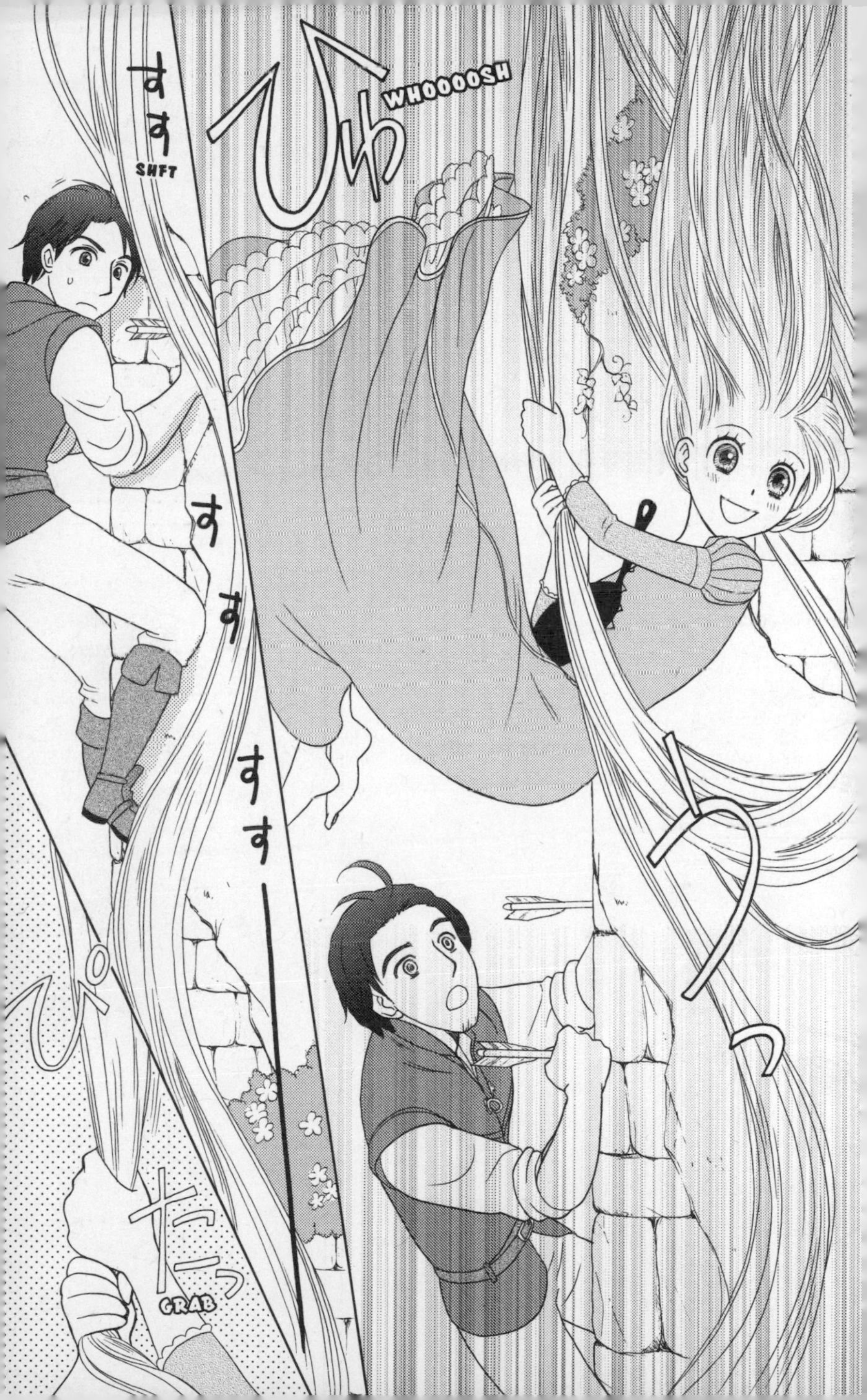

ひゅ
WHOOOOSH
すす
SHFT
すす
すす
すすー
GRAB

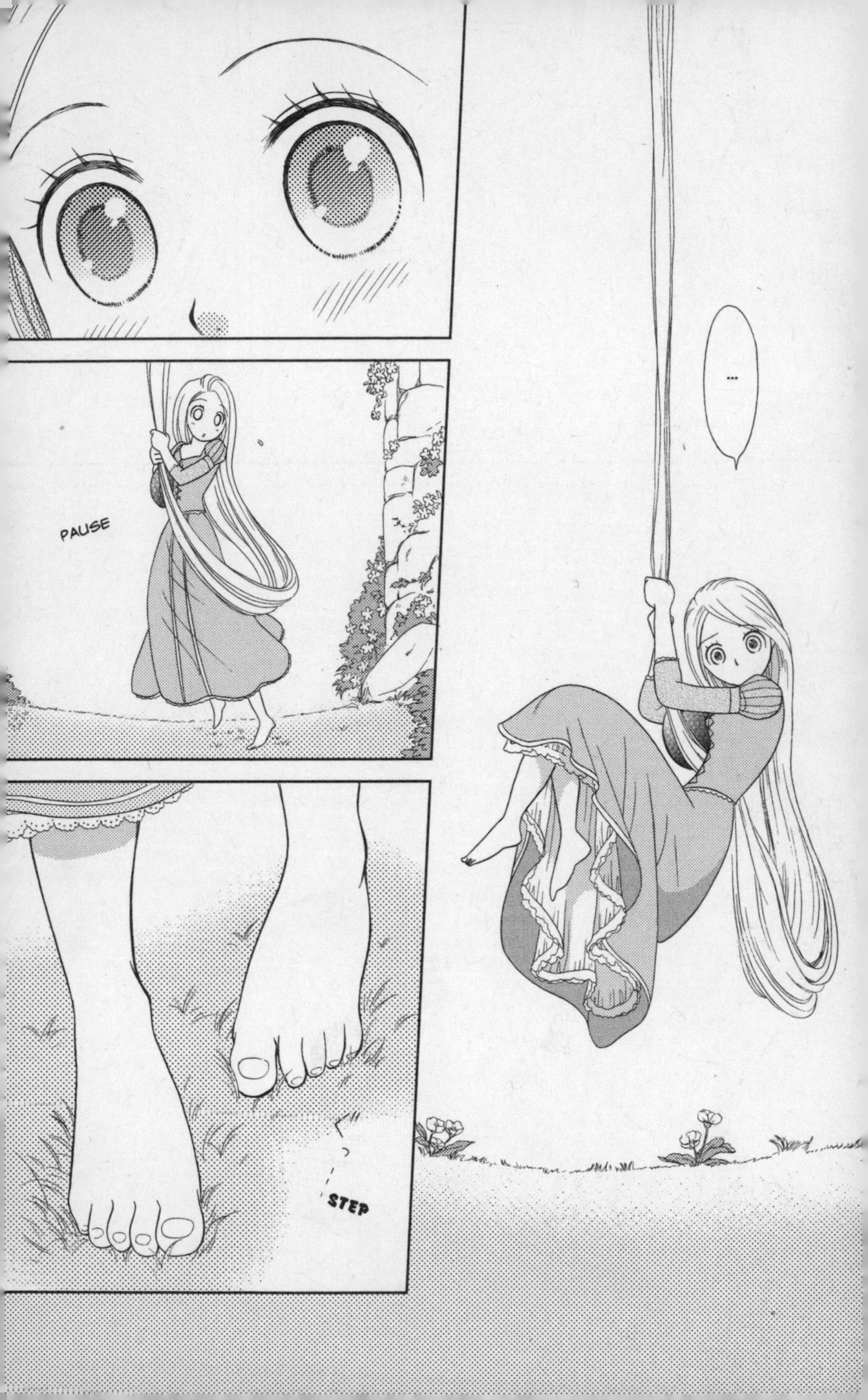
...
PAUSE
STEP

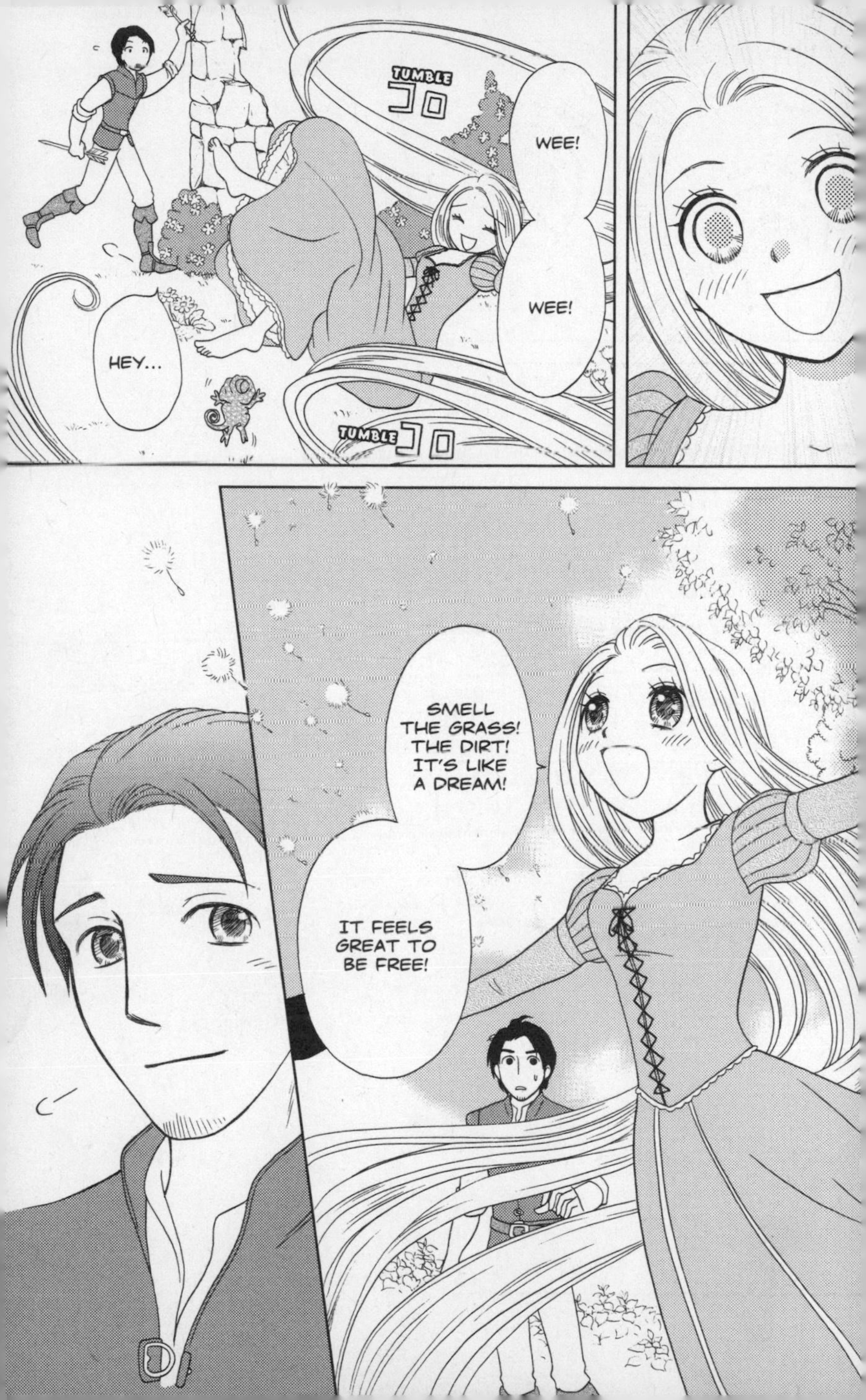
TUMBLE コロ
WEE!
WEE!
HEY...
TUMBLE コロ
SMELL THE GRASS! THE DIRT! IT'S LIKE A DREAM!
IT FEELS GREAT TO BE FREE!

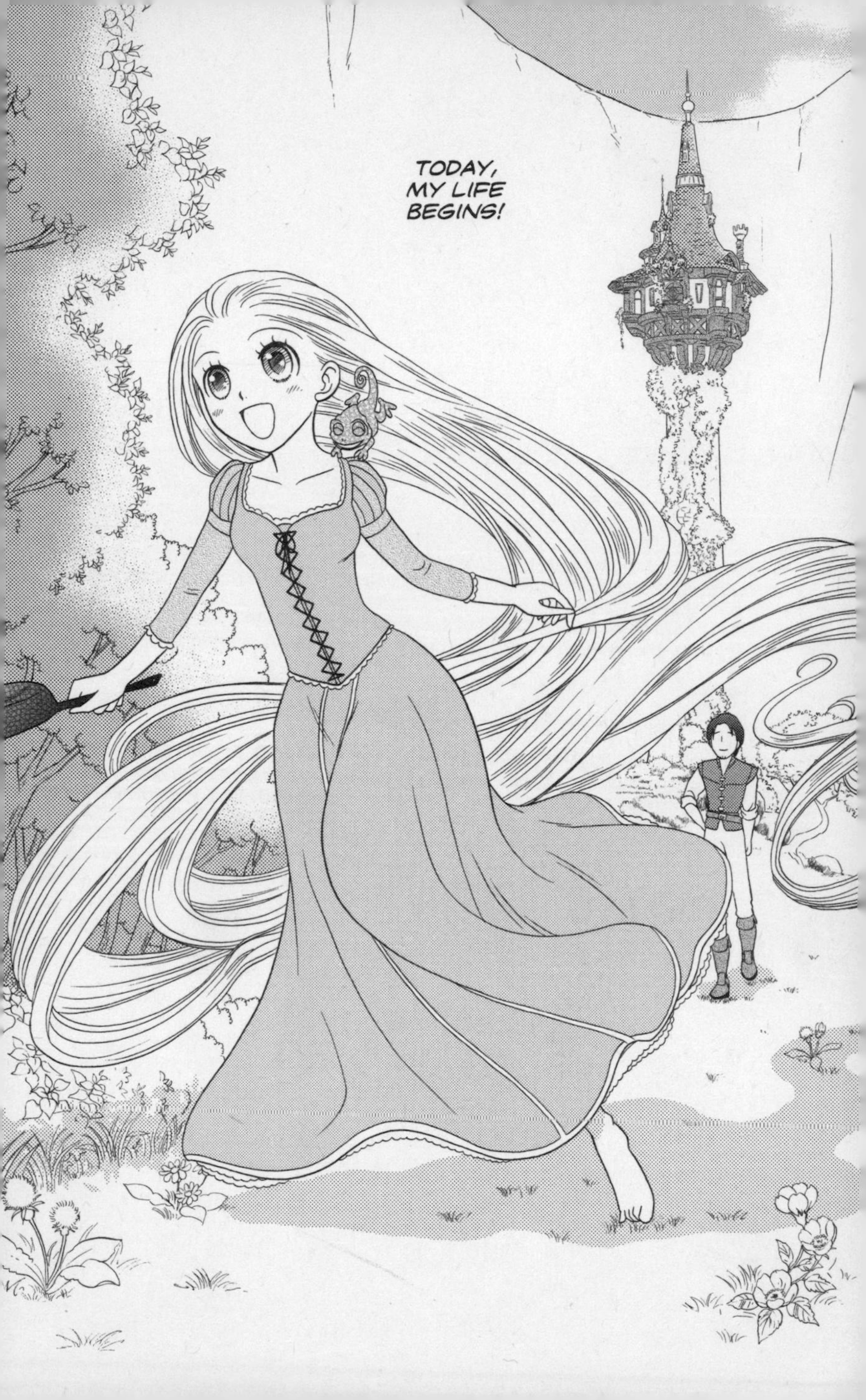
TODAY, MY LIFE BEGINS!

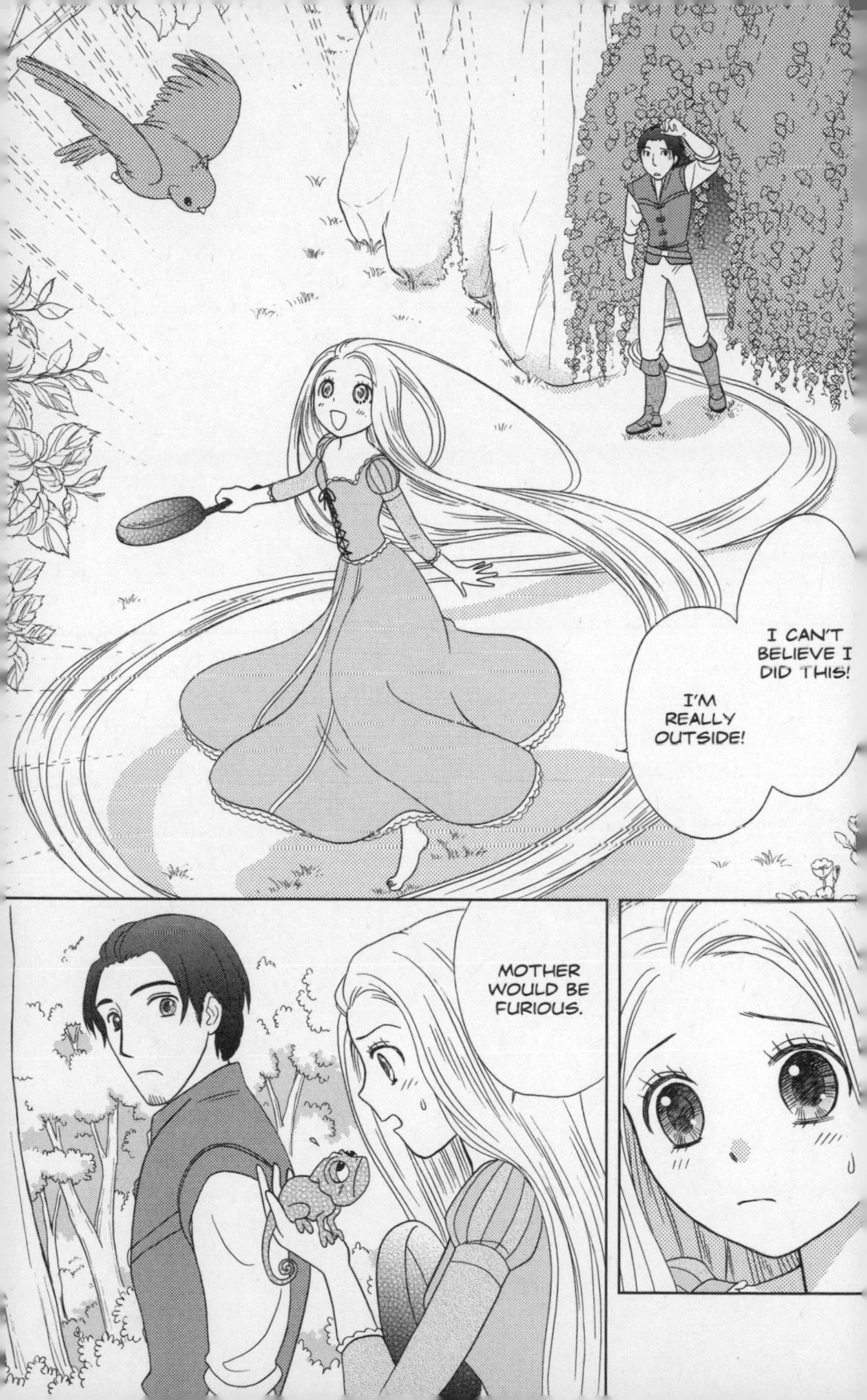
I CAN'T BELIEVE I DID THIS!
I'M REALLY OUTSIDE!
MOTHER WOULD BE FURIOUS.

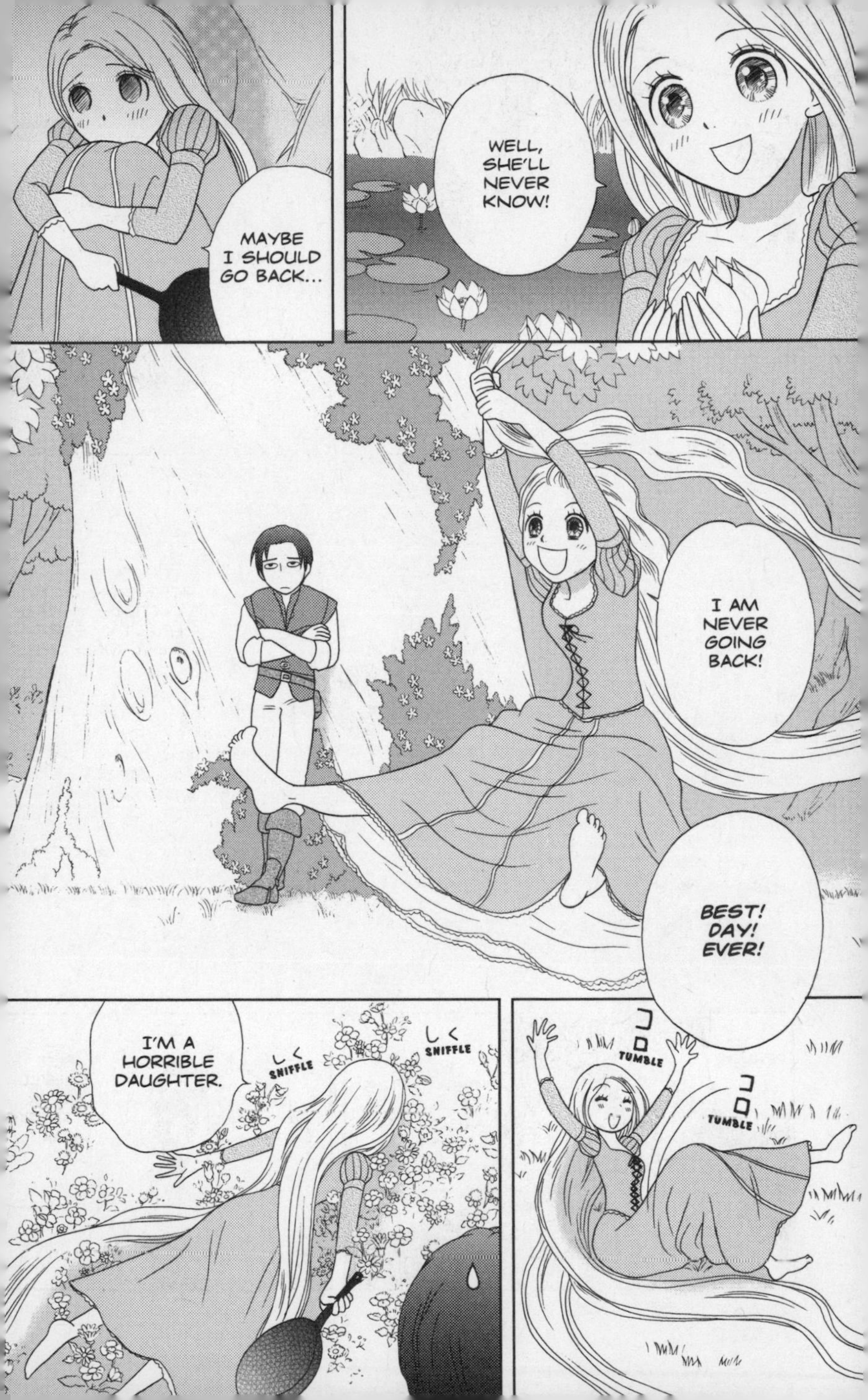
WELL, SHE'LL NEVER KNOW!
MAYBE I SHOULD GO BACK...
I AM NEVER GOING BACK!
BEST! DAY! EVER!
コロ TUMBLE
コロ TUMBLE
しく SNIFFLE
しく SNIFFLE
I'M A HORRIBLE DAUGHTER.

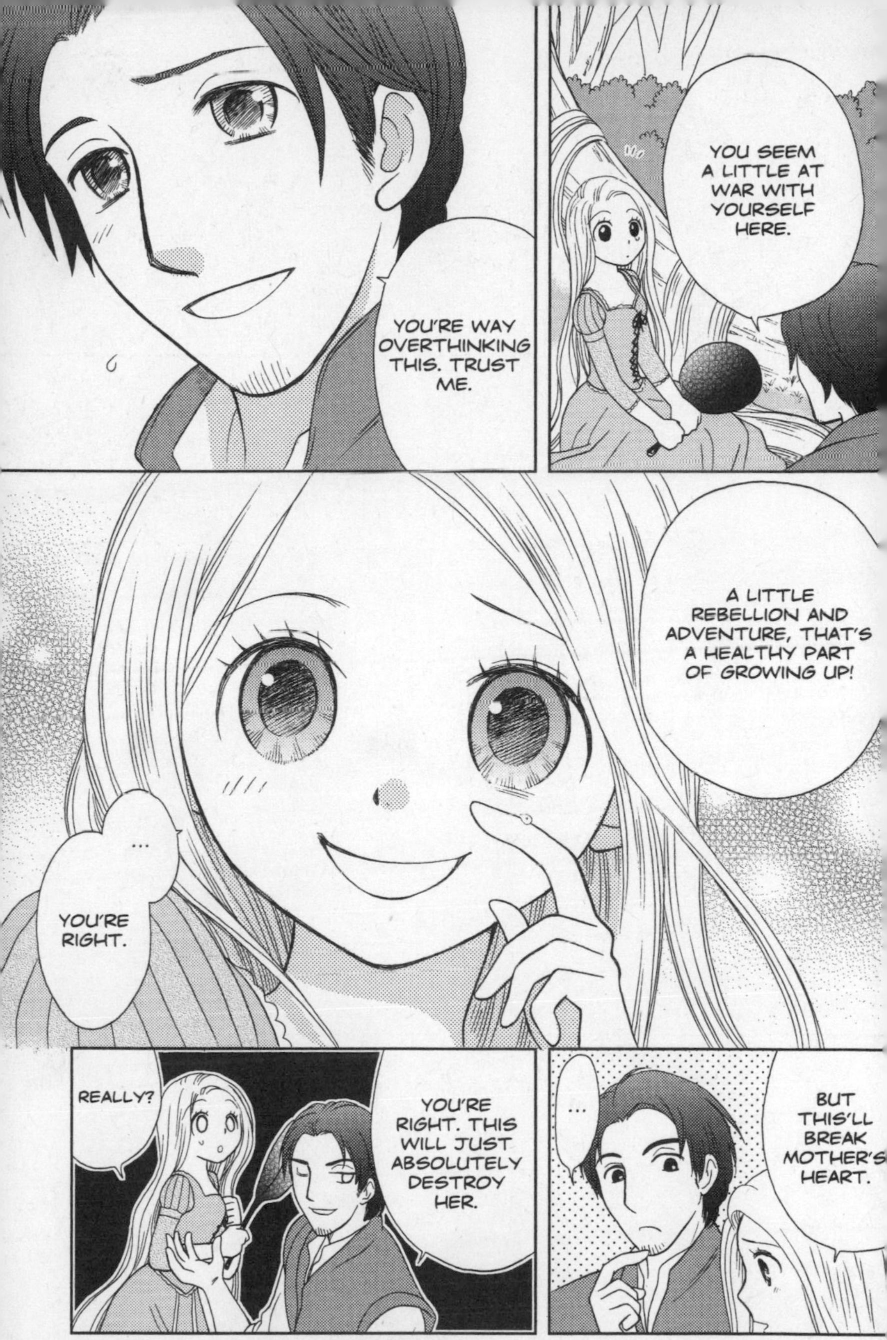
YOU SEEM A LITTLE AT WAR WITH YOURSELF HERE.
YOU'RE WAY OVERTHINKING THIS. TRUST ME.
A LITTLE REBELLION AND ADVENTURE, THAT'S A HEALTHY PART OF GROWING UP!
... YOU'RE RIGHT.
BUT THIS'LL BREAK MOTHER'S HEART.
...
YOU'RE RIGHT. THIS WILL JUST ABSOLUTELY DESTROY HER.
REALLY?

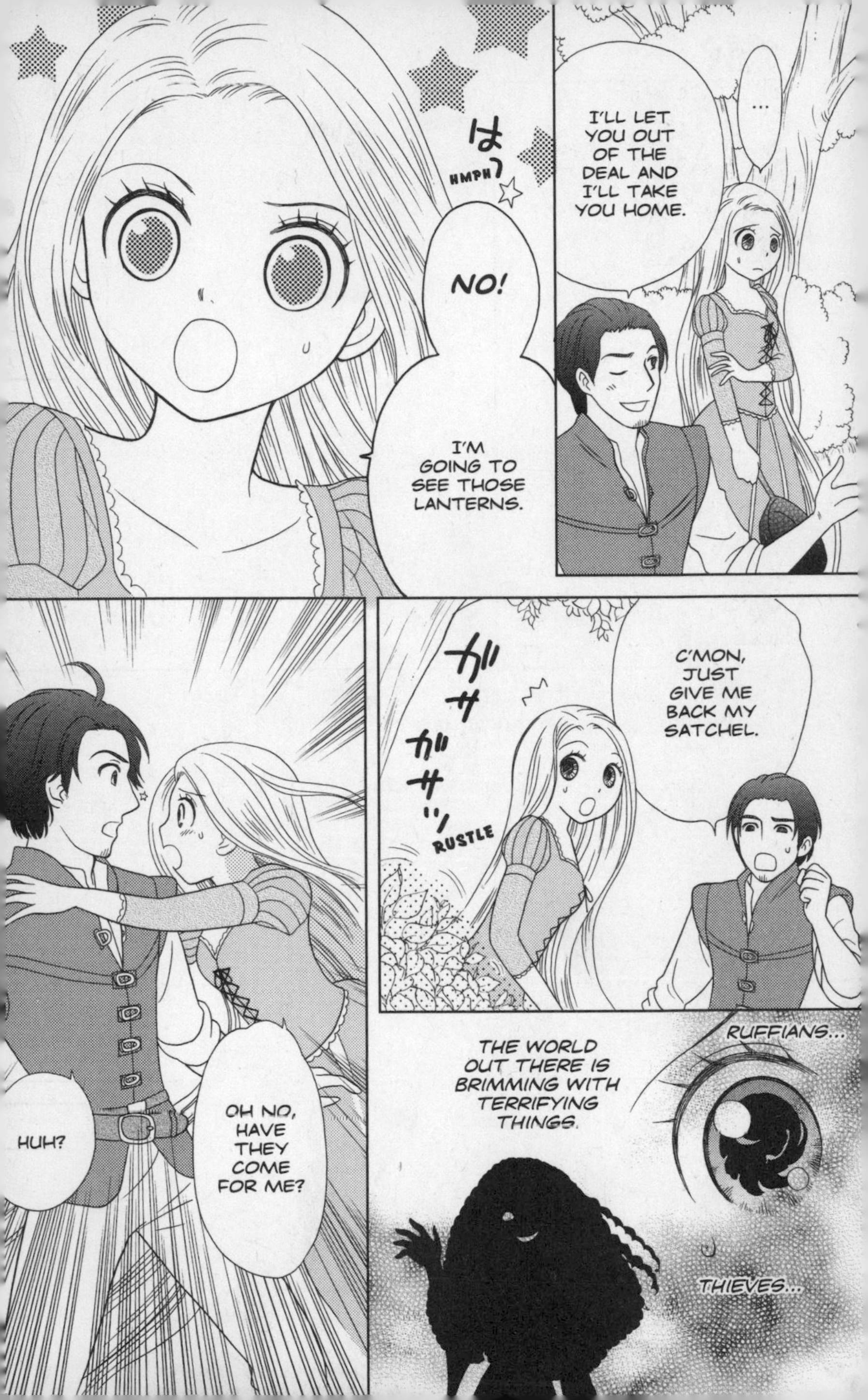
...
I'LL LET YOU OUT OF THE DEAL AND I'LL TAKE YOU HOME.
はっ
HMPH
NO!
I'M GOING TO SEE THOSE LANTERNS.
C'MON, JUST GIVE ME BACK MY SATCHEL.
ガサガサッ
RUSTLE
RUFFIANS...
THE WORLD OUT THERE IS BRIMMING WITH TERRIFYING THINGS.
THIEVES...
OH NO, HAVE THEY COME FOR ME?
HUH?

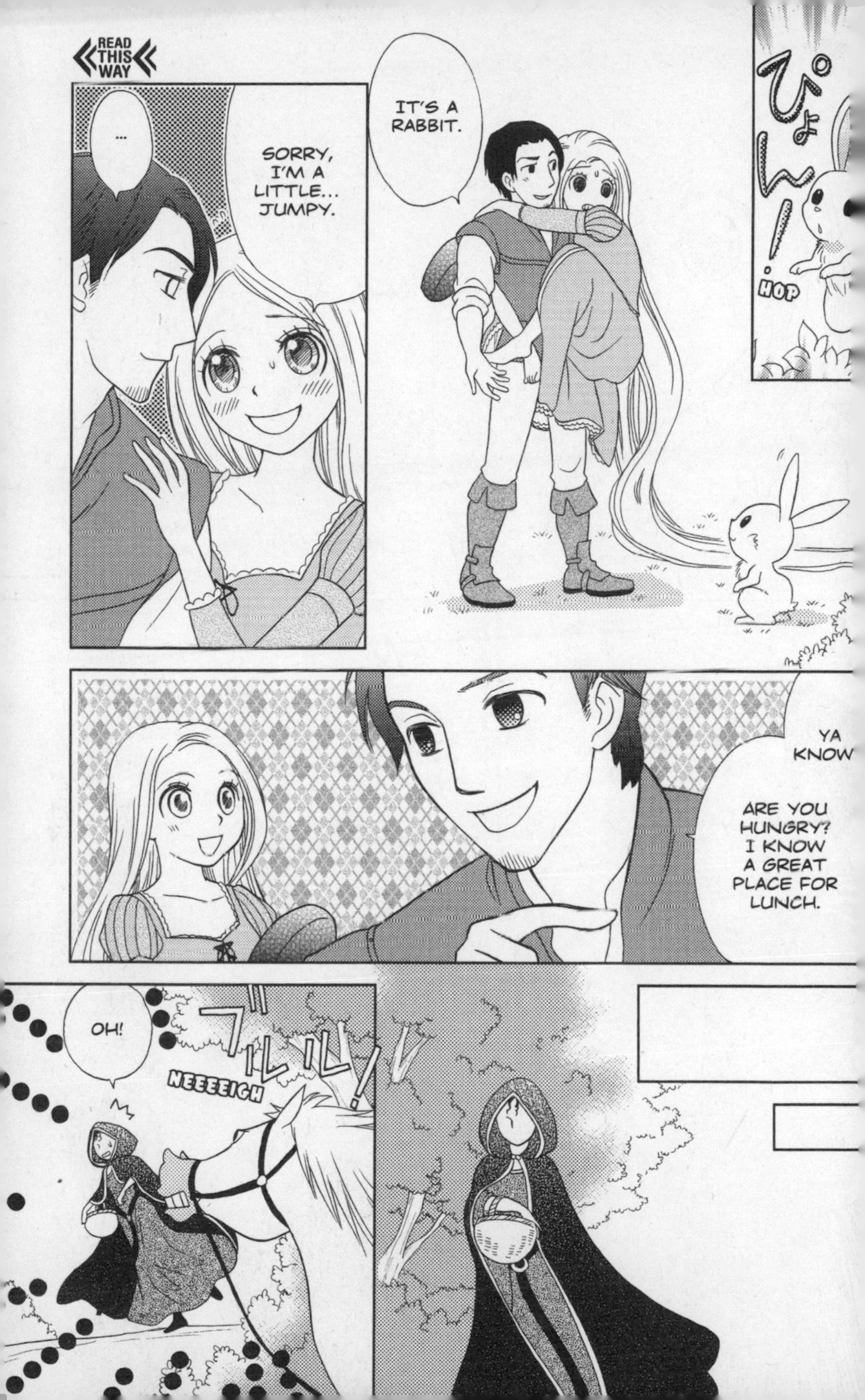
ぴょん!
HOP
IT'S A RABBIT.
SORRY, I'M A LITTLE... JUMPY.
...
YA KNOW
ARE YOU HUNGRY? I KNOW A GREAT PLACE FOR LUNCH.
ブルル!
NEEEEEIGH
OH!

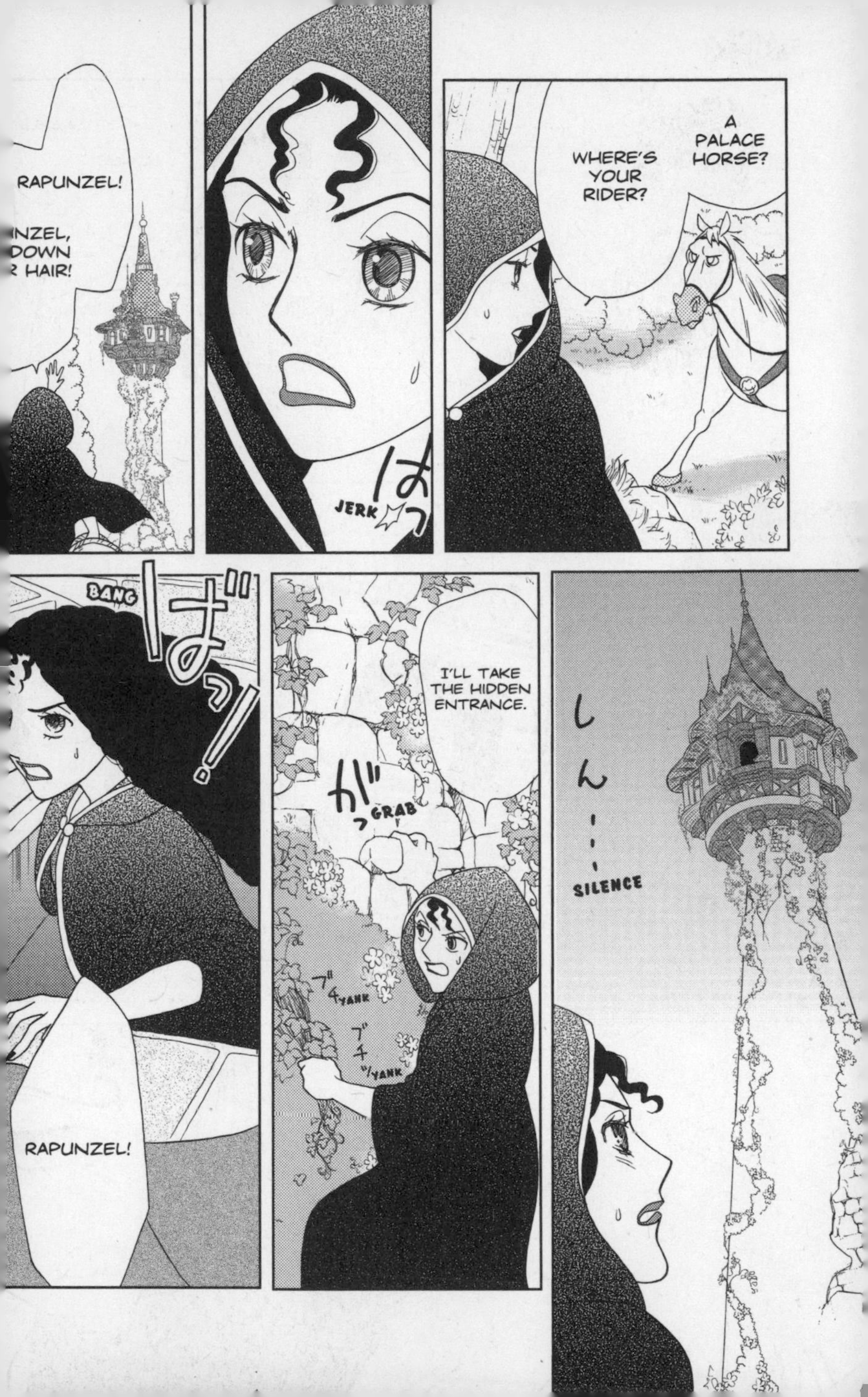
A PALACE HORSE?
WHERE'S YOUR RIDER?
はっ
JERK
RAPUNZEL!
NZEL, DOWN R HAIR!
しん…
SILENCE
I'LL TAKE THE HIDDEN ENTRANCE.
がっ
GRAB
ブチ
YANK
ブチ
YANK
ばっ!
BANG
RAPUNZEL!

HEAD THIS WAY

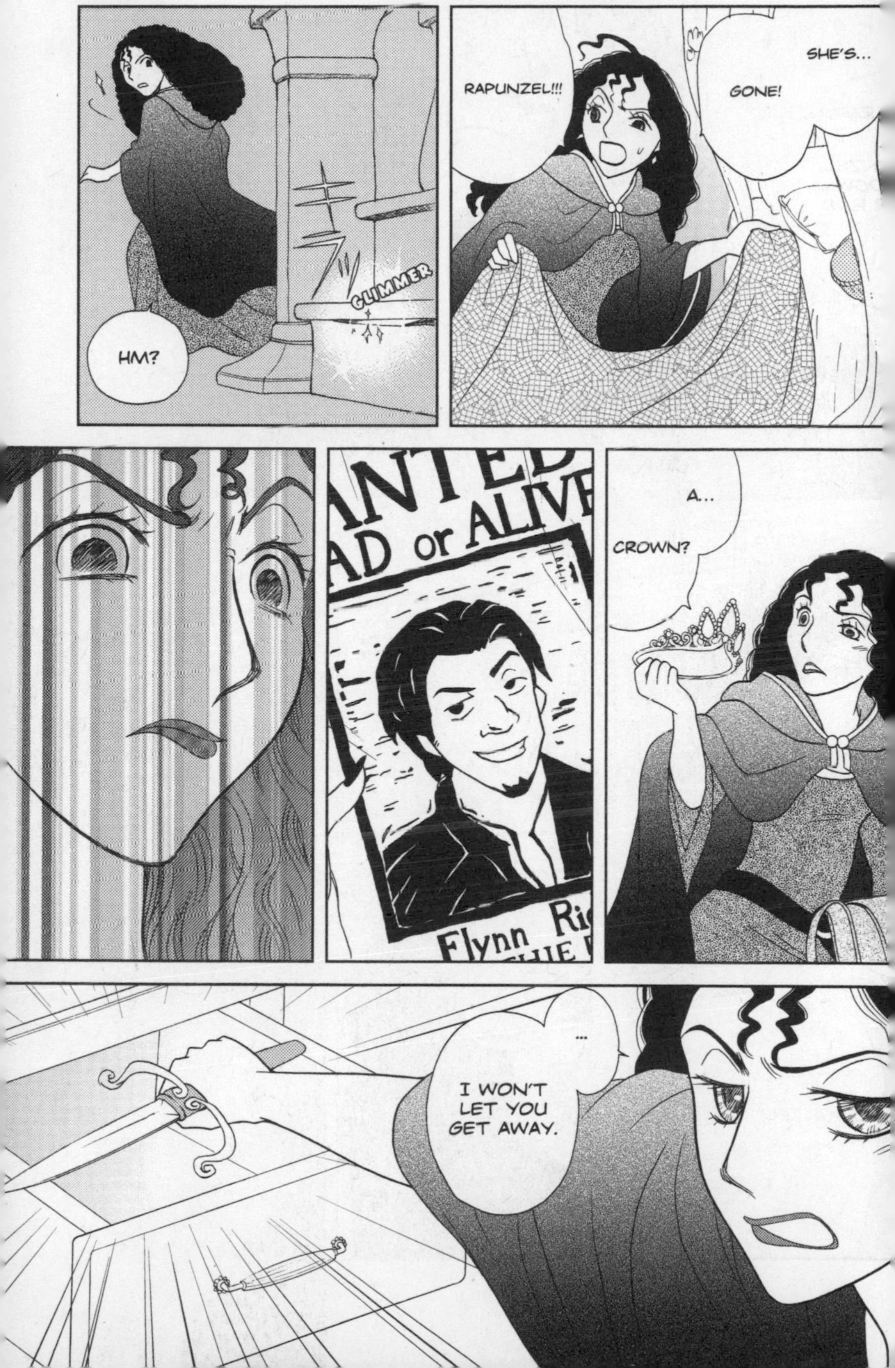
SHE'S...
GONE!
RAPUNZEL!!!
GLIMMER
HM?
A...
CROWN?
AD or ALIVE
Flynn
...
I WON'T LET YOU GET AWAY.

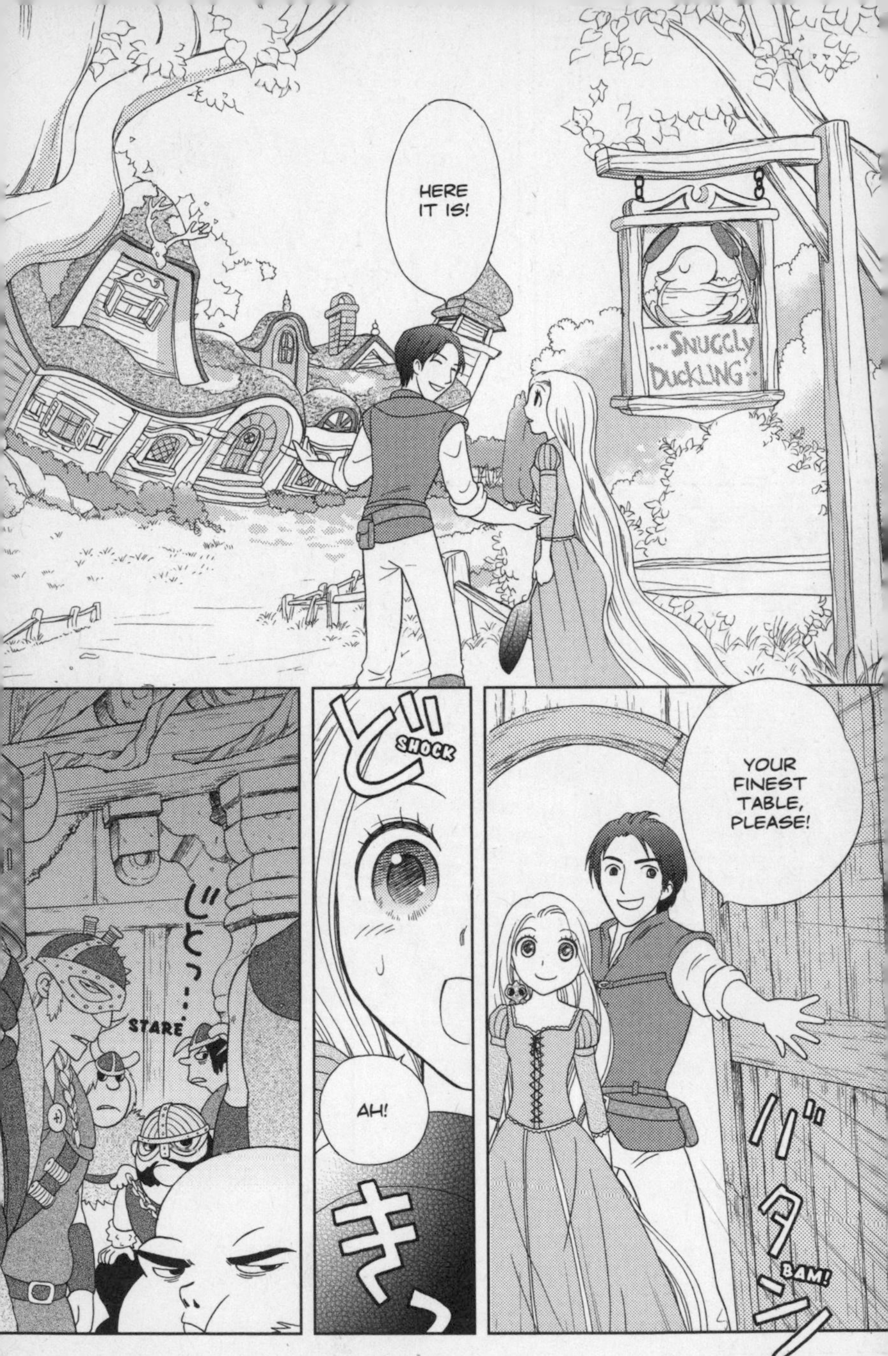
...SNUGGLY DUCKLING...
HERE IT IS!
YOUR FINEST TABLE, PLEASE!
バタン!
BAM!
ど
SHOCK
AH!
きっ
じとっ…
STARE

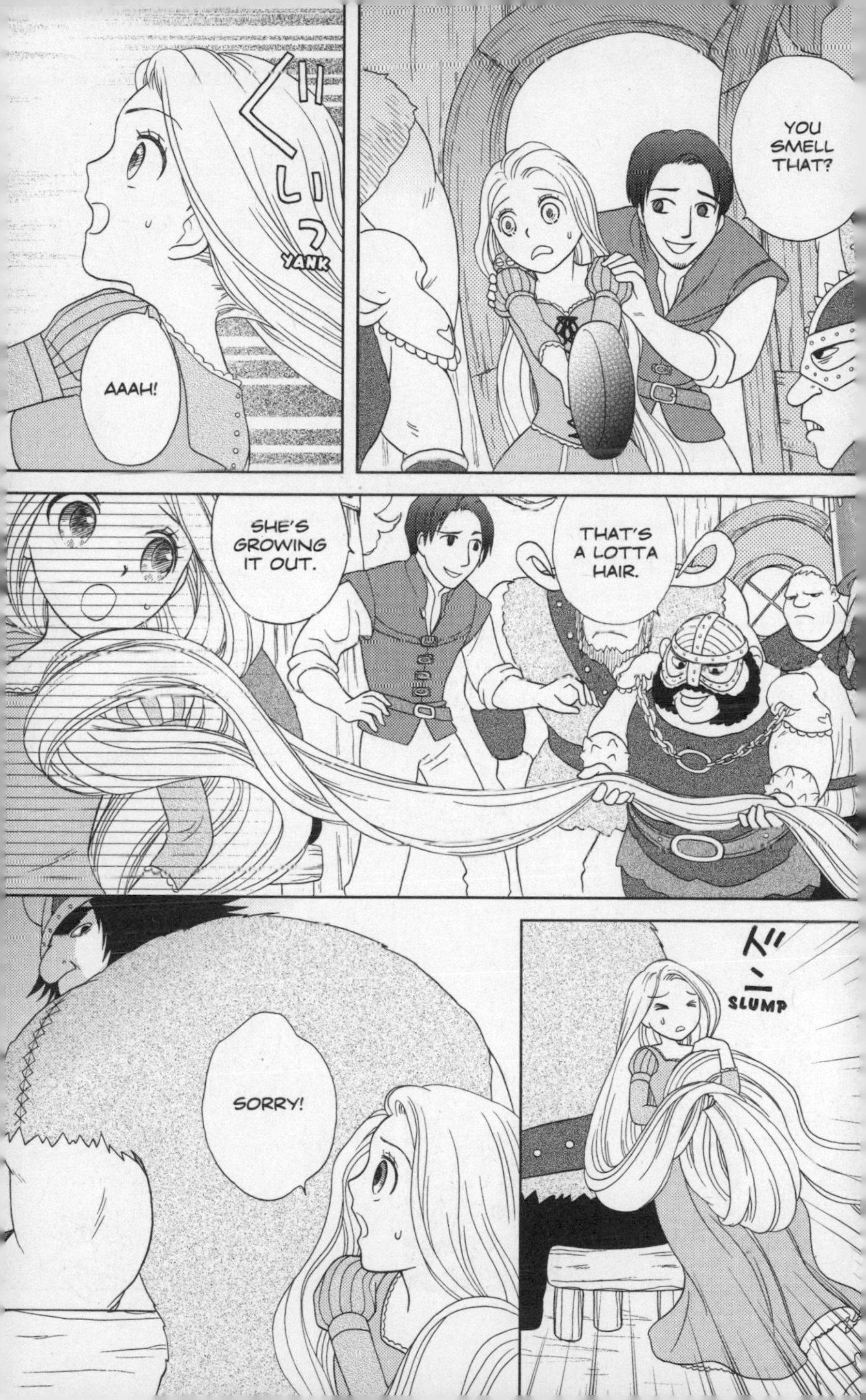
YOU SMELL THAT?
YANK
AAAH!
THAT'S A LOTTA HAIR.
SHE'S GROWING IT OUT.
SLUMP
SORRY!

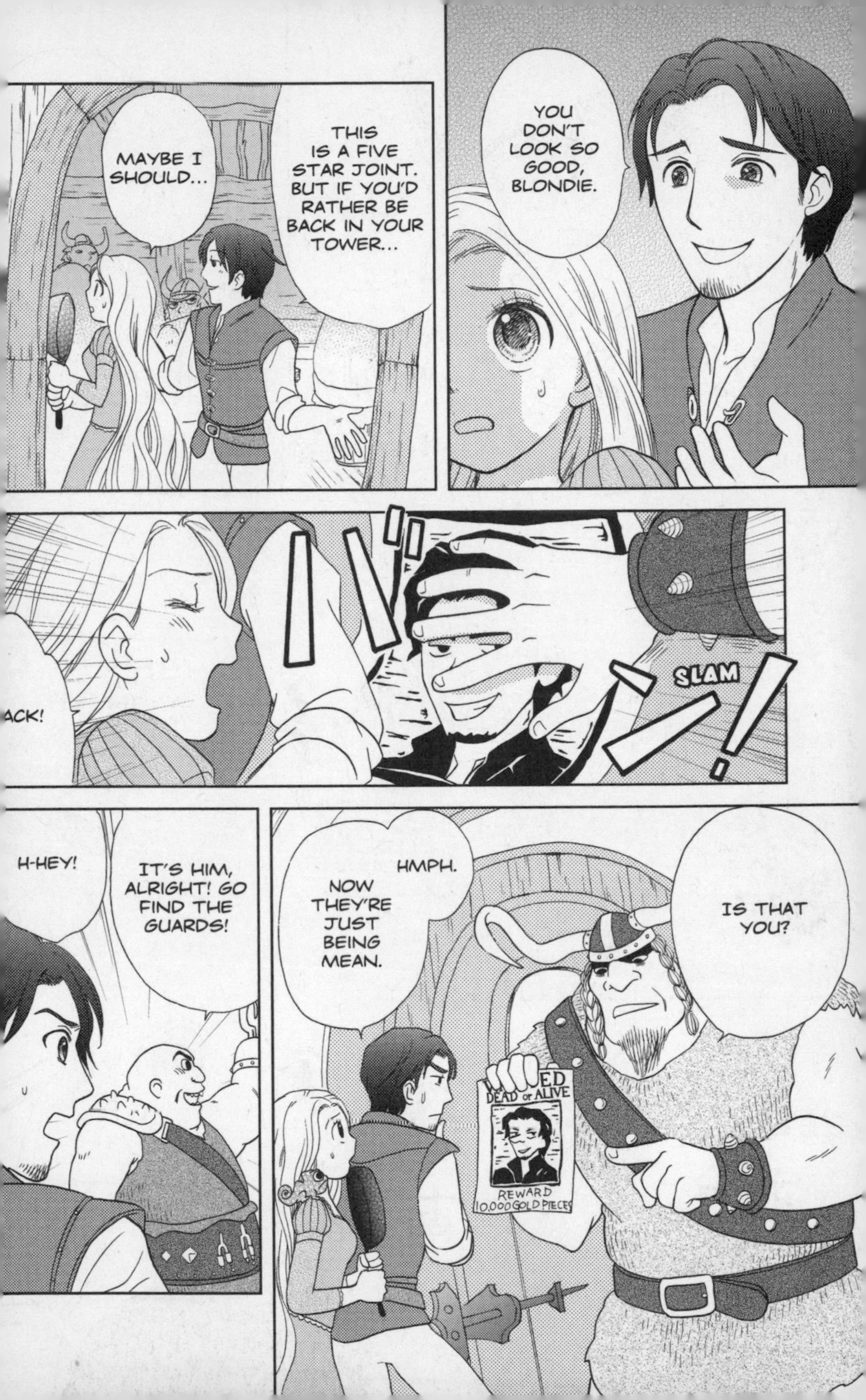
YOU DON'T LOOK SO GOOD, BLONDIE.
THIS IS A FIVE STAR JOINT. BUT IF YOU'D RATHER BE BACK IN YOUR TOWER...
MAYBE I SHOULD...
SLAM
ACK!
IS THAT YOU?
DEAD or ALIVE
REWARD
10,000 GOLD PIECES
HMPH.
NOW THEY'RE JUST BEING MEAN.
IT'S HIM, ALRIGHT! GO FIND THE GUARDS!
H-HEY!

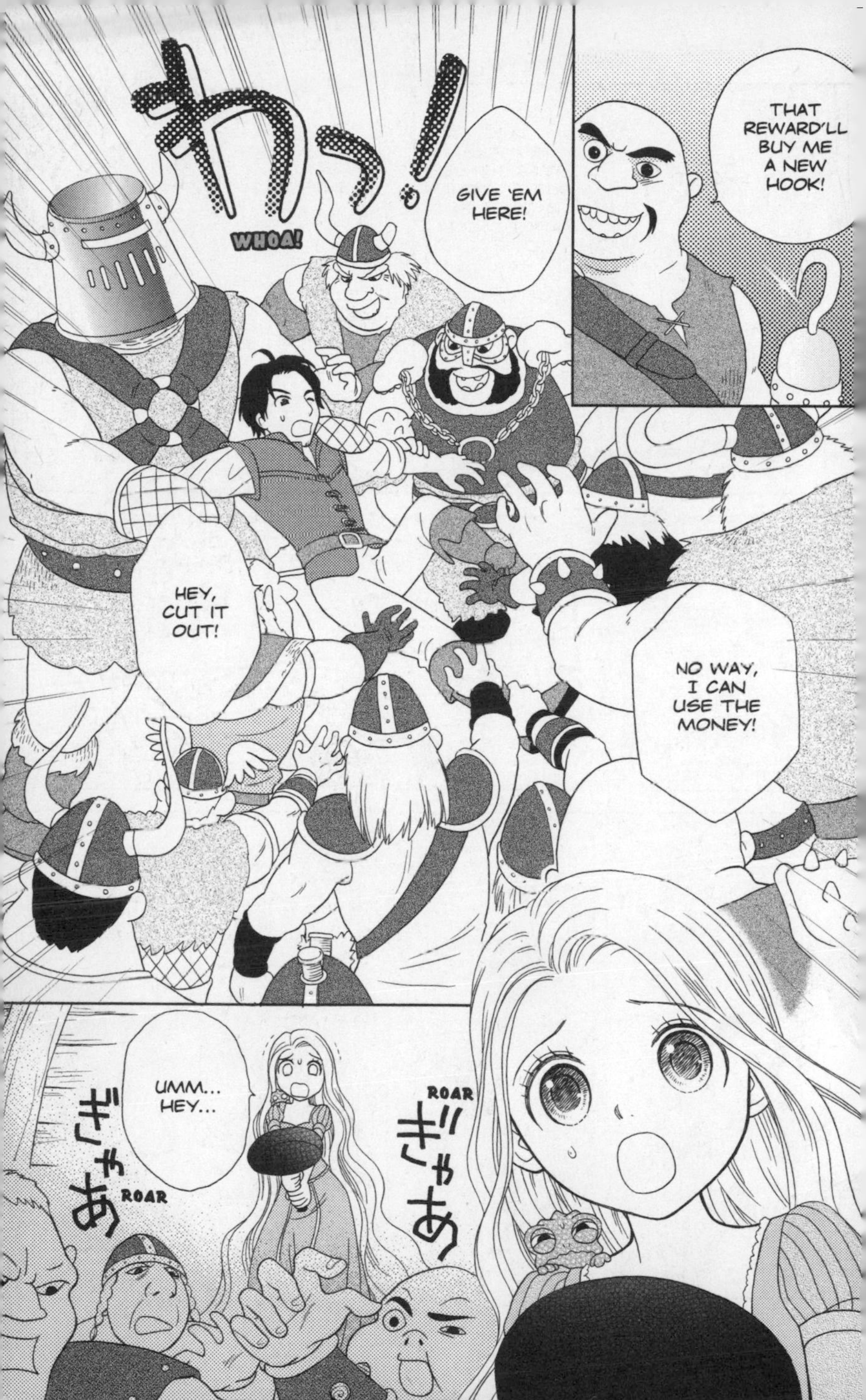
THAT REWARD'LL BUY ME A NEW HOOK!
わっ!
WHOA!
GIVE 'EM HERE!
NO WAY, I CAN USE THE MONEY!
HEY, CUT IT OUT!
ぎゃあ
ROAR
UMM... HEY...
ぎゃあ
ROAR

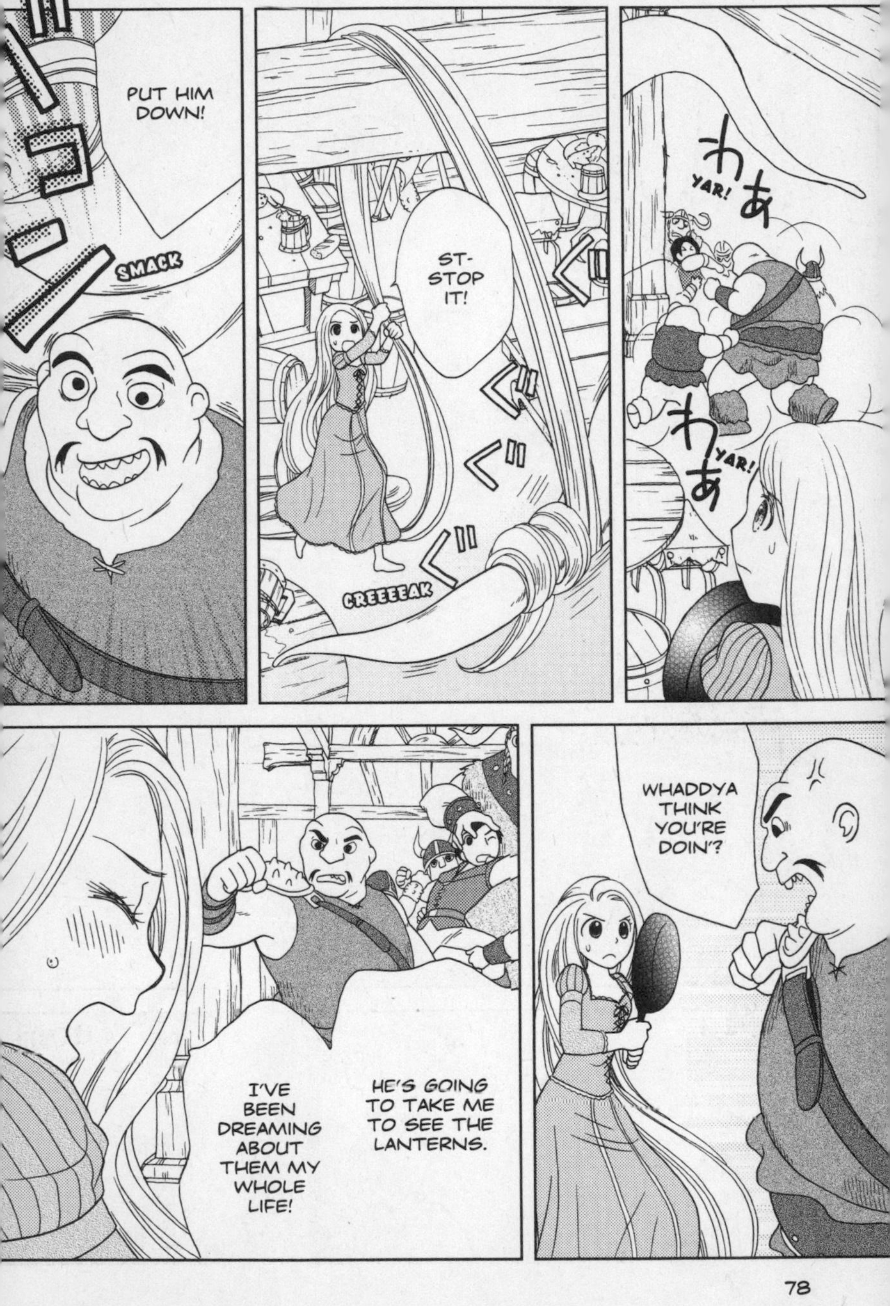
わあ
YAR!
わあ
YAR!
ST-STOP IT!
ぐぐぐぐ
CREEEEAK
SMACK
PUT HIM DOWN!
WHADDYA THINK YOU'RE DOIN'?
HE'S GOING TO TAKE ME TO SEE THE LANTERNS.
I'VE BEEN DREAMING ABOUT THEM MY WHOLE LIFE!

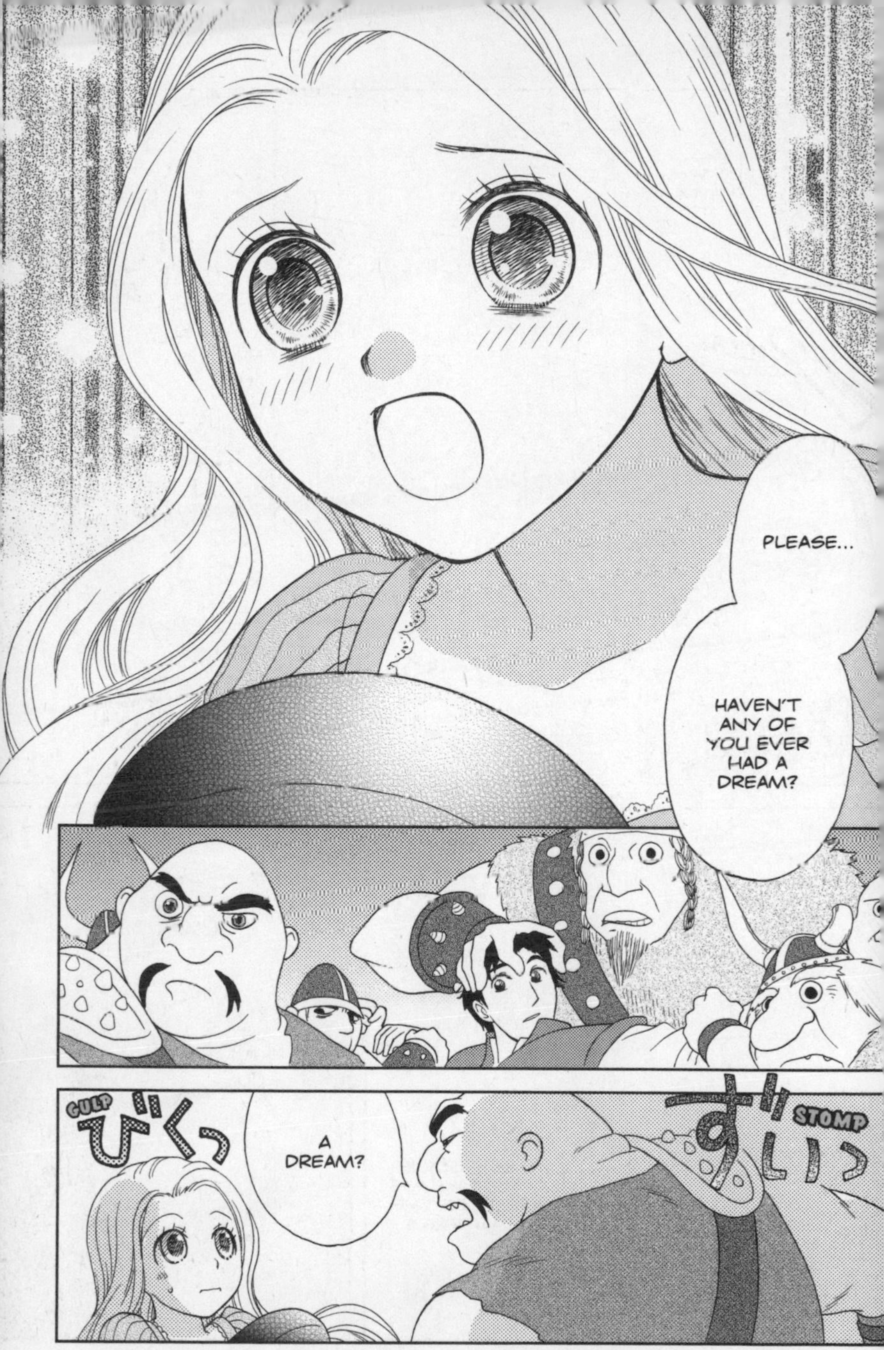
PLEASE...
HAVEN'T ANY OF YOU EVER HAD A DREAM?
STOMP
ずいっ
A DREAM?
GULP
びくっ

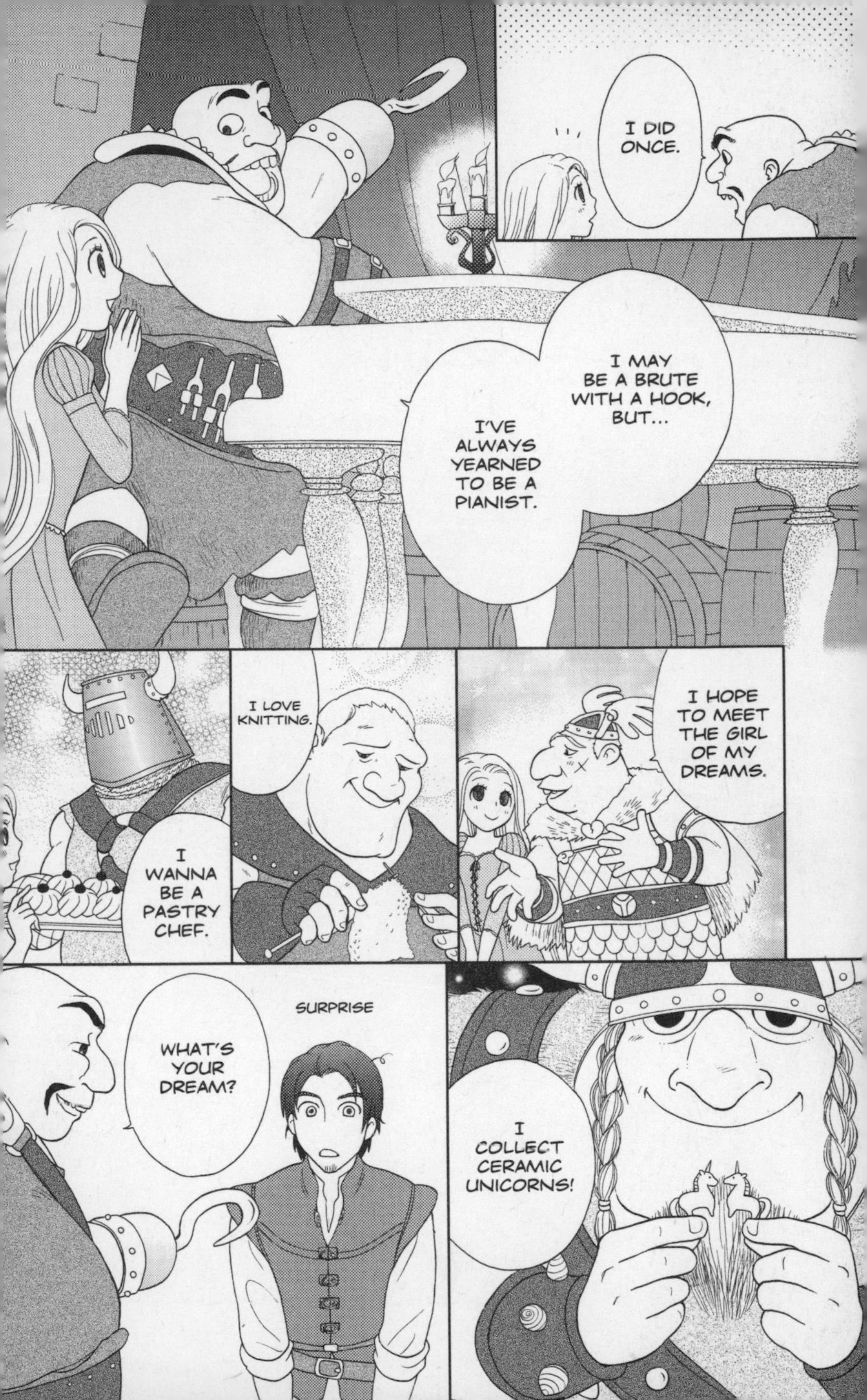
I DID ONCE.
I MAY BE A BRUTE WITH A HOOK, BUT...
I'VE ALWAYS YEARNED TO BE A PIANIST.
I HOPE TO MEET THE GIRL OF MY DREAMS.
I LOVE KNITTING.
I WANNA BE A PASTRY CHEF.
I COLLECT CERAMIC UNICORNS!
SURPRISE
WHAT'S YOUR DREAM?

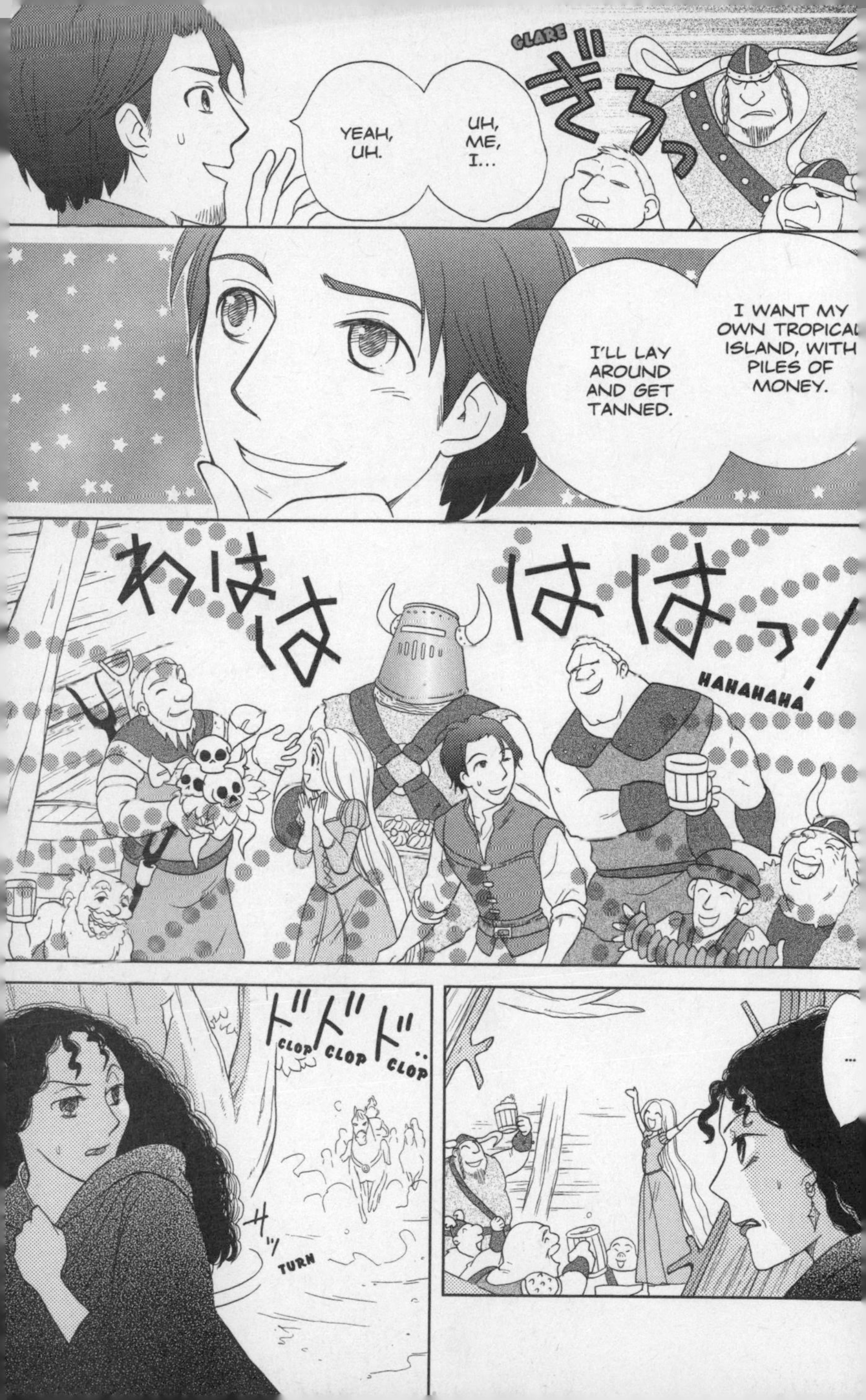
ぎろっ
GLARE
UH, ME, I...
YEAH, UH.
I WANT MY OWN TROPICAL ISLAND, WITH PILES OF MONEY.
I'LL LAY AROUND AND GET TANNED.
わははははっ!
HAHAHAHA
...
ドドド..
CLOP CLOP CLOP
サッ
TURN

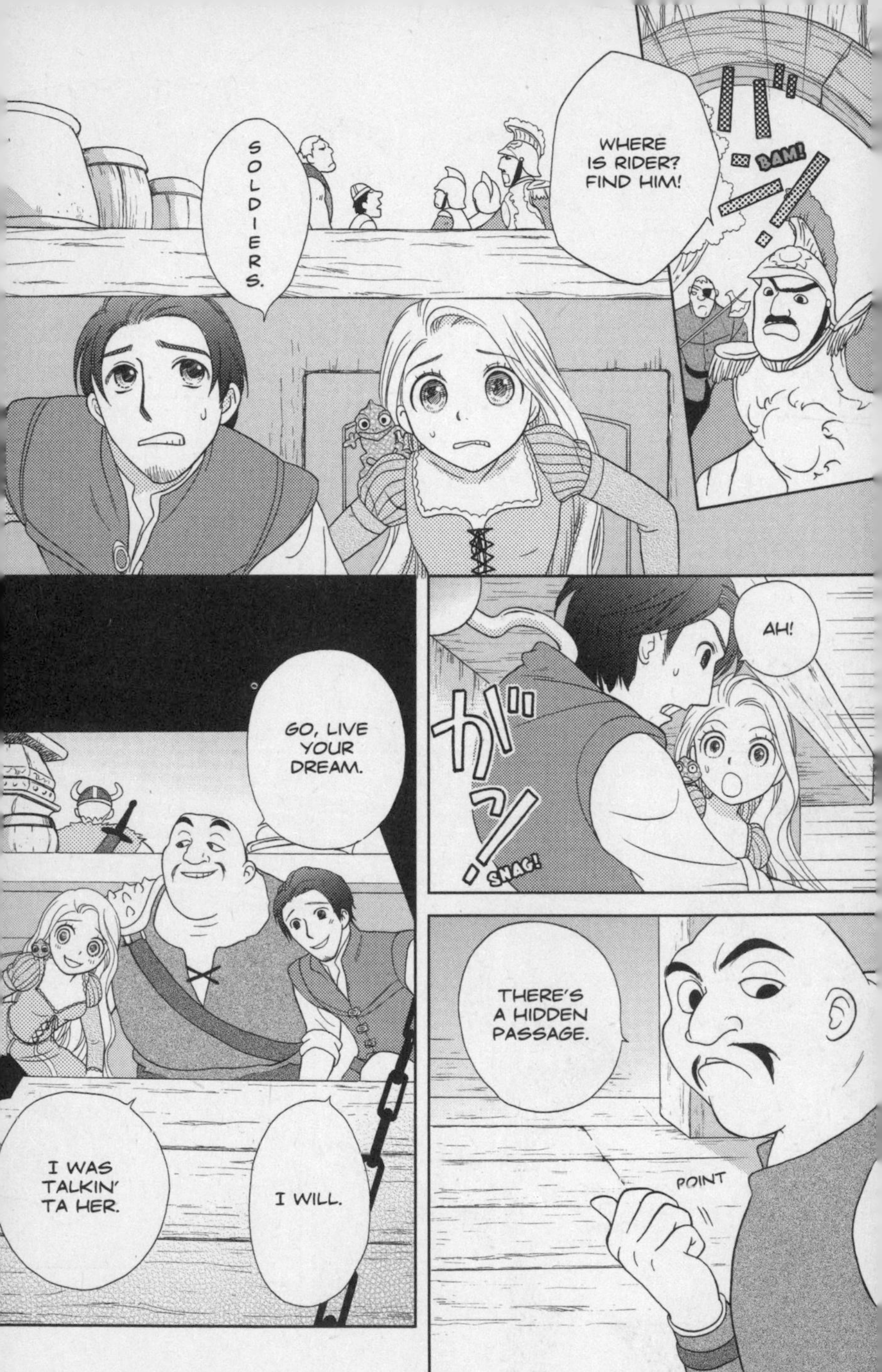
BAM!
WHERE IS RIDER? FIND HIM!
SOLDIERS.
AH!
がっ
SNAG!
THERE'S A HIDDEN PASSAGE.
POINT
GO, LIVE YOUR DREAM.
I WILL.
I WAS TALKIN' TA HER.

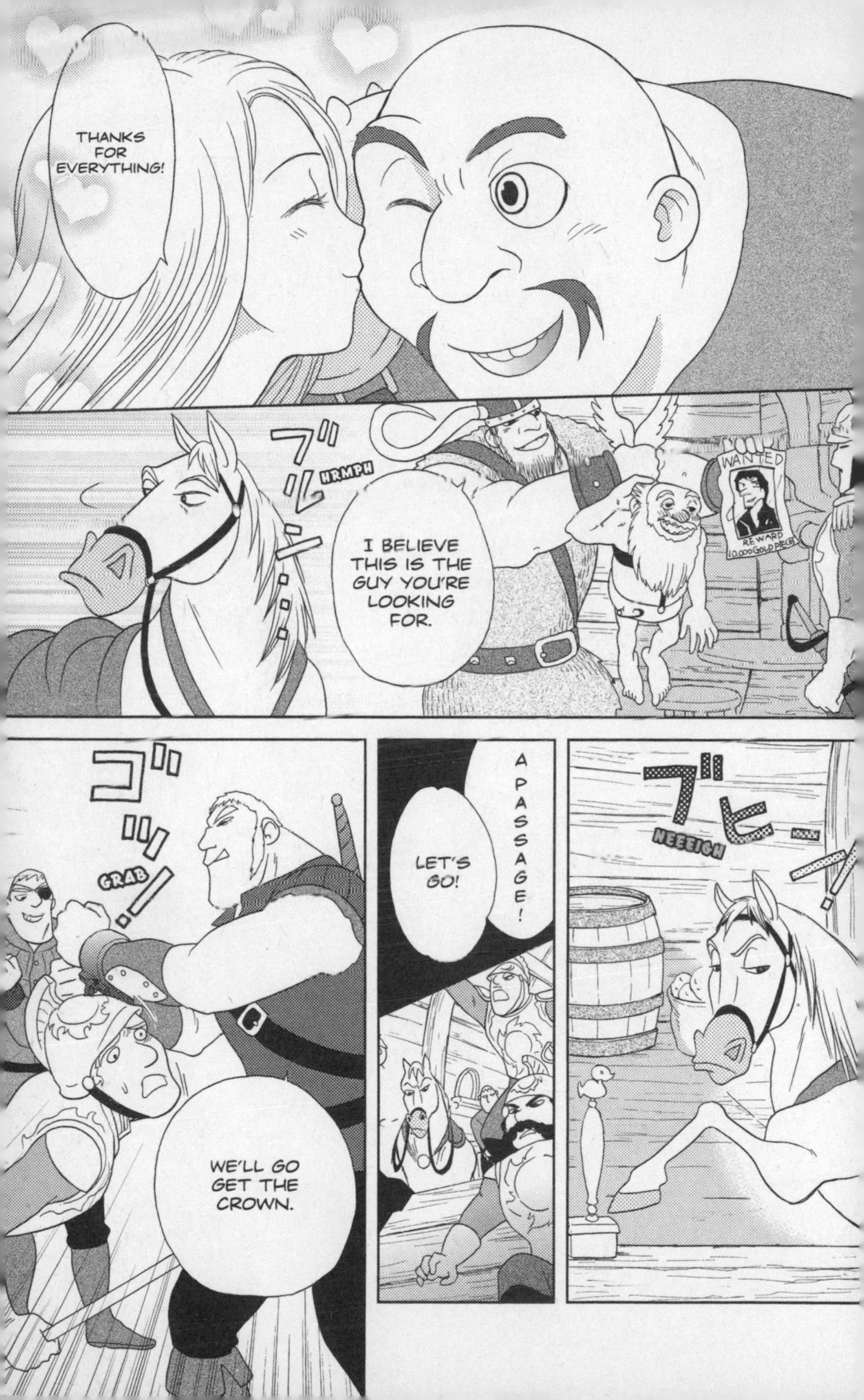
THANKS FOR EVERYTHING!
I BELIEVE THIS IS THE GUY YOU'RE LOOKING FOR.
HRMPH
NEEEIGH
A PASSAGE!
LET'S GO!
GRAB
WE'LL GO GET THE CROWN.

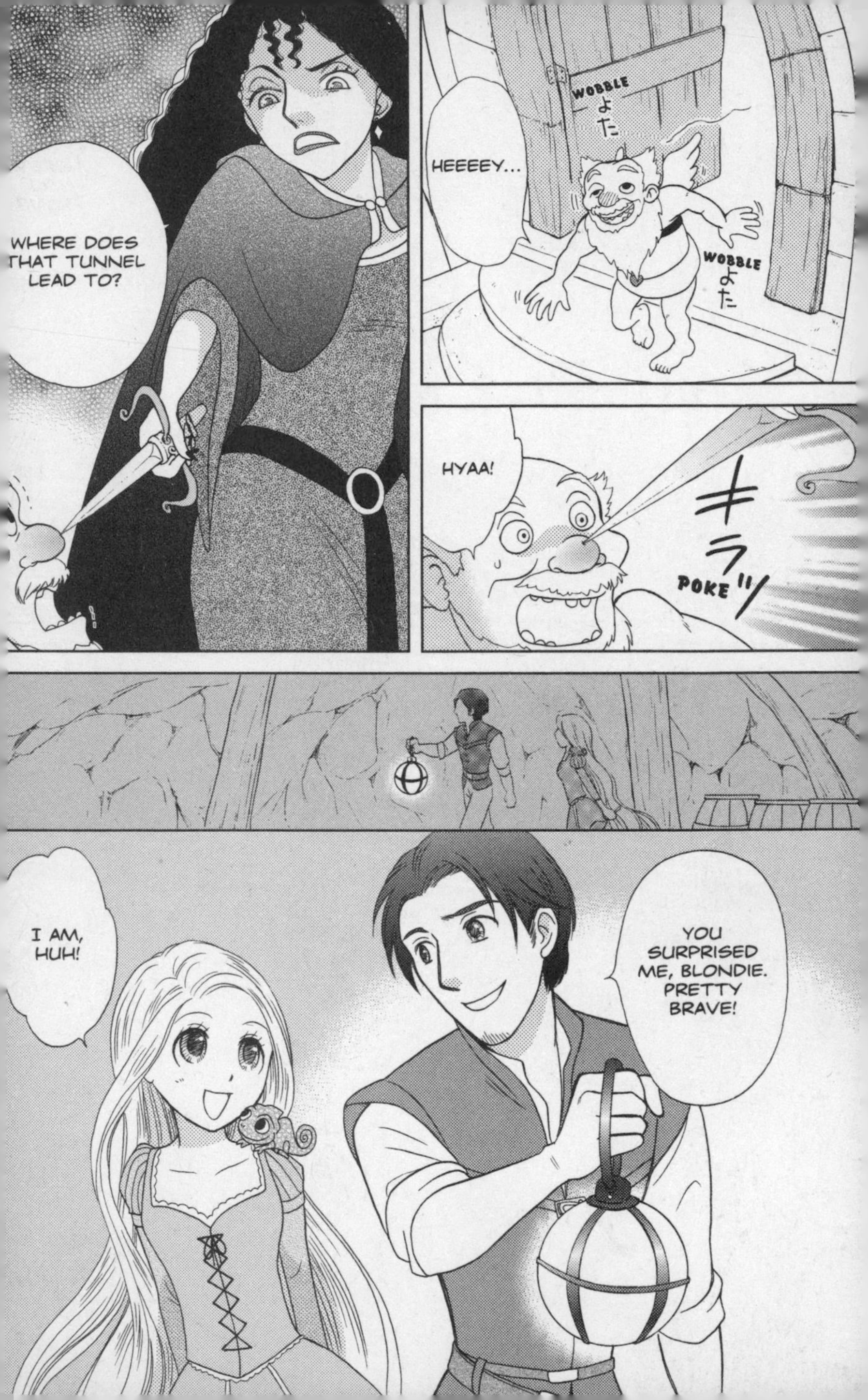
WOBBLE よた
HEEEEY...
WOBBLE よた
HYAA!
キラッ POKE
WHERE DOES THAT TUNNEL LEAD TO?
YOU SURPRISED ME, BLONDIE. PRETTY BRAVE!
I AM, HUH!

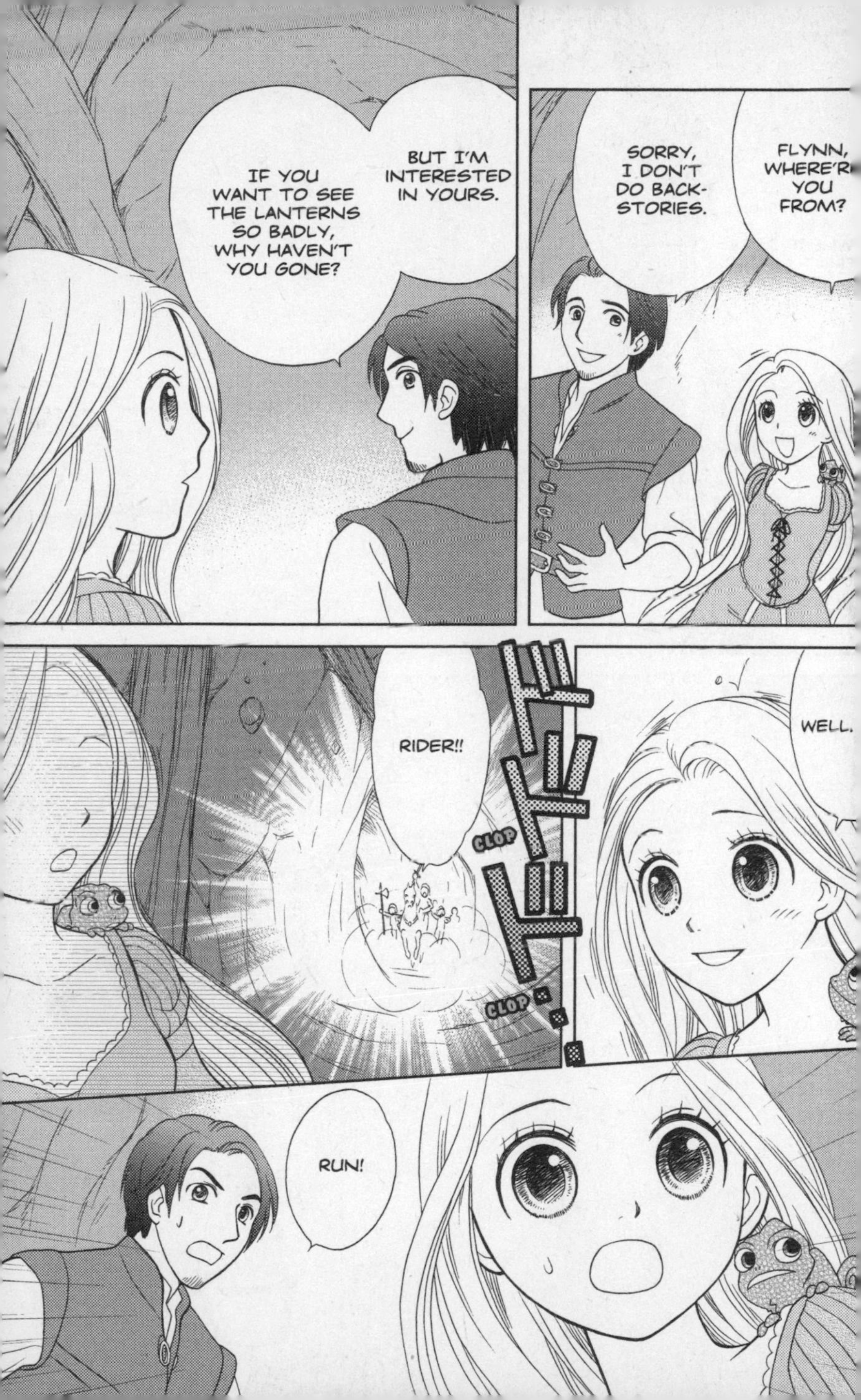
FLYNN, WHERE'R YOU FROM?
SORRY, I DON'T DO BACK-STORIES.
BUT I'M INTERESTED IN YOURS.
IF YOU WANT TO SEE THE LANTERNS SO BADLY, WHY HAVEN'T YOU GONE?
WELL...
ドドドド
CLOP
CLOP
RIDER!!
RUN!

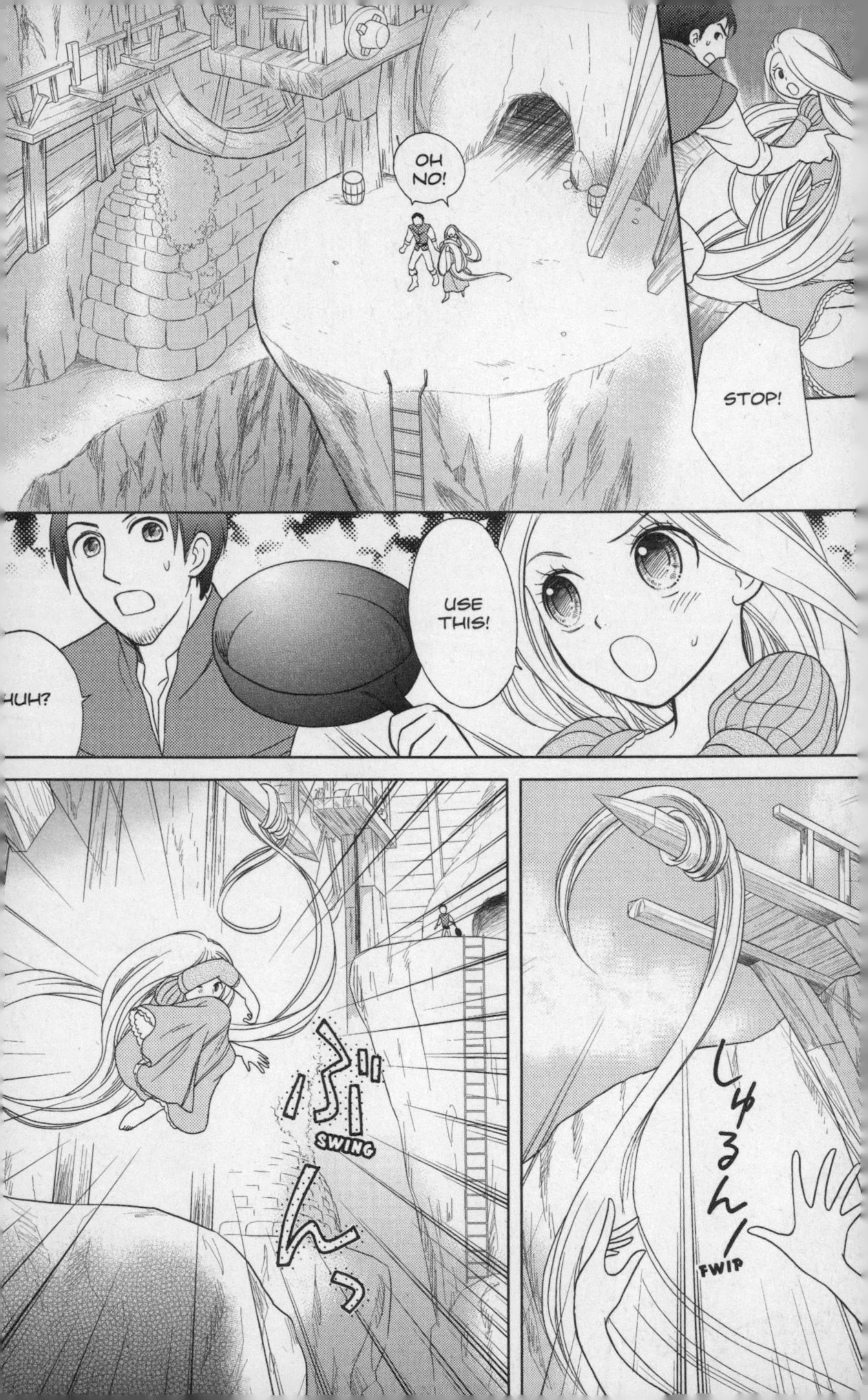
STOP!
OH NO!
USE THIS!
HUH?
しゅるん!
FWIP
ぶんっ
SWING

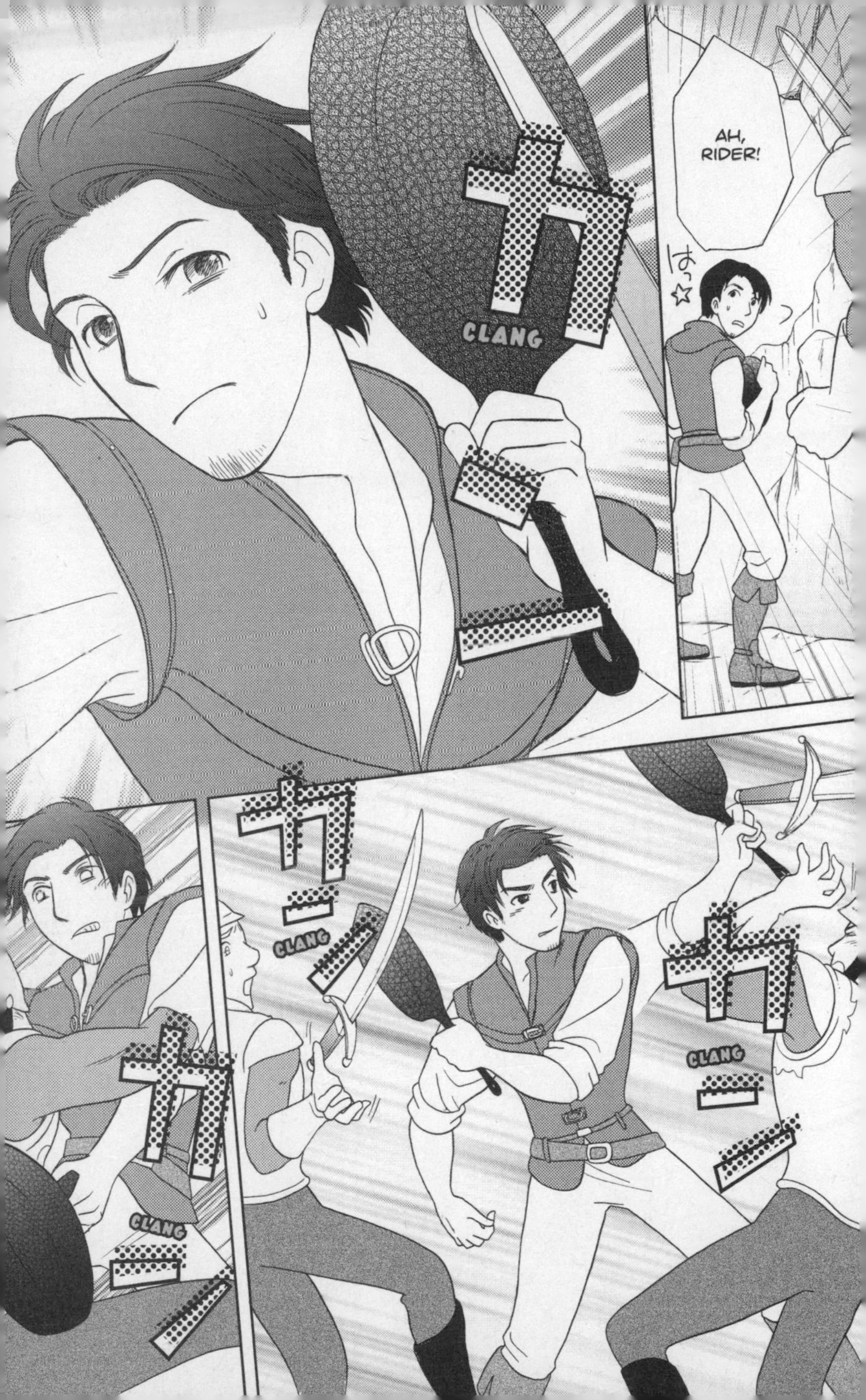
AH, RIDER!
はっ
CLANG
CLANG
CLANG
CLANG

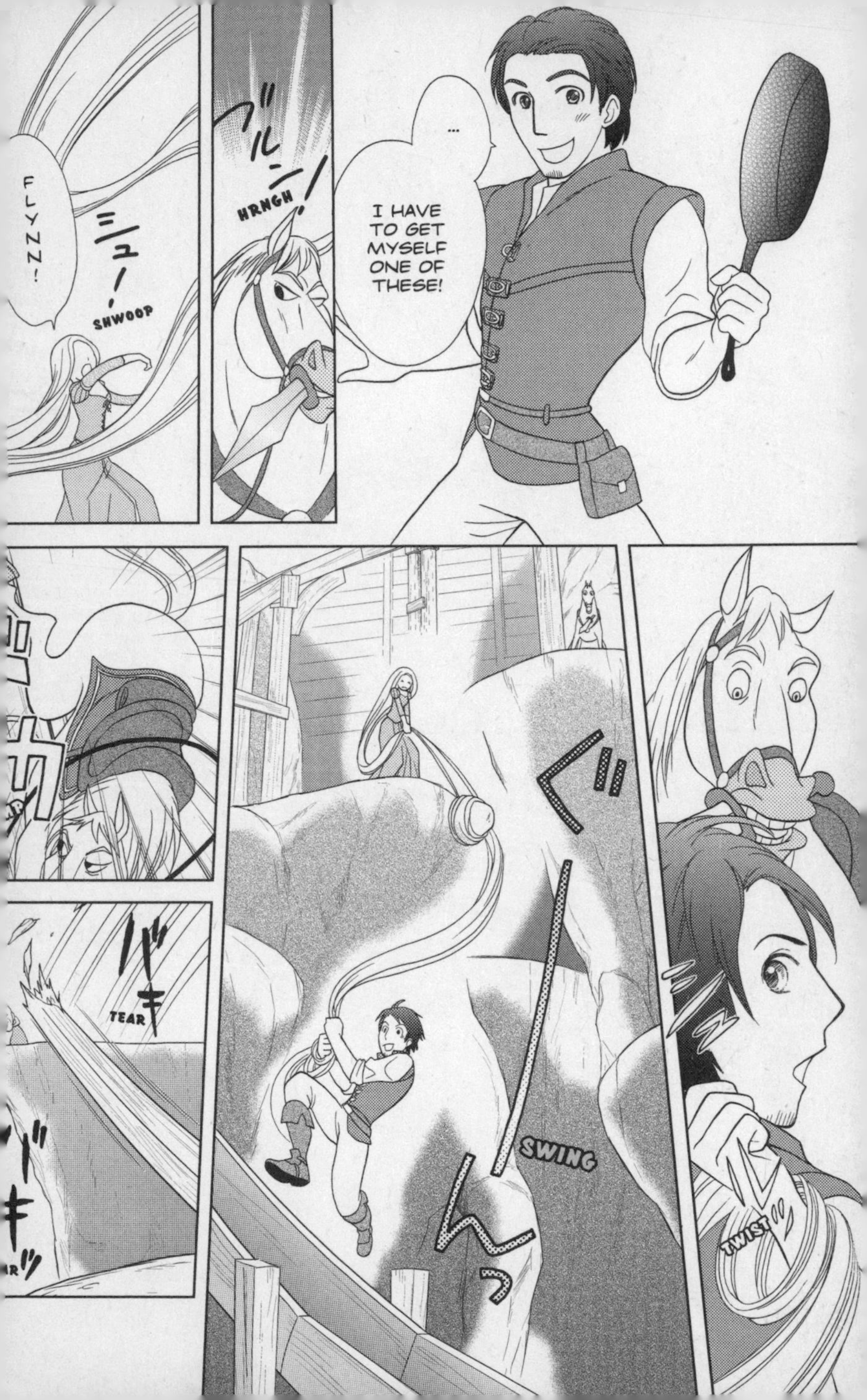
...
I HAVE TO GET MYSELF ONE OF THESE!
ブルン
HRNGH
FLYNN!
シュ
SHWOOP
ギュ
TWIST
ぐい
ぶんっ
SWING
バキ
TEAR
バキ

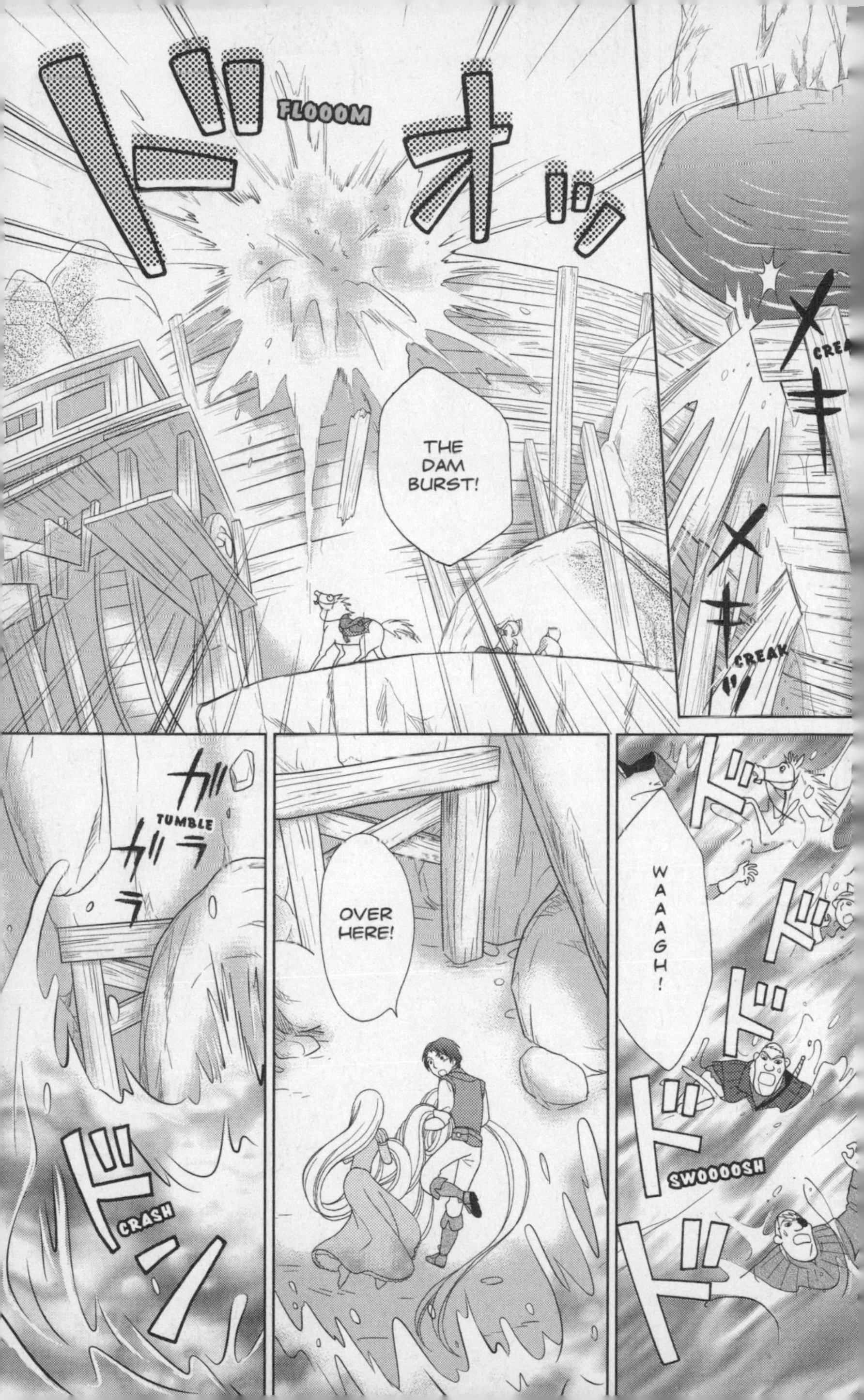
CREA
CREAK
FLOOOM
THE DAM BURST!
WAAAAGH!
SWOOOOSH
OVER HERE!
TUMBLE
CRASH

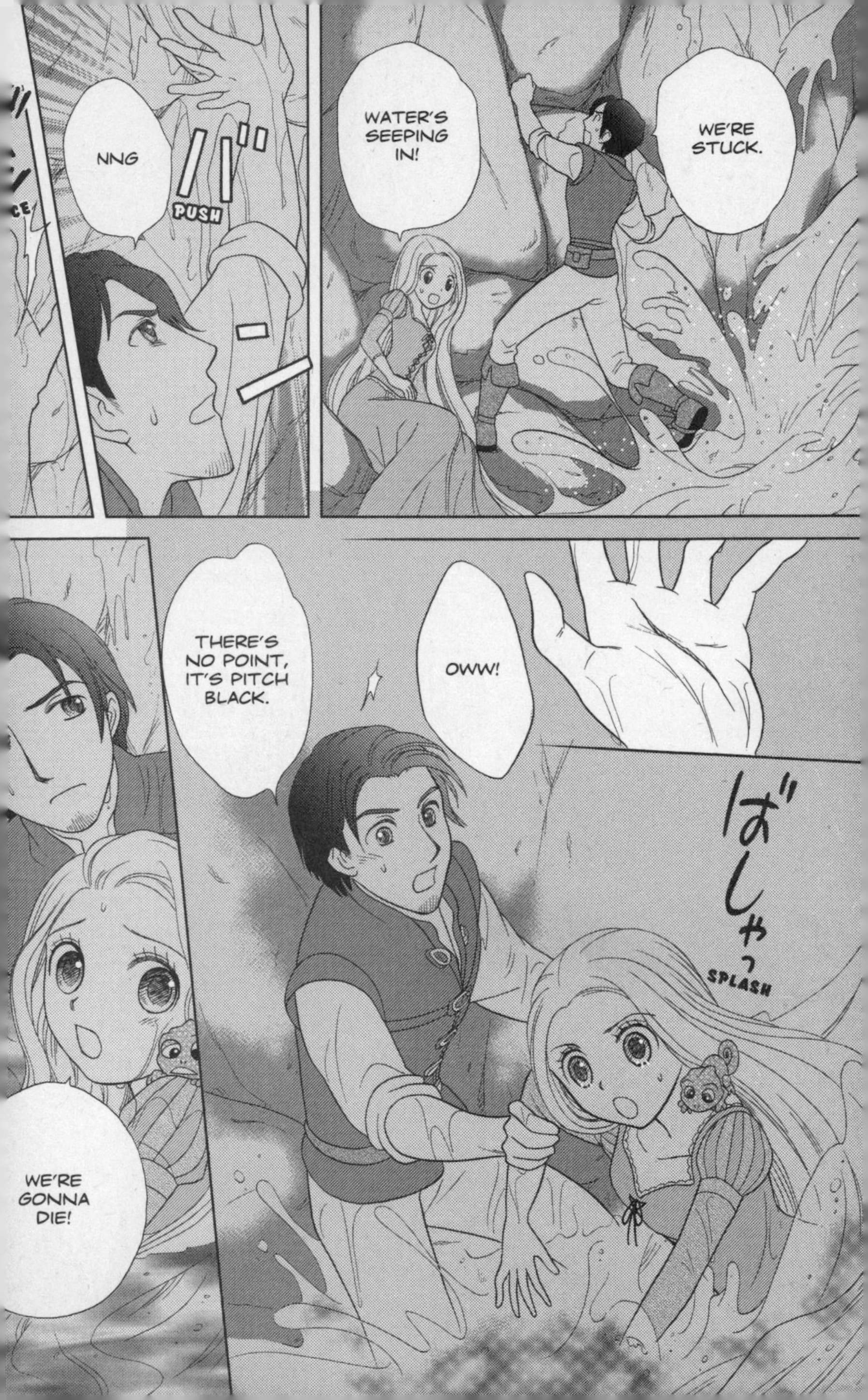
WE'RE STUCK.
WATER'S SEEPING IN!
NNG
PUSH
OWW!
ばしゃっ
SPLASH
THERE'S NO POINT, IT'S PITCH BLACK.
WE'RE GONNA DIE!

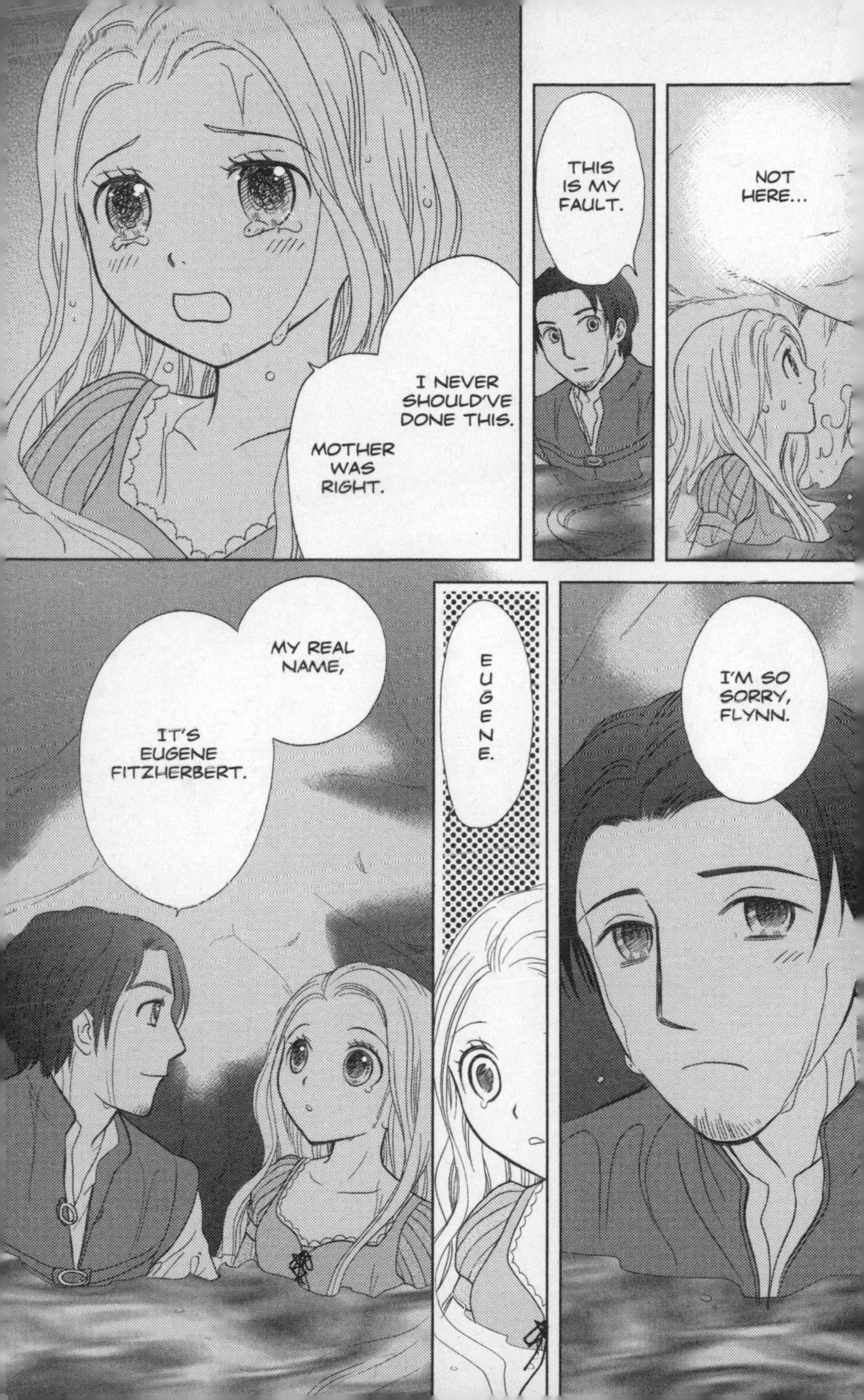
NOT HERE...
THIS IS MY FAULT.
I NEVER SHOULD'VE DONE THIS.
MOTHER WAS RIGHT.
I'M SO SORRY, FLYNN.
EUGENE.
MY REAL NAME,
IT'S EUGENE FITZHERBERT.

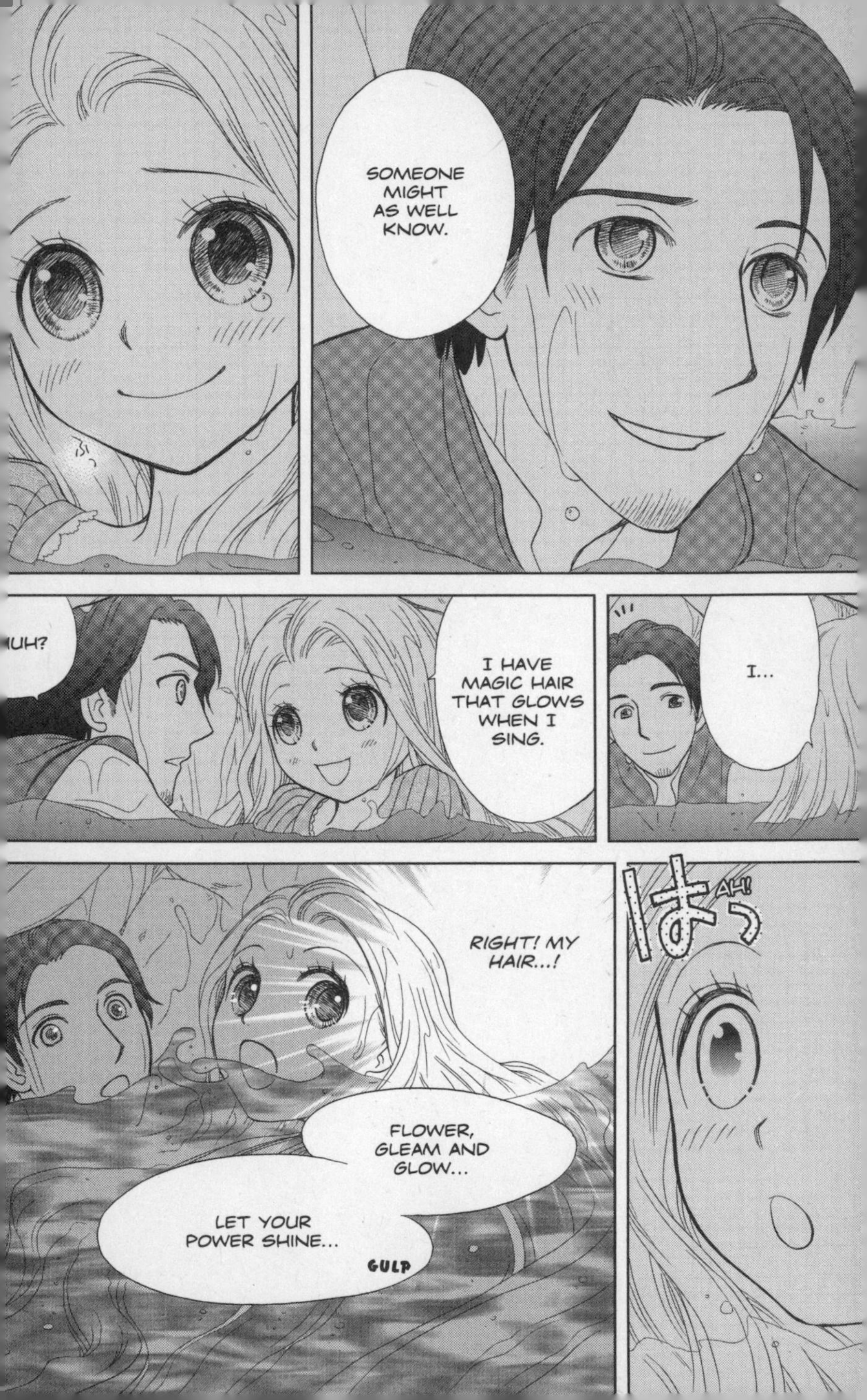
SOMEONE MIGHT AS WELL KNOW.
I...
I HAVE MAGIC HAIR THAT GLOWS WHEN I SING.
HUH?
はっ
AH!
RIGHT! MY HAIR...!
FLOWER, GLEAM AND GLOW...
LET YOUR POWER SHINE...
GULP

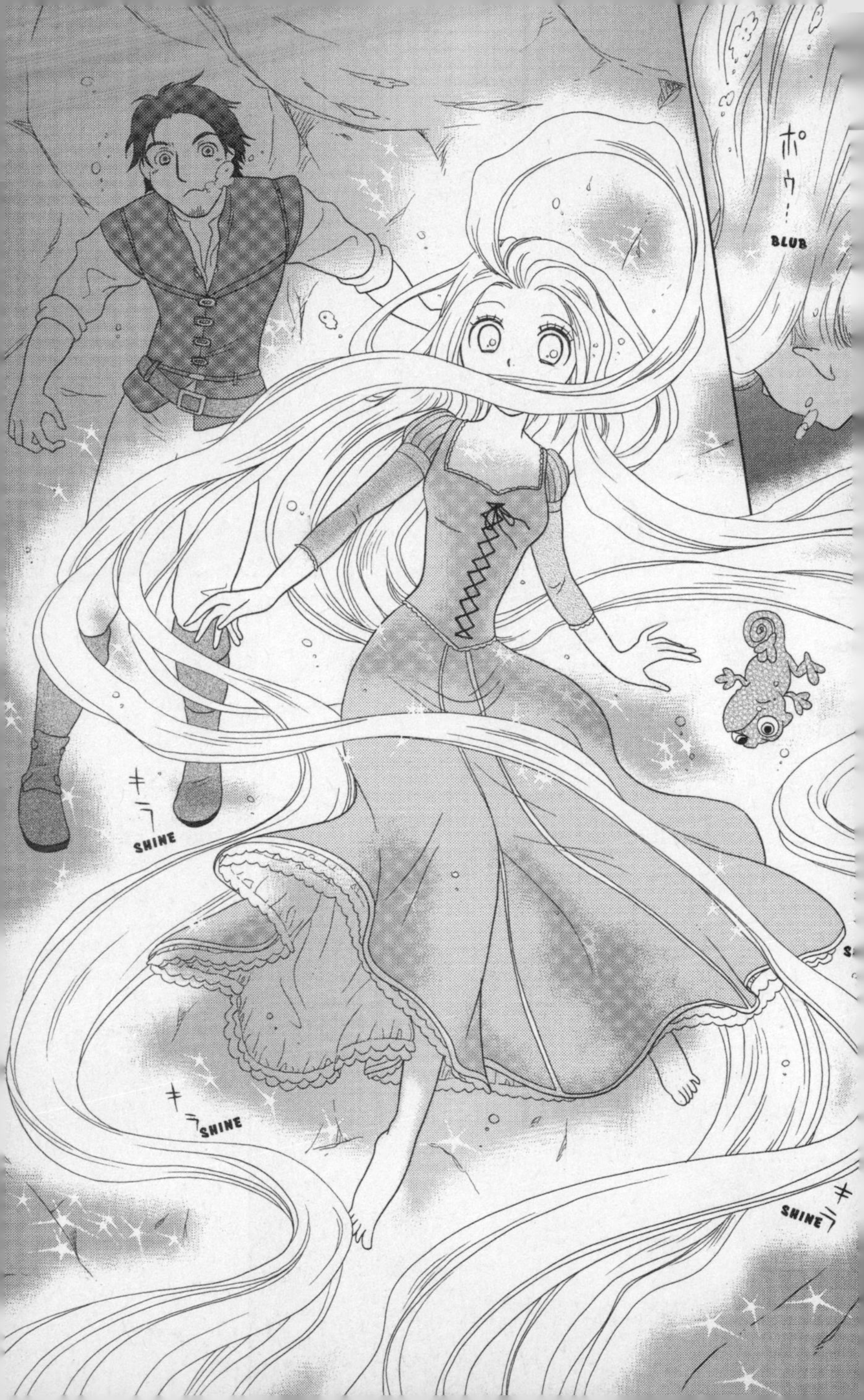

ポウ…
BLUB
キラ
SHINE
キラ
SHINE
キラ
SHINE

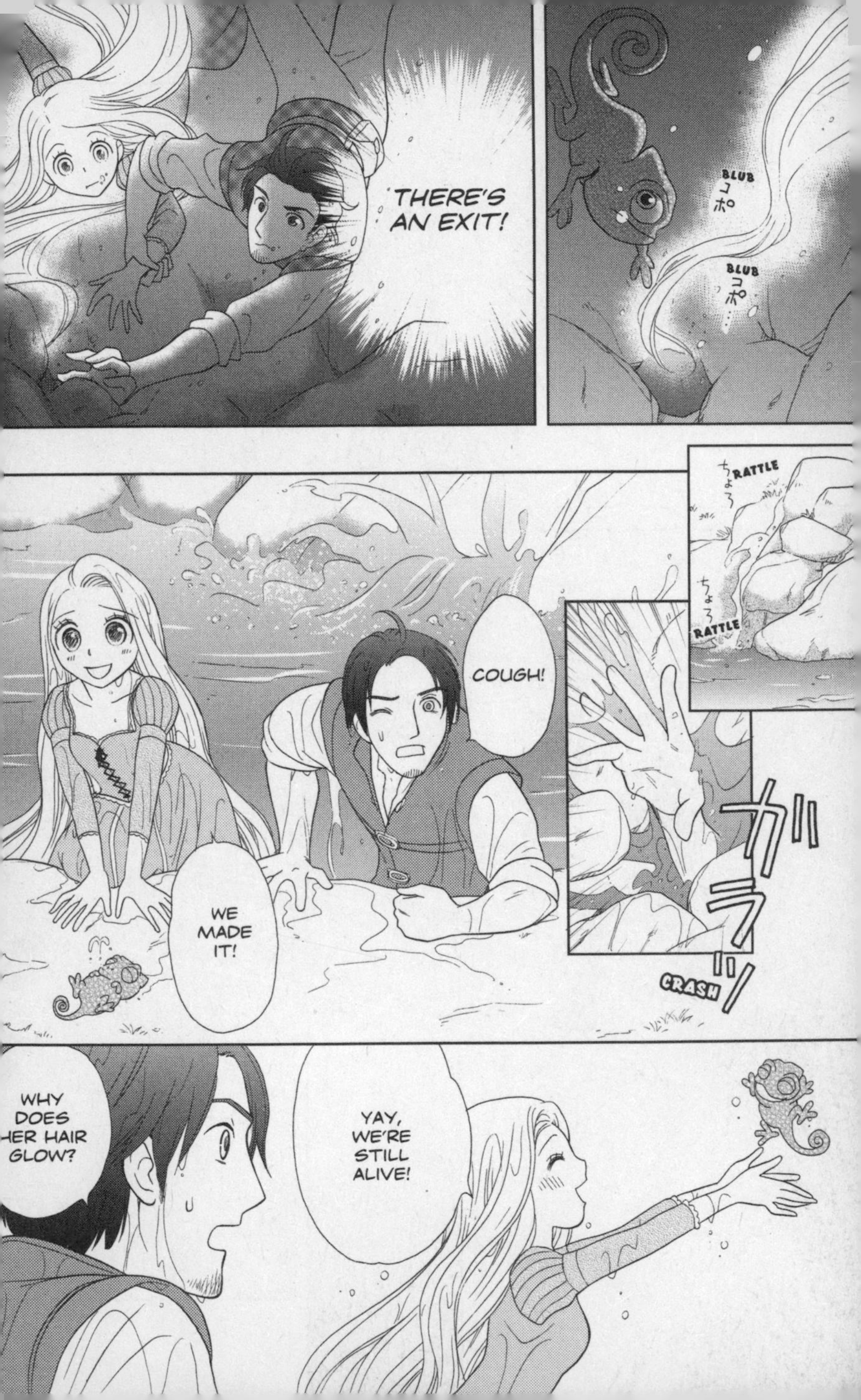
BLUB
コポ
BLUB
コポ…
THERE'S AN EXIT!
ちょろ
RATTLE
ちょろ
RATTLE
ガラッ
CRASH
COUGH!
WE MADE IT!
YAY, WE'RE STILL ALIVE!
WHY DOES HER HAIR GLOW?

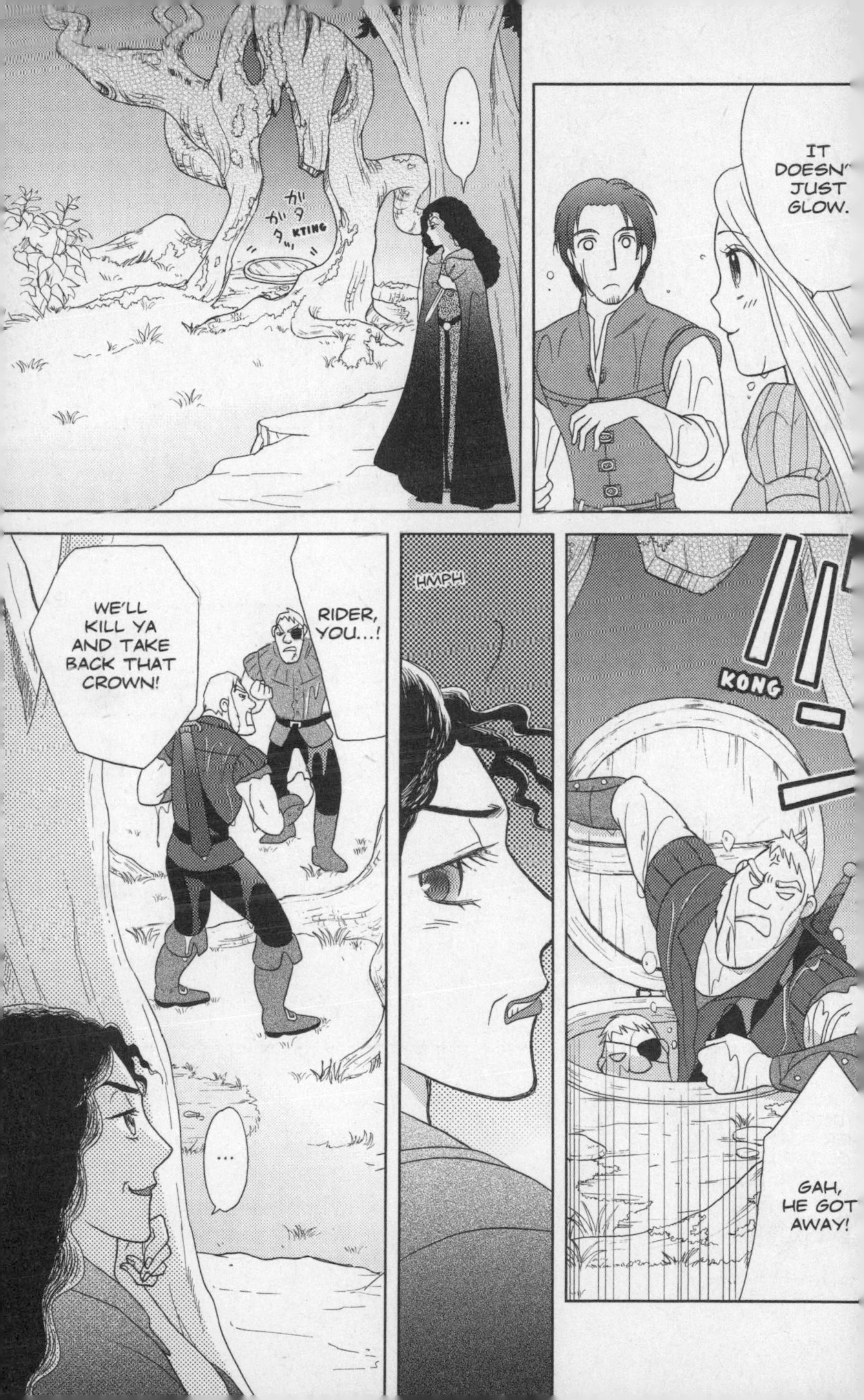
IT DOESN'T JUST GLOW.
...
KTING
KONG
GAH, HE GOT AWAY!
HMPH
RIDER, YOU...!
WE'LL KILL YA AND TAKE BACK THAT CROWN!
...

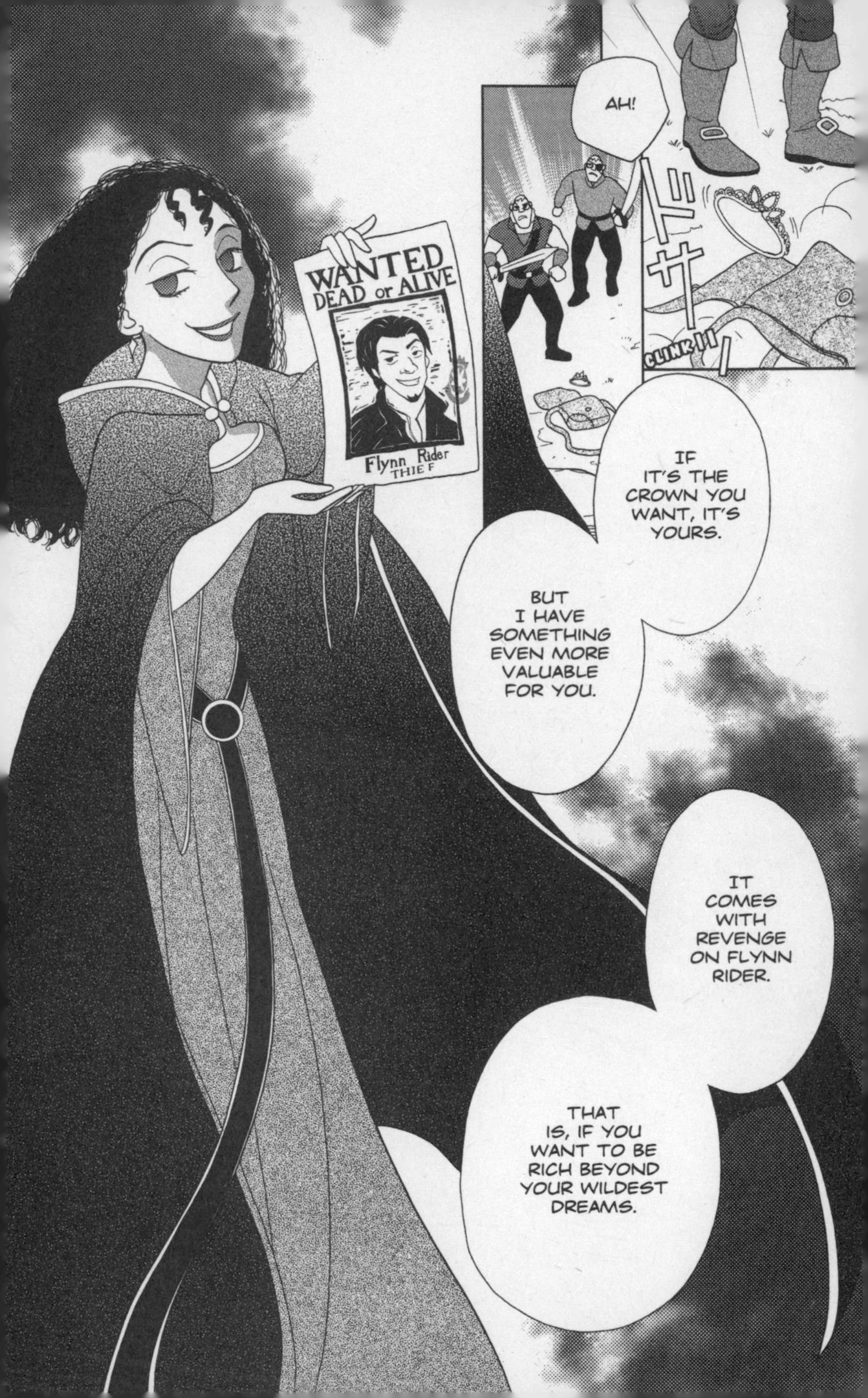
AH!
CLINK!!
WANTED DEAD or ALIVE
Flynn Rider THIEF
IF IT'S THE CROWN YOU WANT, IT'S YOURS.
BUT I HAVE SOMETHING EVEN MORE VALUABLE FOR YOU.
IT COMES WITH REVENGE ON FLYNN RIDER.
THAT IS, IF YOU WANT TO BE RICH BEYOND YOUR WILDEST DREAMS.

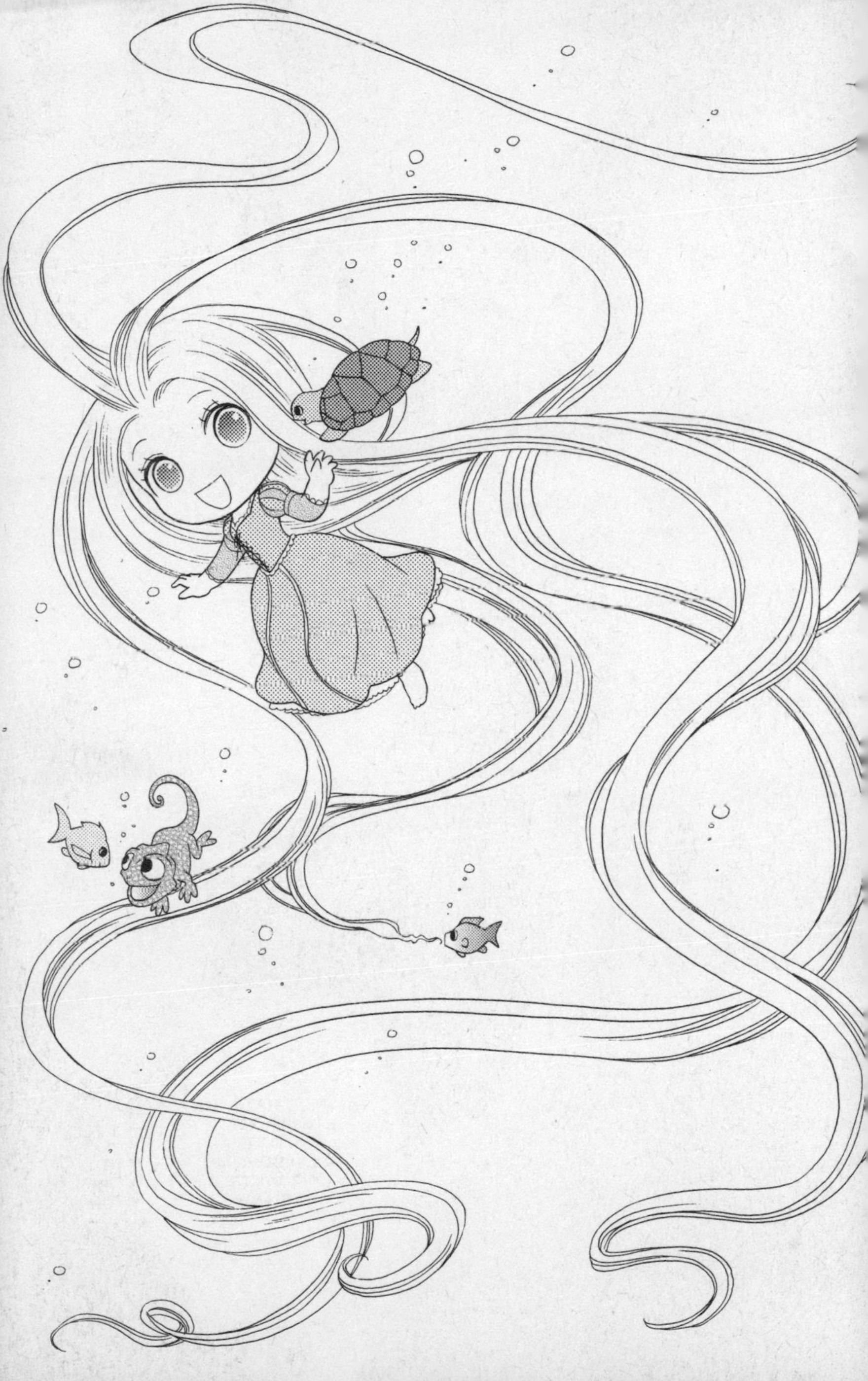

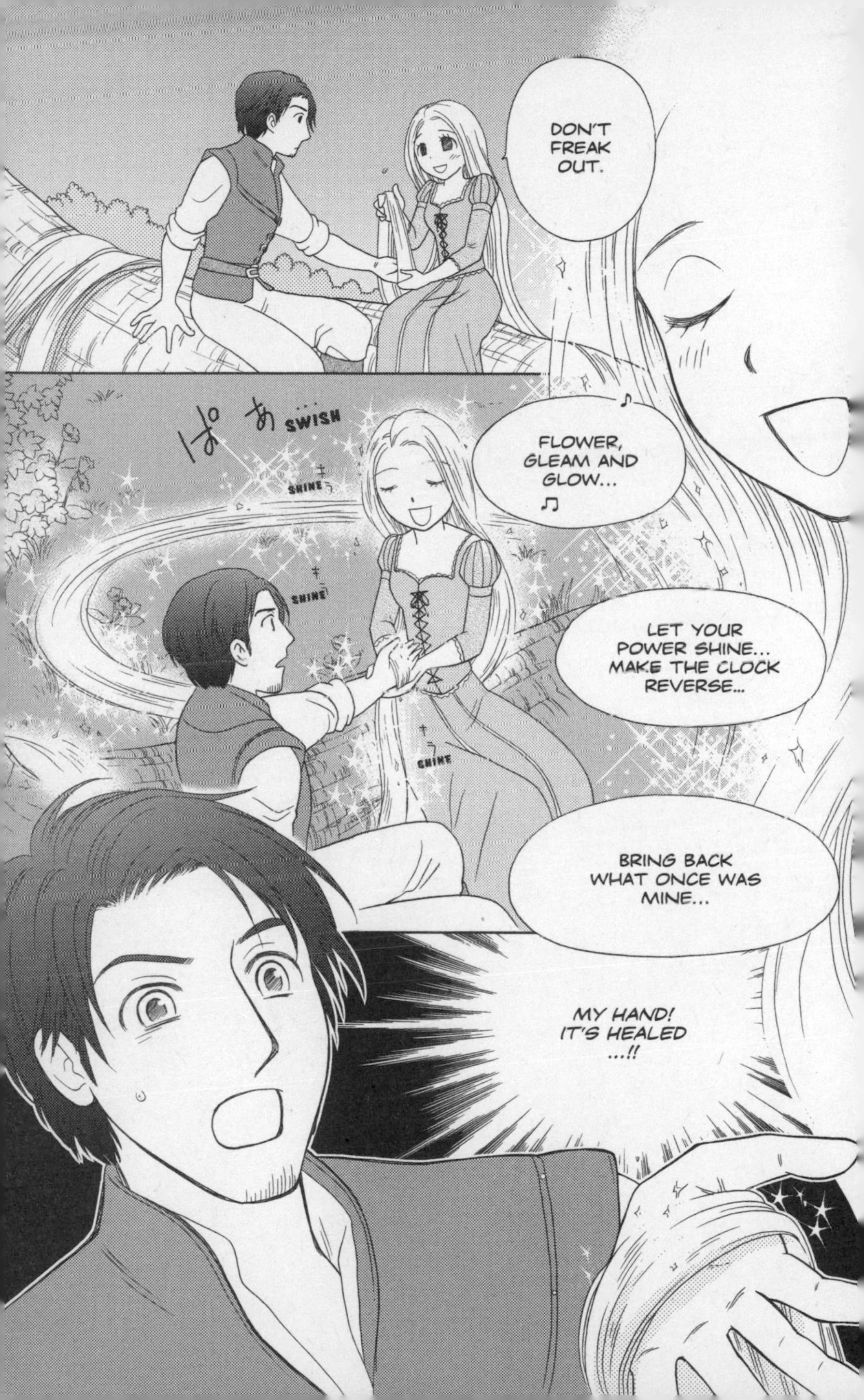
DON'T FREAK OUT.
FLOWER, GLEAM AND GLOW... ♪
ぱあ
SWISH
SHINE
SHINE
SHINE
LET YOUR POWER SHINE... MAKE THE CLOCK REVERSE...
BRING BACK WHAT ONCE WAS MINE...
MY HAND! IT'S HEALED ...!!

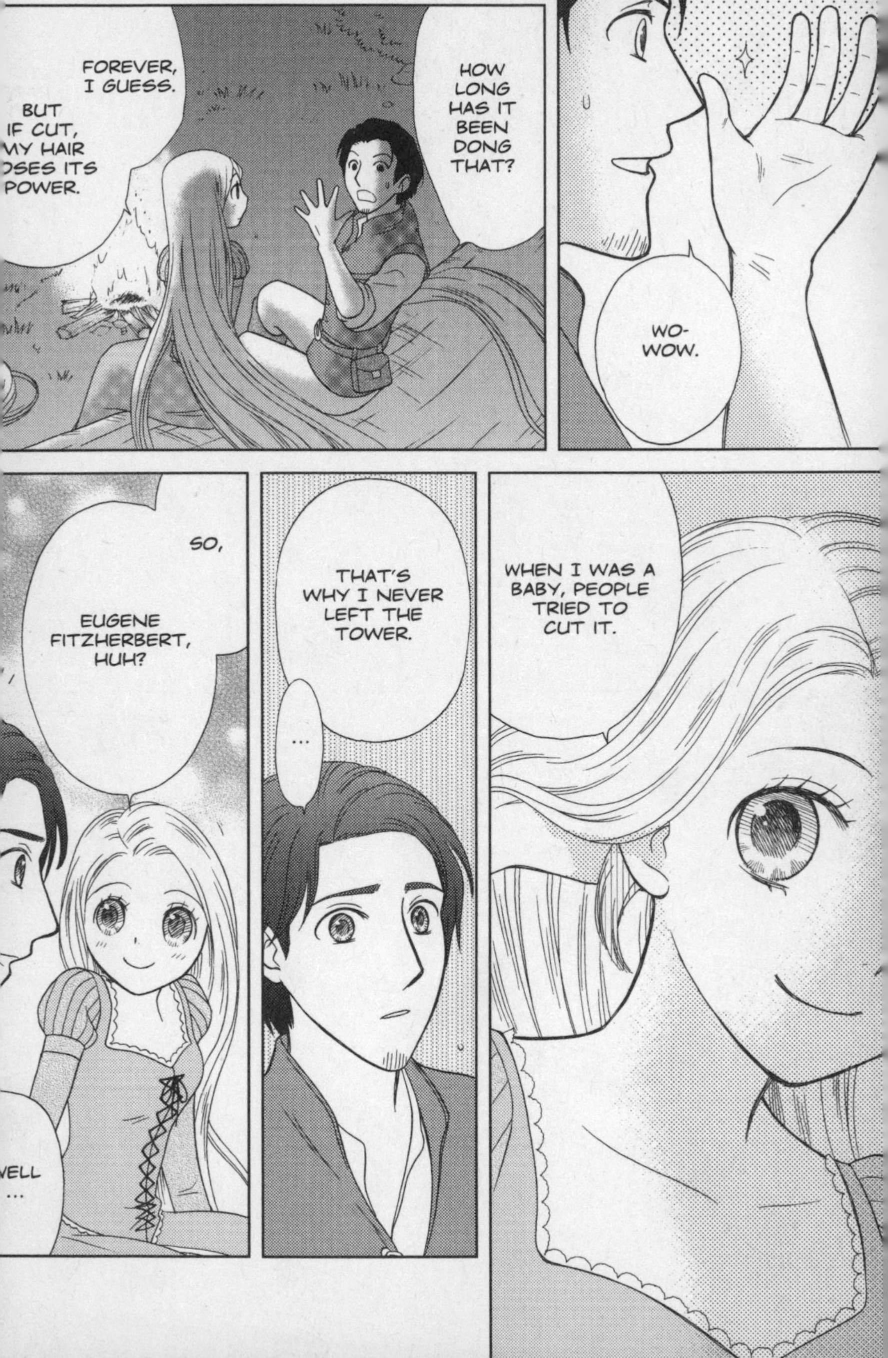
WO-WOW.
HOW LONG HAS IT BEEN DONG THAT?
FOREVER, I GUESS.
BUT IF CUT, MY HAIR OSES ITS POWER.
WHEN I WAS A BABY, PEOPLE TRIED TO CUT IT.
THAT'S WHY I NEVER LEFT THE TOWER.
...
SO,
EUGENE FITZHERBERT, HUH?
VELL ...

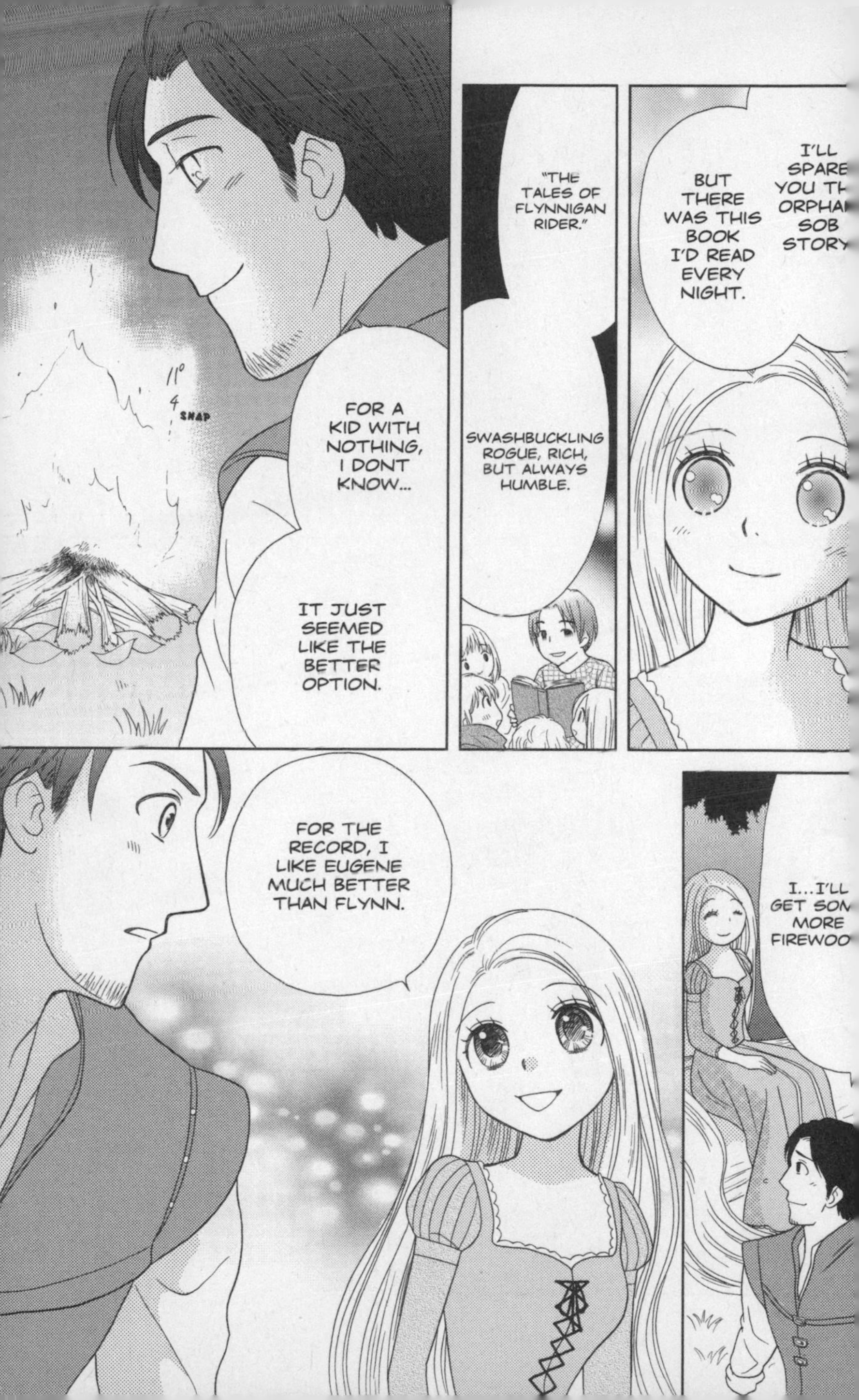
I'LL SPARE YOU TH ORPHA SOB STORY
BUT THERE WAS THIS BOOK I'D READ EVERY NIGHT.
"THE TALES OF FLYNNIGAN RIDER."
SWASHBUCKLING ROGUE, RICH, BUT ALWAYS HUMBLE.
SNAP
FOR A KID WITH NOTHING, I DONT KNOW...
IT JUST SEEMED LIKE THE BETTER OPTION.
I...I'LL GET SOM MORE FIREWOO
FOR THE RECORD, I LIKE EUGENE MUCH BETTER THAN FLYNN.

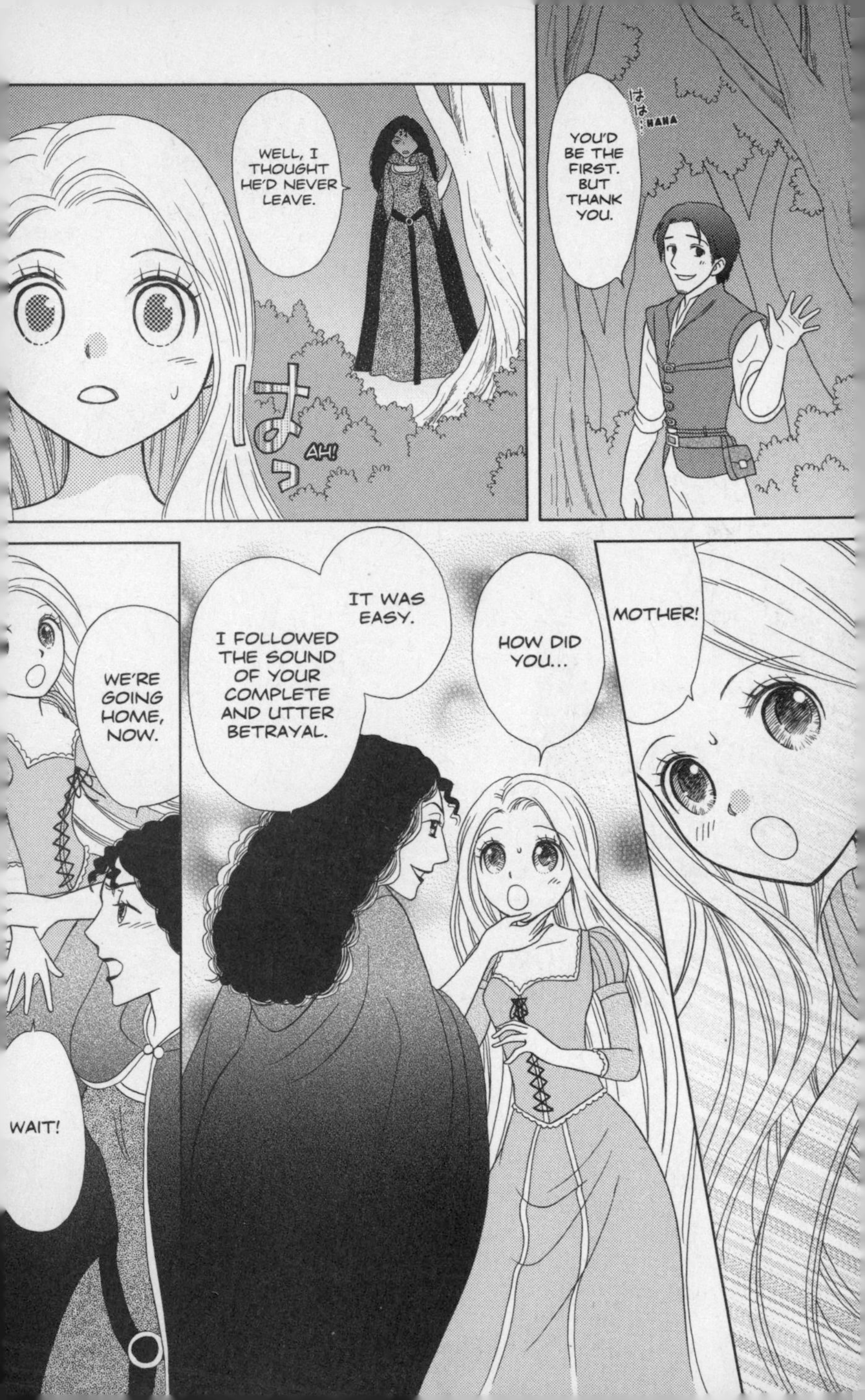
はは HAHA
YOU'D BE THE FIRST. BUT THANK YOU.
WELL, I THOUGHT HE'D NEVER LEAVE.
はっ AH!
MOTHER!
HOW DID YOU...
IT WAS EASY.
I FOLLOWED THE SOUND OF YOUR COMPLETE AND UTTER BETRAYAL.
WE'RE GOING HOME, NOW.
WAIT!

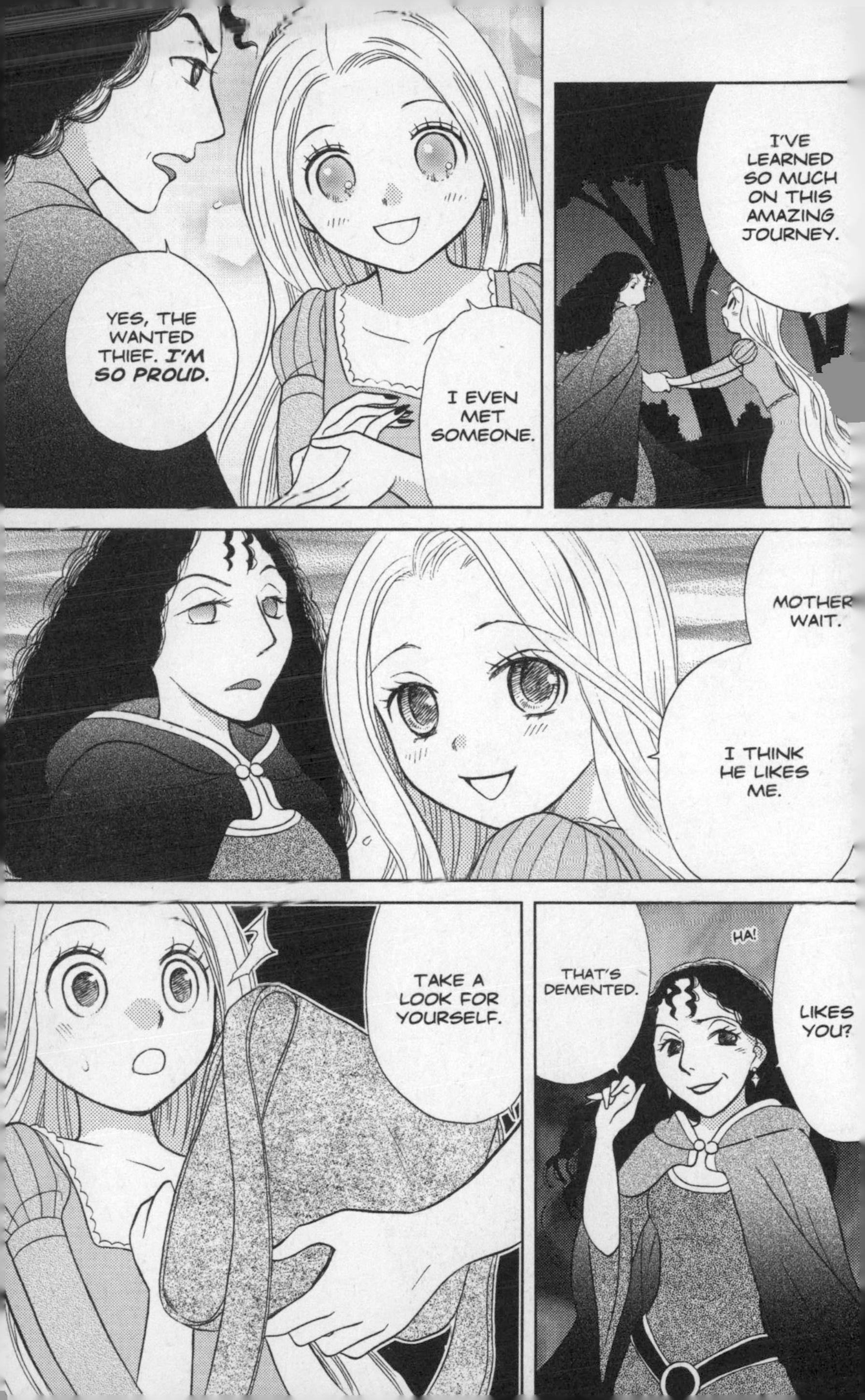
I'VE LEARNED SO MUCH ON THIS AMAZING JOURNEY.
I EVEN MET SOMEONE.
YES, THE WANTED THIEF. *I'M SO PROUD.*
MOTHER WAIT.
I THINK HE LIKES ME.
HA!
LIKES YOU?
THAT'S DEMENTED.
TAKE A LOOK FOR YOURSELF.

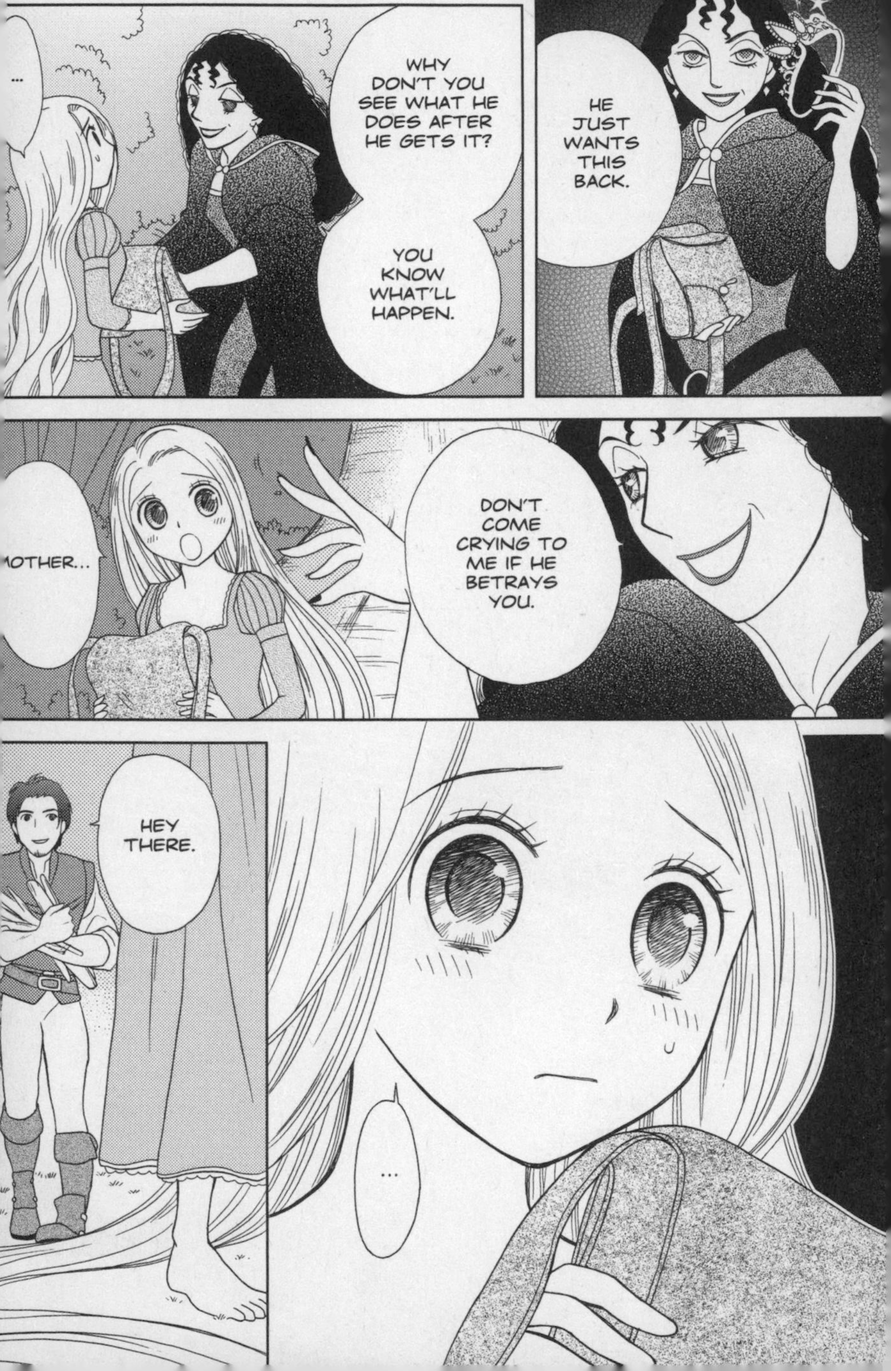
HE JUST WANTS THIS BACK.
WHY DON'T YOU SEE WHAT HE DOES AFTER HE GETS IT?
YOU KNOW WHAT'LL HAPPEN.
...
DON'T COME CRYING TO ME IF HE BETRAYS YOU.
MOTHER...
...
HEY THERE.

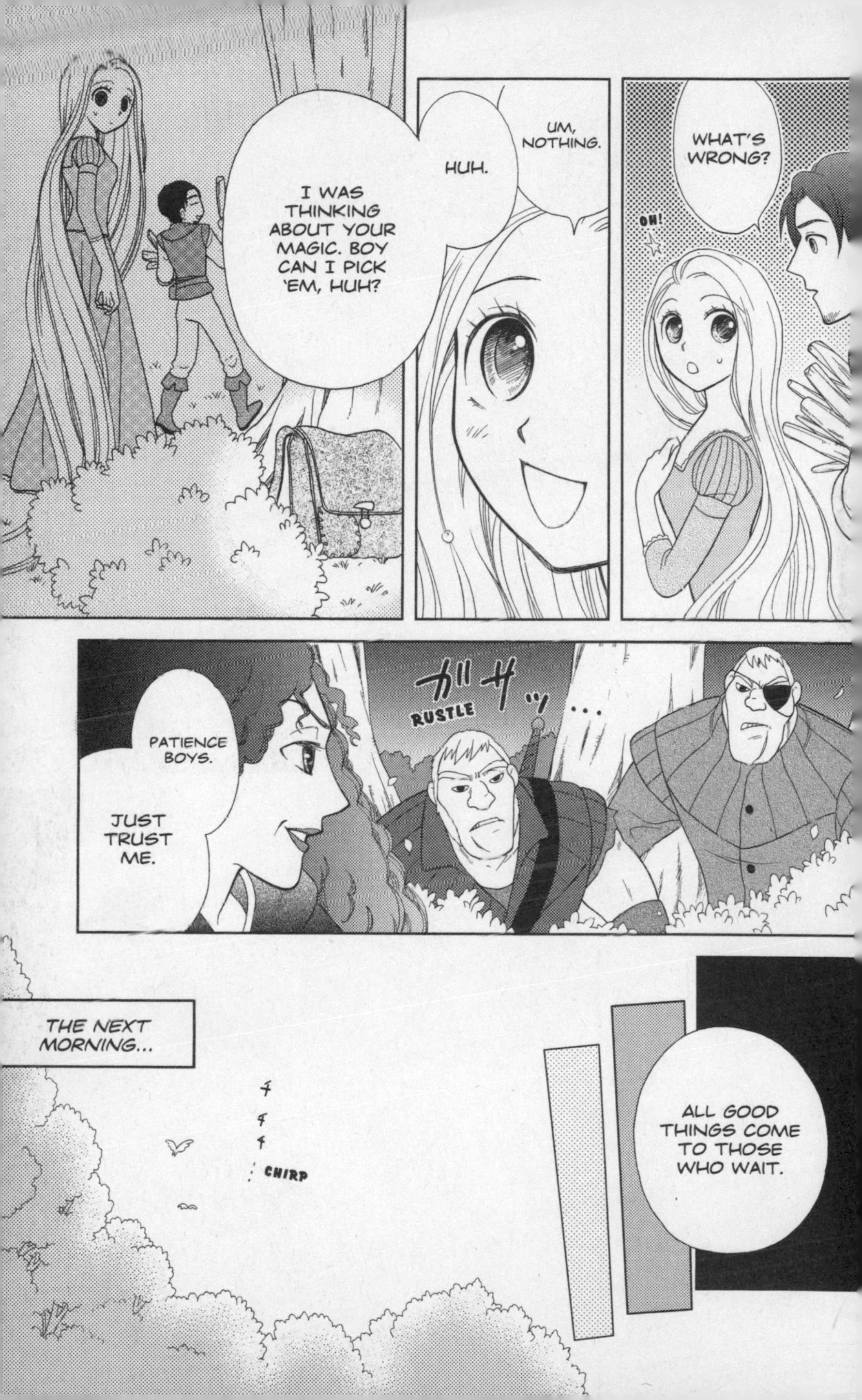
WHAT'S WRONG?
OH!
UM, NOTHING.
HUH.
I WAS THINKING ABOUT YOUR MAGIC. BOY CAN I PICK 'EM, HUH?
ガサッ
RUSTLE
...
PATIENCE BOYS.
JUST TRUST ME.
ALL GOOD THINGS COME TO THOSE WHO WAIT.
THE NEXT MORNING...
チチチ
CHIRP

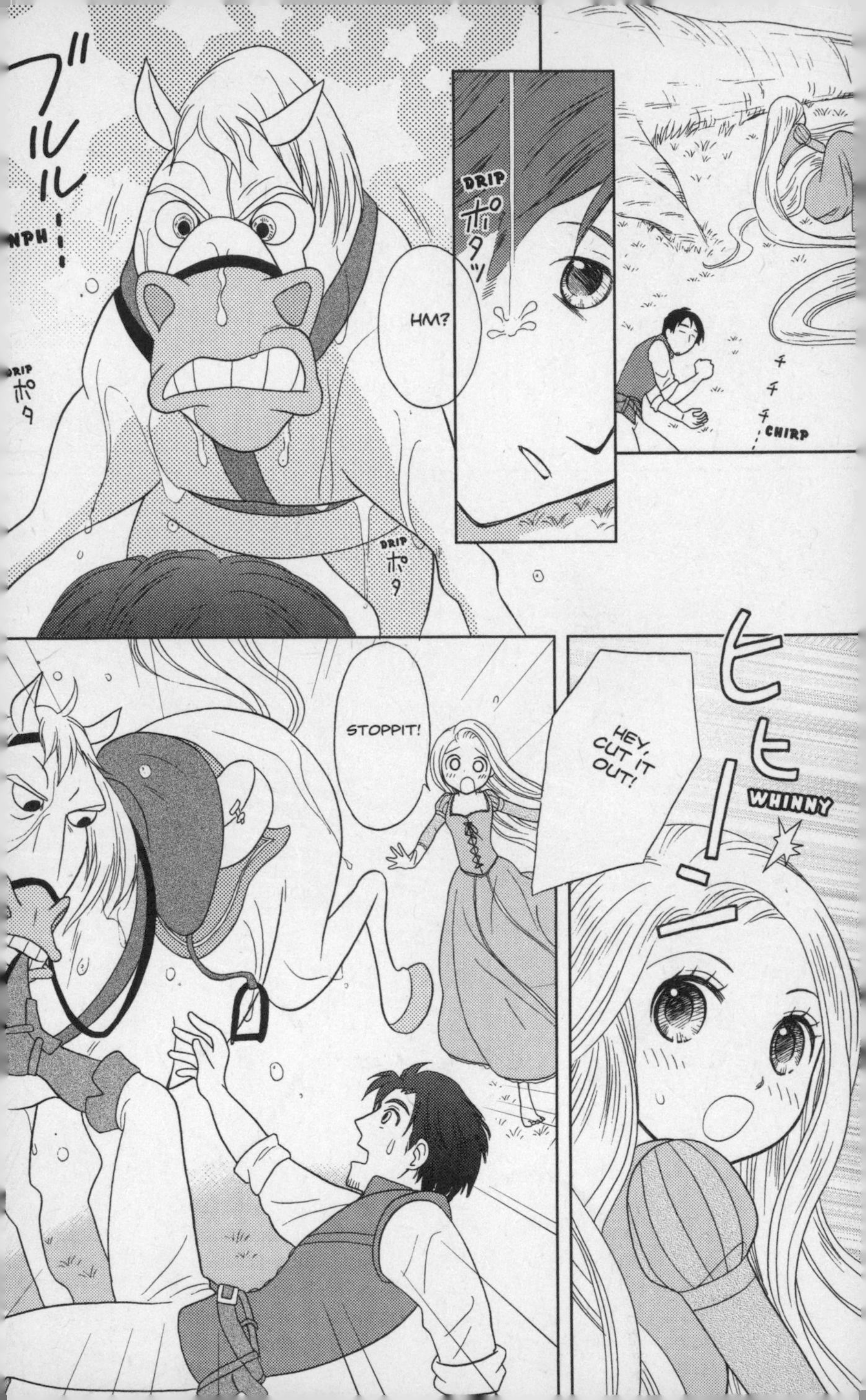

チチチ
CHIRP
DRIP
ポタッ
HM?
ブルル…
NPH
DRIP
ポタ
DRIP
ポタ
HEY, CUT IT OUT!
ヒヒーー
WHINNY
STOPPIT!

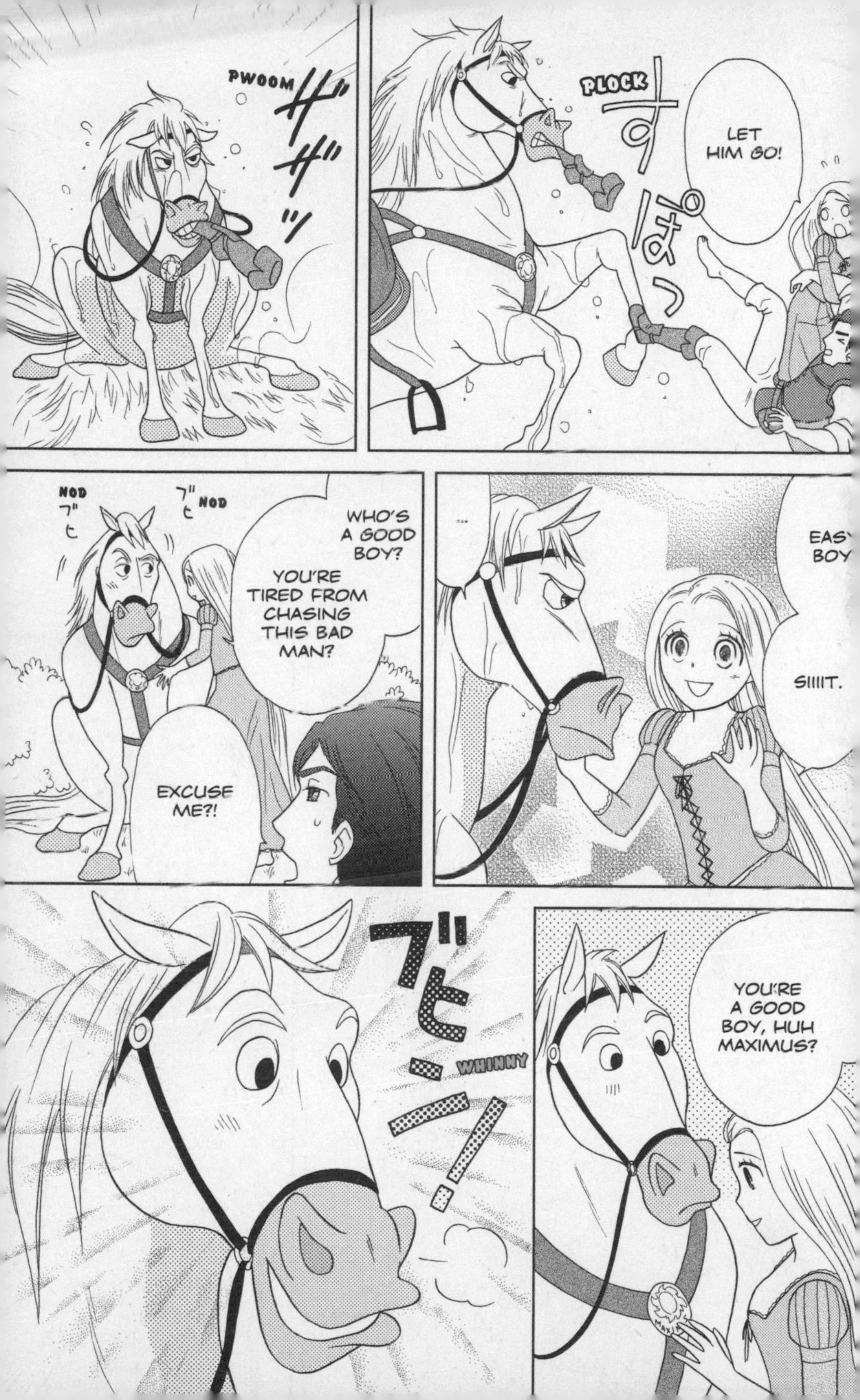

PLOCK
すぽっ
LET HIM GO!
PWOOM
ザザザッ
EASY BOY
SIIIT.
...
WHO'S A GOOD BOY?
YOU'RE TIRED FROM CHASING THIS BAD MAN?
ブヒ NOD
NOD ブヒ
EXCUSE ME?!
YOU'RE A GOOD BOY, HUH MAXIMUS?
ブヒーッ!
WHINNY

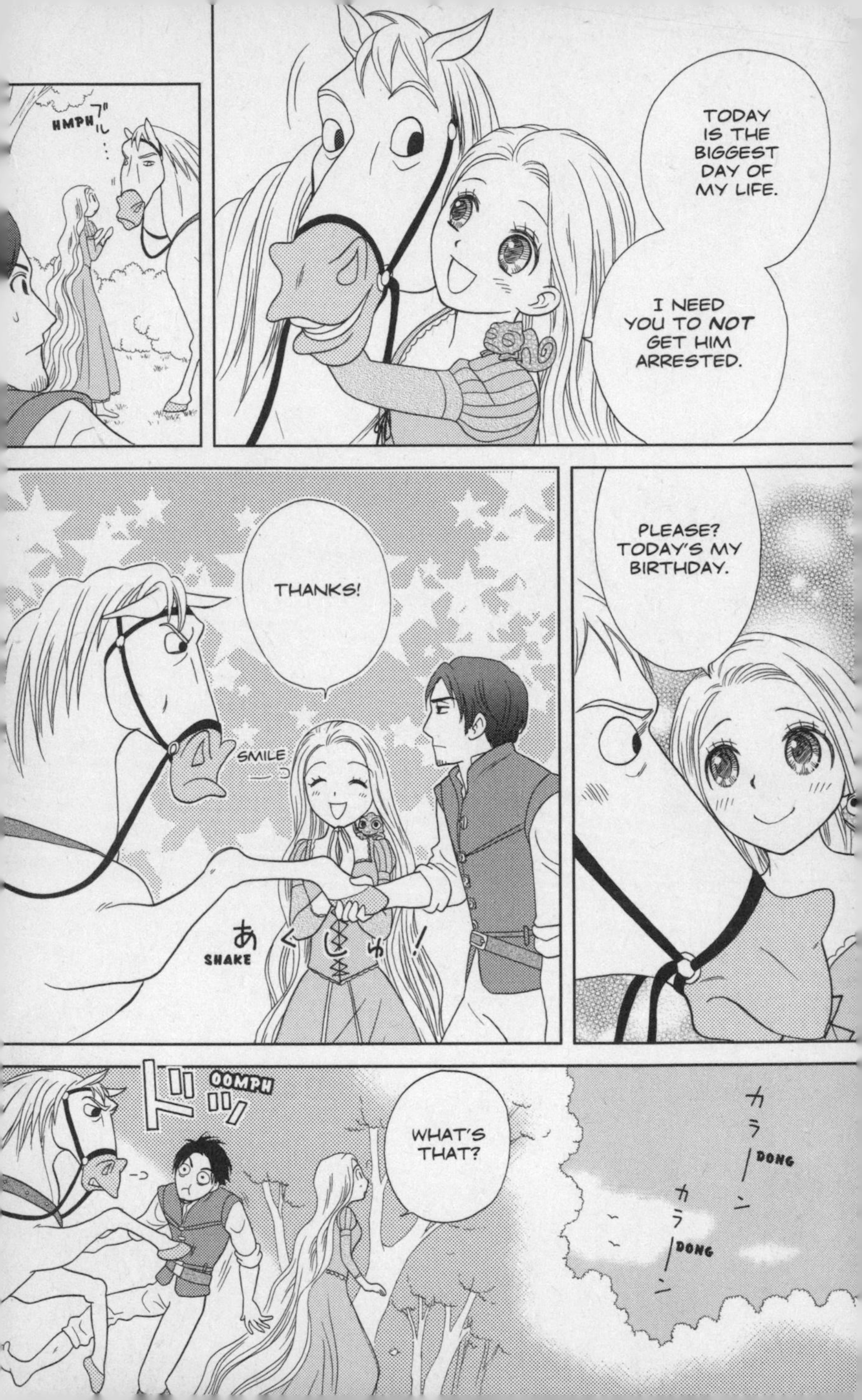
TODAY IS THE BIGGEST DAY OF MY LIFE.
I NEED YOU TO NOT GET HIM ARRESTED.
HMPH
ブル…
PLEASE? TODAY'S MY BIRTHDAY.
THANKS!
SMILE
SHAKE
あくしゅ!
カラーン
DONG
カラーン
DONG
WHAT'S THAT?
OOMPH

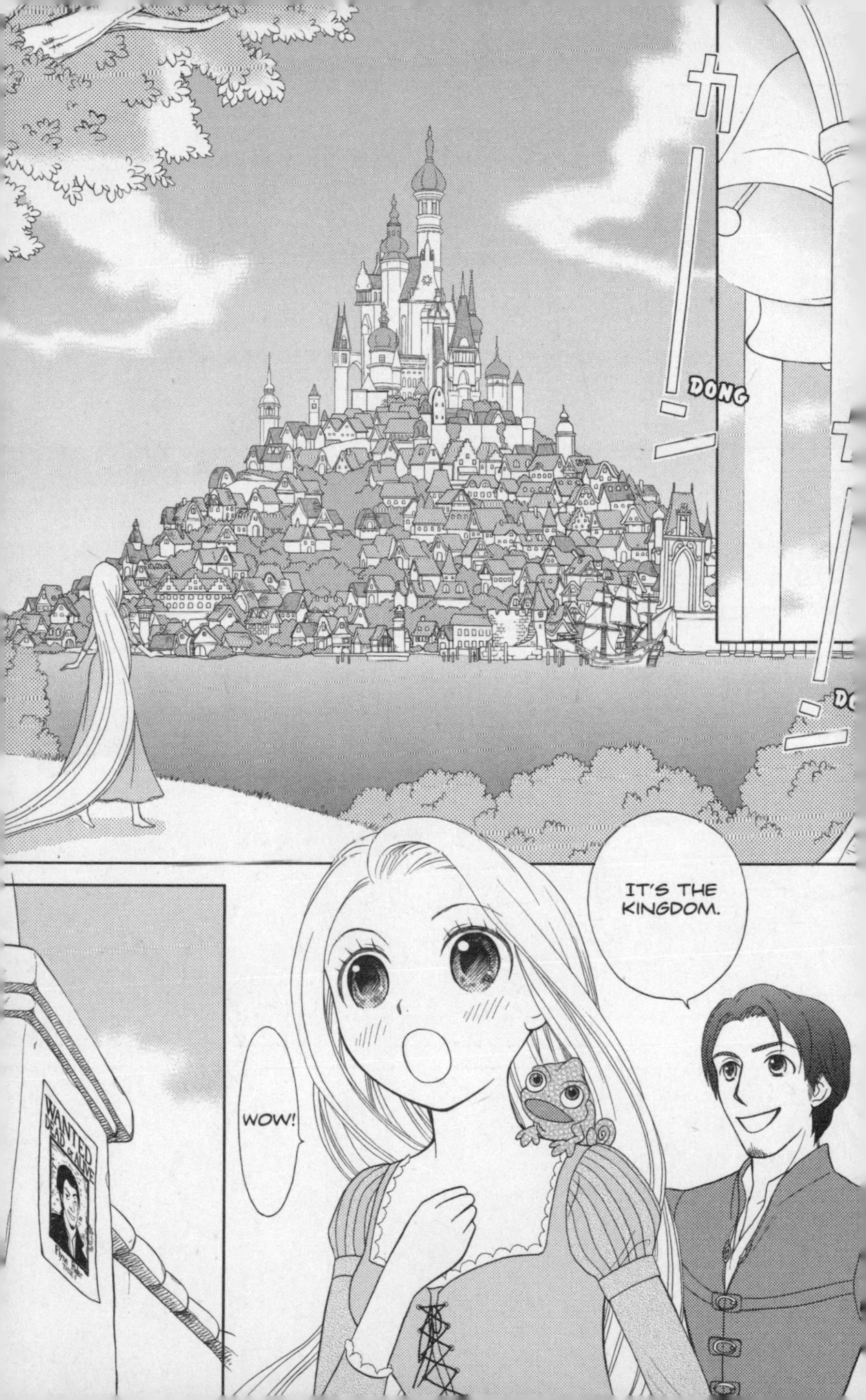
DONG
IT'S THE KINGDOM.
WOW!
WANTED
DEAD OR ALIVE

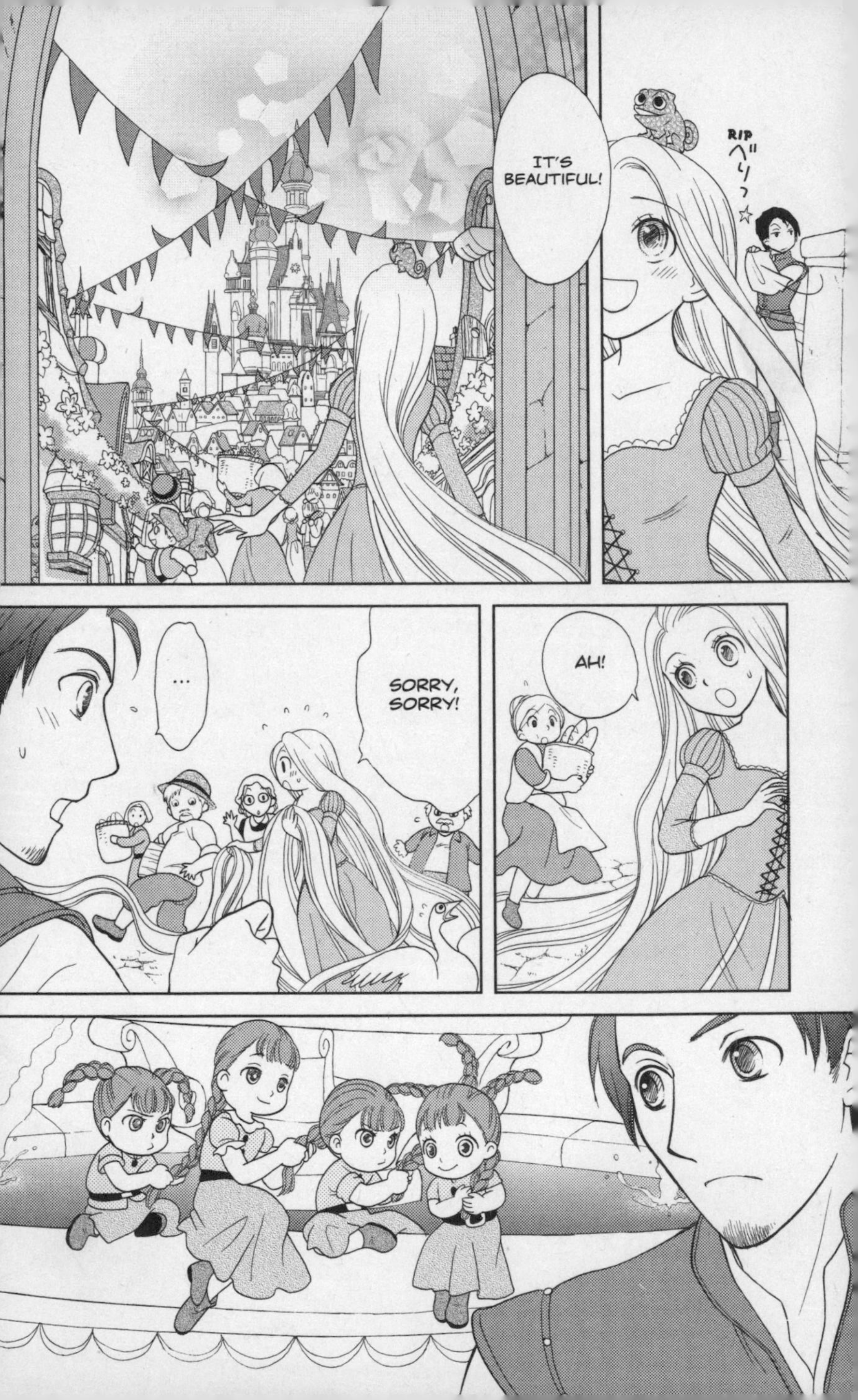

RIP
べりっ
IT'S BEAUTIFUL!
AH!
SORRY, SORRY!
...

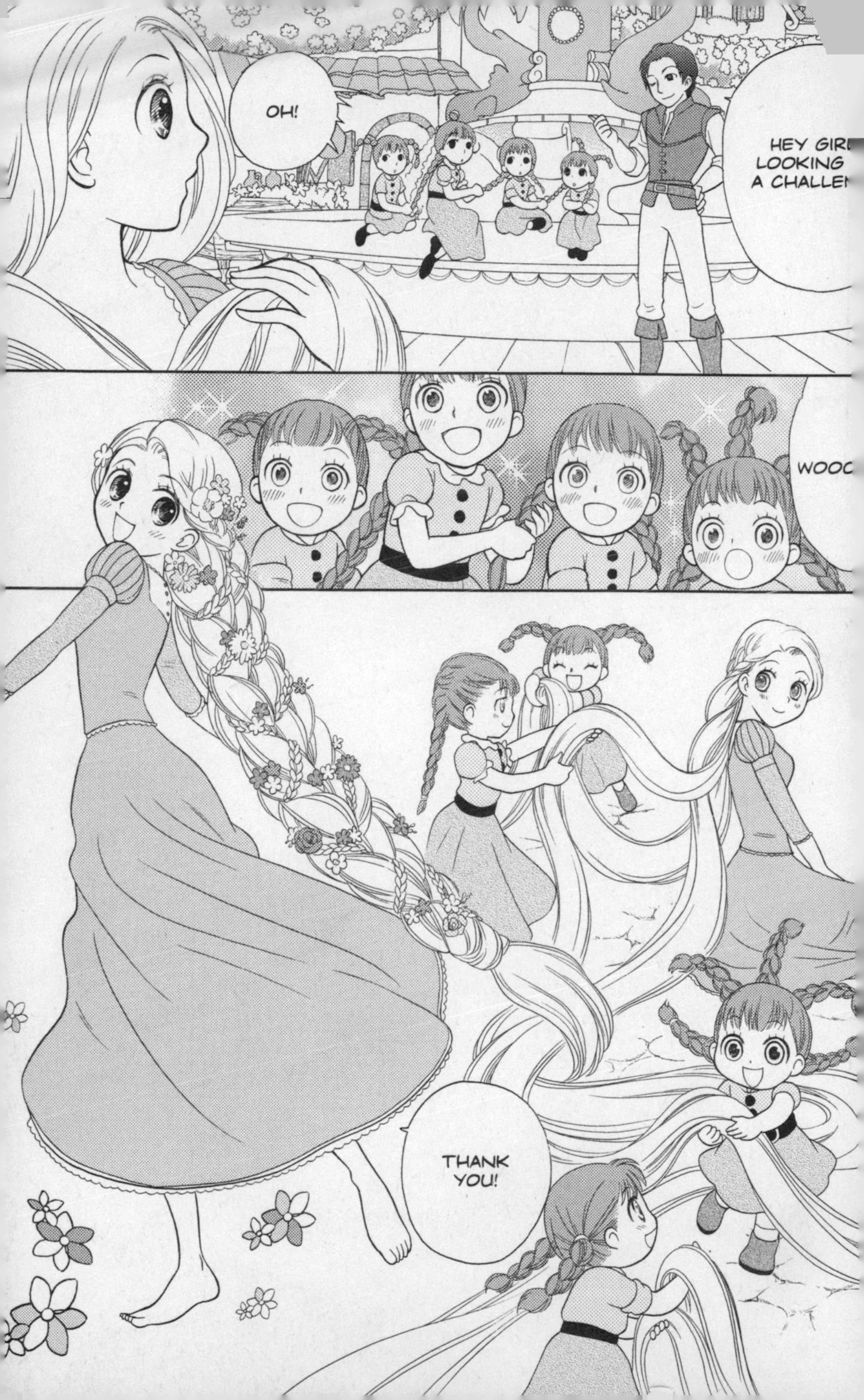
HEY GIR
LOOKING
A CHALLE
OH!
WOO
THANK YOU!

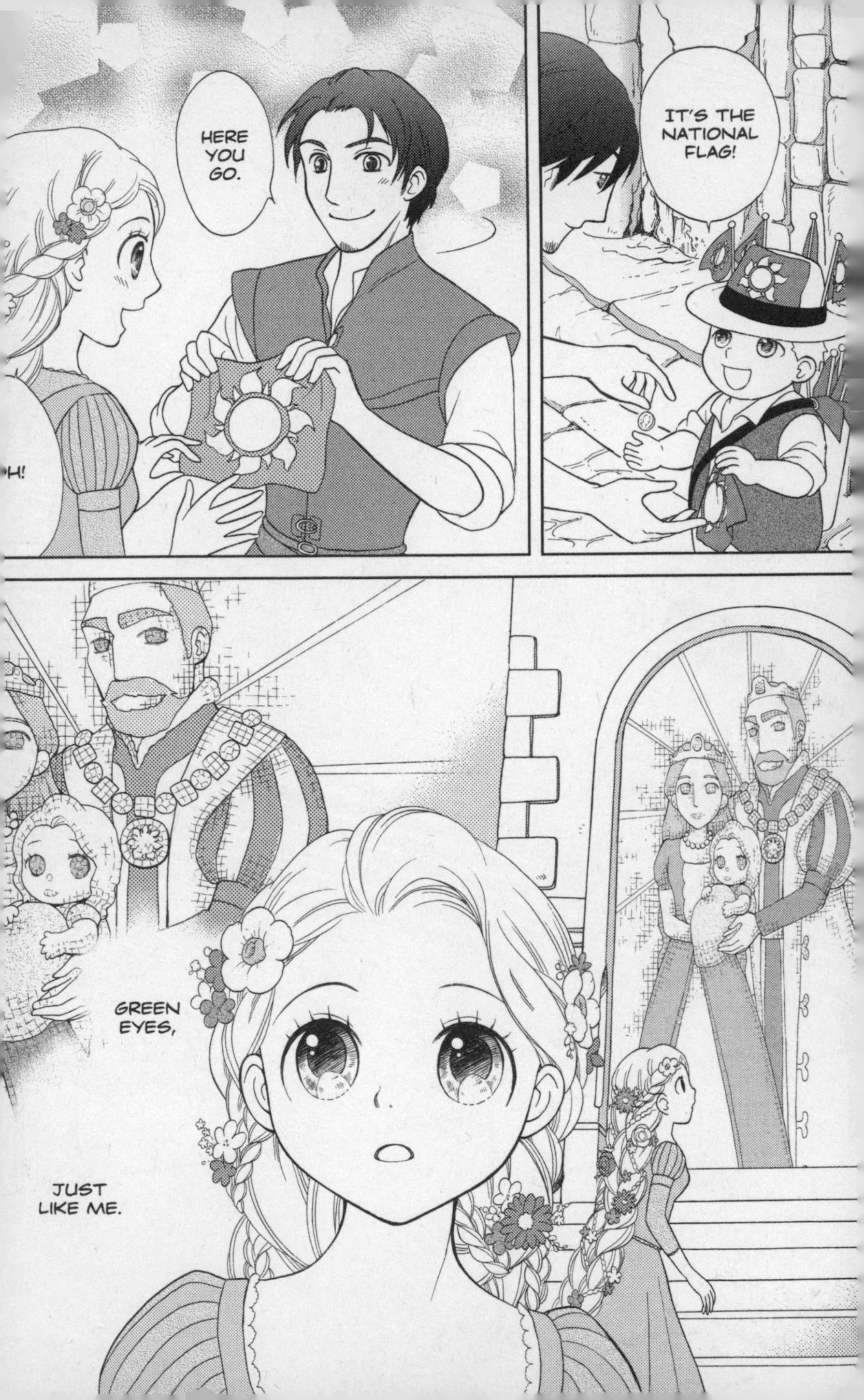
IT'S THE NATIONAL FLAG!
HERE YOU GO.
GREEN EYES,
JUST LIKE ME.

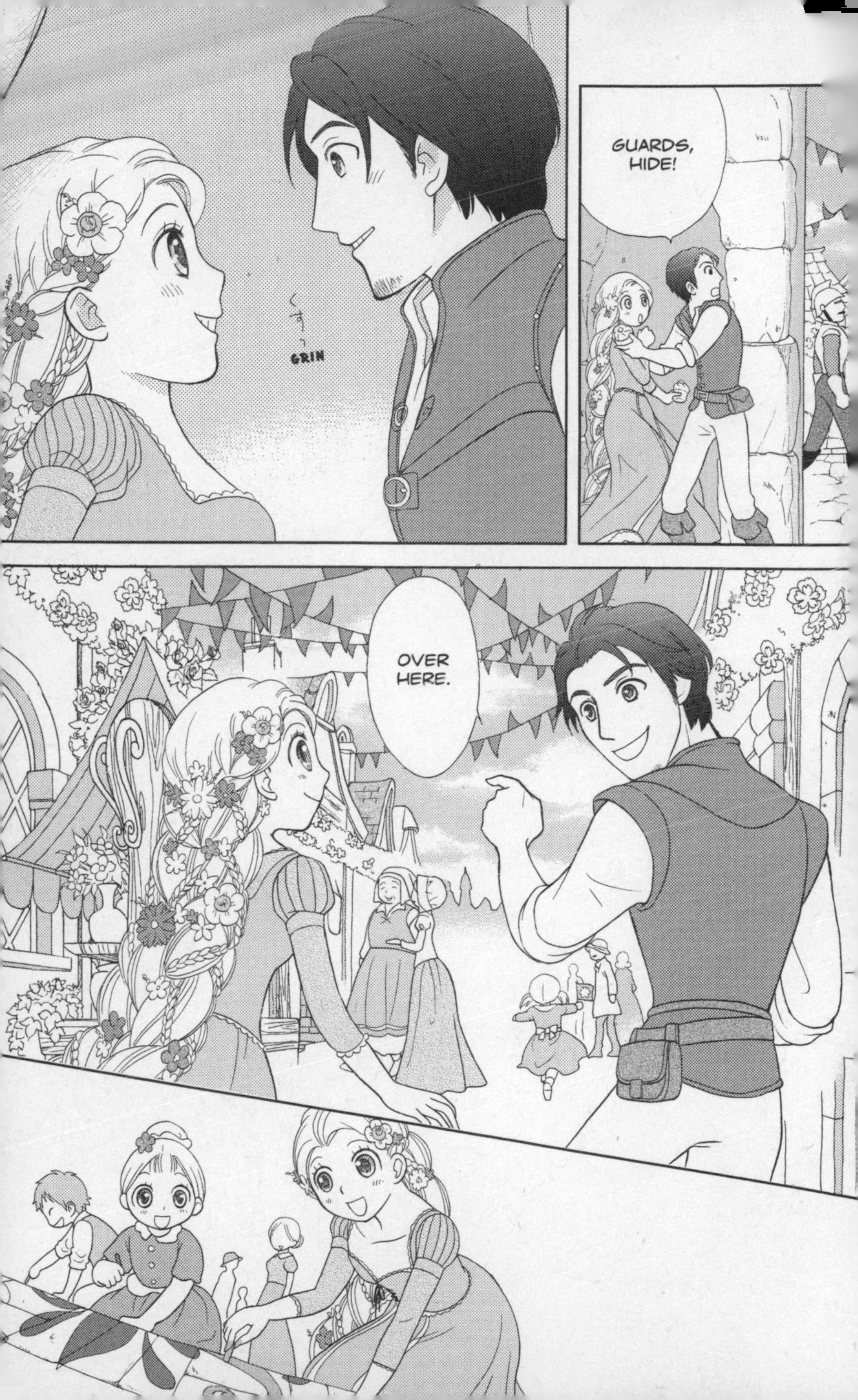
GUARDS, HIDE!
くすっ
GRIN
OVER HERE.

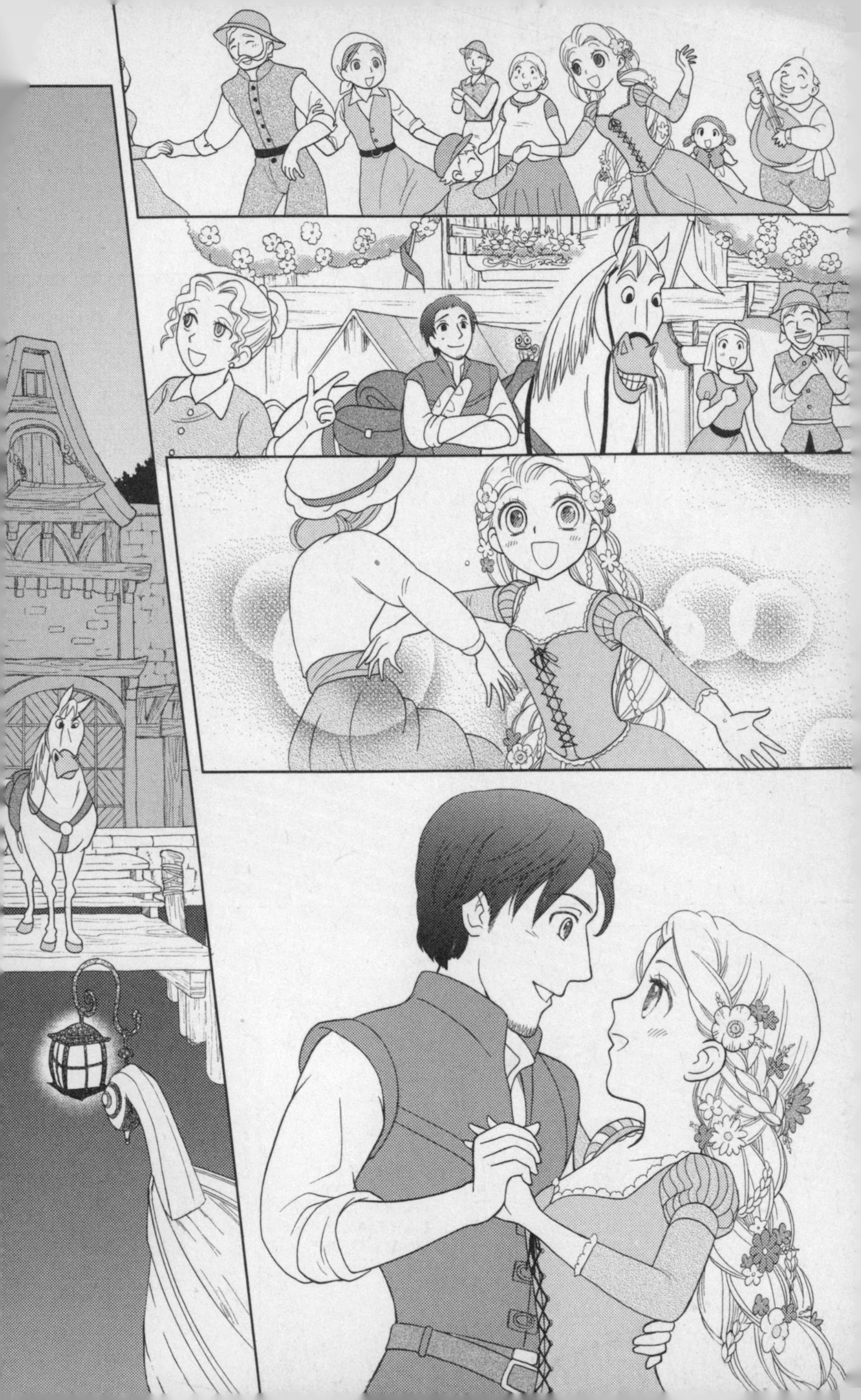

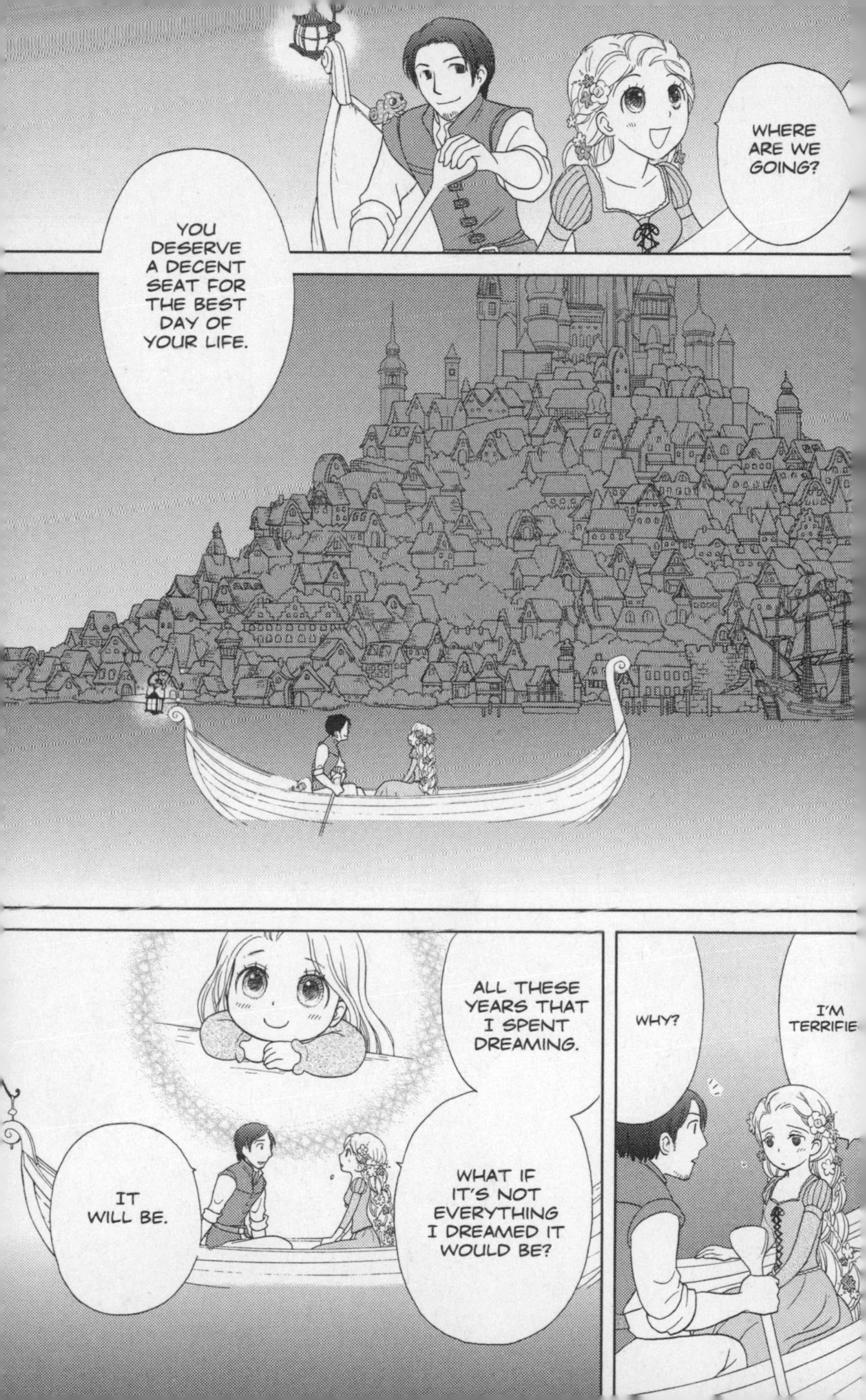
WHERE ARE WE GOING?
YOU DESERVE A DECENT SEAT FOR THE BEST DAY OF YOUR LIFE.
I'M TERRIFIE
WHY?
ALL THESE YEARS THAT I SPENT DREAMING.
WHAT IF IT'S NOT EVERYTHING I DREAMED IT WOULD BE?
IT WILL BE.

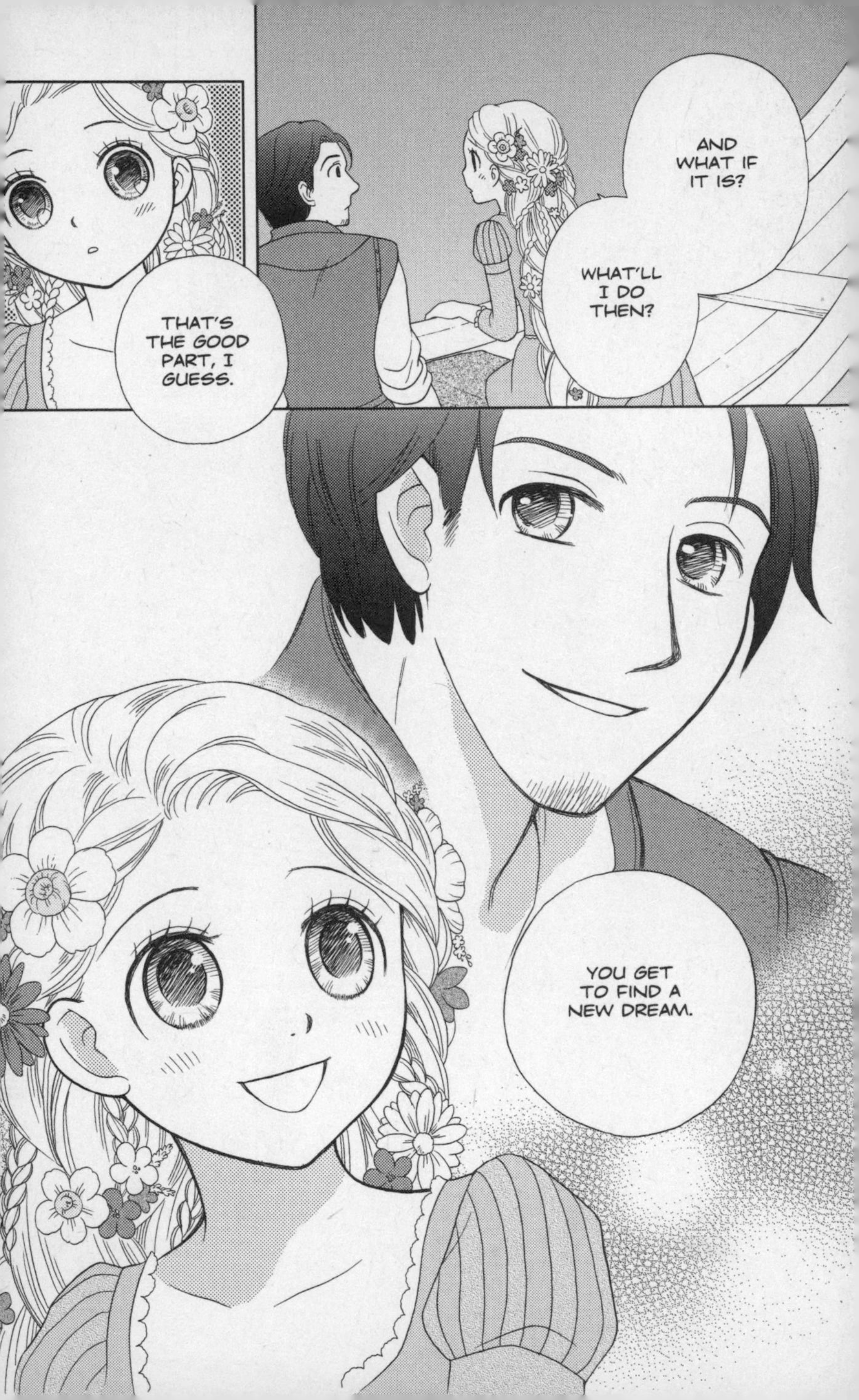
AND WHAT IF IT IS?
WHAT'LL I DO THEN?
THAT'S THE GOOD PART, I GUESS.
YOU GET TO FIND A NEW DREAM.

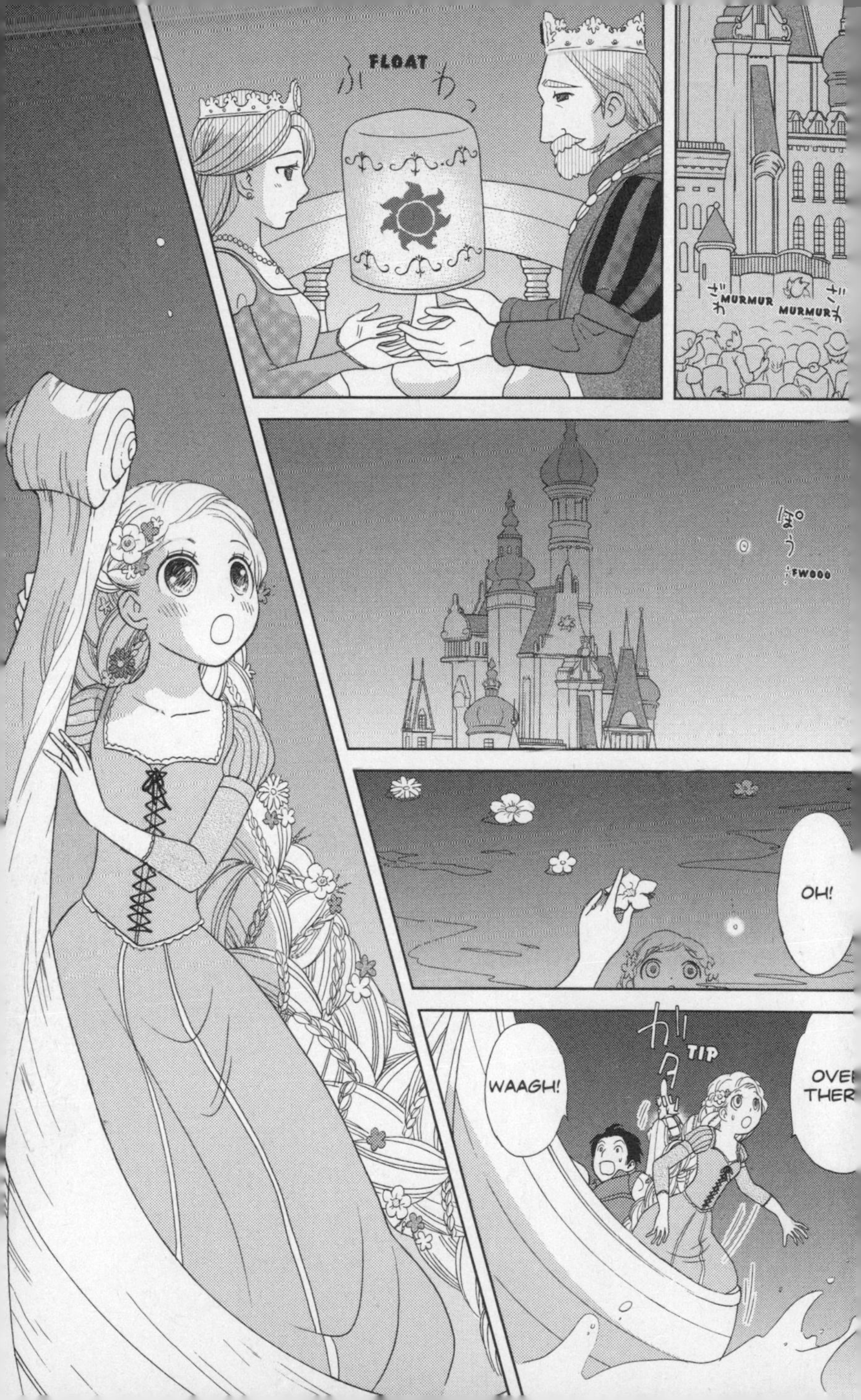

ざわ MURMUR
MURMUR ざわ
ふわっ FLOAT
ぽう FWOOO
OH!
OVE
THER
ガタ TIP
WAAGH!

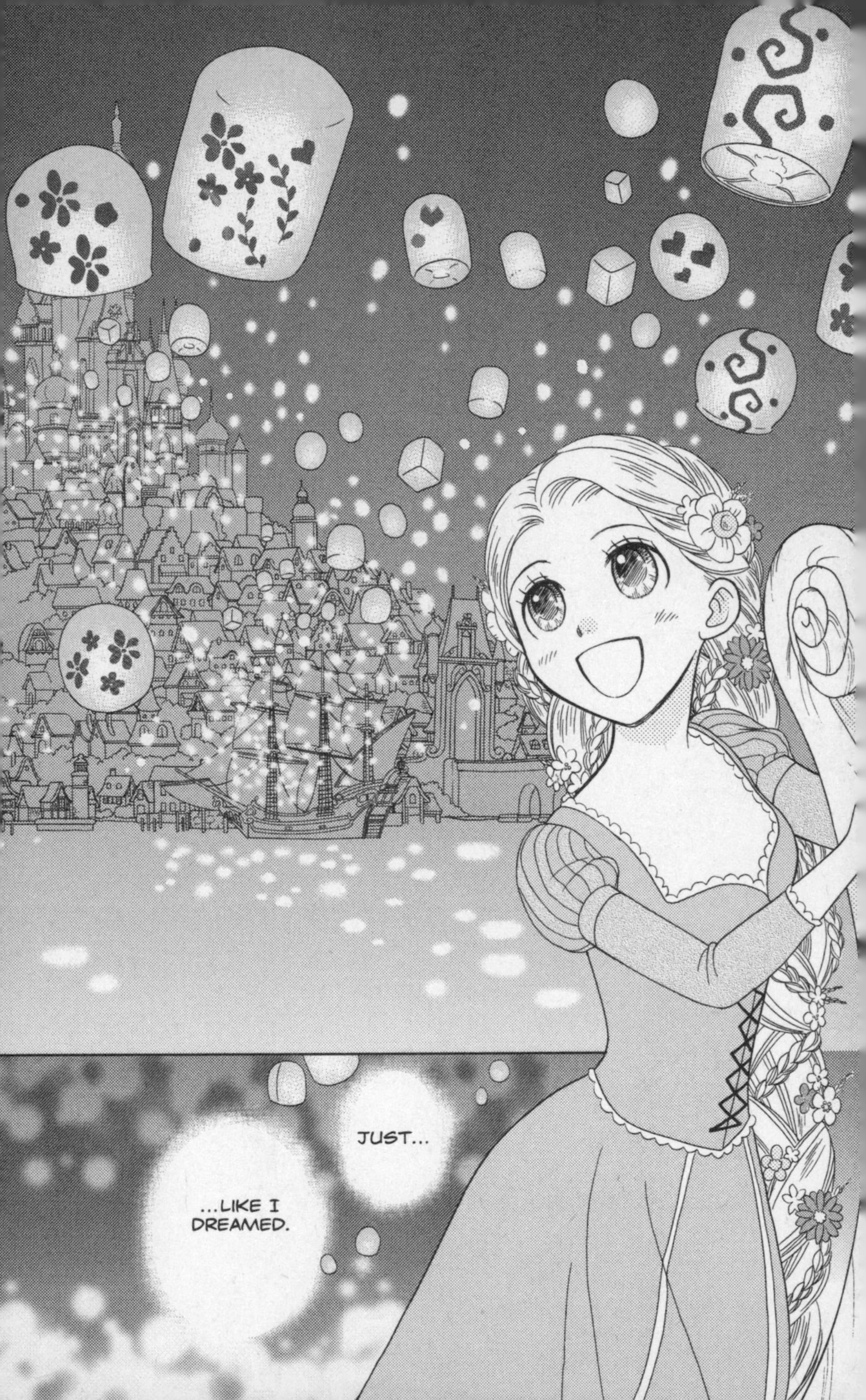
JUST...
...LIKE I DREAMED.

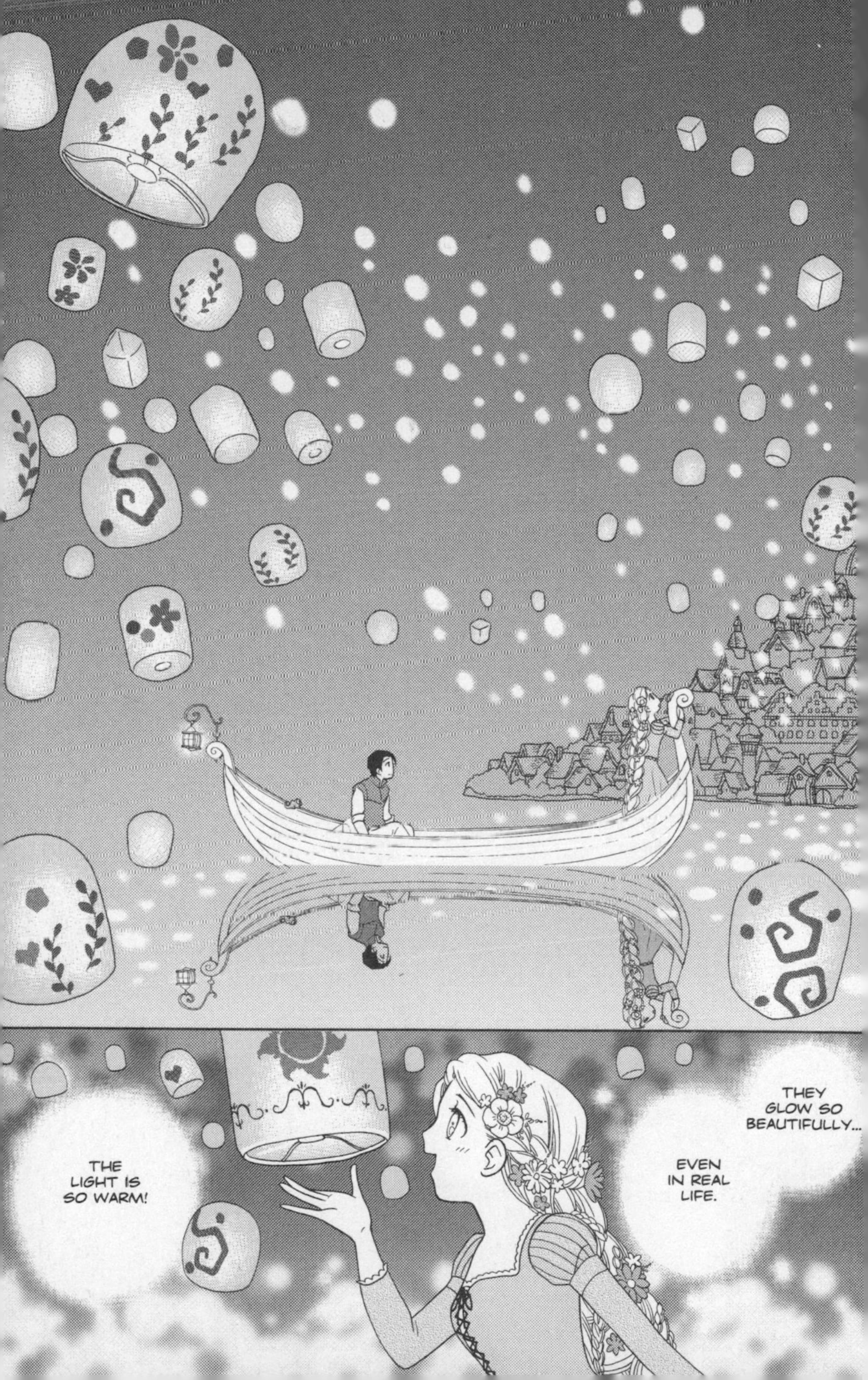
THEY GLOW SO BEAUTIFULLY...
EVEN IN REAL LIFE.
THE LIGHT IS SO WARM!

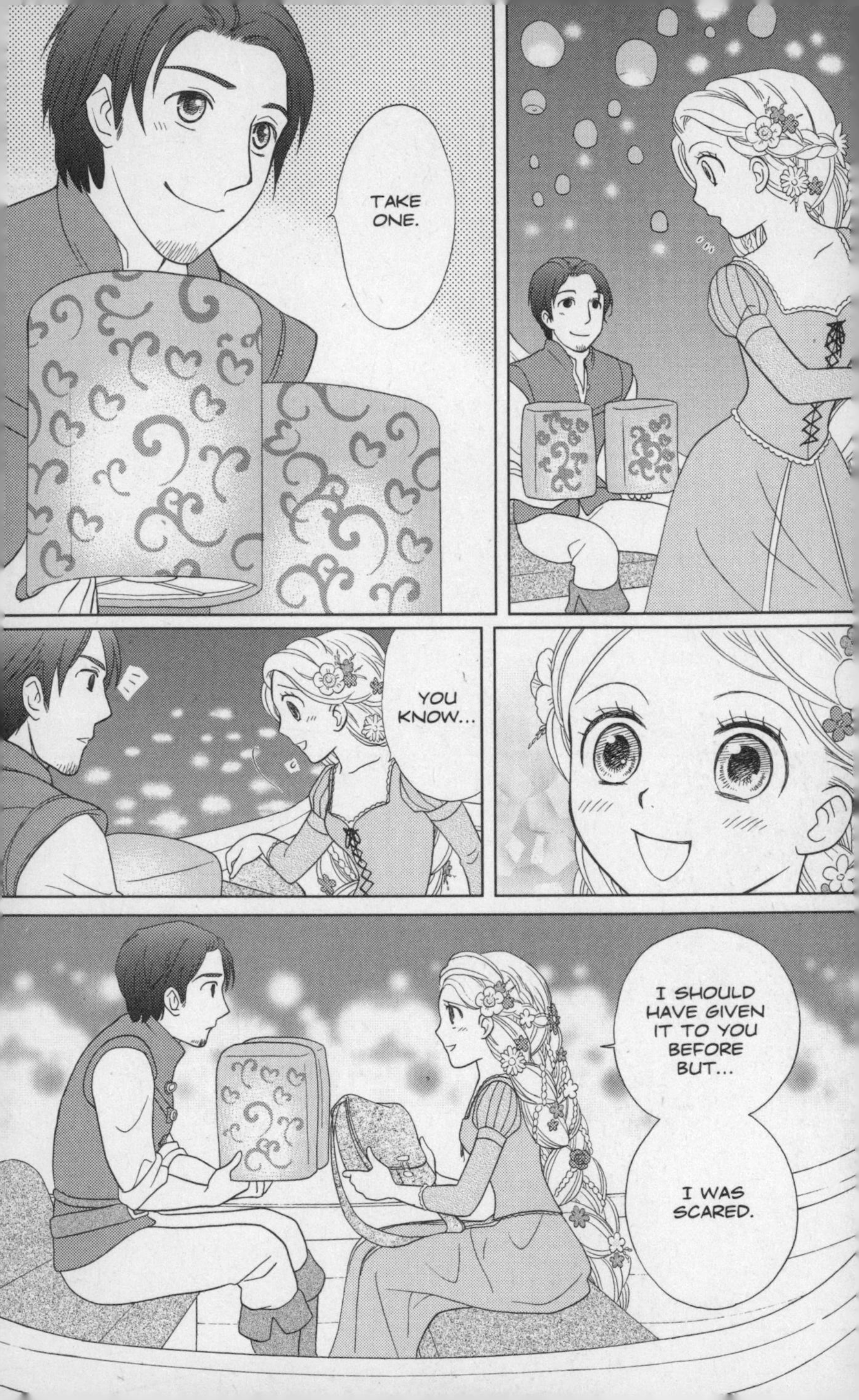
TAKE ONE.
YOU KNOW...
I SHOULD HAVE GIVEN IT TO YOU BEFORE BUT...
I WAS SCARED.

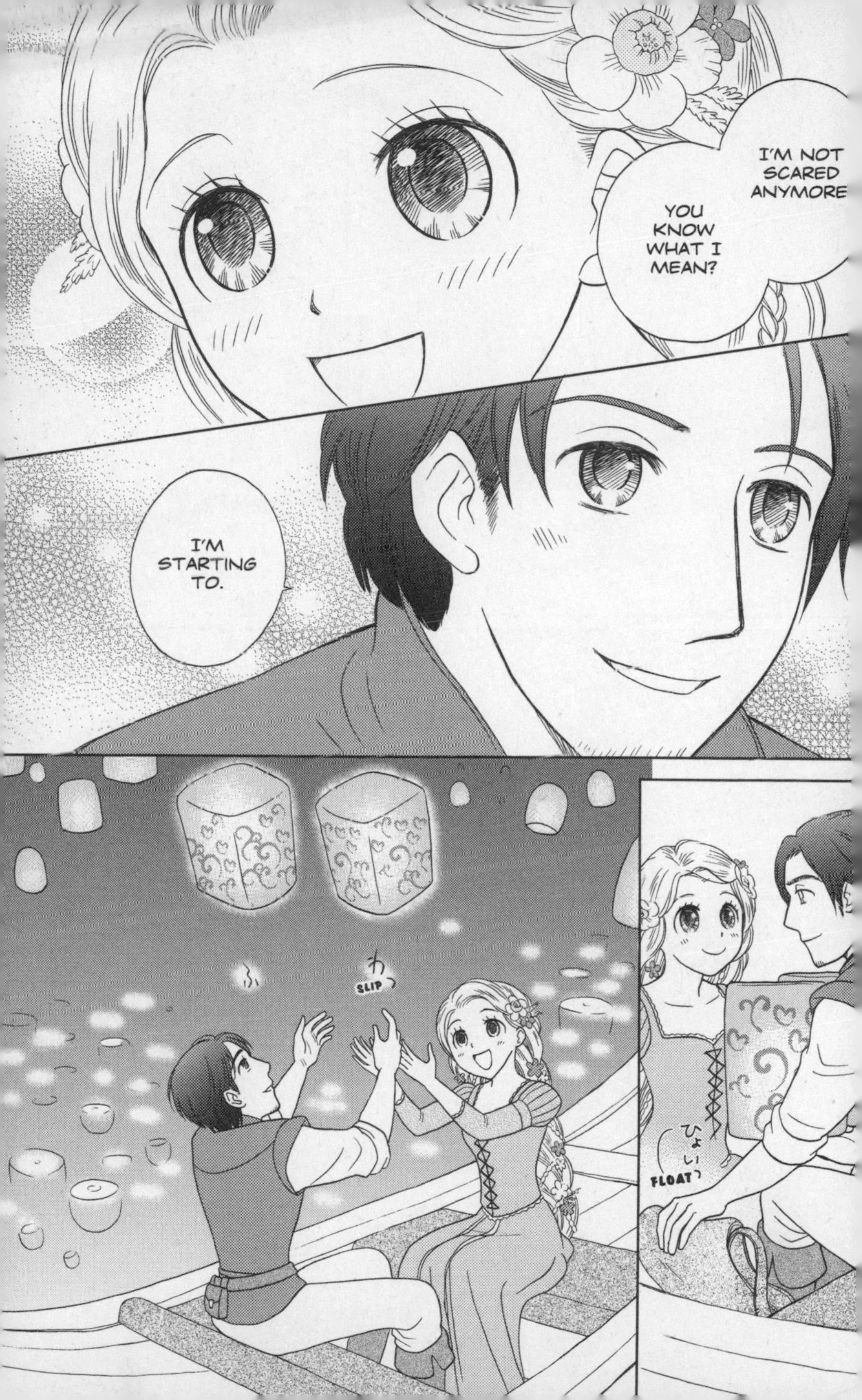
I'M NOT SCARED ANYMORE
YOU KNOW WHAT I MEAN?
I'M STARTING TO.
ひょいっ
FLOAT
わっ
SLIP
ふ

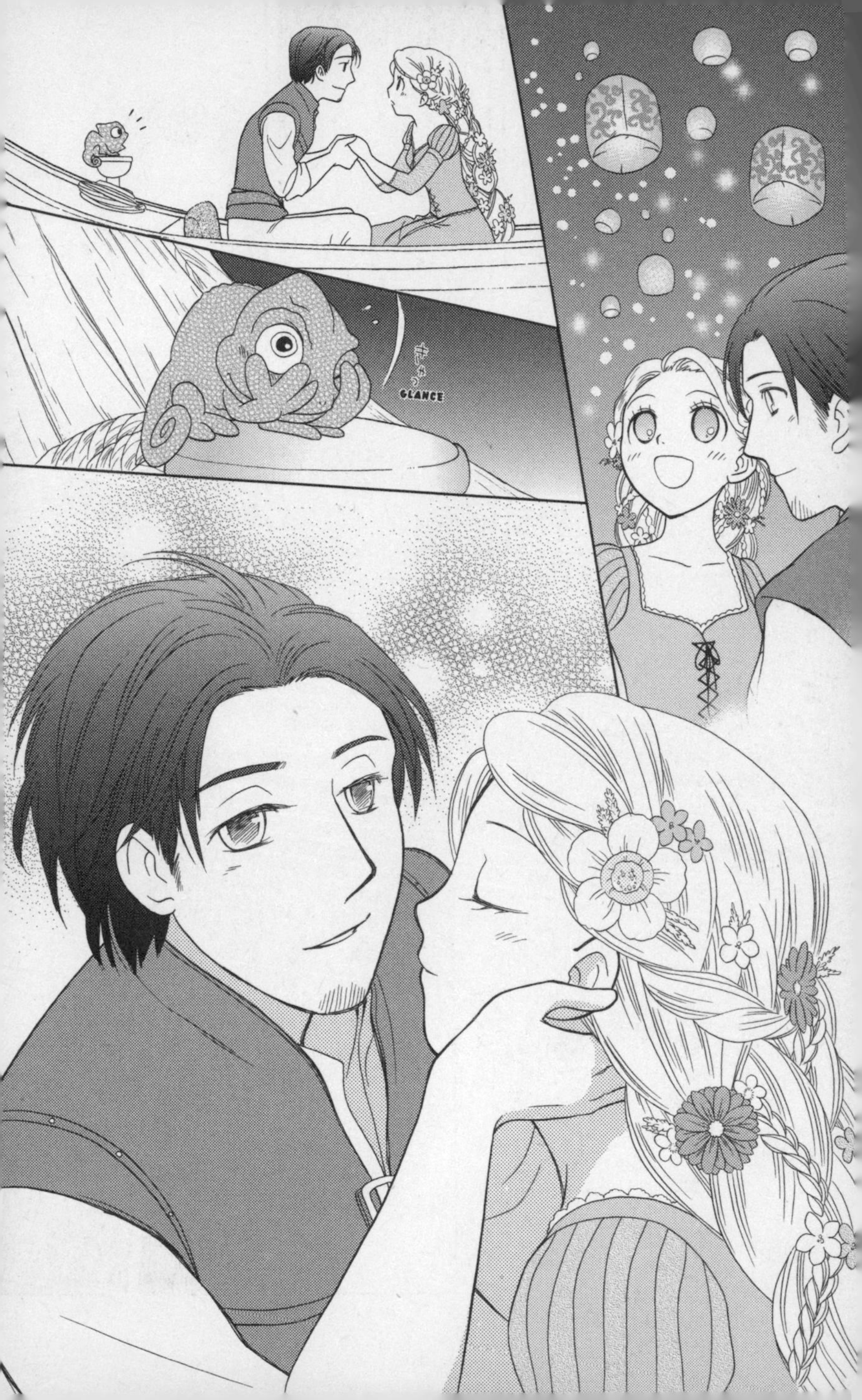
GLANCE

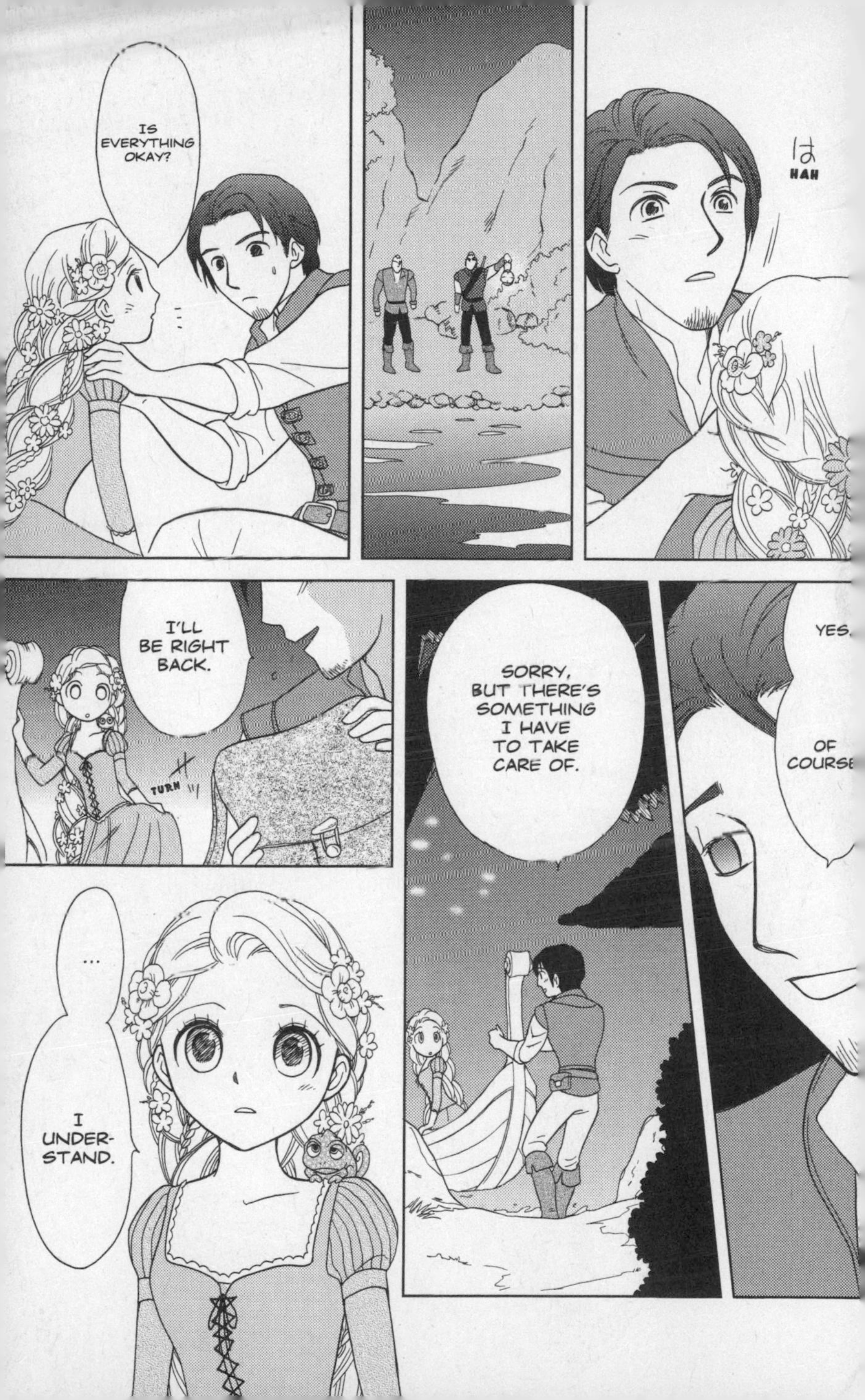
は
HAH
IS EVERYTHING OKAY?
YES.
OF COURSE
SORRY, BUT THERE'S SOMETHING I HAVE TO TAKE CARE OF.
I'LL BE RIGHT BACK.
TURN
...
I UNDERSTAND.

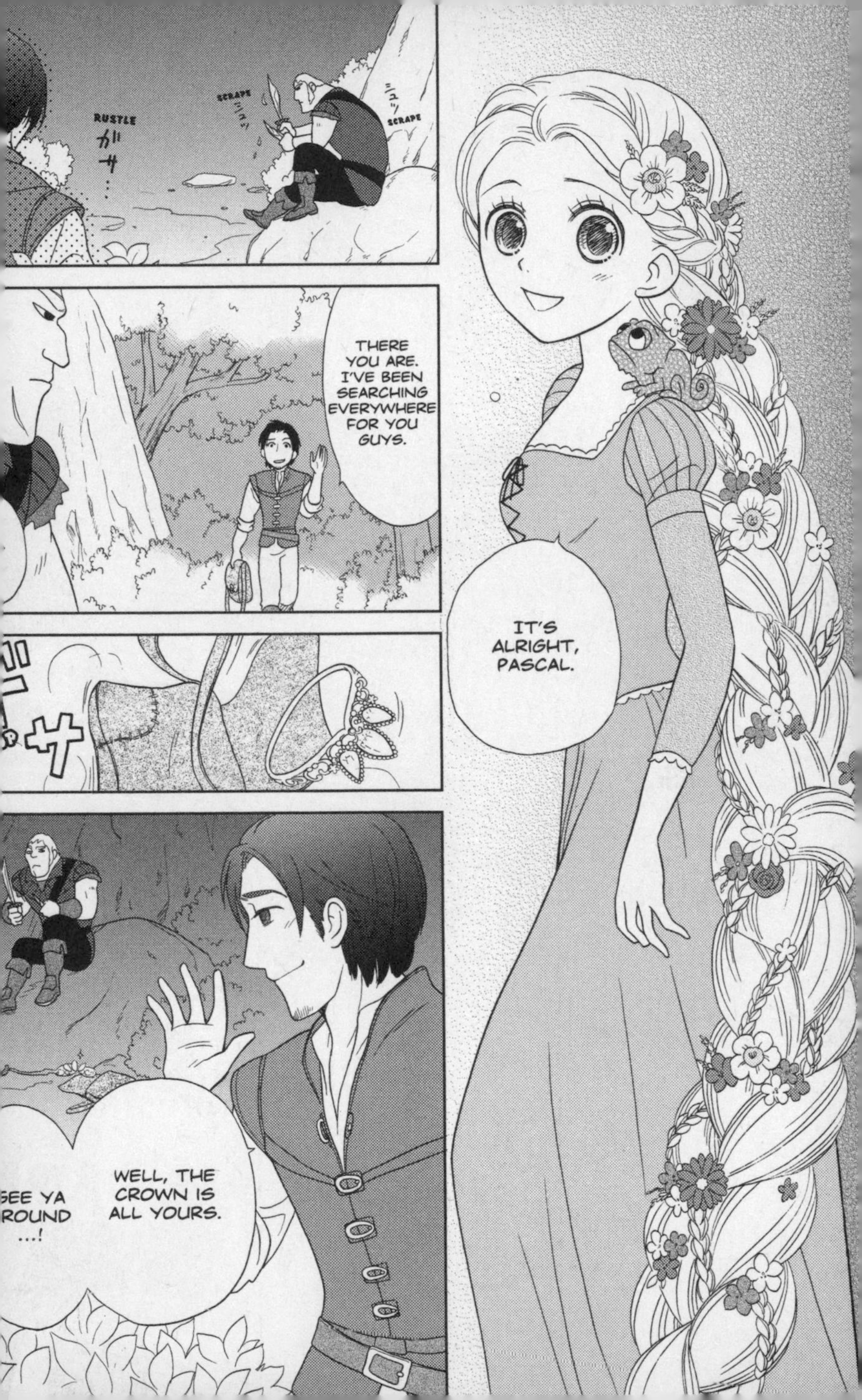
IT'S ALRIGHT, PASCAL.
SCRAPE
SCRAPE
RUSTLE
THERE YOU ARE. I'VE BEEN SEARCHING EVERYWHERE FOR YOU GUYS.
WELL, THE CROWN IS ALL YOURS.
SEE YA ROUND ...!

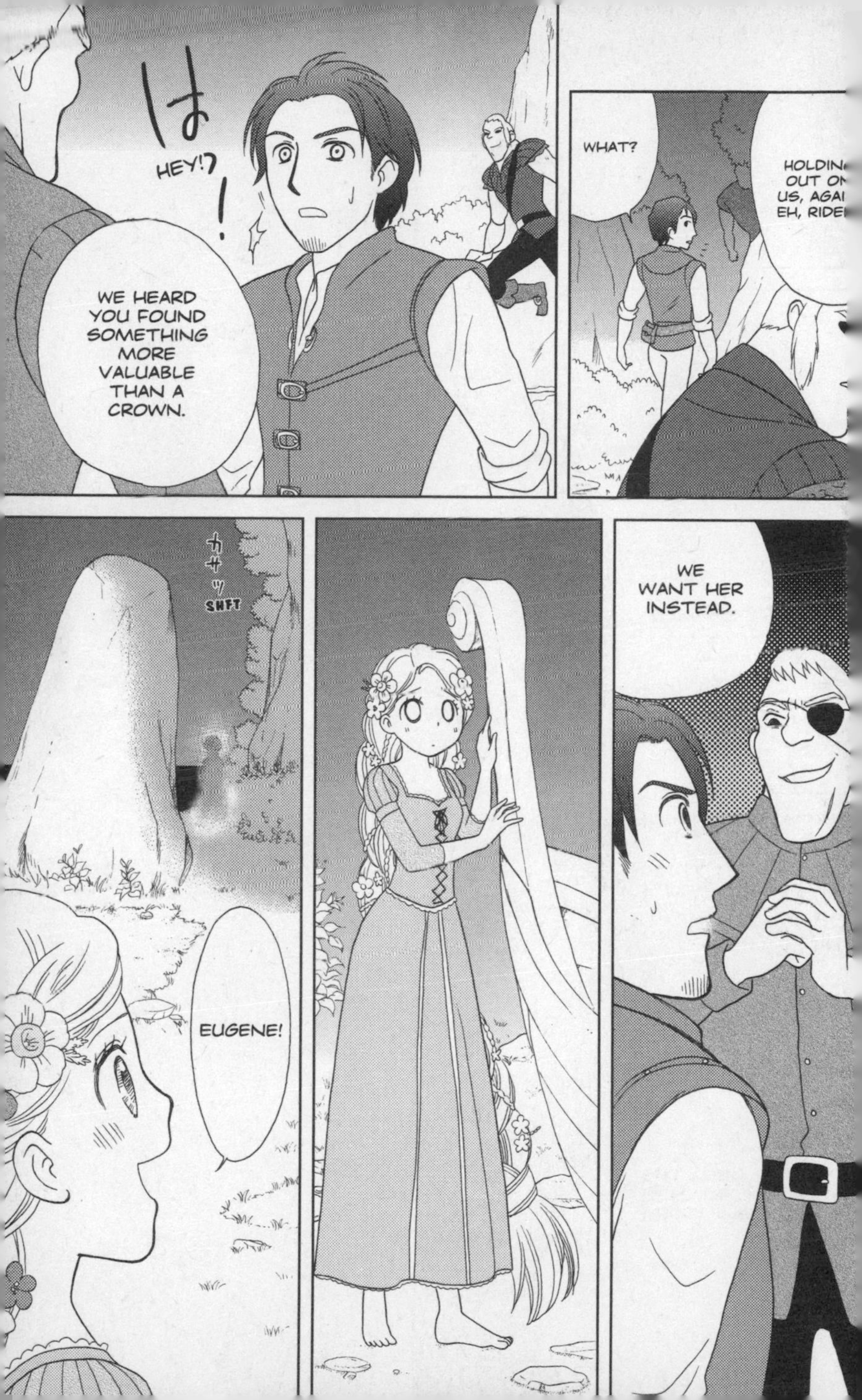
HOLDIN OUT ON US, AGAI EH, RIDE
WHAT?
は
HEY!?
WE HEARD YOU FOUND SOMETHING MORE VALUABLE THAN A CROWN.
WE WANT HER INSTEAD.
カサッ
SHFT
EUGENE!

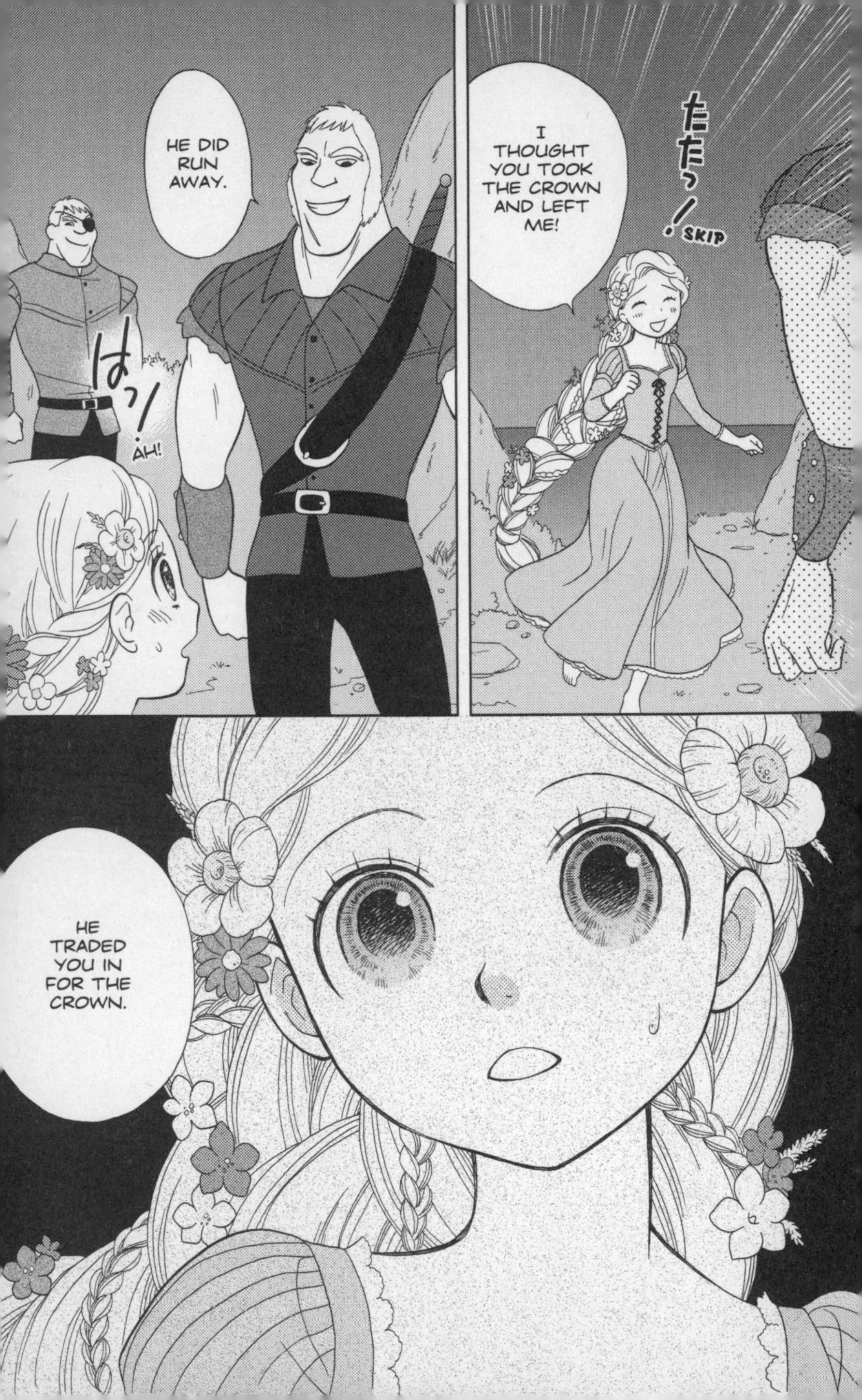

I THOUGHT YOU TOOK THE CROWN AND LEFT ME!
たたっ！
SKIP
HE DID RUN AWAY.
はっ！
AH!
HE TRADED YOU IN FOR THE CROWN.

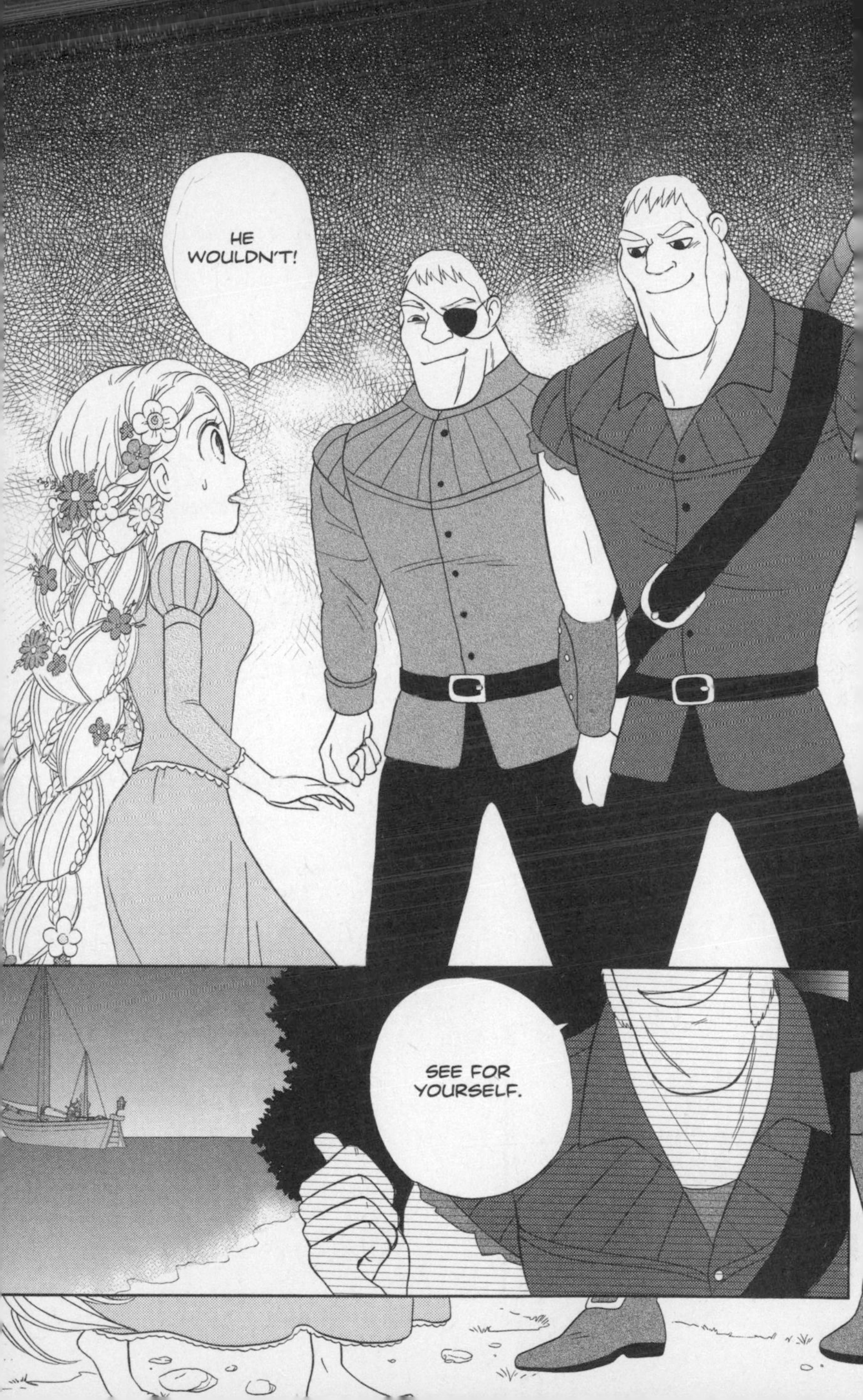
HE WOULDN'T!
SEE FOR YOURSELF.

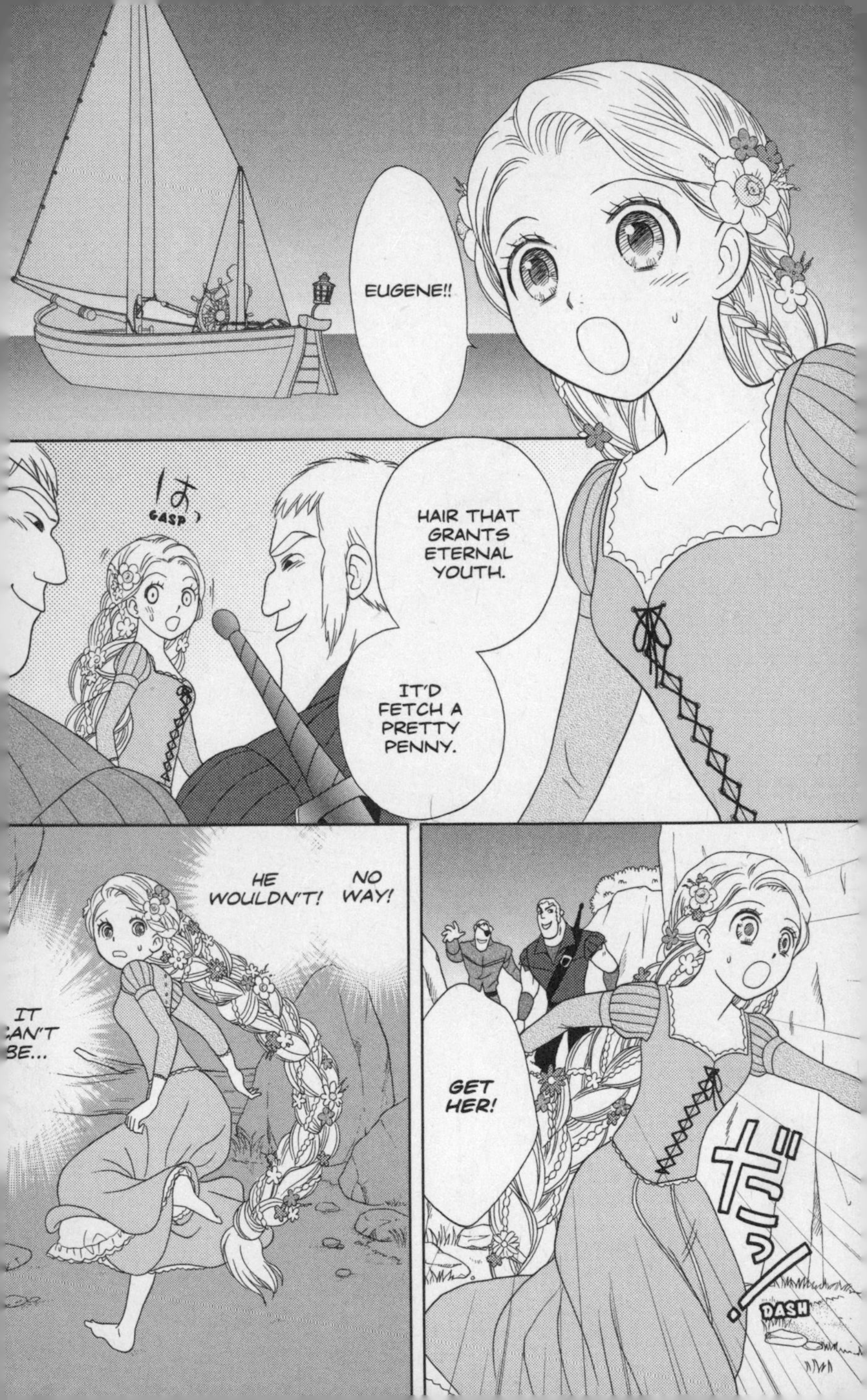
EUGENE!!
GASP
HAIR THAT GRANTS ETERNAL YOUTH.
IT'D FETCH A PRETTY PENNY.
GET HER!
ダッ
DASH
NO WAY!
HE WOULDN'T!
IT CAN'T BE...

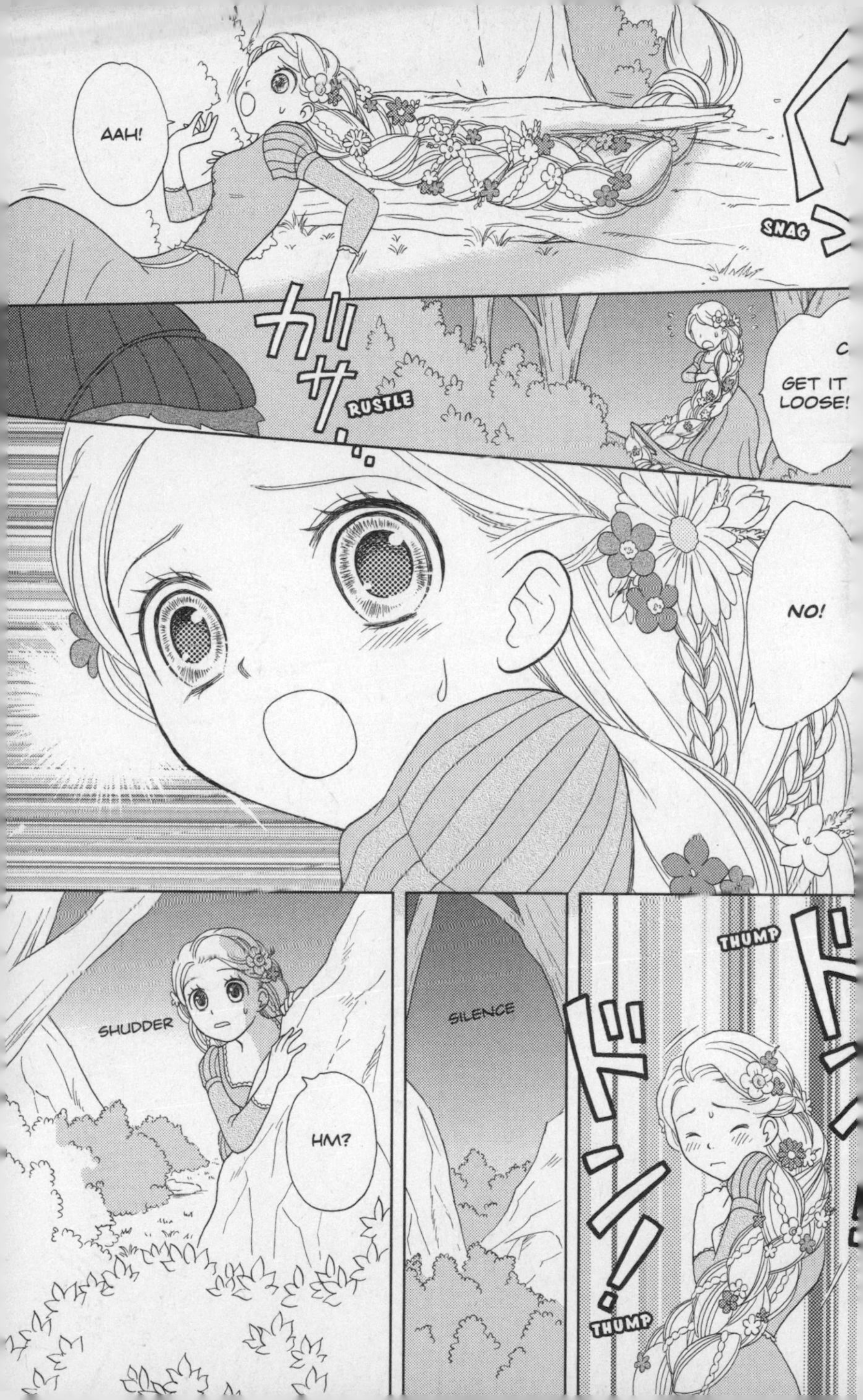
SNAG
AAH!
GET IT LOOSE!
RUSTLE
NO!
THUMP
THUMP
SILENCE
SHUDDER
HM?

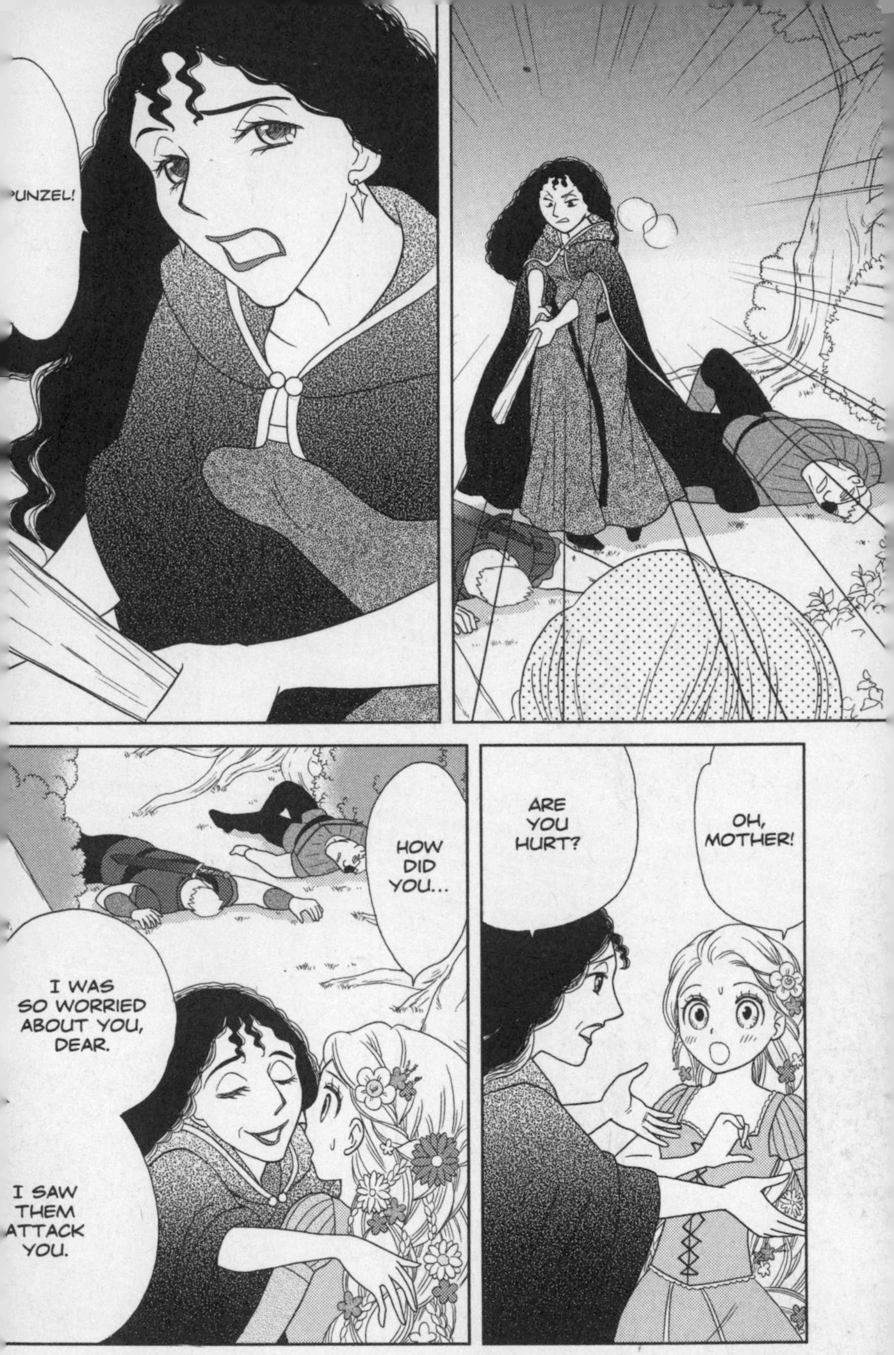
PUNZEL!
OH, MOTHER!
ARE YOU HURT?
HOW DID YOU...
I WAS SO WORRIED ABOUT YOU, DEAR.
I SAW THEM ATTACK YOU.

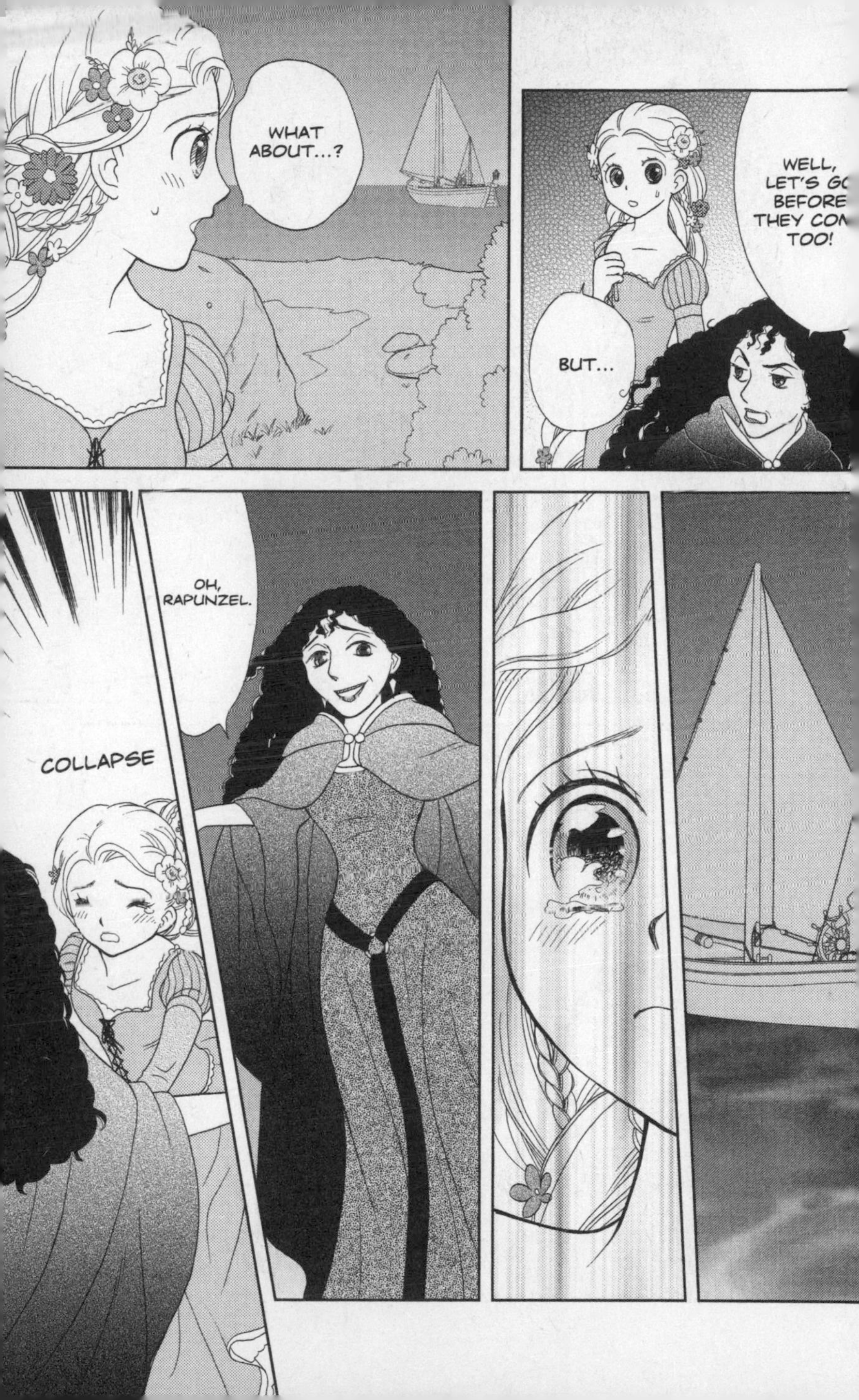

WELL, LET'S G BEFORE THEY COM TOO!
BUT...
WHAT ABOUT...?
OH, RAPUNZEL.
COLLAPSE

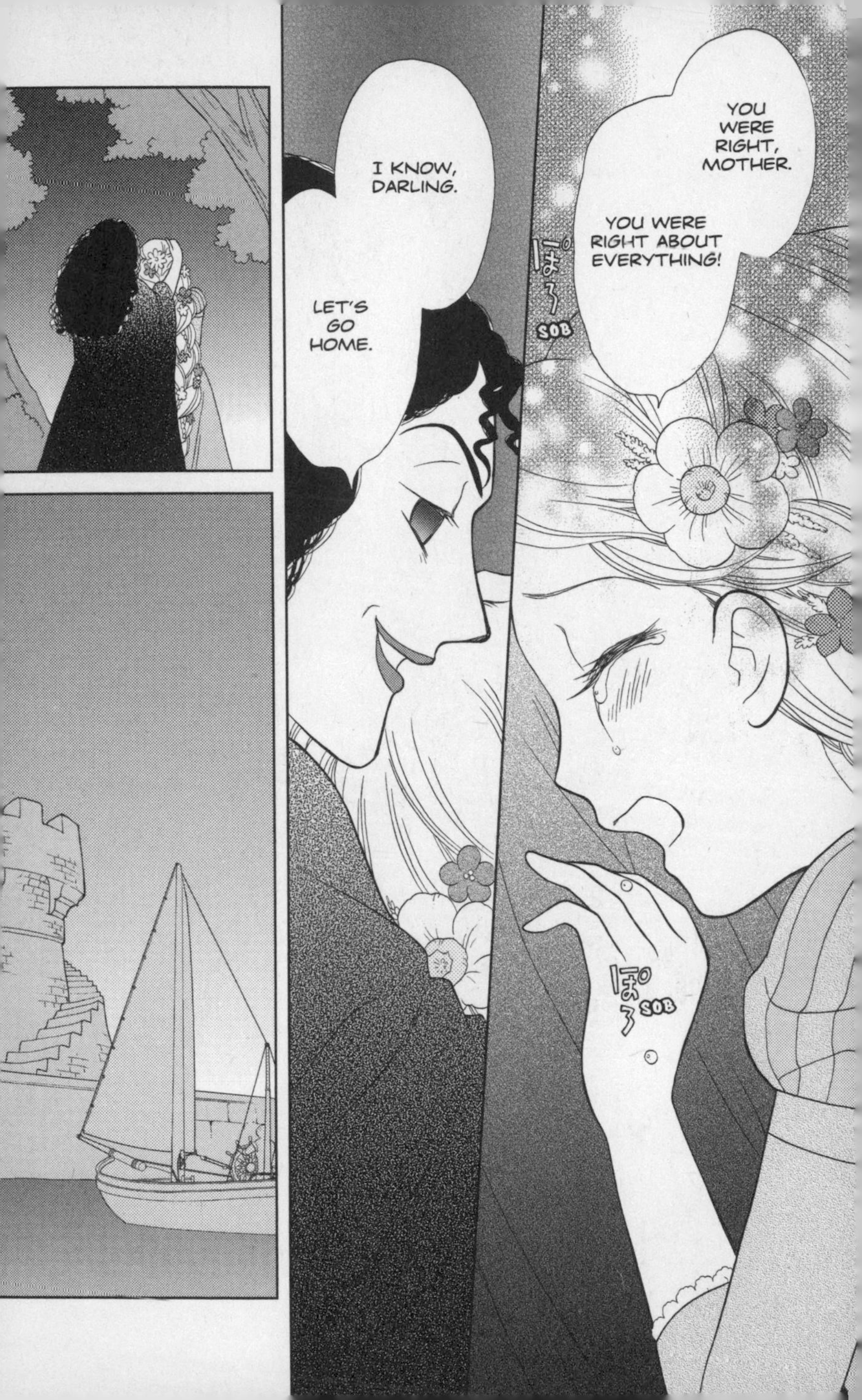
YOU WERE RIGHT, MOTHER.
YOU WERE RIGHT ABOUT EVERYTHING!
ぽろ SOB
ぽろ SOB
I KNOW, DARLING.
LET'S GO HOME.

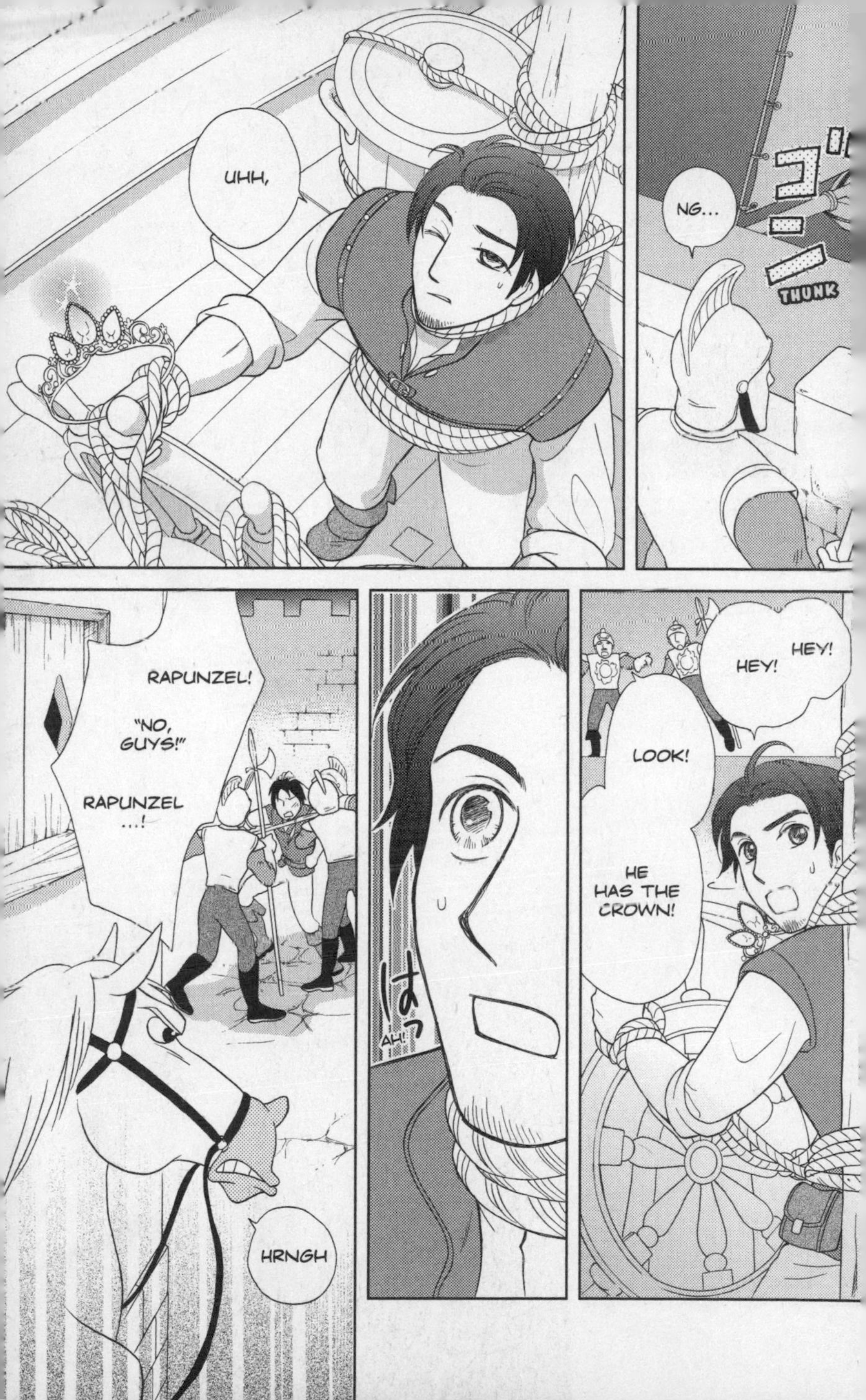
NG...
THUNK
UHH,
HEY!
HEY!
LOOK!
HE HAS THE CROWN!
はっ
AH!
RAPUNZEL!
"NO, GUYS!"
RAPUNZEL ...!
HRNGH

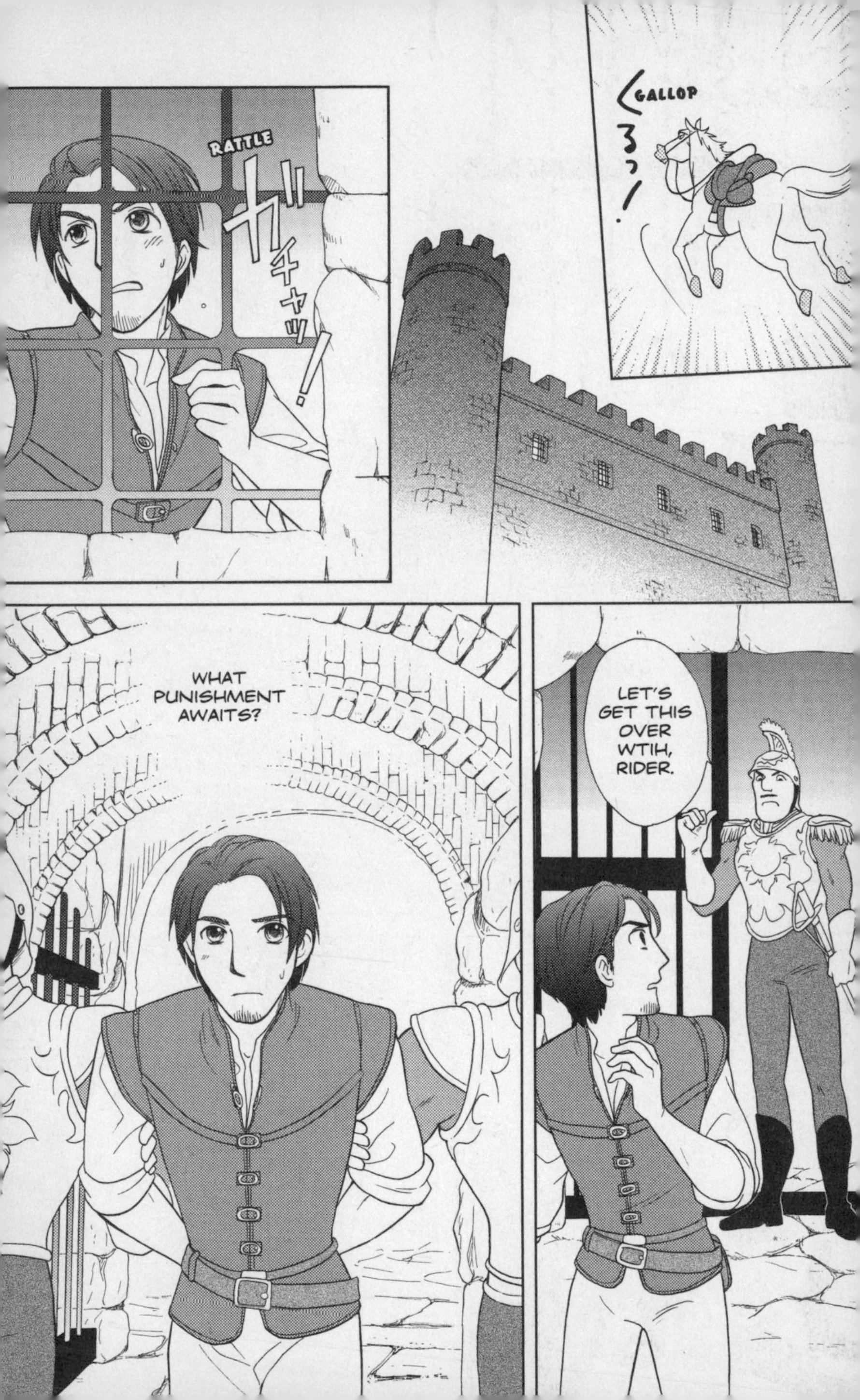
GALLOP
RATTLE
ガチャッ!
LET'S GET THIS OVER WTIH, RIDER.
WHAT PUNISHMENT AWAITS?

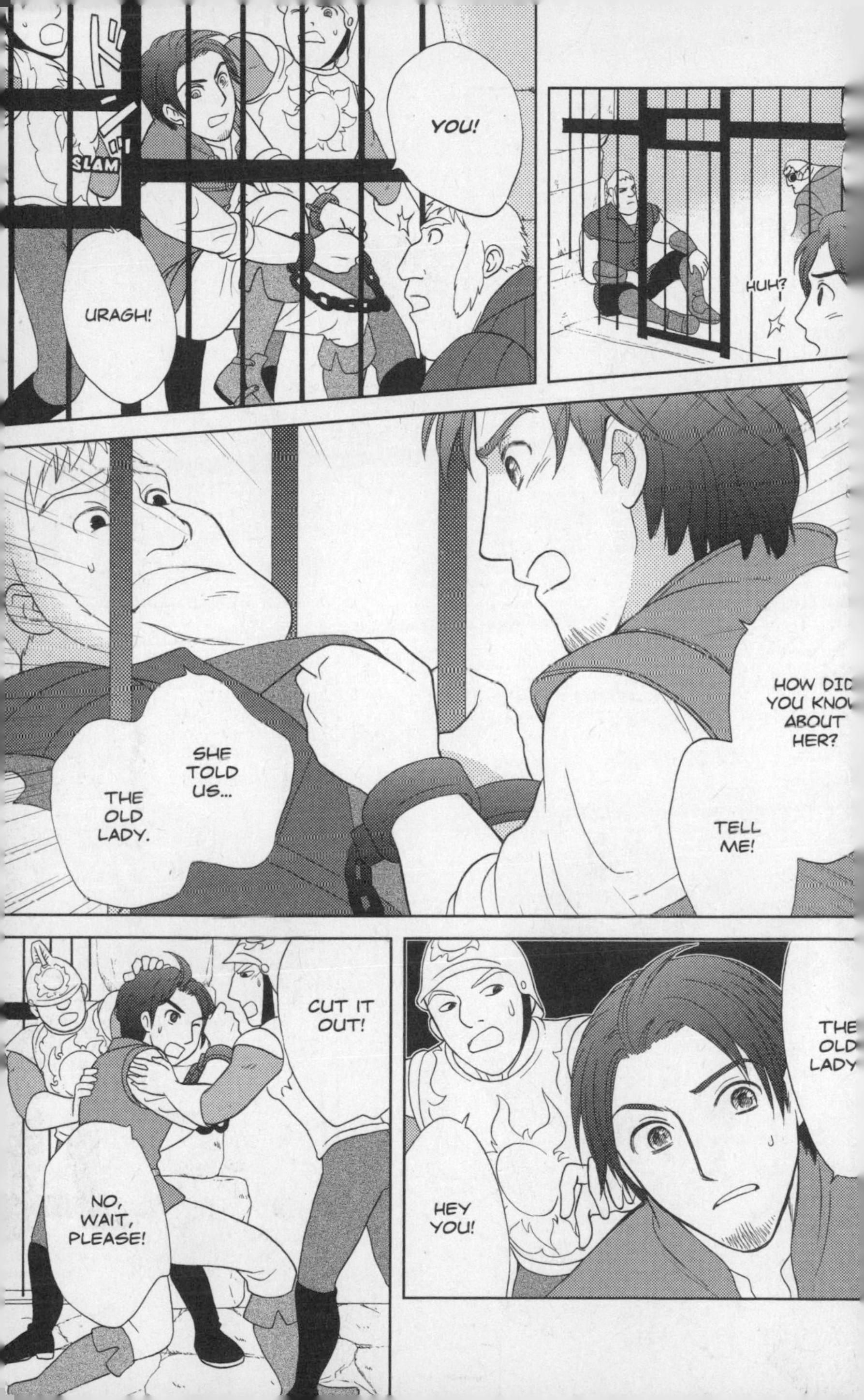

HUH?
YOU!
SLAM
URAGH!
HOW DID YOU KNOW ABOUT HER?
TELL ME!
SHE TOLD US...
THE OLD LADY.
THE OLD LADY
HEY YOU!
CUT IT OUT!
NO, WAIT, PLEASE!

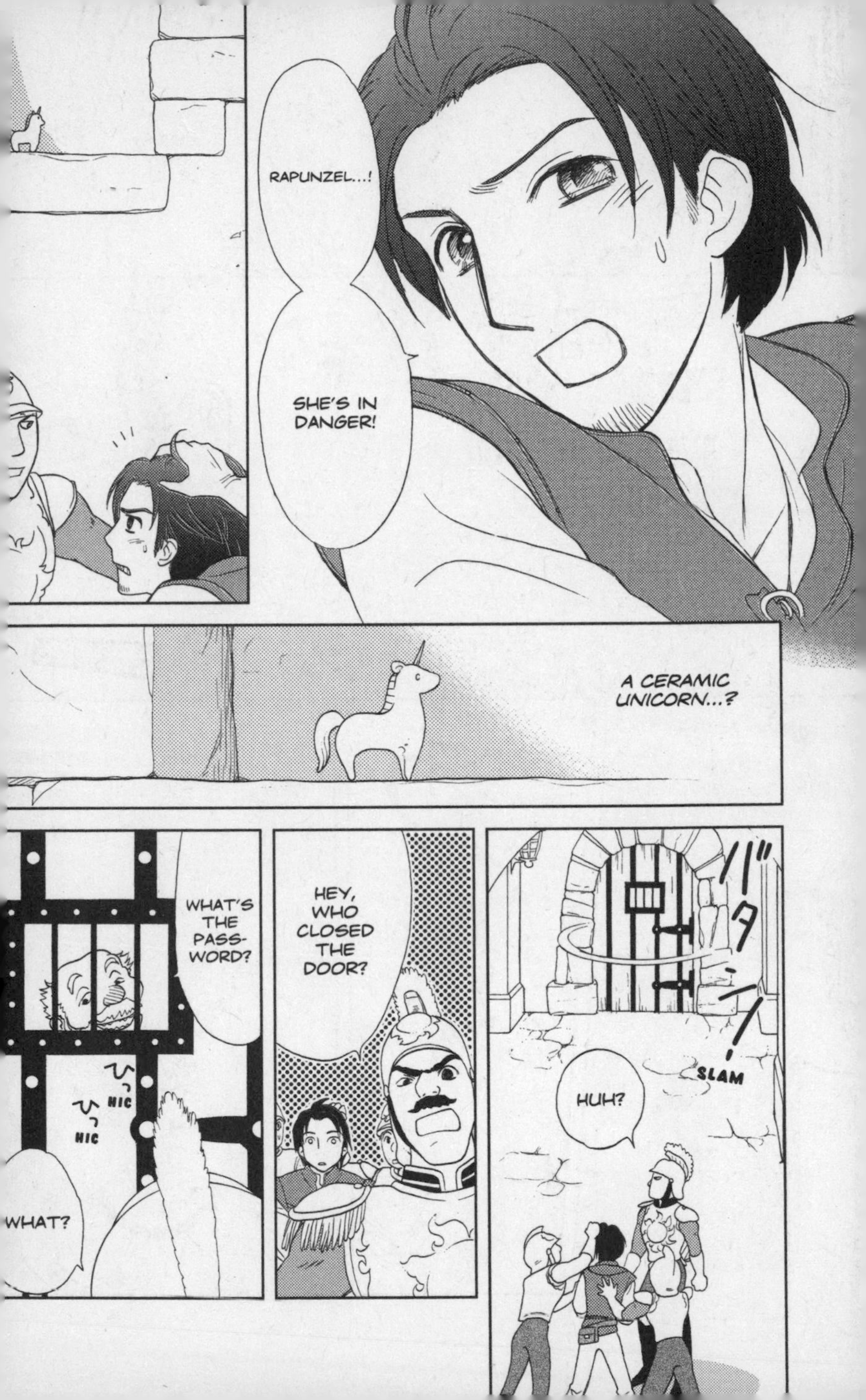
RAPUNZEL...!
SHE'S IN DANGER!
A CERAMIC UNICORN...?
SLAM
HUH?
HEY, WHO CLOSED THE DOOR?
WHAT'S THE PASS-WORD?
ひっ HIC
ひっ HIC
WHAT?

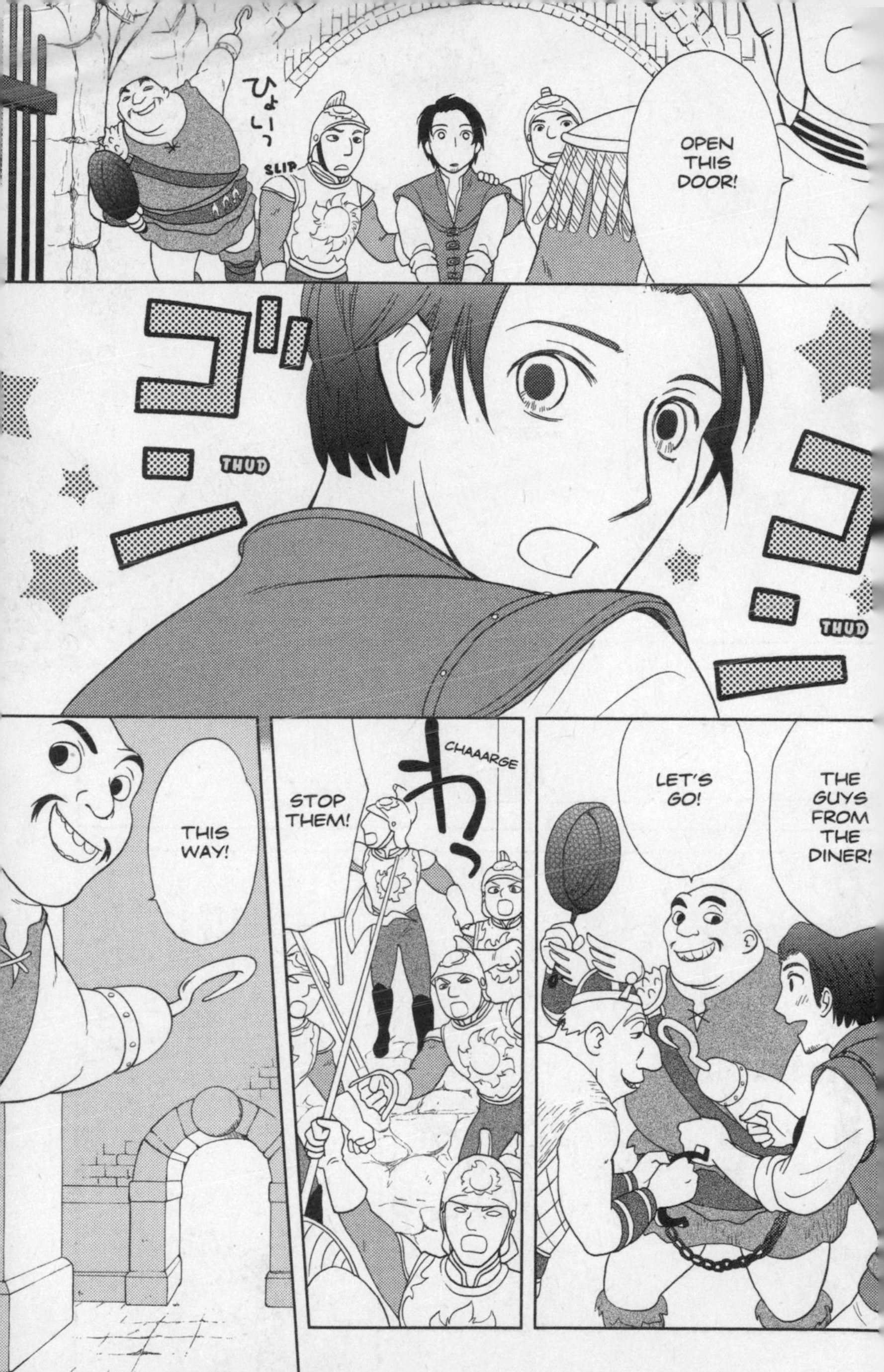
OPEN THIS DOOR!
ひょいっ
SLIP
THUD
THUD
THE GUYS FROM THE DINER!
LET'S GO!
わっ
CHAAARGE
STOP THEM!
THIS WAY!

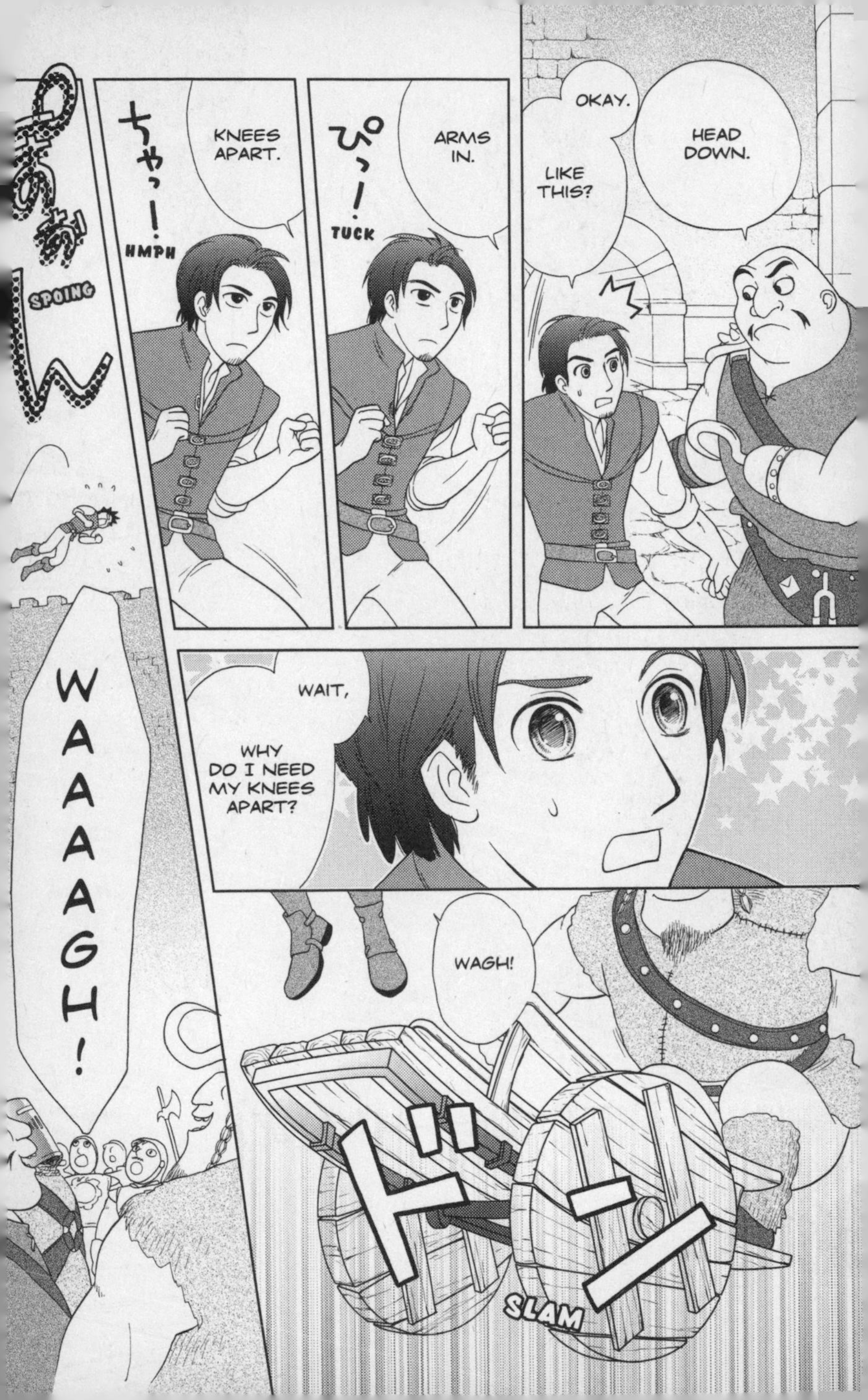
HEAD DOWN.
OKAY.
LIKE THIS?
ARMS IN.
ぴっ!
TUCK
KNEES APART.
ちゃっ!
HMPH
SPOING
WAIT,
WHY DO I NEED MY KNEES APART?
WAGH!
ドーン
SLAM
WAAAAGH!

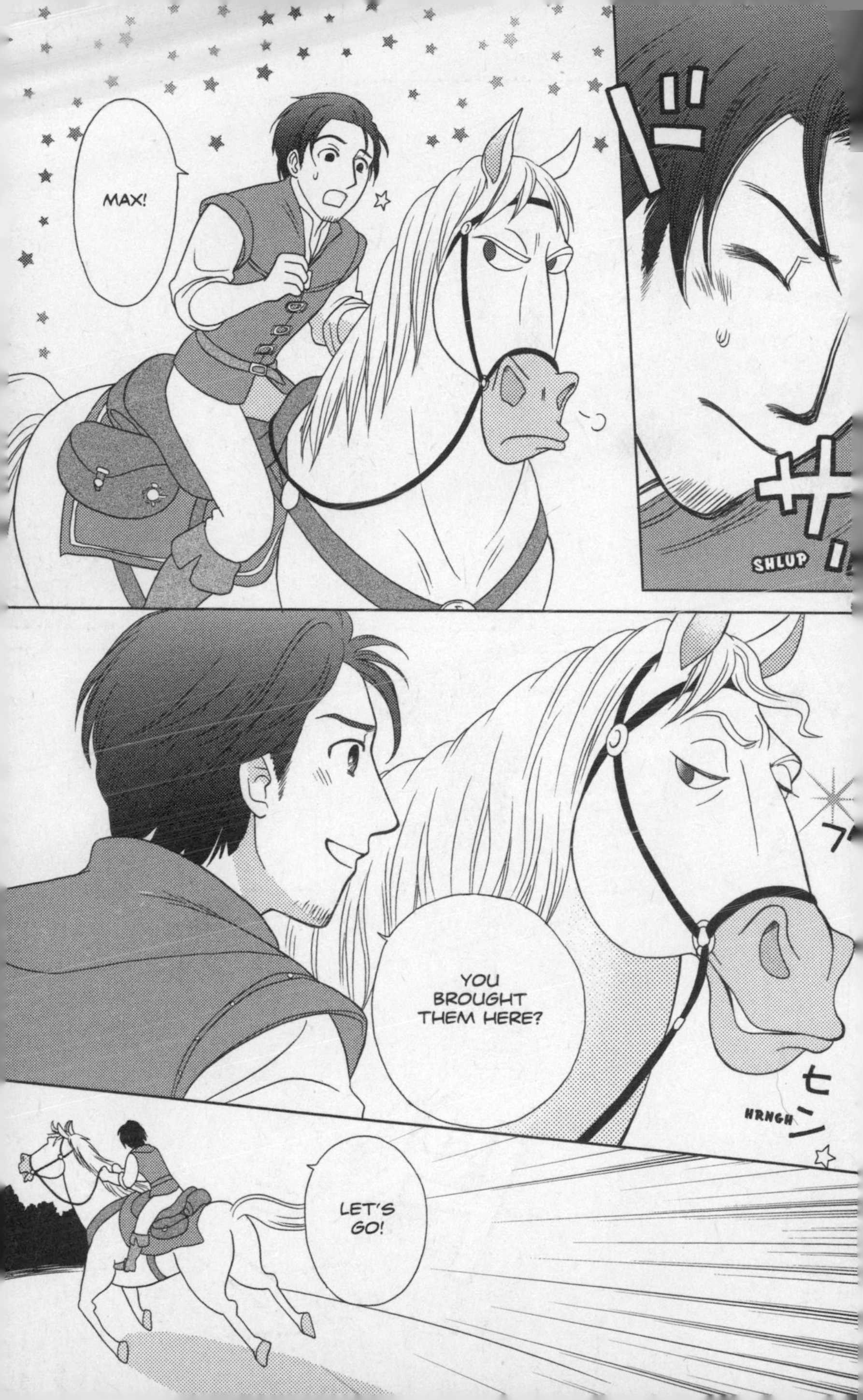
SHLUP
MAX!
YOU BROUGHT THEM HERE?
HRNGH
LET'S GO!

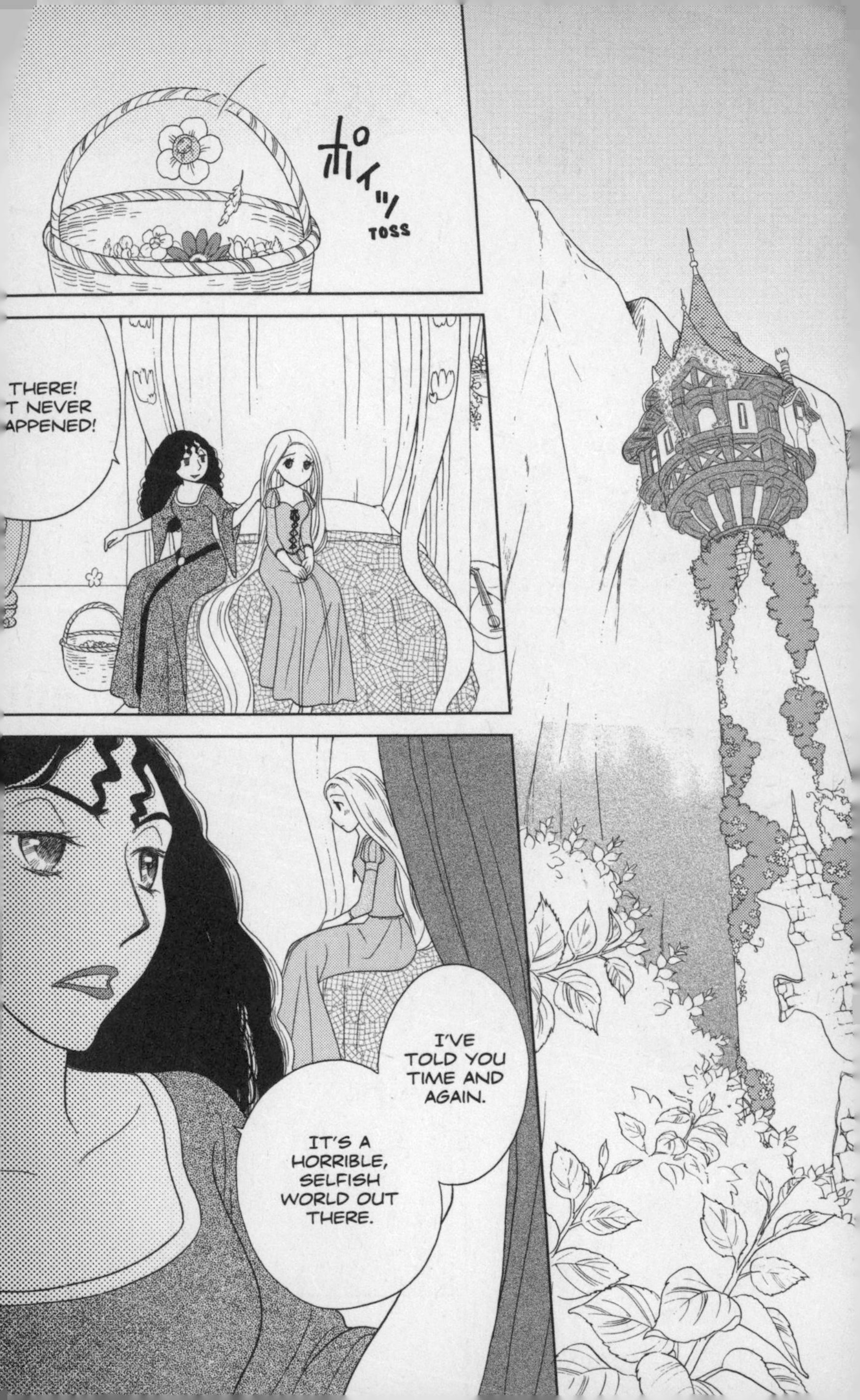
ポイッ
TOSS
THERE! T NEVER APPENED!
I'VE TOLD YOU TIME AND AGAIN.
IT'S A HORRIBLE, SELFISH WORLD OUT THERE.

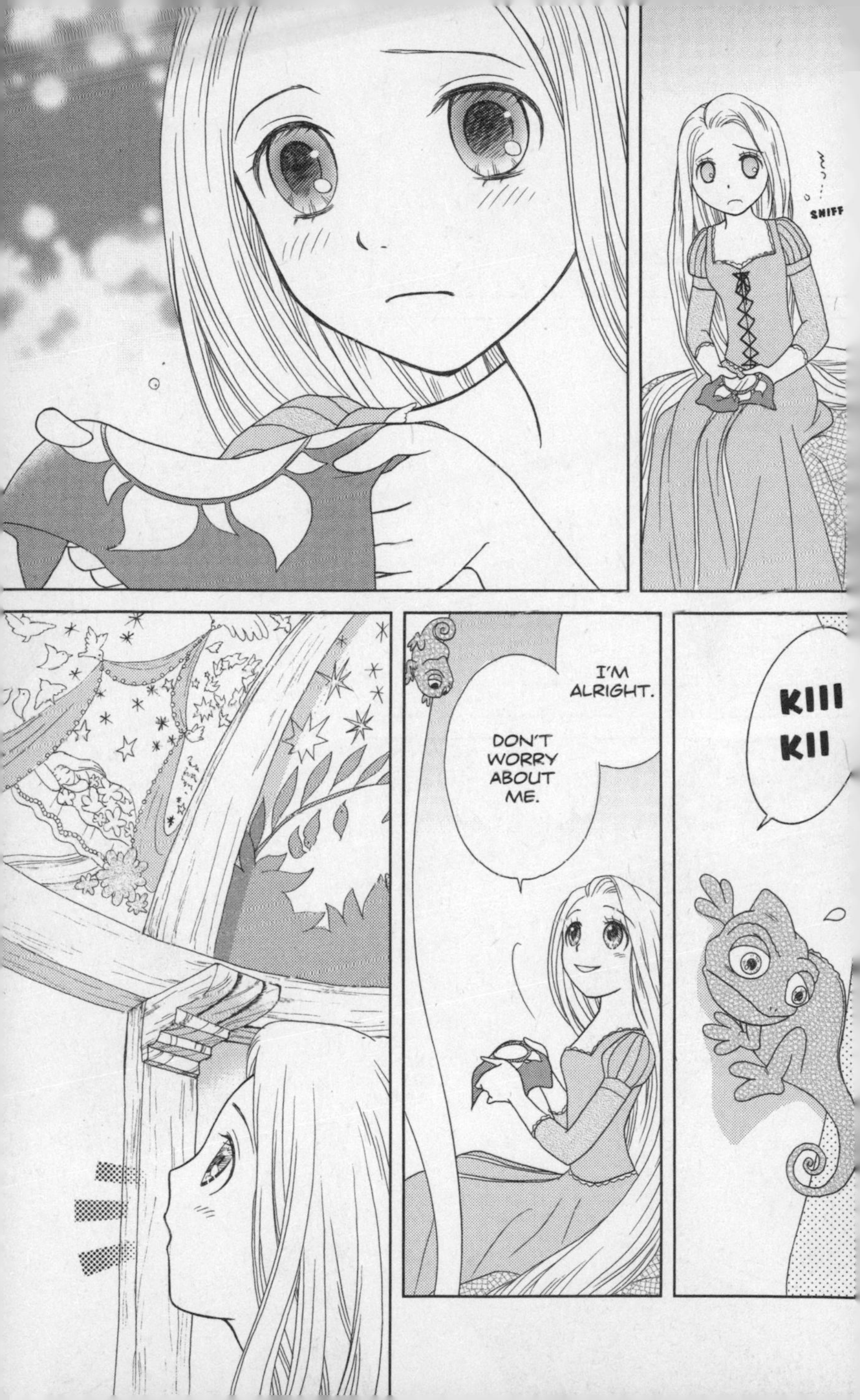
SNIFF
KIII KII
I'M ALRIGHT.
DON'T WORRY ABOUT ME.

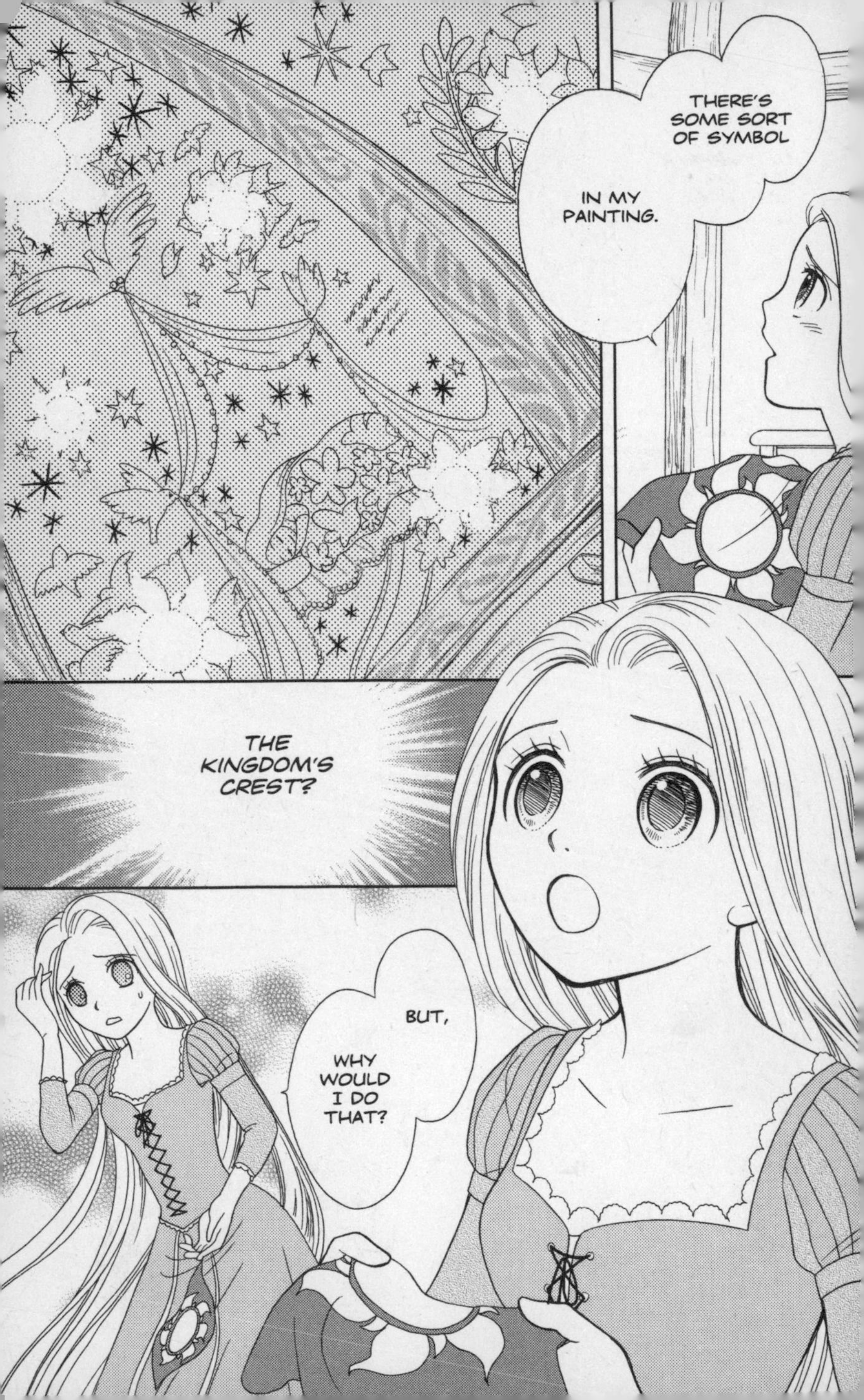
THERE'S SOME SORT OF SYMBOL
IN MY PAINTING.
THE KINGDOM'S CREST?
BUT,
WHY WOULD I DO THAT?

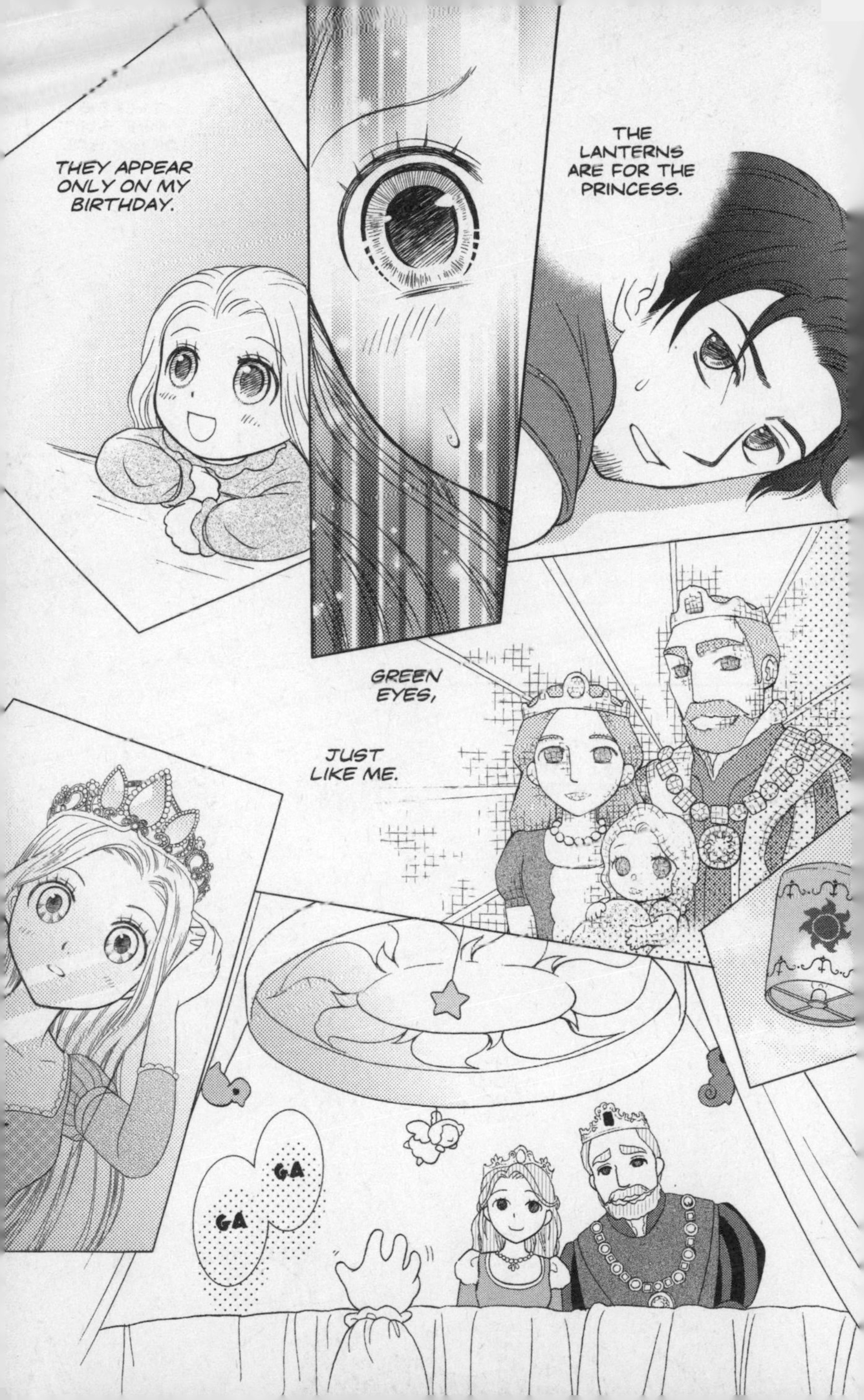
THE LANTERNS ARE FOR THE PRINCESS.
THEY APPEAR ONLY ON MY BIRTHDAY.
GREEN EYES,
JUST LIKE ME.
GA
GA

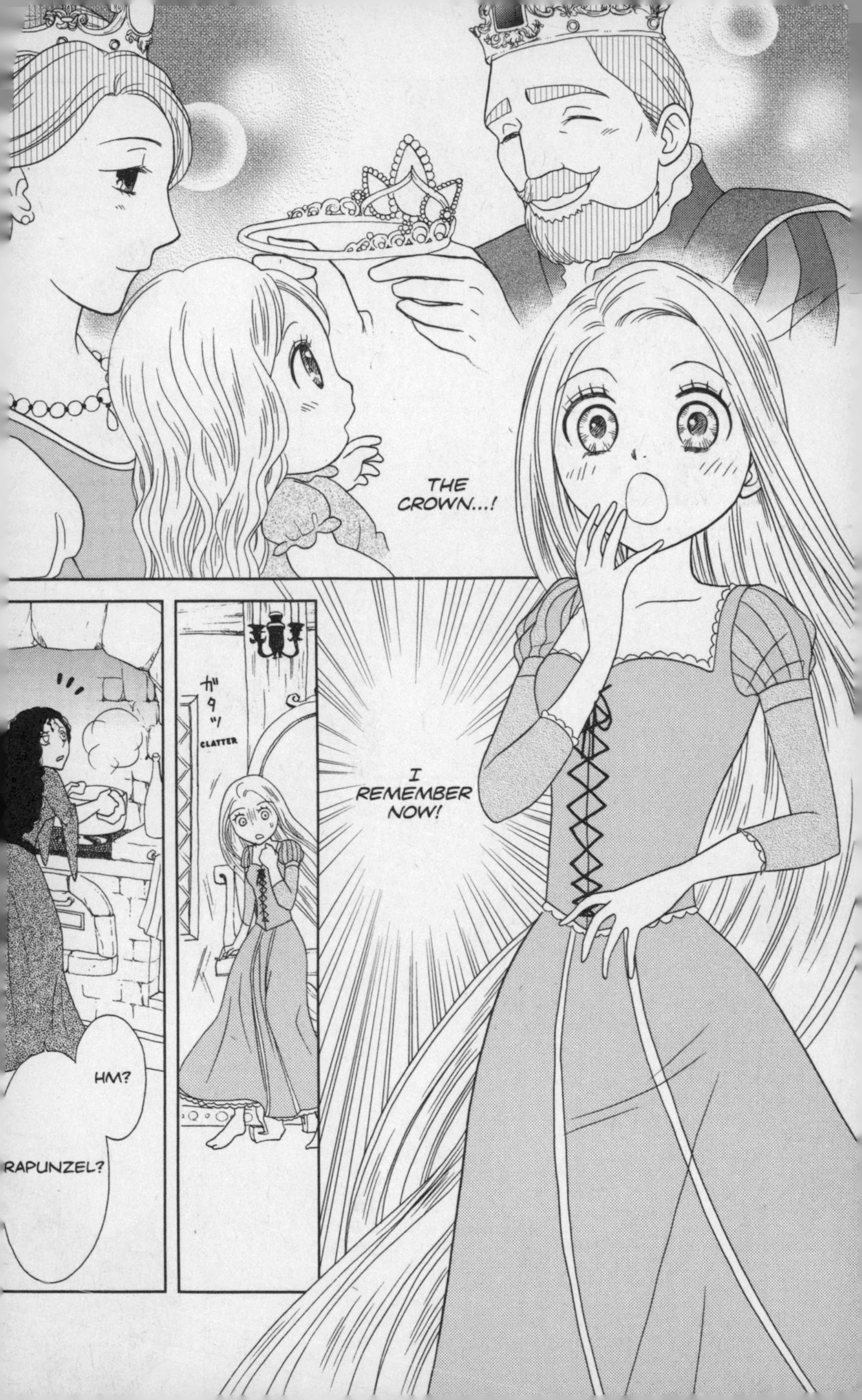
THE CROWN...!
I REMEMBER NOW!
ガタッ
CLATTER
HM?
RAPUNZEL?

READ THIS WAY

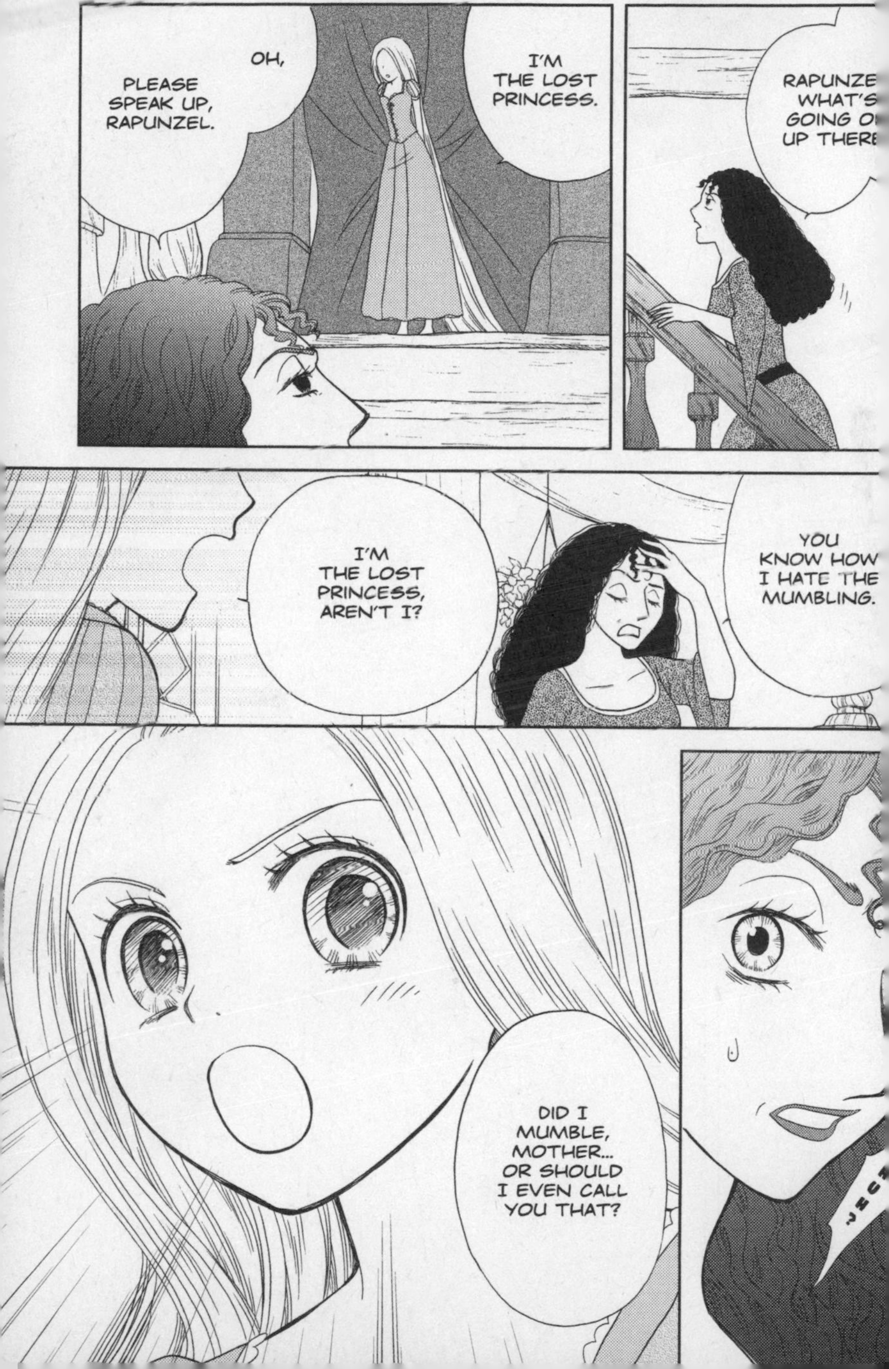
RAPUNZE WHAT'S GOING O UP THERE
I'M THE LOST PRINCESS.
OH, PLEASE SPEAK UP, RAPUNZEL.
YOU KNOW HOW I HATE THE MUMBLING.
I'M THE LOST PRINCESS, AREN'T I?
DID I MUMBLE, MOTHER... OR SHOULD I EVEN CALL YOU THAT?

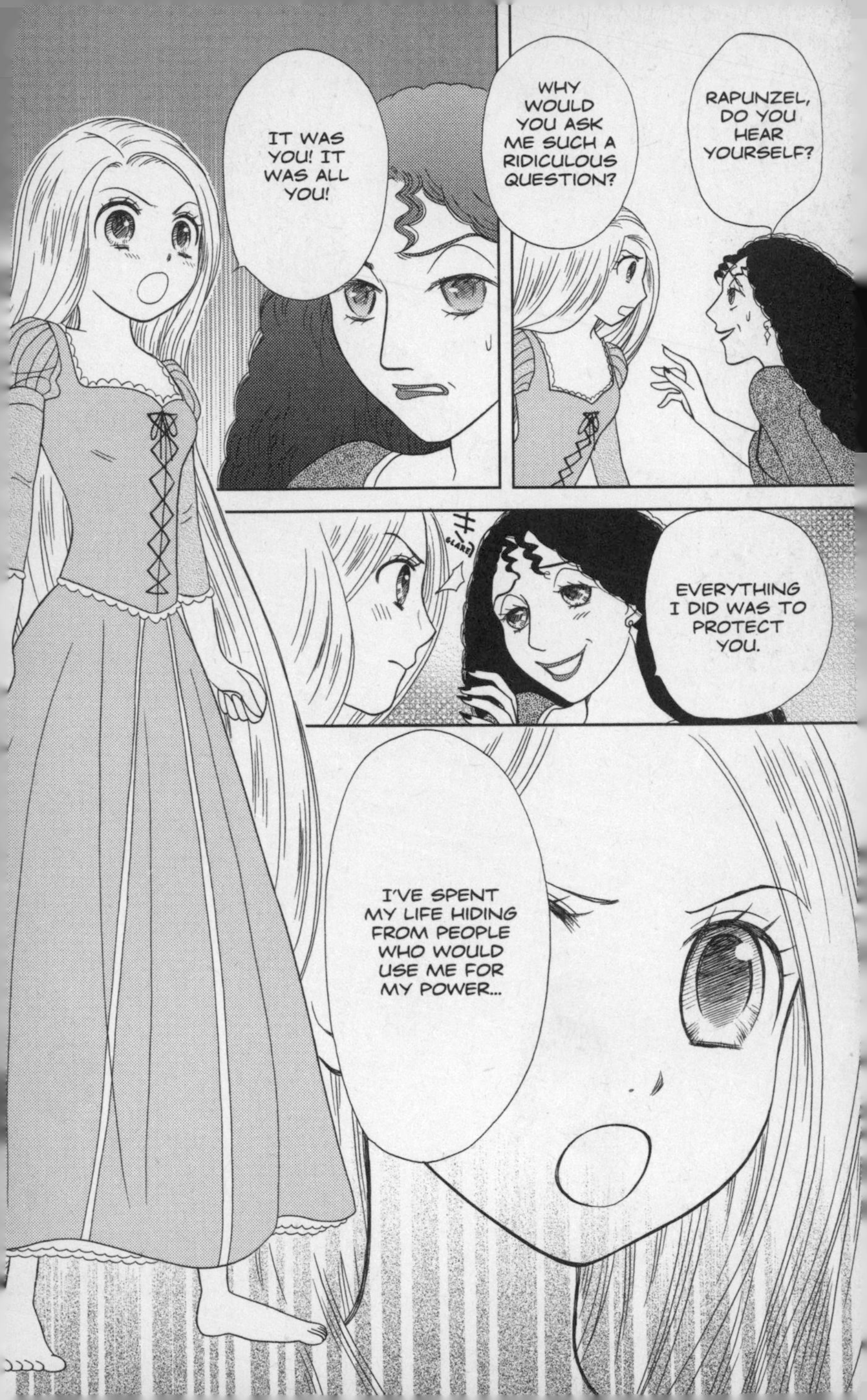
RAPUNZEL, DO YOU HEAR YOURSELF?
WHY WOULD YOU ASK ME SUCH A RIDICULOUS QUESTION?
IT WAS YOU! IT WAS ALL YOU!
GLARE
EVERYTHING I DID WAS TO PROTECT YOU.
I'VE SPENT MY LIFE HIDING FROM PEOPLE WHO WOULD USE ME FOR MY POWER...

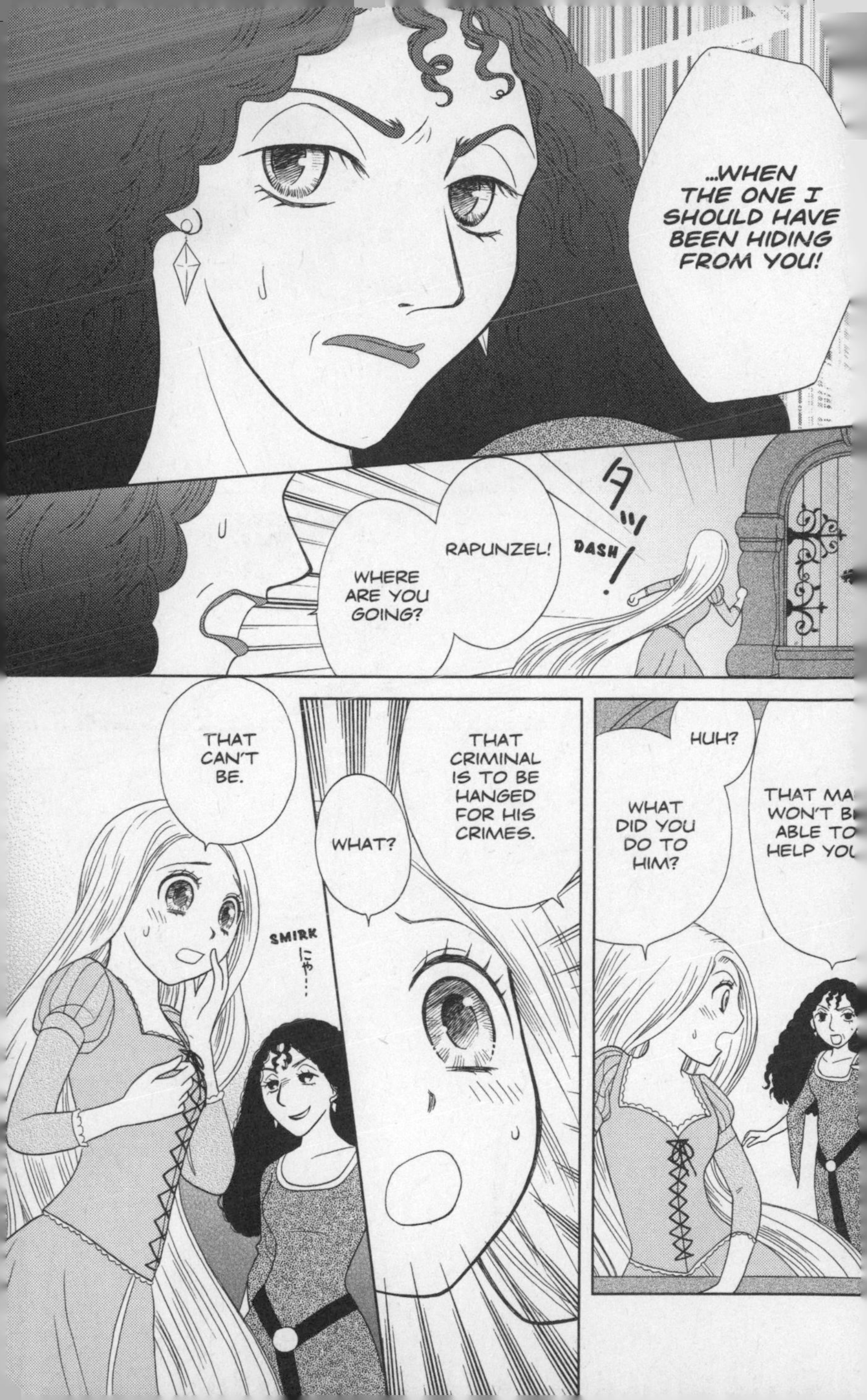
...WHEN THE ONE I SHOULD HAVE BEEN HIDING FROM YOU!
タッ
DASH
RAPUNZEL!
WHERE ARE YOU GOING?
THAT MA WON'T B ABLE TO HELP YO
HUH?
WHAT DID YOU DO TO HIM?
THAT CRIMINAL IS TO BE HANGED FOR HIS CRIMES.
WHAT?
THAT CAN'T BE.
SMIRK
にや…

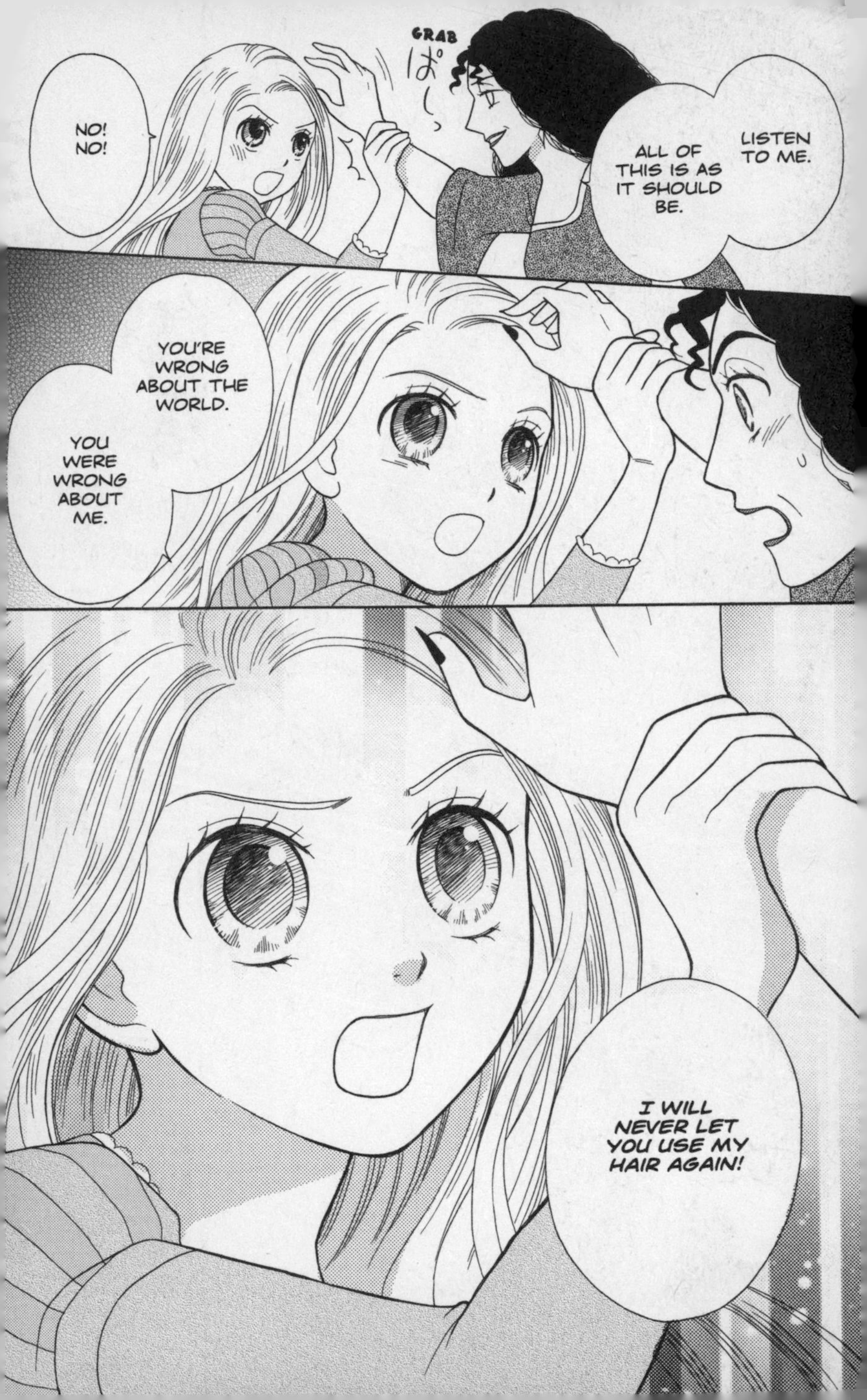
LISTEN TO ME.
ALL OF THIS IS AS IT SHOULD BE.
GRAB
ぱし
NO! NO!
YOU'RE WRONG ABOUT THE WORLD.
YOU WERE WRONG ABOUT ME.
I WILL NEVER LET YOU USE MY HAIR AGAIN!

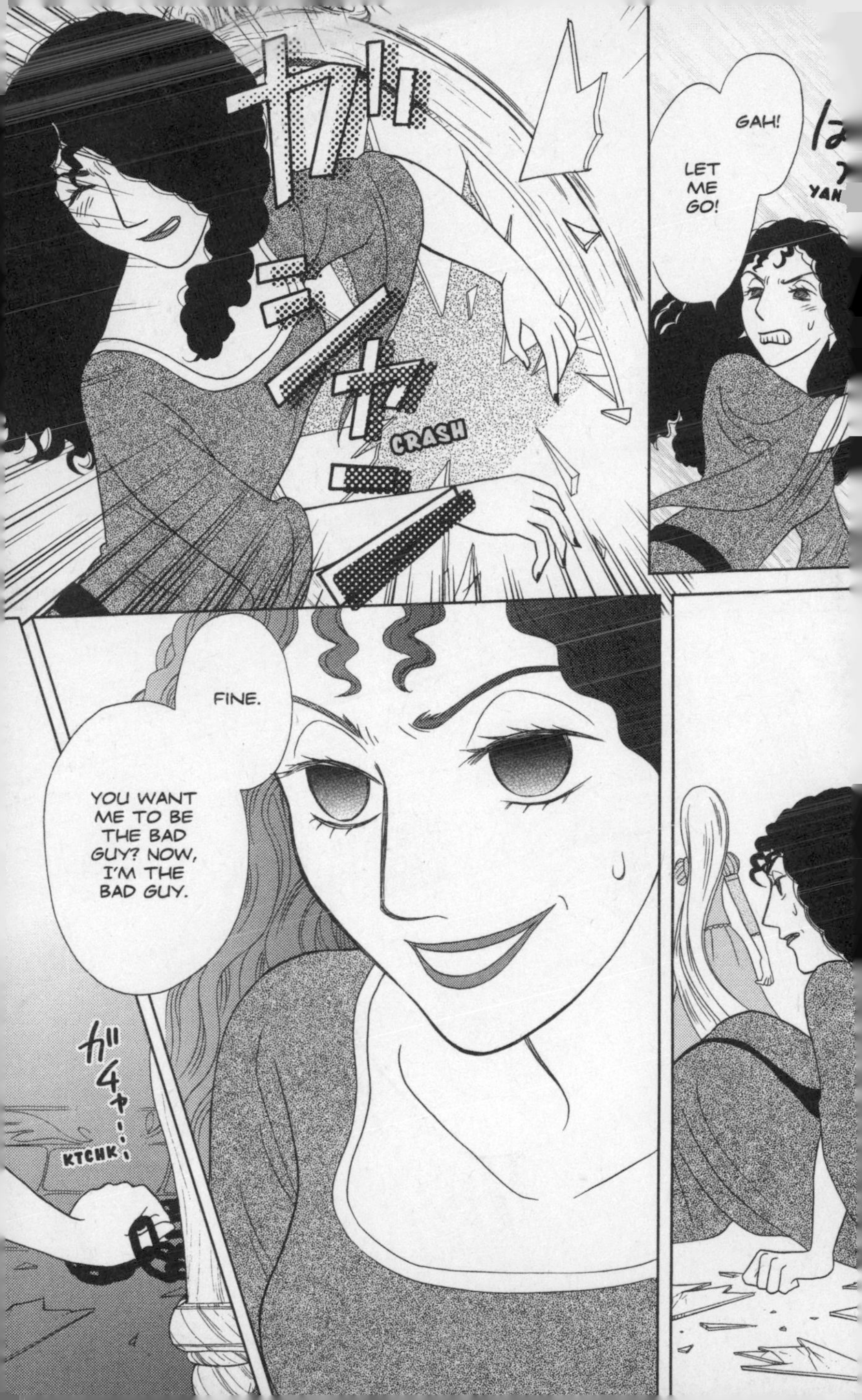
GAH!
LET ME GO!
YAN
CRASH
FINE.
YOU WANT ME TO BE THE BAD GUY? NOW, I'M THE BAD GUY.
KTCHK

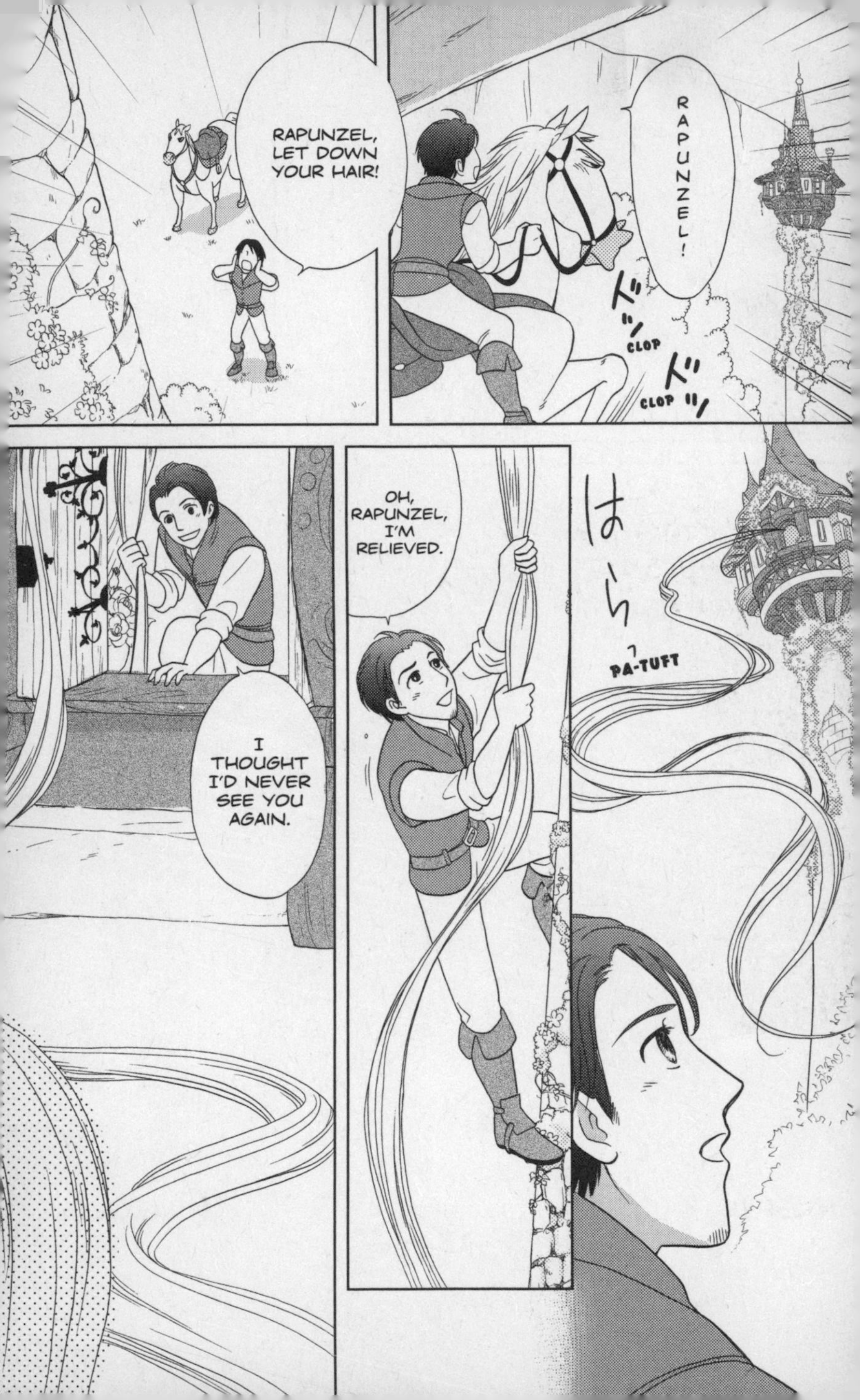
RAPUNZEL!
ドッ
CLOP
ドッ
CLOP
RAPUNZEL, LET DOWN YOUR HAIR!
はら
PA-TUFT
OH, RAPUNZEL, I'M RELIEVED.
I THOUGHT I'D NEVER SEE YOU AGAIN.

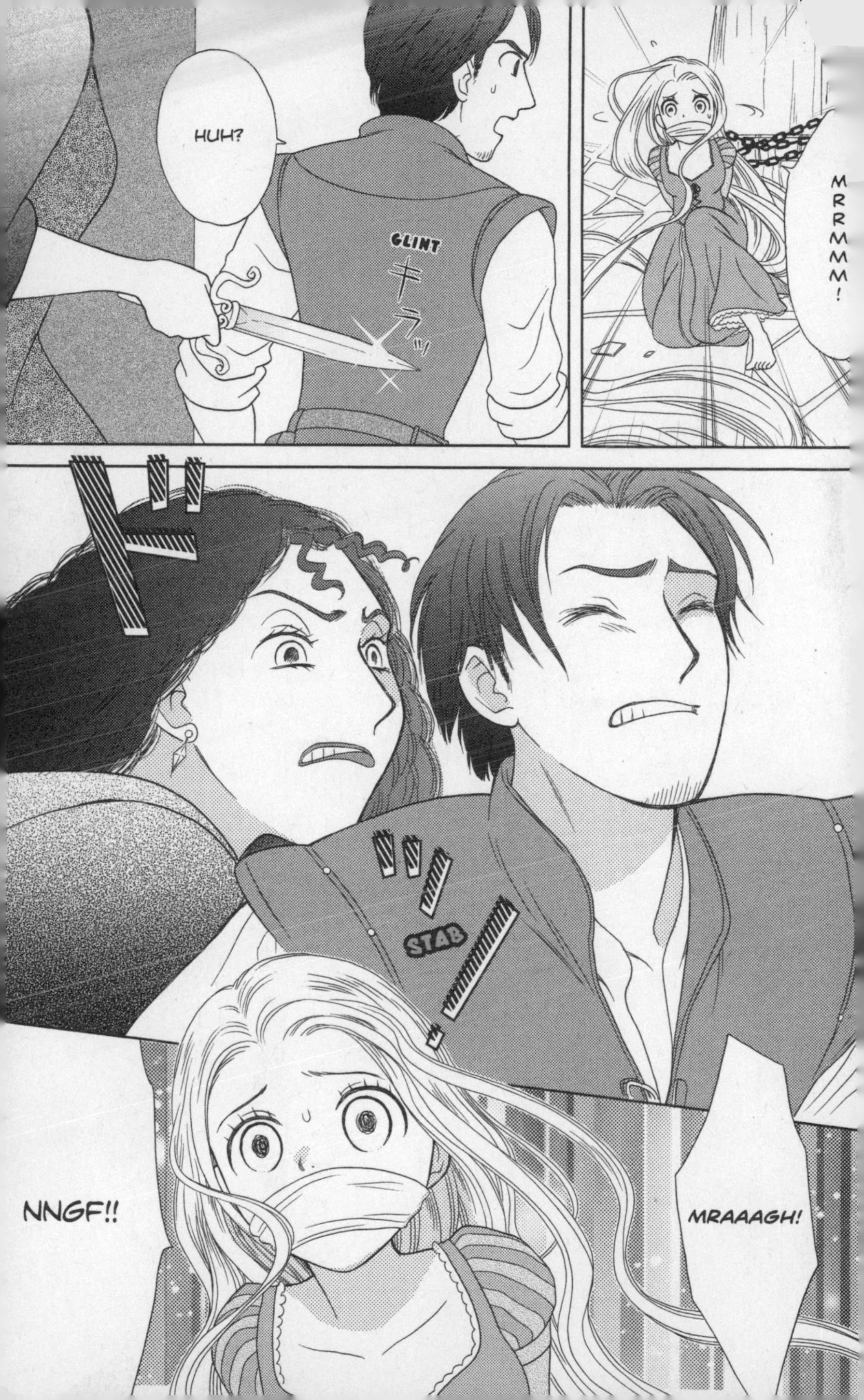
MRRMMM!
HUH?
GLINT
キラッ!!
ド
STAB
MRAAAGH!
NNGF!!

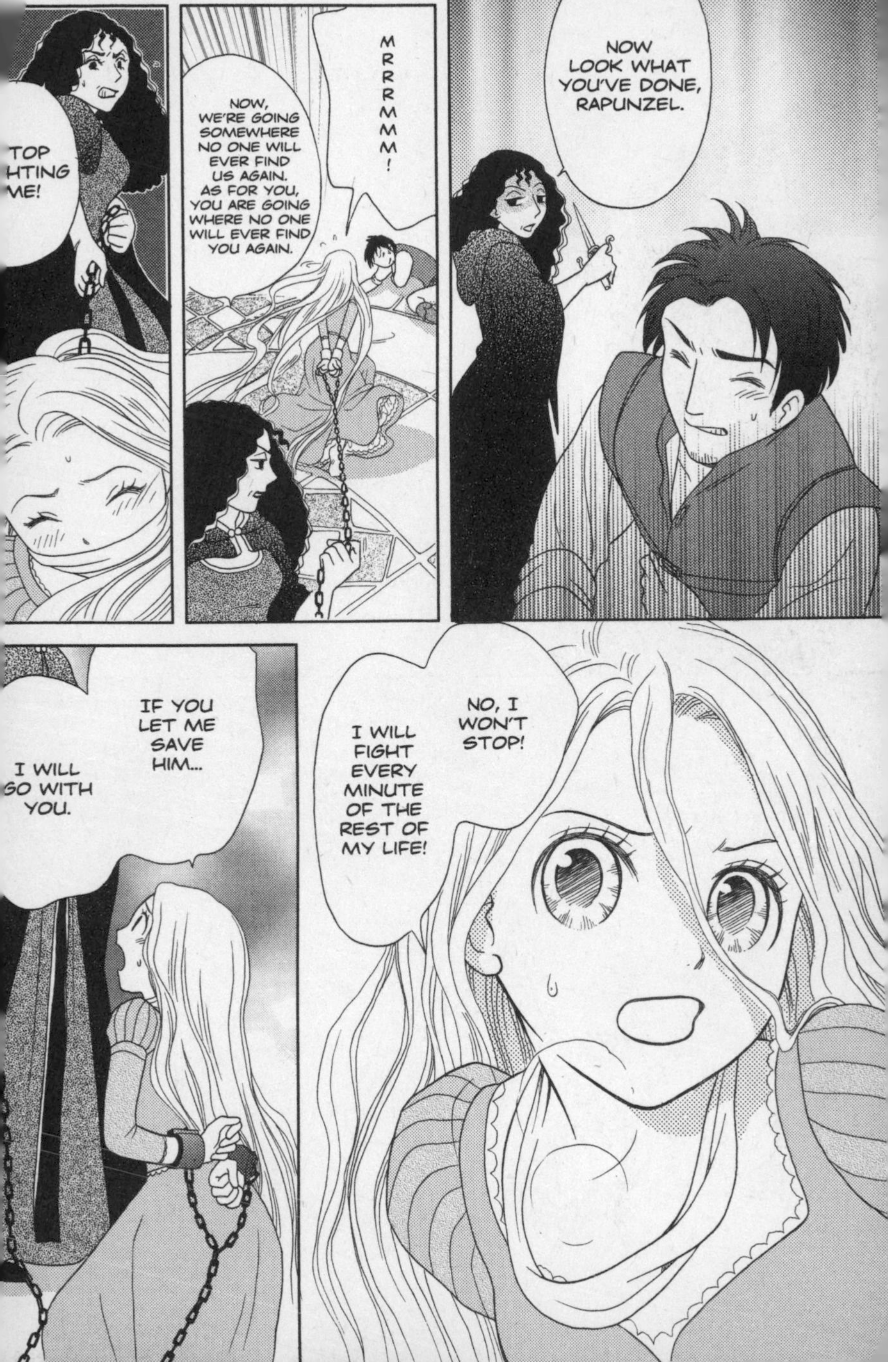
NOW LOOK WHAT YOU'VE DONE, RAPUNZEL.
MRRRMMM!
NOW, WE'RE GOING SOMEWHERE NO ONE WILL EVER FIND US AGAIN. AS FOR YOU, YOU ARE GOING WHERE NO ONE WILL EVER FIND YOU AGAIN.
TOP HTING ME!
NO, I WON'T STOP!
I WILL FIGHT EVERY MINUTE OF THE REST OF MY LIFE!
IF YOU LET ME SAVE HIM...
I WILL GO WITH YOU.

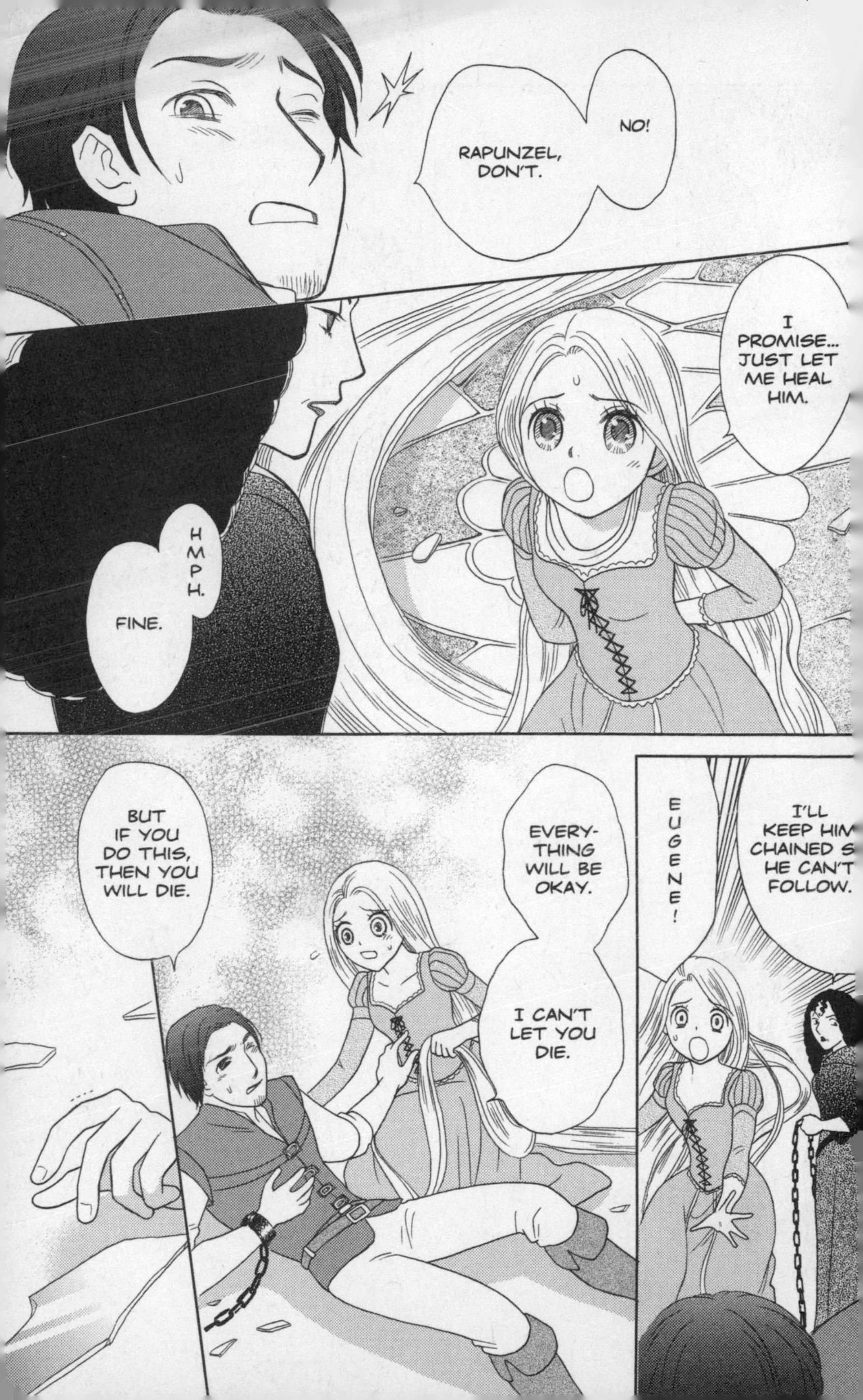
NO!
RAPUNZEL, DON'T.
I PROMISE... JUST LET ME HEAL HIM.
HMPH.
FINE.
I'LL KEEP HIM CHAINED S HE CAN'T FOLLOW.
EUGENE!
EVERY-THING WILL BE OKAY.
BUT IF YOU DO THIS, THEN YOU WILL DIE.
I CAN'T LET YOU DIE.

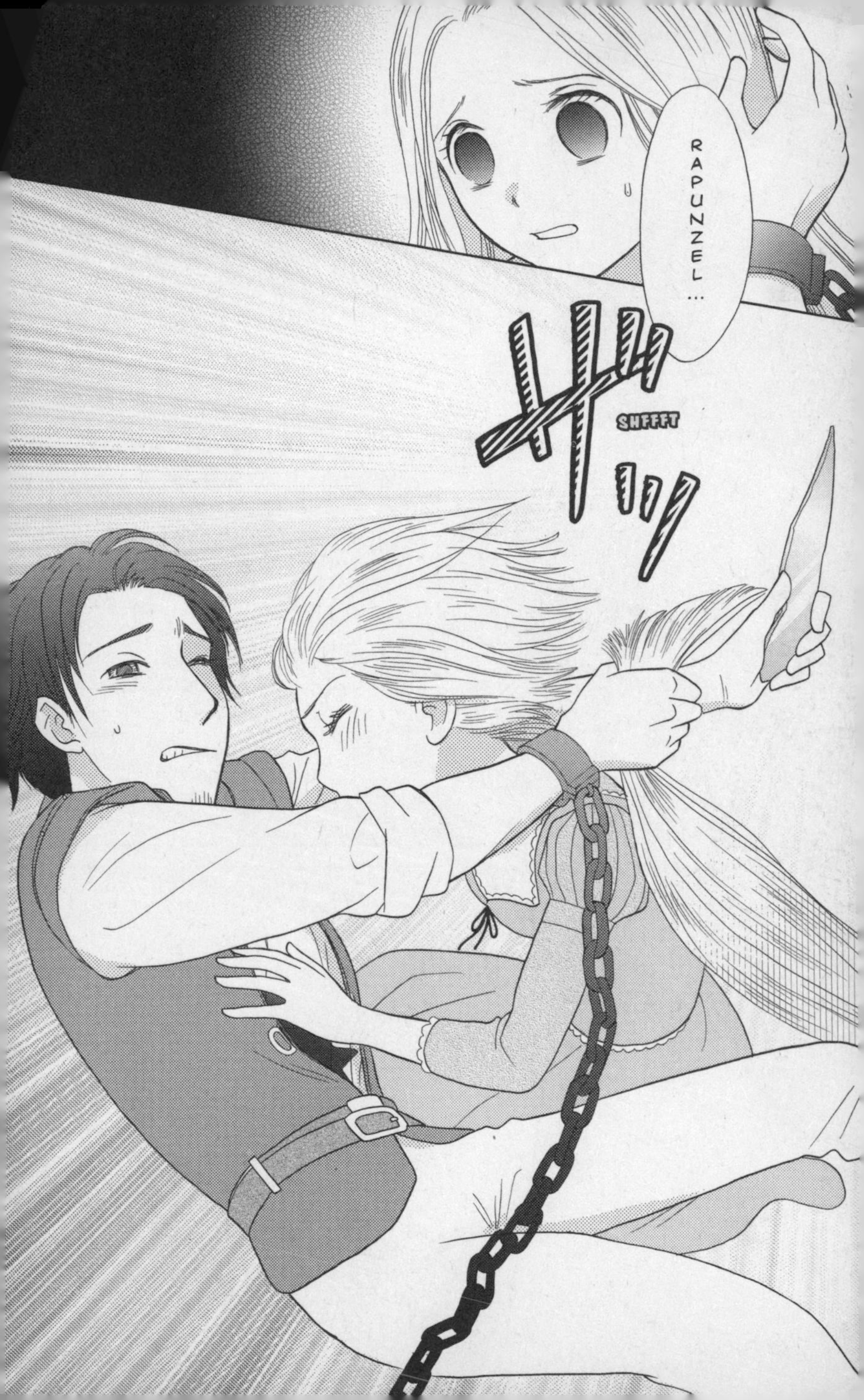
RAPUNZEL...
SHFFFT

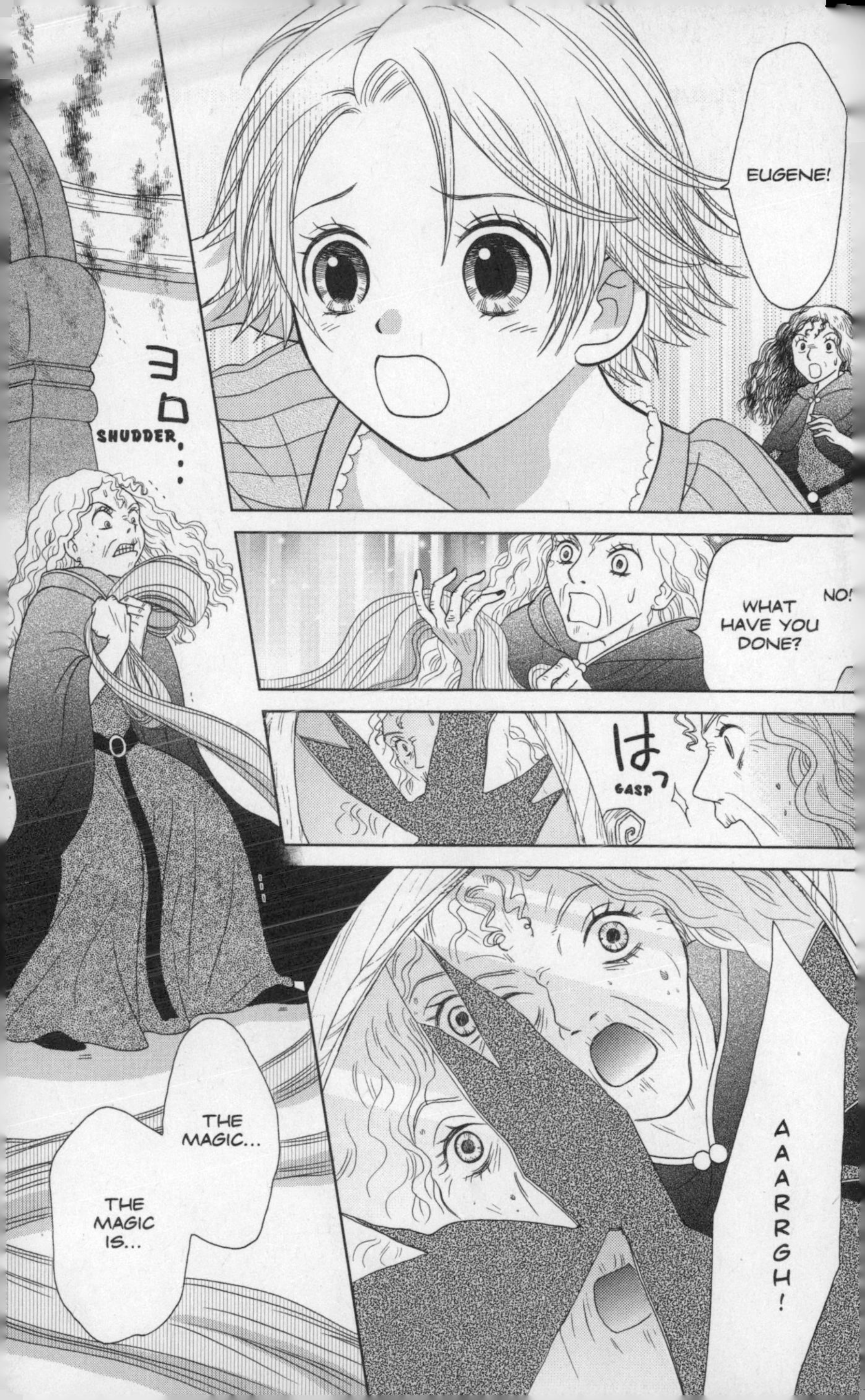
EUGENE!
NO!
WHAT HAVE YOU DONE?
はっ
GASP
AAARRGH!
ヨロ
SHUDDER...
THE MAGIC...
THE MAGIC IS...

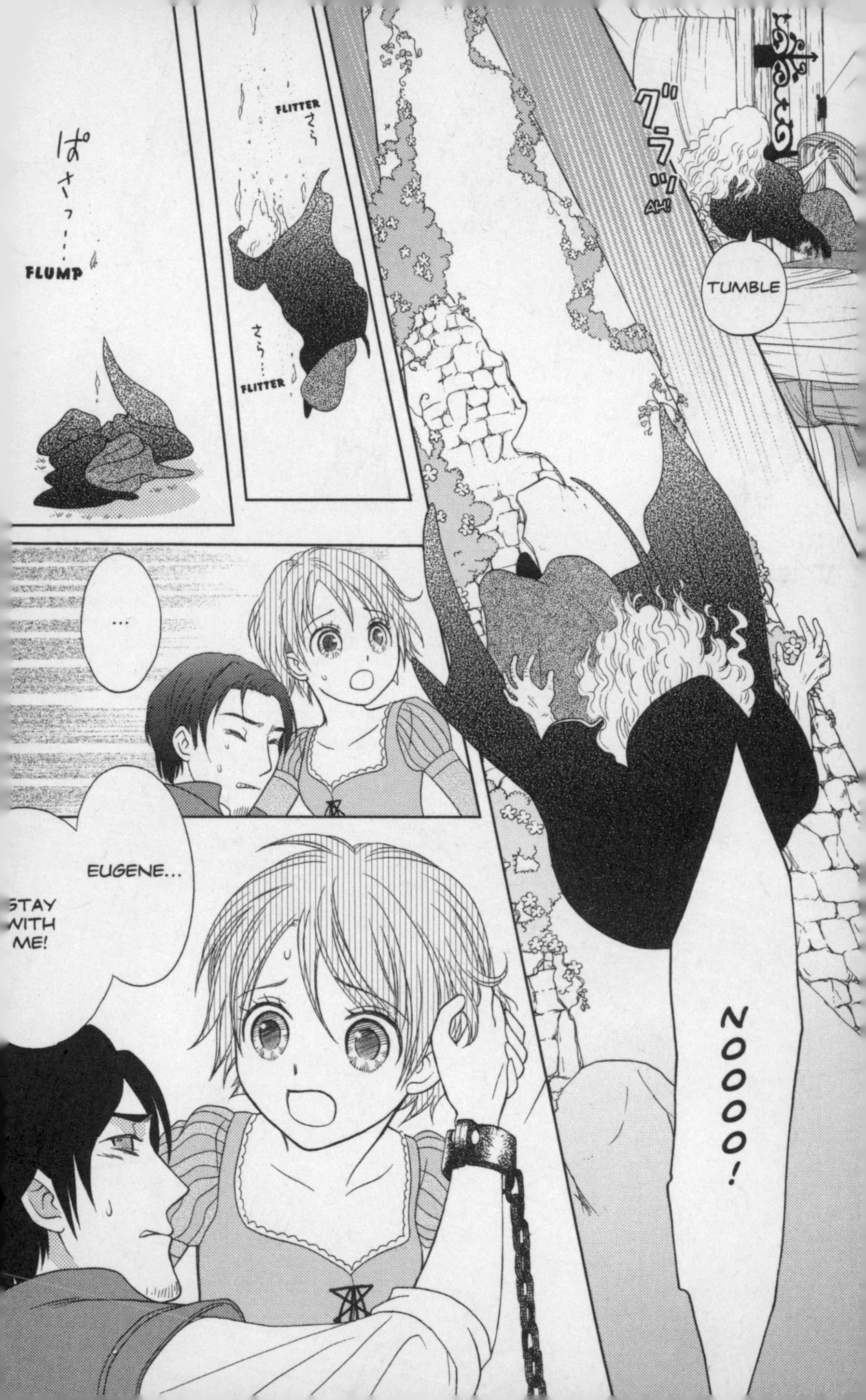
グラッ
AH!
TUMBLE
NOOOOO!
FLITTER さら
さら… FLITTER
ぱさっ… FLUMP
…
EUGENE…
STAY WITH ME!

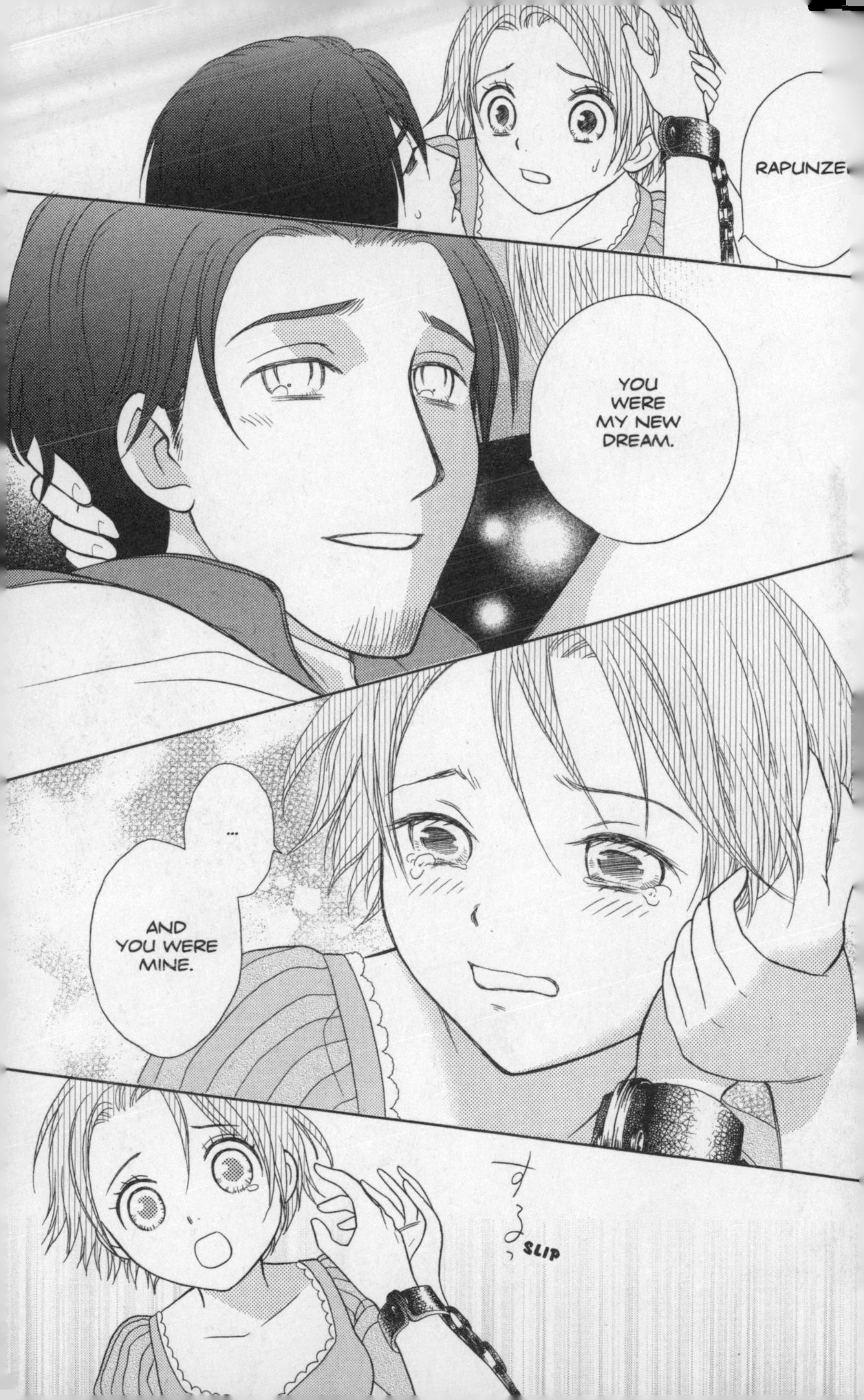
RAPUNZEL
YOU WERE MY NEW DREAM.
...
AND YOU WERE MINE.
する
SLIP

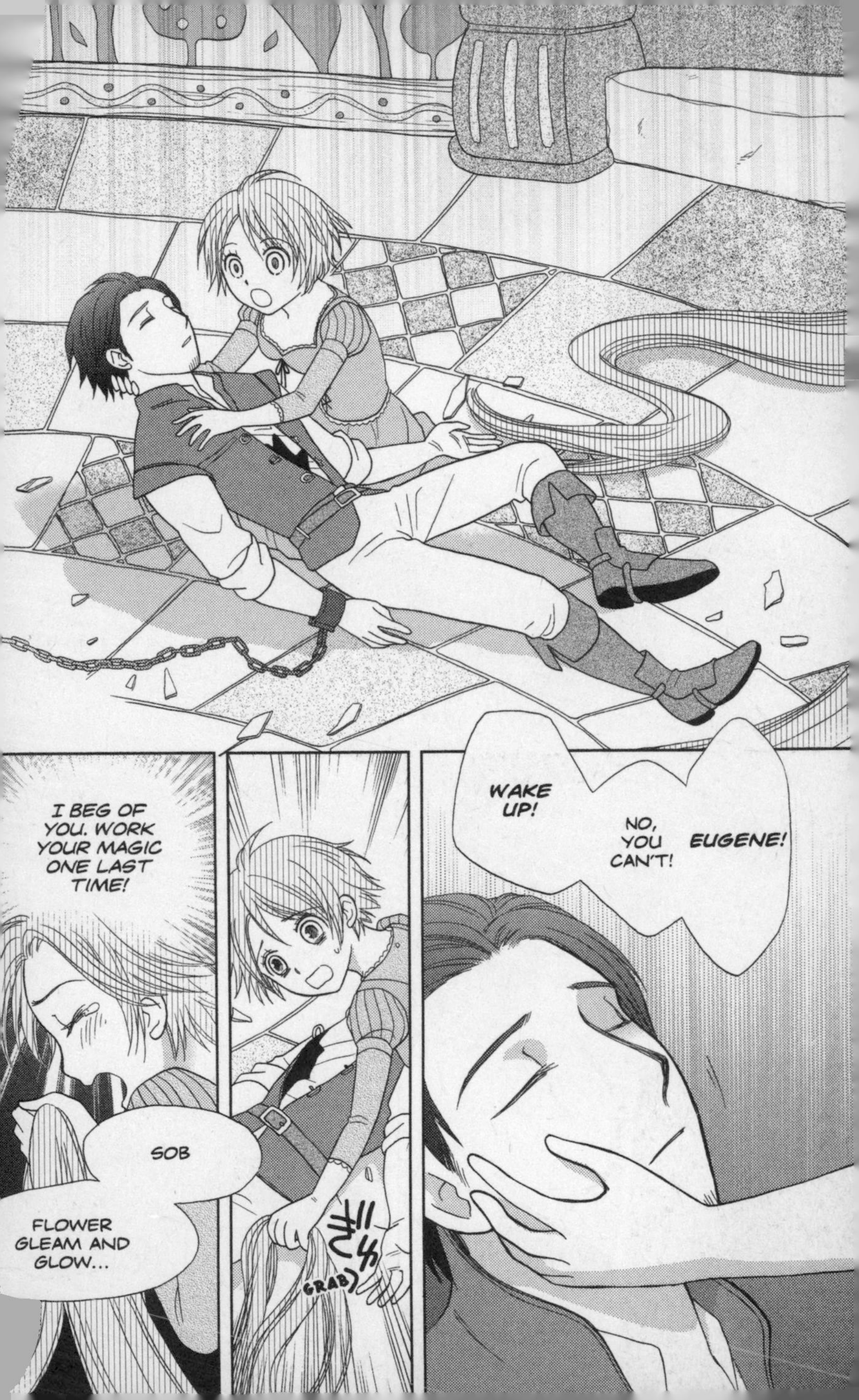
EUGENE!
NO, YOU CAN'T!
WAKE UP!
GRAB
I BEG OF YOU. WORK YOUR MAGIC ONE LAST TIME!
SOB
FLOWER GLEAM AND GLOW...

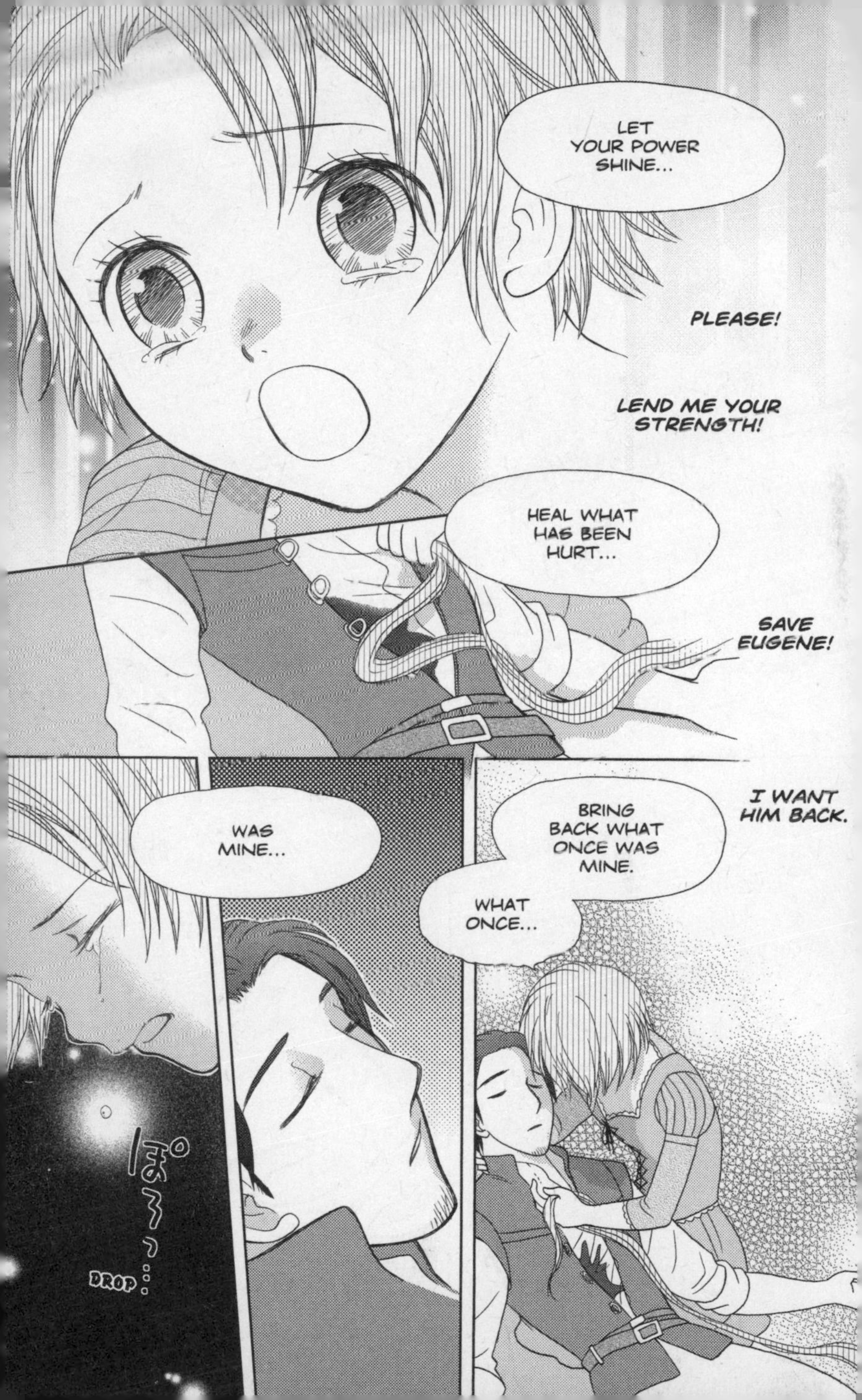
LET YOUR POWER SHINE...
PLEASE!
LEND ME YOUR STRENGTH!
HEAL WHAT HAS BEEN HURT...
SAVE EUGENE!
I WANT HIM BACK.
BRING BACK WHAT ONCE WAS MINE.
WHAT ONCE...
WAS MINE...
ぽろっ…
DROP

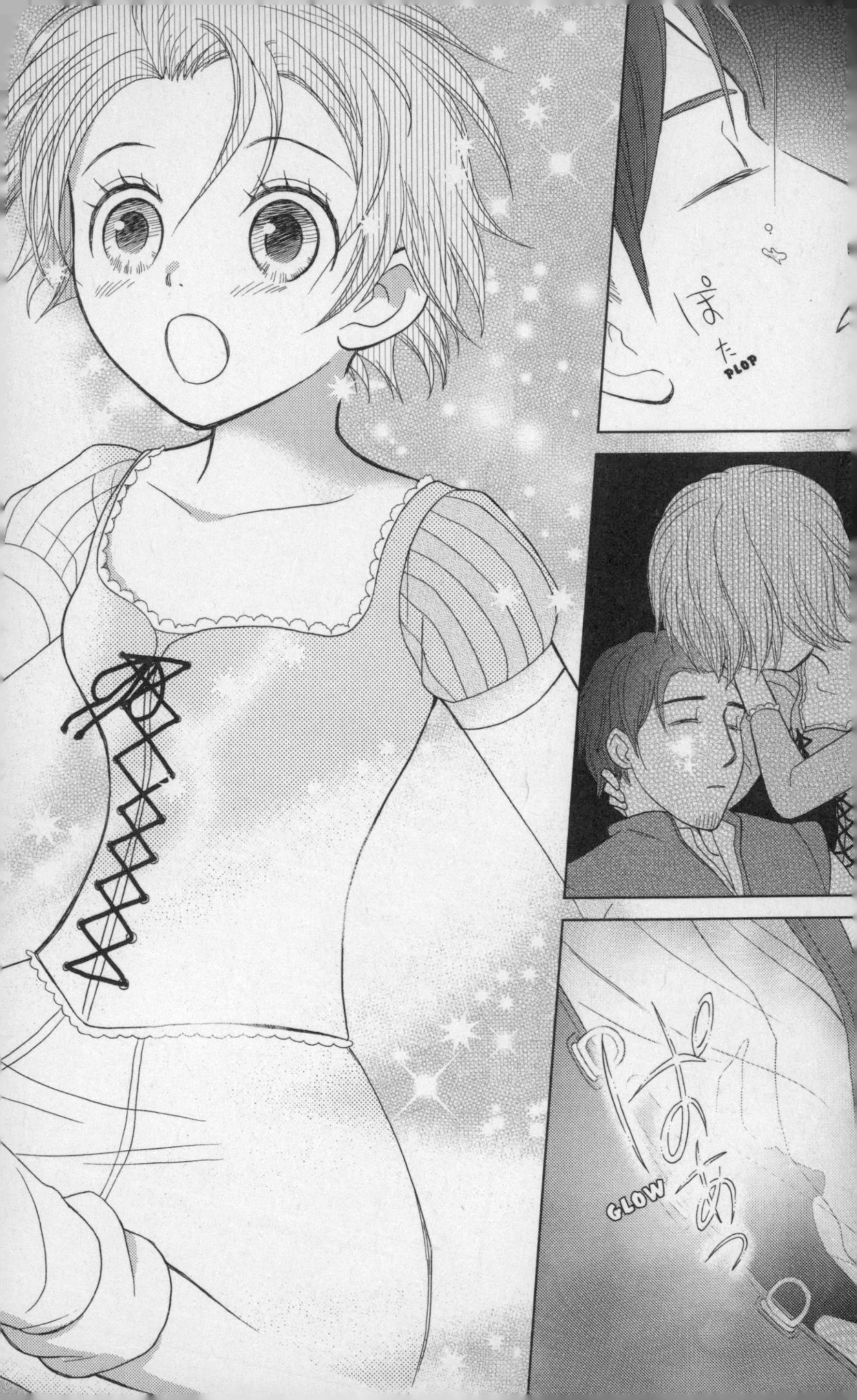
ぽた
PLOP
GLOW

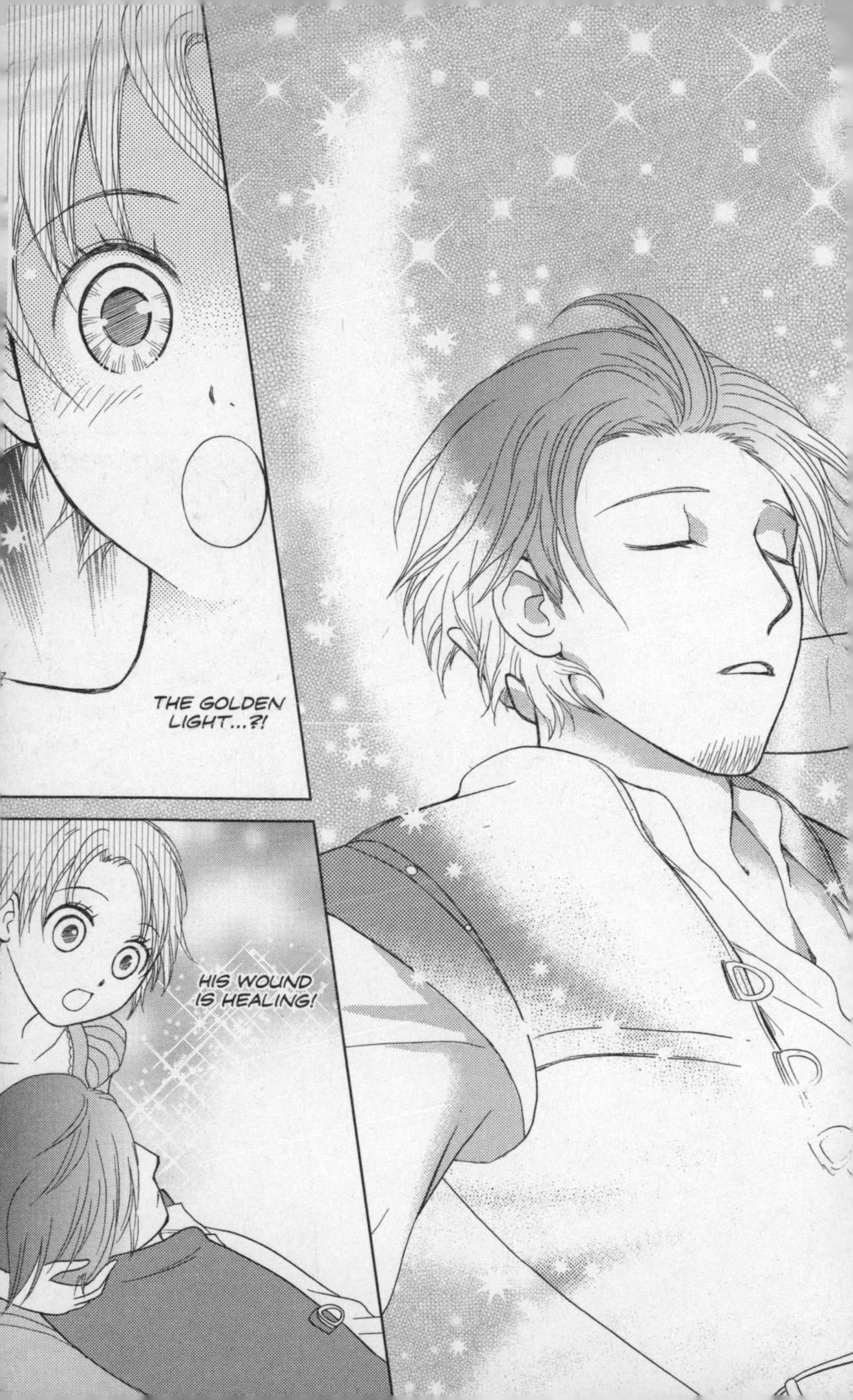
THE GOLDEN LIGHT...?!
HIS WOUND IS HEALING!

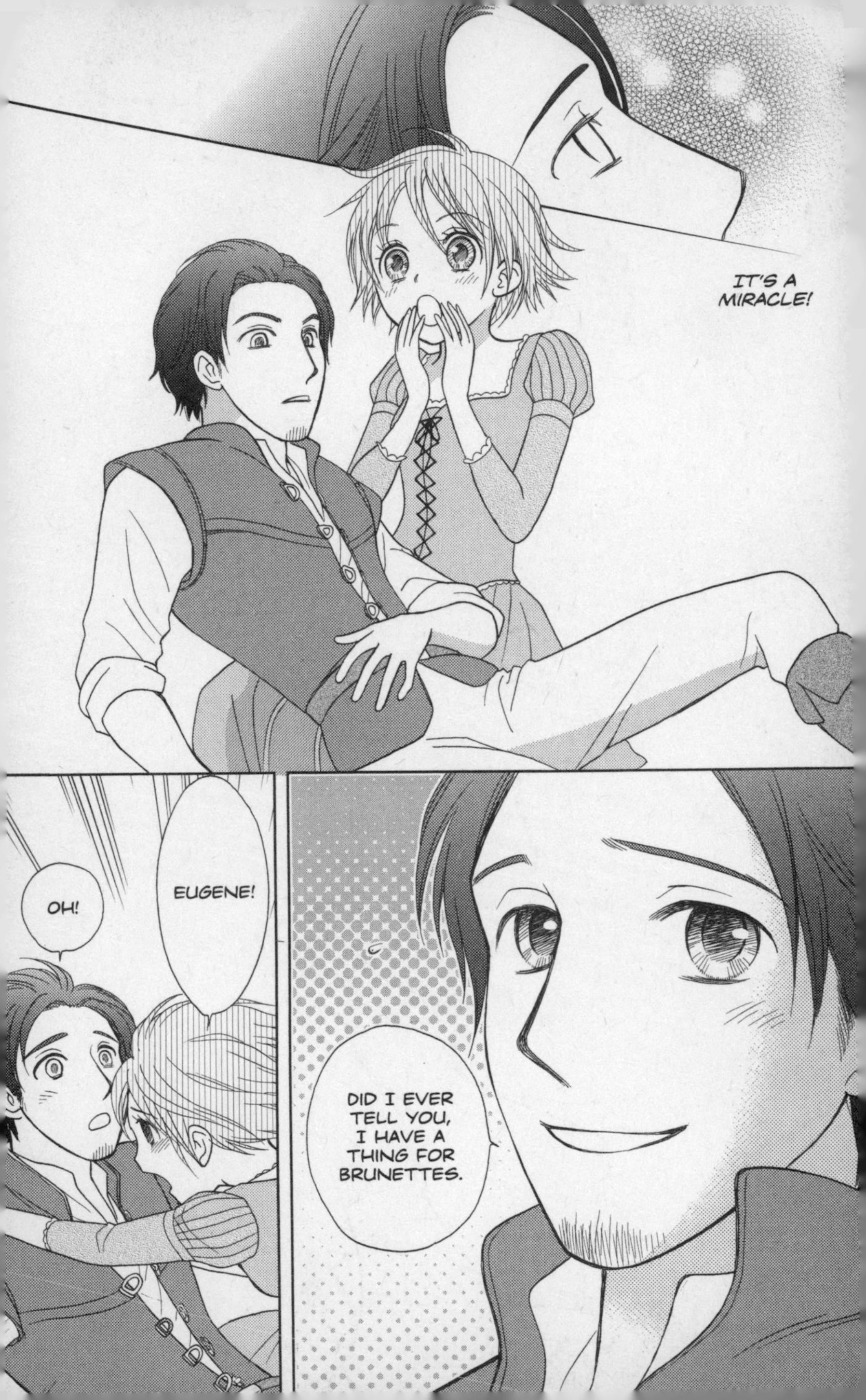
IT'S A MIRACLE!
DID I EVER TELL YOU, I HAVE A THING FOR BRUNETTES.
EUGENE!
OH!

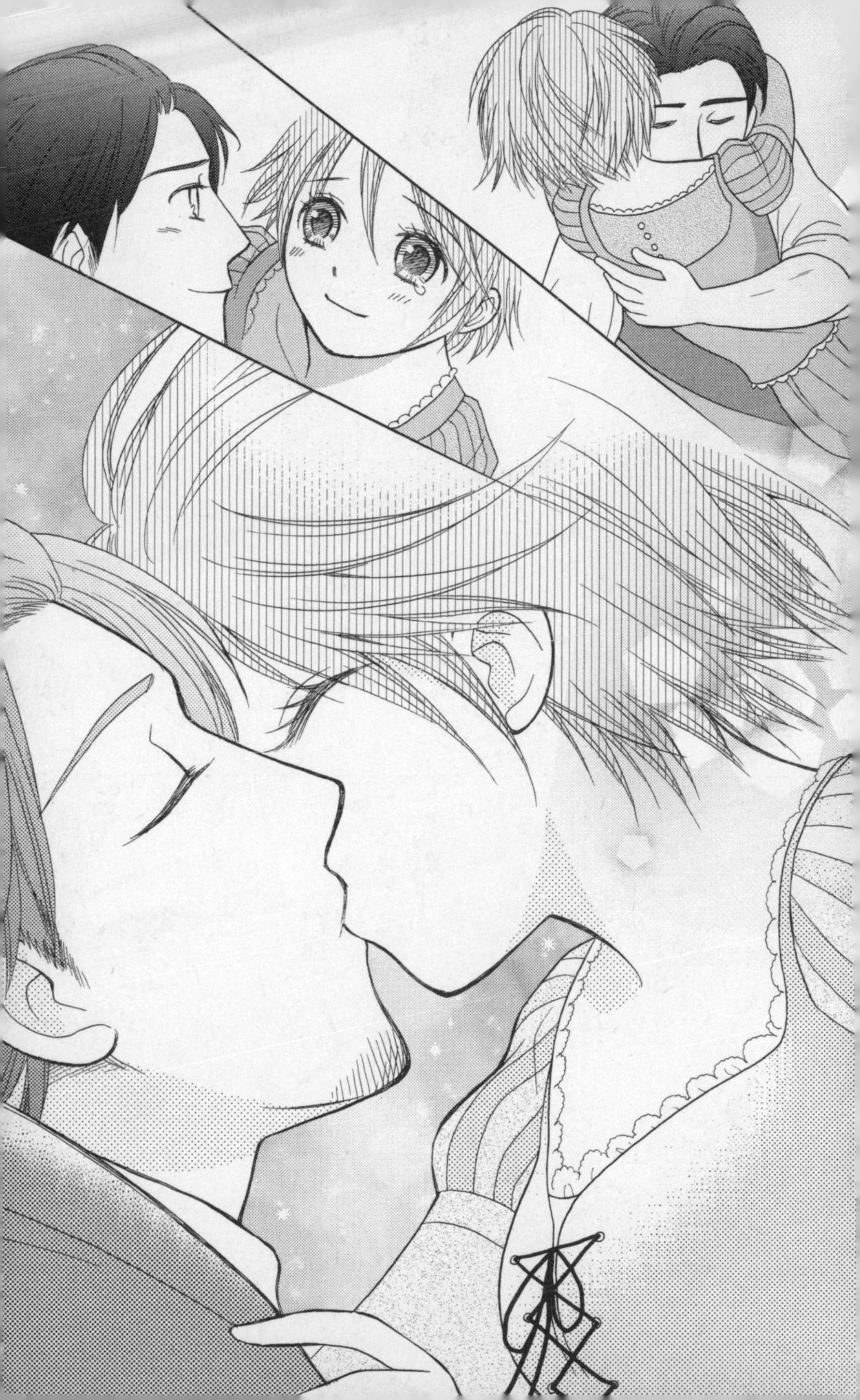

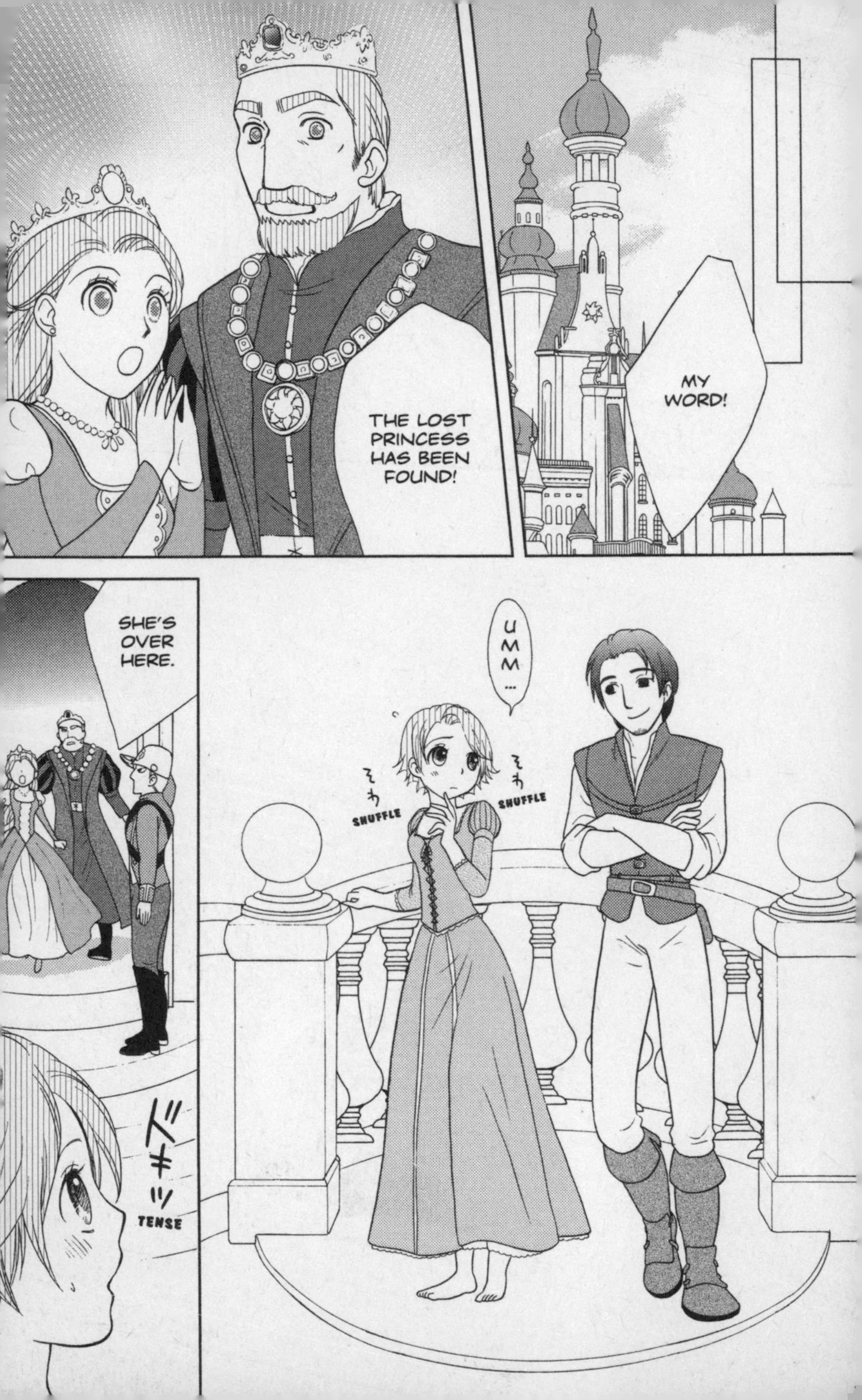
MY WORD!
THE LOST PRINCESS HAS BEEN FOUND!
UMM...
SHUFFLE
SHUFFLE
SHE'S OVER HERE.
ドキッ
TENSE

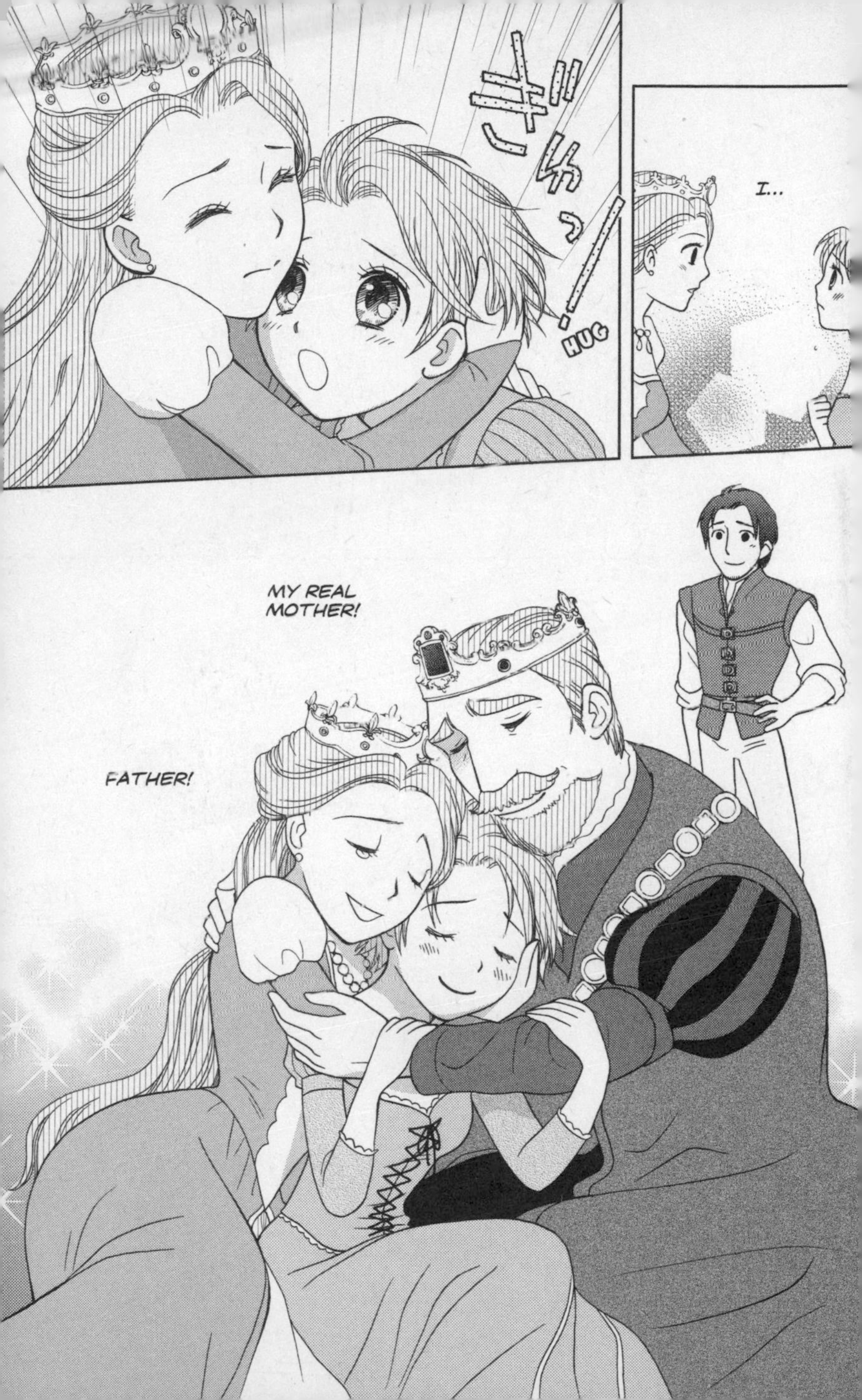
I...
ぎゅっ!
HUG
MY REAL MOTHER!
FATHER!

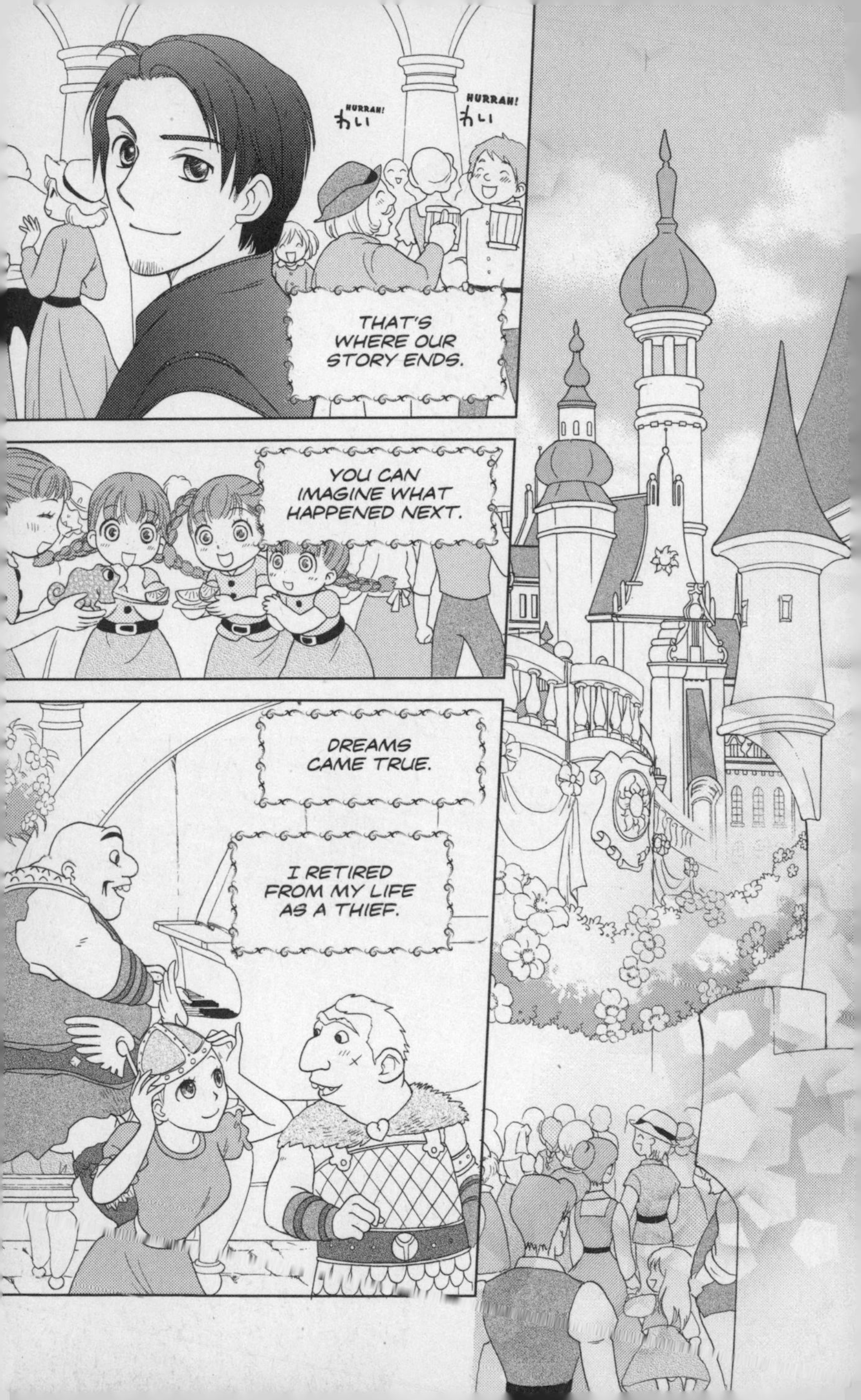
HURRAH! わい
HURRAH! わい
THAT'S WHERE OUR STORY ENDS.
YOU CAN IMAGINE WHAT HAPPENED NEXT.
DREAMS CAME TRUE.
I RETIRED FROM MY LIFE AS A THIEF.

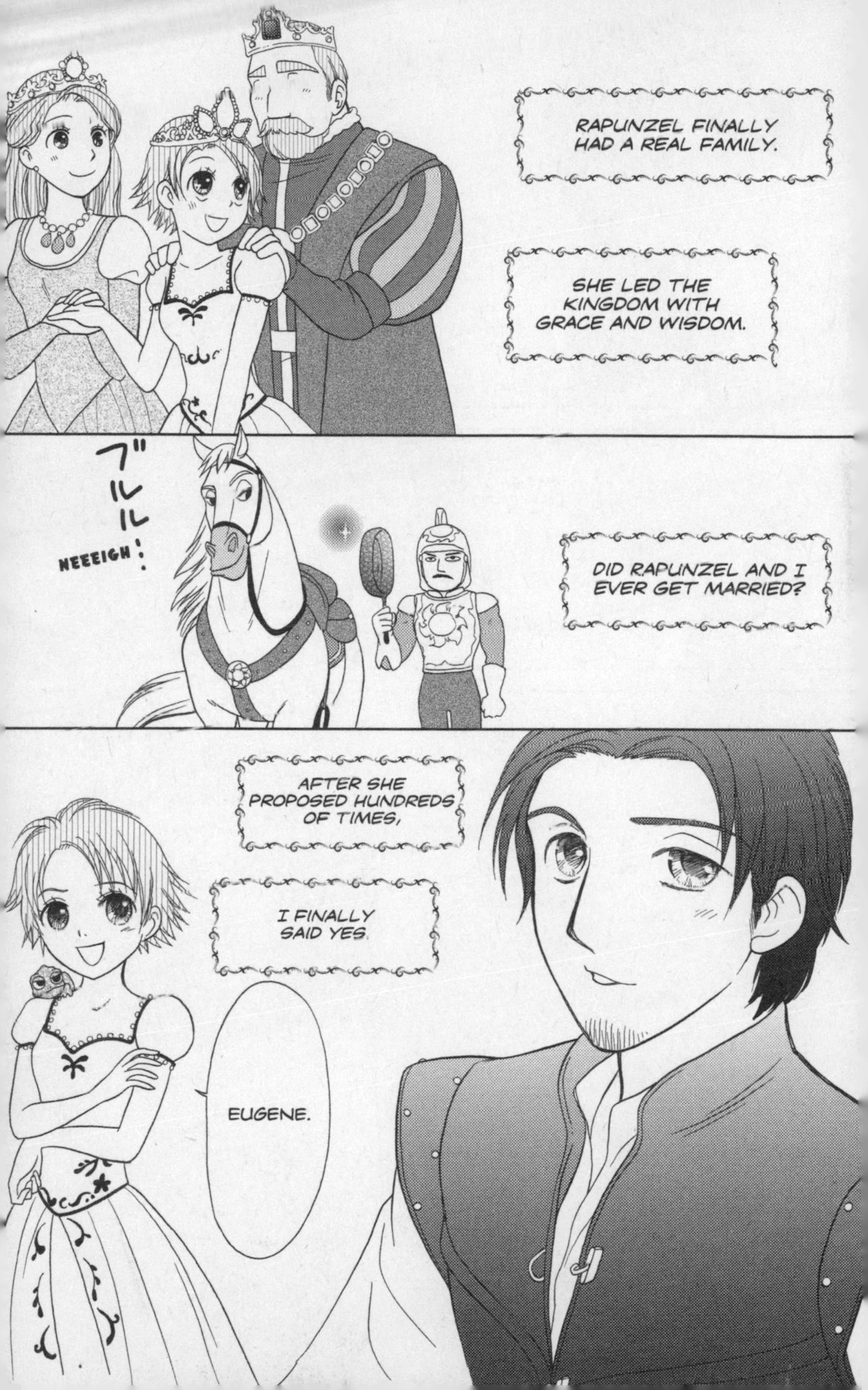
RAPUNZEL FINALLY HAD A REAL FAMILY.
SHE LED THE KINGDOM WITH GRACE AND WISDOM.
DID RAPUNZEL AND I EVER GET MARRIED?
ブルル
NEEEIGH
AFTER SHE PROPOSED HUNDREDS OF TIMES,
I FINALLY SAID YES.
EUGENE.

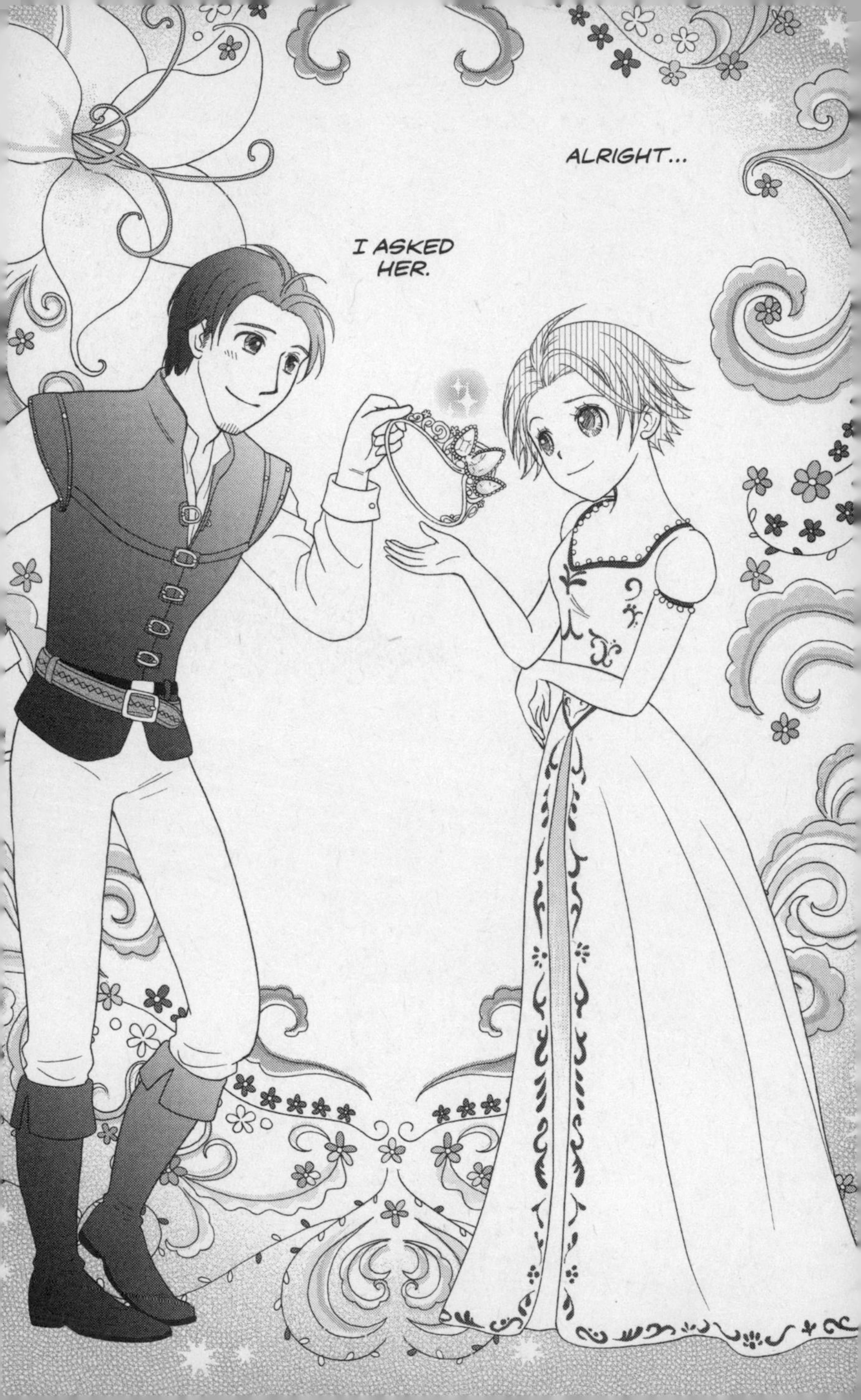
ALRIGHT...
I ASKED HER.

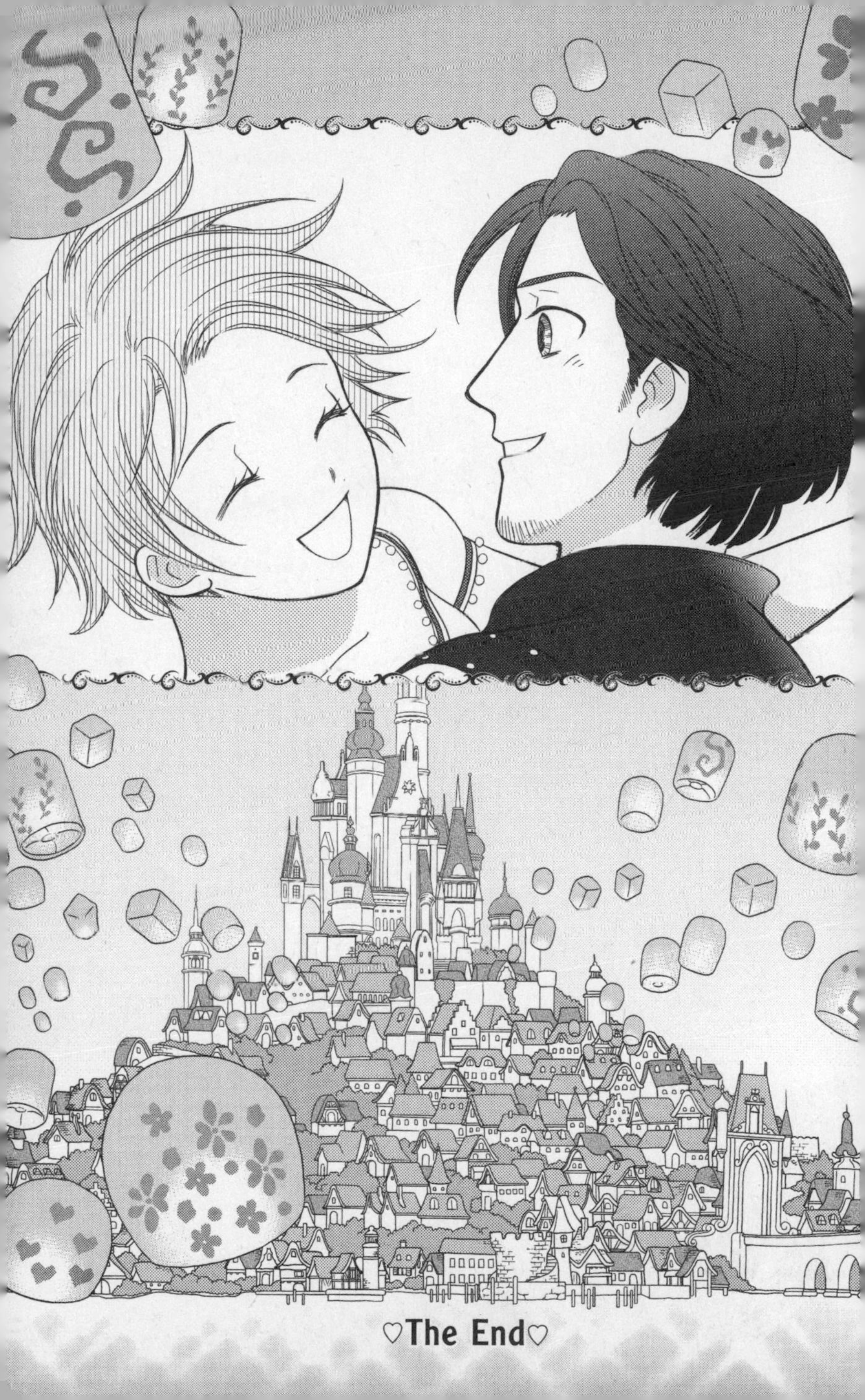
♡The End♡

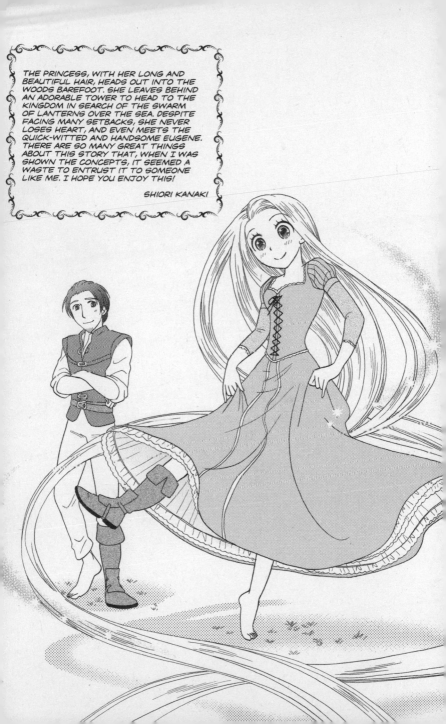

THE PRINCESS, WITH HER LONG AND BEAUTIFUL HAIR, HEADS OUT INTO THE WOODS BAREFOOT. SHE LEAVES BEHIND AN ADORABLE TOWER TO HEAD TO THE KINGDOM IN SEARCH OF THE SWARM OF LANTERNS OVER THE SEA. DESPITE FACING MANY SETBACKS, SHE NEVER LOSES HEART, AND EVEN MEETS THE QUICK-WITTED AND HANDSOME EUGENE. THERE ARE SO MANY GREAT THINGS ABOUT THIS STORY THAT, WHEN I WAS SHOWN THE CONCEPTS, IT SEEMED A WASTE TO ENTRUST IT TO SOMEONE LIKE ME. I HOPE YOU ENJOY THIS!

SHIORI KANAKI

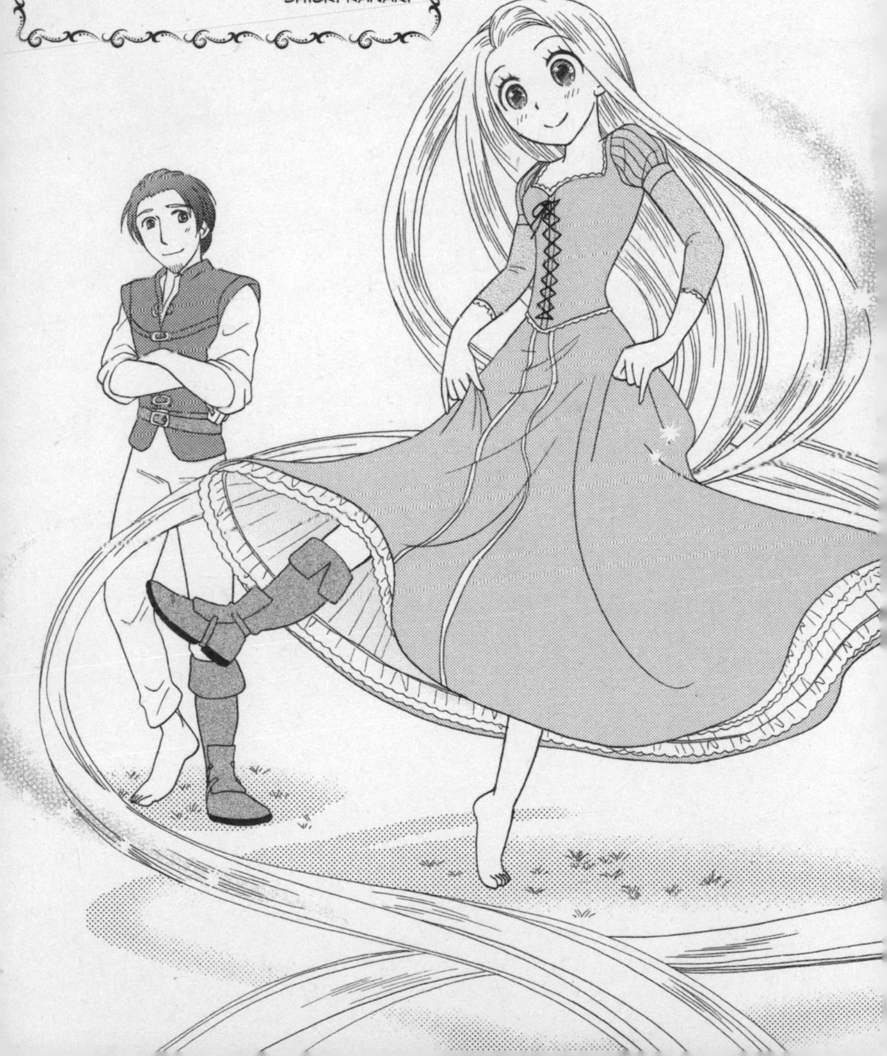

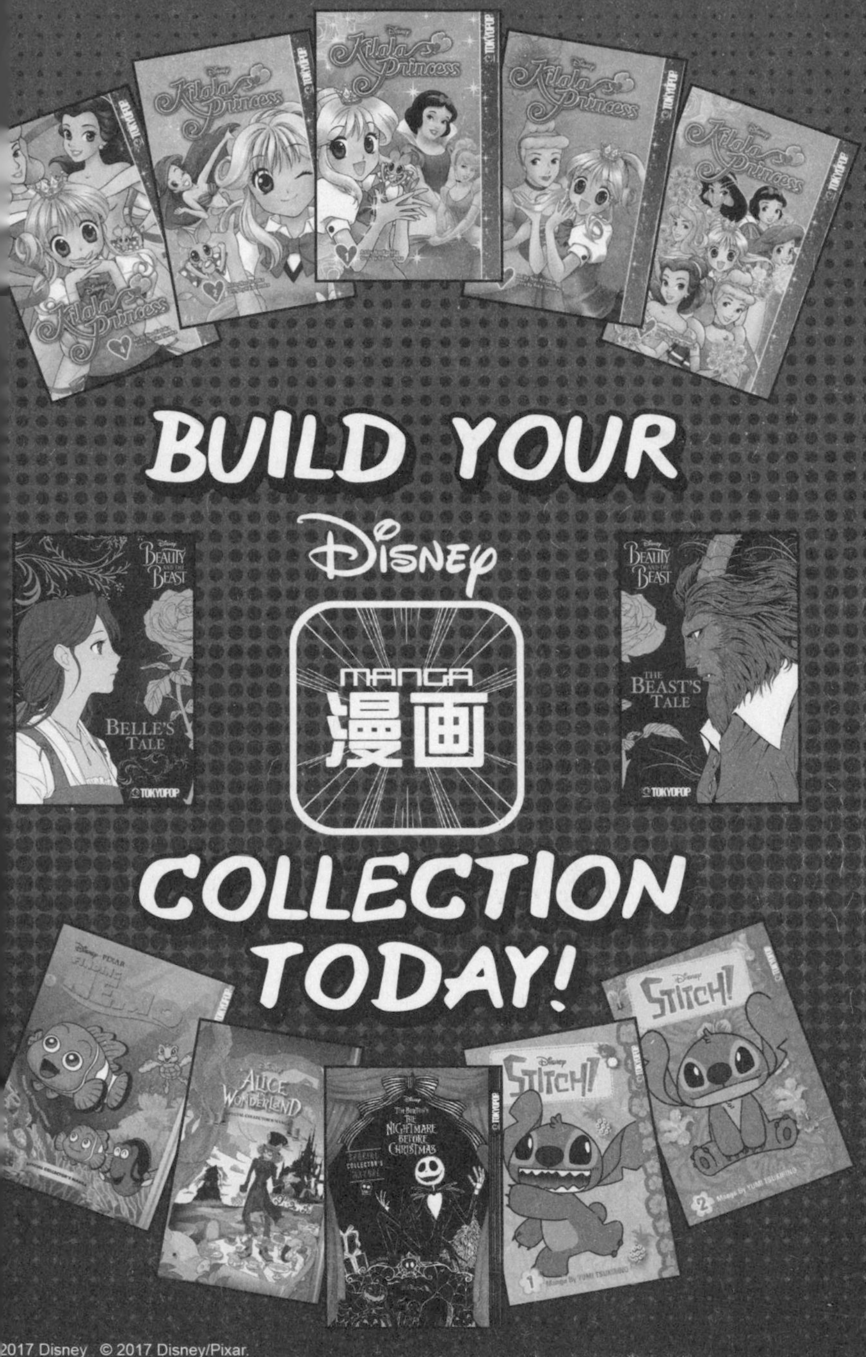
BUILD YOUR
DISNEY
MANGA
漫画
COLLECTION
TODAY!
Kilala Princess
TOKYOPOP
Beauty and the Beast
Belle's Tale
The Beast's Tale
Alice in Wonderland
Tim Burton's The Nightmare Before Christmas
Stitch!

Disney Tangled Manga
Manga by Shiori Kanaki

Publishing Assistant - Janae Young
Marketing Assistant - Kae Winters
Technology and Digital Media Assistant - Phillip Hong
Retouching and Lettering - Vibrraant Publishing Studio
Translations - Jason Muell
Graphic Designer - Phillip Hong
Copy-Editor - Daniella Orihuela-Gruber
Editor-in-Chief & Publisher - Stu Levy

A  Manga

TOKYOPOP and 🐾 are trademarks or registered trademarks of TOKYOPOP Inc.

TOKYOPOP inc.
5200 W Century Blvd
Suite 705
Los Angeles, CA 90045 USA

E-mail: info@TOKYOPOP.com
Come visit us online at www.TOKYOPOP.com

f www.facebook.com/TOKYOPOP
🐦 www.twitter.com/TOKYOPOP
▶ www.youtubc.com/TOKYOPOPTV
📌 www.pinterest.com/TOKYOPOP
📷 www.instagram.com/TOKYOPOP
t. TOKYOPOP.tumblr.com

ISBN: 978-1-4278-5704-0

First TOKYOPOP Printing: July 2017
10 9 8 7 6 5 4 3 2 1
Printed in CANADA

STOP

THIS IS THE BACK OF THE BOOK!

How do you read manga-style? It's simple! To learn,
just start in the top right panel and follow the numbers: